Class Politics and the Radical Right

One of the most significant events in European politics during the past two decades is the emergence of radical right-wing parties, mobilizing against immigration and multiethnic societies. Such parties have established themselves in a large number of countries, often with voter shares exceeding 10 percent and sometimes even 20 percent. Many of these parties exert a real influence on policy within their respective country.

The emergence of the recent wave of radical right-wing party politics has generated a large and growing literature, spanning a variety of dimensions— such as ideology, voting, and policy impact. This volume will cover all these dimensions, but it will in particular focus on two questions: why is it that the working class tends to be especially attracted by the radical right-wing parties? And what does the radical right-wing parties' growing electoral success mean for social democracy and the traditional left in Europe, which are meeting growing competition from the radical right over working class voters?

Bringing together the leading scholars within this field, this book makes a unique contribution by focusing on the relationship between class politics and the radical right.

Jens Rydgren holds the Chair in Sociology at the Department of Sociology, Stockholm University, Sweden.

Routledge studies in extremism and democracy
Series Editors:
Roger Eatwell
University of Bath
and
Matthew Goodwin
University of Nottingham

Founding Series Editors:
Roger Eatwell
University of Bath
and
Cas Mudde
University of Antwerp—UFSIA

This new series encompasses academic studies within the broad fields of 'extremism' and 'democracy'. These topics have traditionally been considered largely in isolation by academics. A key focus of the series, therefore, is the (inter-)*relation* between extremism and democracy. Works will seek to answer questions such as to what extent 'extremist' groups pose a major threat to democratic parties, or how democracy can respond to extremism without undermining its own democratic credentials.

The books encompass two strands:

Routledge Studies in Extremism and Democracy includes books with an introductory and broad focus, which are aimed at students and teachers. These books will be available in hardback and paperback. Titles include:

Understanding Terrorism in America
From the Klan to al Qaeda
Christopher Hewitt

Fascism and the Extreme Right
Roger Eatwell

Racist Extremism in Central and Eastern Europe
Edited by Cas Mudde

Political Parties and Terrorist Groups (2nd Edition)
Leonard Weinberg, Ami Pedahzur and Arie Perliger

The New Extremism in 21st Century Britain
Edited by Roger Eatwell and Matthew Goodwin

New British Fascism
Rise of the British National Party
Matthew Goodwin

The End of Terrorism?
Leonard Weinberg

Mapping the Extreme Right in Contemporary Europe
From local to transnational
Edited by Andrea Mammone, Emmanuel Godin and Brian Jenkins

Varieties of Right-Wing Extremism in Europe
Edited by Andrea Mammone, Emmanuel Godin and Brian Jenkins

Routledge Research in Extremism and Democracy offers a forum for innovative new research intended for a more specialist readership. These books will be in hardback only. Titles include:

1 **Uncivil Society?**
Contentious politics in post-Communist Europe
Edited by Petr Kopecky and Cas Mudde

2 **Political Parties and Terrorist Groups**
Leonard Weinberg and Ami Pedahzur

3 **Western Democracies and the New Extreme Right Challenge**
Edited by Roger Eatwell and Cas Mudde

4 **Confronting Right Wing Extremism and Terrorism in the USA**
George Michael

5 **Anti-Political Establishment Parties**
A comparative analysis
Amir Abedi

6 **American Extremism**
History, politics and the militia
D. J. Mulloy

7 **The Scope of Tolerance**
Studies on the costs of free expression and freedom of the press
Raphael Cohen-Almagor

8 **Extreme Right Activists in Europe**
Through the magnifying glass
Bert Klandermans and Nonna Mayer

Class Politics and the Radical Right

Edited by Jens Rydgren

Routledge
Taylor & Francis Group

LONDON AND NEW YORK

First published 2013
by Routledge
2 Park Square, Milton Park, Abingdon, Oxon OX14 4RN

Simultaneously published in the USA and Canada
by Routledge
711 Third Avenue, New York, NY 10017

Routledge is an imprint of the Taylor & Francis Group, an informa business

British Library Cataloguing in Publication Data
A catalogue record for this book is available from the British Library

Library of Congress Cataloging in Publication Data
A catalog record has been requested for this book

ISBN: 978-0-415-69052-2 (hbk)
ISBN: 978-0-203-07954-6 (ebk)

Typeset in Times New Roman
by Wearset Ltd, Boldon, Tyne and Wear

MIX
Paper from
responsible sources
FSC
www.fsc.org   FSC® C004839

Printed and bound in Great Britain by
TJ International Ltd, Padstow, Cornwall

Contents

Figures and tables

Figures

Tables

About the authors

Kai Arzheimer is Professor of Political Science at the University of Mainz and Visiting Fellow at the Department of Government, University of Essex. Among his publications are "Contextual Factors and the Extreme Right Vote in Western Europe, 1980–2002" in the *American Journal of Political Science* 53 (2009).

Tim Bale was educated at Cambridge, Northwestern and Sheffield. He is now Professor of Politics at Queen Mary, University of London. His main interest is party politics in Britain and Europe. His latest book, *The Conservatives since 1945: The Drivers of Party Change*, will be published by Oxford University Press in September 2012. He is also the author of *European Politics: A Comparative Introduction*, the third edition of which will be out soon.

Inger Baller is currently a PhD student at the University of Antwerp. She has recently completed the Research Masters in Social Sciences at the University of Amsterdam with a thesis on the support for Dutch right-wing populist parties.

Hans-Georg Betz is Adjunct Professor at the University of Zurich. Among his major publications are: *Radical Right-Wing Populism in Western Europe* (1994), *Extrême et démocrate: La droite populiste en Europe* (2004), and *États-Unis: Une nation divisée* (2008).

Simon Bornschier is a Senior Researcher at the Institute for Political Science at the University of Zurich, and a Post-Doctoral Fellow at the University of St Gallen. He is the author of *Cleavage Politics and the Populist Right. The New Cultural Conflict in Western Europe* (Temple University Press, 2010) and co-author of *West European Politics in the Age of Globalization* (with H. Kriesi, E. Grande, R. Lachat, M. Dolezal, and T. Frey, Cambridge University Press, 2008). He currently works on cleavage structures and evolving citizen-party linkages in Latin America.

Hilde Coffé is a Senior Lecturer in the Political Science and International Relations Programme at Victoria University of Wellington. Her main research interests include voting behavior, political participation, and public opinion. She has written a book on the radical right in Belgium and some of her recent work has been published in *Electoral Studies*, *Party Politics*, *British Journal of Sociology*, *Social Science Quarterly*, and *Political Studies*.

David Cutts is a Senior Lecturer in the Department of Politics, Languages and International Studies at the University of Bath. With Matthew Goodwin, he has published a number of articles on far right extremism in Britain. He has also published on a wide range of issues including political engagement and participation, voter turnout, and voting behaviour, with a particular focus on the interaction between individuals and the local context. David Cutts has published in many high quality journals including the *American Journal of Political Science, Canadian Journal of Political Science, Journal of Politics* and *European Journal of Political Research*.

Sarah de Lange is Assistant Professor in the Department of Political Science at the University of Amsterdam. Her dissertation, entitled *From Pariah to Power: Explanations for the Government Participation of Radical Right-Wing Populist Parties in West European Parliamentary Democracies*, was nominated for the thesis award of the Dutch Political Science Association (NKWP), in 2009. Her publications have appeared in journals such as *Acta Politica, Comparative European Politics*, and *Party Politics*.

Marie Demker is Professor in Political Science at the University of Gothenburg. She has written several books, including *Colonial Power and National Identity*. Another text that deserves to be mentioned is *Pierre Mendès France and the History of French Decolonisation* (Santérus, 2008). She has also published articles in *Party Politics, Punishment & Society* and the *International Review of Sociology*. Her most recent publication is a chapter on Scandinavian right-wing populism in *Mapping the Extreme Right in Contemporary Europe* (Mammone, Godin, Jenkins (eds), Routledge, 2012).

Meindert Fennema is Professor in Political Theory at the Department of Political Science at the University of Amsterdam. With Wouter van der Brug and Jean Tillie he has published extensively on anti-immigrant parties and on the social capital of immigrant communities and their political participation. He has also published several articles on corporate governance. In Dutch he has published a textbook on the history of democratic theory (2012) and a biography of the most powerful Dutch civil servant during Nazi occupation, Hans Max Hirschfeld (2007). He has also written a political biography of the anti-Islamic politician Geert Wilders (*Tovenaarsleerling*, Bert Bakker, 2010).

Matthew J. Goodwin is Lecturer in Politics at the School of Politics and International Relations, University of Nottingham, and Associate Fellow at Chatham House. He is the author and co-editor of several major studies of right-wing extremism, including *New British Fascism: Rise of the British National Party* (Routledge, 2011), *The New Extremism in 21st Century Britain* (Routledge, 2010), and the Chatham House report, *Right Response: Understanding and Countering Populist Extremism in Europe*. Matthew is an advisor to national and local government and security services, and is currently working on a book manuscript, *Voting for Extremists*, with Dr Robert Ford.

Florent Gougou is a PhD candidate at the Center for European Studies at Sciences Po, Paris. His research focuses on elections, voting behavior, cleavages and realignment theory. His articles have appeared in French Politics and he recently coauthored a chapter on class and religious voting in France (in G. Evans, N.D. De Graaf (eds.), *Political Choice Matters*, Oxford University Press, forthcoming).

Dan Hough is a Reader in Politics at the University of Sussex in the UK. He is also Director of the Sussex Centre for the Study of Corruption. His most recent publications include *The Politics of the New Germany* (co-written with Simon Green and Alister Miskimmon, Palgrave, 2011) and at the end of 2012 he will publish a book entitled *Corruption, Anti-Corruption and Governance* (Palgrave).

Elisabeth Ivarsflaten is Associate Professor and Vice-Head at the Department of Comparative Politics, University of Bergen. She wrote her PhD on populist right parties in Western Europe at the University of Oxford where she also worked as a Postdoctoral Prize Research Fellow. She currently coordinates the Norwegian branch of the Nordic Populism network (NOPO). Her publications on populist right parties and voters and public opinion in the immigration and minority domain have appeared in several books and journals, including *Comparative Political Studies* and the *European Journal of Political Research*.

Herbert Kitschelt is George V. Allen Professor of International Relations at Duke University. Among his many books are *Patrons or Policies? Patterns of Democratic Accountability and Political Competition* (Cambridge University Press, 2007), *Continuity and Change in Contemporary Capitalism* (Cambridge University Press, 1999), *The Radical Right in Western Europe: A Comparative Analysis* (University of Michigan Press, 1995), and *The Transformation of European Social Democracy* (Cambridge University Press, 1994).

Hanspeter Kriesi holds the Chair in Comparative Politics at the Department of Political Science at the University of Zurich. Previously, he has been teaching at the universities of Amsterdam and Geneva. His wide-ranging research interests include the study of direct democracy, social movements, political parties and interest groups, public opinion, the public sphere, and the media. He is the director of a Swiss national research program, "Challenges to Democracy in the Twenty-First Century".

Nonna Mayer is Research Professor at the Centre for European Studies (Sciences Po—National Centre for Scientific Research) and teaches in the Political Science Doctoral School of Sciences, Po. She is President of the French Political Science Association (AFSP). Her research fields are electoral behavior, racism and anti-Semitism and right-wing extremism. Recent publications include: *Ces Français qui votent Le Pen* (Flammarion, 2002); *Extreme Right Activists in Europe: Through the Magnifying Glass* (with B. Klandermans, Routledge, 2006); *Sociologie des comportements politiques* (A. Colin, 2010); and "Why

Extremes Don't Meet: Le Pen and Besancenot Voters in the 2007 French Presidential Election", *French Politics, Culture and Society*, Winter 2011.

Susi Meret is Assistant Professor at the Institute for Culture and Global Studies at Aalborg University. She is the main coordinator of the research network on Nordic Populism.

Michael Minkenberg is Professor of Comparative Politics at the European University Viadrina in Frankfurt (Oder). From 2007–2010 he held the Max Weber Chair for German and European Studies at NYU. He received his MA in American Government from Georgetown University in 1984, and his PhD in Political Science from the University of Heidelberg in 1989. Since then, he has taught at the universities of Göttingen and Heidelberg, and at Cornell University and Columbia University. Among his recent publications are: *The Radical Right in Europe. An Overview* (Guetersloh, 2008), and "The Tea Party Movement and American Populism Today: Between Protest, Patriotism, and Paranoia", *dms—der moderne staat* (February 2011).

Daniel Oesch is Assistant Professor at the Institute of Social Sciences at the University of Lausanne and is teaching a Master's course at the University of Geneva. He is the author of *Redrawing the Class Map. Stratification and Institutions in Britain, Germany, Sweden and Switzerland* (Palgrave Macmillan, 2006).

Maria Oskarson is Associate Professor of Political Science at the University of Gothenburg.

Bartek Pytlas is a PhD candidate at the Chair of Comparative Politics at the European University Viadrina in Frankfurt (Oder). He received his BA in Cultural Sciences from the same university in 2005, and his MA in European Studies in 2008. His dissertation project aims at analyzing party competition mechanisms in regard to right-wing radical frames in Central Eastern Europe. The thesis research is being funded by a scholarship grant from the Heinrich Böll Foundation.

Jens Rydgren is Professor (Chair) of Sociology at Stockholm University. He is working in the areas of political sociology, ethnic relations, and social networks. He is the author and editor of several books, and his research has been published in journals such as the *Annual Review of Sociology*, the *European Journal of Political Research*, and *Rationality and Society*.

Rune Stubager is Associate Professor of Political Science at Aarhus University. His research has appeared in journals such as the *British Journal of Political Science*, the *British Journal of Sociology*, and *Political Psychology*.

Wouter van der Brug is Professor of Political Science at the University of Amsterdam. His research interests focus on comparative research in collective political behavior, in particular electoral behavior, right-wing populism, political communication, political trust and support, and political parties. His work has been published in various international journals, such as the *European Journal of Political Research*, the *British Journal of Political Science*, and *Electoral Studies*. His most recent monograph, called *The Economy and the Vote* (co-authored by Cees van der Eijk and Mark Franklin), was published in 2007 by Cambridge University Press.

Stijn van Kessel completed his doctorate in 2011 at the University of Sussex. He has subsequently been Visiting Lecturer at the Radboud University Nijmegen and the VU University Amsterdam. His doctoral research focused on the concept of populism and the electoral performance of populist political parties in Europe in a comparative perspective. He has published several book chapters, as well as journal articles in *Acta Politica* and *Perspectives on European Politics and Society*.

Introduction

Class politics and the radical right

Jens Rydgren

Introduction

Radical right-wing parties are today established in a majority of Western European party systems, and increasingly so also in Eastern Europe. The emergence of the recent wave of radical right-wing party politics has generated a large and growing literature, spanning a variety of dimensions—such as ideology, voting, and policy impact. This volume will cover all these dimensions, but it will in particular focus on two questions: why is it that the working class tends to be especially attracted by the radical right-wing parties? And what does the radical right-wing parties' growing electoral success mean for social democracy and the traditional left in Europe, which are meeting growing competition from the radical right over working-class voters?

The chapters in this volume address these questions in different but overlapping ways, and present evidence from a large spectrum of countries. Several chapters present new takes on one of the more popular explanations for the emergence of radical right-wing parties: that post-industrialization and globalization have restructured social stratification in Western societies, creating new frustrations among the losers in these processes, that is, chiefly among people who lack higher education and who tend to work in sectors that are shrinking in Western Europe (such as manual workers). At the same time, however, as demonstrated in several of the chapters, working-class voters' electoral support of the radical right can be explained not by socio-economic preferences but is rather filtered by socio-cultural policy preferences—where the quest for reduced immigration is the most fundamental. Hence, the over-representation of working-class voters within the radical right-wing parties' electorates can partly be explained by the fact that workers on average tend to be more socio-culturally authoritarian than other voters (due to lower levels of education and/or more instrumental and mechanic working conditions), partly by the fact that they increasingly find socio-cultural politics to be more salient than socio-economic politics. As is also discussed in several of the chapters, changes in the economic-political programs of the radical right-wing parties—which for many of the parties have changed from neo-liberal positions to centrist or even slightly leftist positions on economic policy during the past decade and a half—have made the radical right more attractive for working-class voters. The combination of ethnic nationalism and anti-immigration messages on the one hand and a pro-welfare rhetoric on the other seems to be the new winning formula for radical right-wing parties, which partly explains why these parties have become increasingly popular among workers. As is discussed in Betz and Meret's contribution to this volume, some radical right-wing parties—such as the French Front National under its new party leader Marine Le Pen—are currently in the process of sharpening their economic-political profiles by calling for a halt to economic (and not only cultural) globalization. It is also possible to find examples of when the radical right has actively tried to mobilize workers by appealing to social class and by appropriating working-class symbols.

The remainder of this short introduction will be structured in the following way. First, I will briefly discuss the definition of the party family of radical right-wing parties. Second, I will make a modest attempt to fill a gap (or at least a less-developed area) in previous research on the radical right. Although, as is reflected in this volume, research on the radical right has become much more sophisticated the past decade and a half, it is still largely preoccupied with macro-structural explanations of voters' behavior. What are less developed, however, are the micro-level foundations to such explanations. Several attempts have been made, such as "frustration" (that is, "losers of modernity and globalization processes are becoming frustrated, and such frustration is canalized into support for the radical right), and "ethnic competition" (that is, immigration increases competition over scarce resources, making voters more likely to support strict immigration policy) (see Rydgren 2007 for discussion and references)—but however useful these attempts are there is still room for improvement. Borrowing from social movement theory and the sociology of emotions, I will in the second part of this introduction discuss alternative micro-level foundations, in particular the role of the articulation of negative emotions.

I will not discuss the individual chapters in greater detail, since that would be redundant and (I think) tiresome for the readers. Instead, I have asked Herbert Kitschelt to provide a critical commentary on the other contributions to this book; this is integrated in his chapter, which is the final chapter of the volume.

Radical right-wing parties: how should they be defined?

The radical right-wing parties share an emphasis on ethno-nationalism rooted in myths about the distant past. Their program is directed toward strengthening the nation by making it more ethnically homogeneous. They also tend to be populists in accusing elites of putting internationalism ahead of the nation and of putting their own narrow self-interests, and various special interests, ahead of the interests of the people. The radical right-wing parties share a core of ethno-nationalist xenophobia and anti-establishment populism. In their political platforms this ideological core is often embedded in a general socio-cultural authoritarianism that stresses themes such as law and order and family values (Rydgren 2005).

One common way to distinguish between left and right is to view the former as egalitarian and the latter as nonegalitarian (Bobbio 1996) or the left as universalistic and the right as particularistic (e.g., Eatwell 2004). Two problems with this distinction, of course, are that it is unclear on what policies parties should be judged and that parties can, for instance, be nonegalitarian and universalistic at the same time. More specifically, we may define a party as left or right according to its position on socio-economic politics, which concerns the degree of state involvement in the economy (i.e., economic socialism versus economic liberalism), or on its position on socio-cultural politics, which relate to value-laden issues such as national identity, law and order, immigration policy, abortion, and so on (i.e., socio-cultural liberalism versus authoritarianism). The new radical right is right wing primarily in the socio-cultural sense of the term.

The new radical right gives priority to socio-cultural issues, in particular to issues related to national identity, and its central political program can be understood as "a response to the erosion of the system of 'ethno-national dominance', which characterized much of the history of modern nation states" (Betz and Johnson 2004: 323). More specifically, the radical right builds on the idea of ethno-pluralism, a concept that is in line with right-wing ideas going back to Herder (Berlin 1976; Holmes 2000) and that in modern times was elaborated by the French *Nouvelle Droite*. The *Nouvelle Droite* was a composite term for intellectual groups that, inspired by Gramsci's notion of cultural hegemony, formed in France during the late 1960s and 1970s to counter the intellectual and cultural dominance of the left. For the *Nouvelle Droite*, as for related groups in Italy and Germany, the principal aim was *Kulturkampf*, and not party politics (Minkenberg 2000). Departing from the left's notion of *différence*—on which the doctrine of multiculturalism (that is, the idea that migrants should have the right to preserve the habits and traditions of their home countries) is largely based—the notion of ethno-pluralism states that, to preserve the unique national characters of different peoples, they have to be kept separate. Mixing of different ethnicities only leads to cultural extinction (see Griffin 2000; Minkenberg 1997; Taguieff 1988). Moreover, in this doctrine, which claims that difference, culture and ethnicity are deterministic and monolithic, chances for individual change and in-group variation are believed to be slight. Yet, contrary to the traditional conception of racism, the doctrine of ethno-pluralism, as such, is not hierarchical: different ethnicities are not necessarily superior or inferior, only different, incompatible, and incommensurable (Betz and Johnson 2004; Taguieff 1988). Hence, whereas old racism, common in colonial settings, aimed at subordination, the ethno-pluralist doctrine basically aims at expulsion (Fennema 2005).

The French Front National adopted this notion from the *Nouvelle Droite* and made it the core of the party's political program and rhetorical profile. Today it is the most distinguishing ideological characteristic of the new radical right party family (Rydgren 2005; see also Betz 2005). By using the ethno-pluralist ideology, the radical right-wing parties claim the right of European national cultures to protect their cultural identity. According to the new radical right, there are several threats against their national identity, of which the alleged invasion of immigrants is the most important. Immigrants from Muslim countries are singled out as particularly threatening to European values, allegedly because they are the least commensurable and the least inclined to assimilation. Other threats are supranational entities such as the European Union and, increasingly, multinational corporations and economic globalization, as well as cosmopolitan elites, and other processes believed to foster universalization and homogenization.

Also, more generally, anti-immigration issues are the core message of the new radical right. These parties have used four arguments to frame immigrants as national/cultural threats: first, as implied above, for the radical right immigrants are a threat to ethno-national identity; second, they are a major cause of criminality and other kinds of social insecurity; third, they are a cause of unemployment; and fourth, they are abusers of the generosity of the welfare states of Western democracies, which results in fewer state subsidies, etc. for natives (see, for example, Rydgren 2003). Using the third and fourth frames, the new radical right-wing parties have promoted the idea of national preference, that is, giving natives priority when it comes to jobs, housing, health care, and so on. Their proposals can be characterized as a sort of reversed affirmative action (e.g., Zaslove 2004a; Rydgren 2003). For all these reasons, radical right-wing parties promote an ethnic view of citizenship (*jus sanguinis*) and oppose models of residential citizenship (*jus soli*) (see Brubaker 1992).

The picture is more ambiguous as far as economic policies are concerned. Most of the radical right-wing parties backed neo-liberal economics of one sort or another during the 1980s, often manifested in campaigns for radical tax cuts. However, during the 1990s, most of the radical right parties changed positions and have become more economically protectionist, which implies a more centrist position on economic policies. As a result, many radical right-wing parties today support the capitalist system nationally, while at the same time strongly opposing globalization (Zaslove 2004b). In this vein, for example, Bruno Mégret, then member of the French Front National, launched the idea of national capitalism (see Rydgren 2003). Simultaneously, as we shall see in this book through several examples, welfare chauvinism became increasingly important to the new radical right-wing parties and led some of them to present themselves as supporters of the welfare state (see also Betz and Johnson 2004; Evans *et al.* 2001).

Some scholars (e.g., Betz 1993, 1994; Taggart 1996, 2000) have argued that populism is a defining characteristic of the new radical right. This is true insofar as these parties tend to view society as "ultimately separated into two homogeneous and antagonistic groups, the 'pure' people versus 'the corrupt elite'"—a worldview that, according to Cas Mudde (2004: 543), is characteristic of populism—and that the populist anti-establishment strategy has been crucial to the success of the new radical right-wing parties. In the case of the new radical right-wing parties, not only elites but other groups as well (immigrants, ethnic minorities) are excluded from the "pure people." A party that uses the anti-establishment strategy tries to construct an image of itself as in opposition to the political class, while trying actively not to appear antidemocratic. A party that is viewed as antidemocratic will be stigmatized and marginalized as long as the overwhelming majority of the electorate is in favor of democracy per se (Schedler 1996; see also van der Brug *et al.* 2005).

To create distance between themselves and the established political parties (i.e., both the government and the anti-incumbent opposition), populist parties aim at recoding the political space, with its diversity of parties, into one single, homogeneous political class. One way of achieving this goal is to argue that the differences between government and established opposition parties are irrelevant surface phenomena. According to the radical right-wing parties, in reality the established parties do not compete but collude (Schedler 1996). Part of their strategy is often also to criticize the established parties for focusing on obsolete issues, while at the same time suppressing political issues associated with the real conflict between national identity and multiculturalism.

The populist anti-establishment strategy makes it possible for the radical right-wing parties to present themselves as the real champions of true democracy—as a new kind of party—which takes the worries and interests of the common man into account (see, e.g., Betz and Johnson 2004; Mudde 2004). Yet, the Manichean worldview of the new radical right-wing parties makes the politics of compromise and bargaining of liberal democracy difficult. Thus, the new radical right-wing parties commonly demand more referenda, which encourage clear yes or no answers, while discouraging compromise (Eatwell 2004).

Yet one can argue that populism is a characteristic but not a distinctive feature of the new radical right. Other parties use the populist anti-establishment strategy as well, and several parties of other political shades in Western Europe can be said to be populist in some way or another.

Frustration, shame, and fear: micro-level explanations of radical right-wing mobilization

Grievance theory forms an important part of popular explanations of radical right-wing support, and in particular gives reasons for working-class voters tending to support these parties. The feeling of being left behind in a rapidly changing world, in which formal education and other forms of cultural capital is increasingly important for life chances, is believed to lead to frustration and even resentment. As is somewhat less noted in previous literature, however, such processes may also give rise to feelings of shame and the perception of threat. According to Kemper (2001), real or perceived losses in status or economic position (in absolute or relative terms) are likely to result in feelings of anger or indignation if they are successfully attributed to the action of others, whereas they will lead to feelings of shame if such losses are blamed on the self. Since shame tends to be less tolerable than anger or indignation, those who are ashamed are often susceptible to political messages trying to demonize outgroups as being responsible for their losses (see Goodwin and Jasper 2007). Since globalization and other structural processes are abstract phenomena, which only "act" in an indirect sense, there is a tendency to personalize problems and to attribute actions to individuals or, rather, groups or categories of individuals. Examples of such groups include elites, and various immigrant groups.

Negative feelings may also operate in other ways than through status losses. In particular, real or perceived threats to the "quotidian" may result in feelings of fear and deep frustration. The quotidian encompasses the taken-for-granted features of the everyday, the routines and established ways of getting along with one's life and with people in one's immediate vicinity, as well as expectations about the near future (Snow *et al.* 2010). The quotidian represents settled times (Swidler 1986), when people feel at ease and do not need to reflect too much on alternative strategies for interpreting the world. When the quotidian is disrupted, routines and settled ways of actions are rendered problematic, giving rise to confusion, frustration, and feelings of insecurity and fear (Snow *et al.* 2010). This state makes people more receptive to political actors offering new frames for how to understand (the now) problematic reality (Swidler 1986), and maybe especially to frames pointing out who are to be blamed for the disruption of the quotidian and who promises to restore the status quo ante. In terms of content such frames can be very different, and can lean both to the left and the right; but the frames offered by radical right-wing parties are clearly one alternative that people may find attractive in unsettled times, in which the quotidian has been disrupted. Even if the disruption of the quotidian is caused by a complex combination of structural factors, frames that scapegoat immigrant groups who are visibly different from the majority population may be particularly effective since they point to changes (increased migration) that are concrete and visible. Frames attributing guilt to structures, and even frames attributing guilt to "global capitalists," may be less effective because of being more abstract. This is a possible explanation as to why immigration-skeptical attitudes (i.e., a preference for reduced immigration) are strongly correlated with voting for radical right-wing parties, whereas xenophobia and racism are not (Rydgren 2008). In fact, opposition to immigration caused by real and perceived disruption of the quotidian may very well be very locally bounded, and closer to "NIMBY" mobilization than genuine xenophobia. In other words, people may view immigrants positively in principle, but have strong preferences for fencing them out of their backyards. As argued by Snow *et al.* (2010: 20), "actual or threatened intrusion into culturally defined zones of privacy and control by strangers, uninvited persons, corporate and/or governmental agents, all else being equal, to generate collective action to re-establish the zone of privacy and control." This is the general principle, and I argue that anti-immigration mobilization at the voter level is often just one manifestation of this principle.

Why then, would workers be especially likely to feel their quotidian disrupted, and be particularly susceptible to frames mobilizing against immigration? One reason is that they have fewer resources, and thus less control over their situations. Compared to people with more resources, they cannot as easily move out of neighborhoods, for example. They often lack exit options. One other reason is that workers on average are less educated, and there are good reasons to assume that the ability to adjust to problematic reality is enhanced by higher education (Lipset 1960; Kriesi *et al.* 2008). Furthermore, mainstream left parties have often failed to present competing frames that find resonance among workers (in particular among male workers). As noted by Kitschelt (2004: 9), "the strategic movement of social democracy toward economic centrism and socio-cultural liberalism," prompted by the strategy of winning middle-class voters, has alienated many working voters. Finally, segments of the working class are more likely to be (or at least perceive themselves to be) in social decline. It is important to note that individuals' worldviews and ideological outlooks not only depend on their present status position, but also on their past and expected future position (see Bourdieu 1984: 453–454).

This gives trajectory a major role in the formation of people's political opinions. The slope of the individual and the collectivity of which he or she is a part influences whether people are turned toward the future and are inclined to social optimism, or turned toward the past and inclined to social pessimism (Bourdieu 1984: 454–455). Individuals who find themselves in social decline are more likely to celebrate traditions of the past, history, and its rituals, because, as Bourdieu (1984: 111) put it, "the best they can expect from the future is the return of the old order, from which they expect the restoration of their social being." In other words, groups of individuals in social decline have a perceived interest in the status quo ante, as well as in a reevaluation of established orders of values. As is argued in several chapters in this volume, recent transformations in the economy, together with cultural and political changes, have increasingly marginalized and excluded segments of the population. People who possess little cultural capital and/or have cultural capital invested in "old" modes of production (i.e., unskilled and semiskilled workers, and segments of the lower middle class, such as some small tradesmen and craftsmen, and other small employers, etc.) have found themselves in social decline in absolute or relative terms, which may foster feelings of relative deprivation (not least of social status). Those individuals, whose objective properties, practices, and opinions can be seen as linked to a past age, might be more likely to become conservative, pessimistic, and resentful, and to reject "politics" and "politicians" of all kinds (Bourdieu 1984: 364, 458). This tendency is likely stronger for individuals who are not politically organized and/or lack strong ties (due to political socialization) to the labor movement.

Hence, the structures of social space, which is also a structure of social comparison, change as a result of macro-structural changes (globalization, post-industrialization). In this process knowledge (not least formal education) increasingly becomes the dominant instrument of stratification. Those lagging behind in this process may be more likely to experience relative deprivation, which in turn leads to frustration and other negative feelings, such as resentment and envy, but also shame (as was discussed above). Generally, the experience of relative deprivation is caused by a gap between expectation and achievement, which and is either from comparisons with other groups of individuals, or from comparisons with one's own past (Brown 1995: 192). People mostly expect their future to be similar to their present, or at least to follow the current trajectory of

If standards of living rise over time, many people will expect future ~ases. As a consequence, it may be predicted that the level of dissatisfaction will be at its highest when a period of increased standards of living is suddenly followed by an economic downturn (Davies 1966). Similarly, people tend to regard the status associated with particular social positions and characteristics, professions in particular, as taken for granted. When their status becomes devalued, some will experience a status deprivation.

An illustrative example of this process can be found in Flecker and colleagues:

> A number of interviews in all the countries under investigation showed clear connections between the conditions and changes in the world of work and the receptiveness to right-wing populism and extremism. One such connection can be located in ... their experience of fear that, in spite of hard work and sacrifices, they are not able to maintain or attain the standard of living and social status they have previously enjoyed or which they aspire to.
>
> (Flecker *et al.* 2007: 41–42)

Hence, when people believe that they run the risk of status deprivation, negative feelings may under certain conditions be channeled into support for the radical right in a variety of ways, of which three will be mentioned here. First, it may be expressed in "nihilist" populism (i.e., "All politicians and capitalists are out to cheat us ordinary people"). Second, people may adopt and support strategies of reevaluation (i.e., to shift the dominant value system toward values based on the status quo ante). Third, and partly overlapping, people may become susceptible to ethno-nationalist protectionism and/or xenophobic welfare chauvinism (i.e., "Those who don't belong here shouldn't share the benefits of our society"). This is more likely to happen in a situation in which the voter groups in question have a low level of trust in the established political parties, in particular when they have lost confidence in the parties that traditionally have represented their interests.

As indicated above, one important question is what happens when individuals find themselves belonging to in-groups that are negatively evaluated in relation to other groups. We may assume that most people, under normal conditions, will accept this situation as a *fait accompli*—especially if they are born into this position. However, in a situation of social decline and (further) deprivation (or the perceived risk of that), that is, when new groups enter into such a position or when socio-economic cleavages are increasing, more people may strive to change this situation. There are three strategies that can be used in such situations: (1) individuals belonging to such groups may leave the group; (2) they may try to change the society's status hierarchy; and (3) they may try to change the established group classification. However, it is not always easy to leave the group one belongs to, especially not social classes or professional groups. It may be particularly difficult to acquire the cultural and social capital needed to move to another, more positively evaluated group. Much of our cultural and social capital is acquired in the family and in formal education during adolescence. Nor is it always easy for individuals with little cultural capital to leverage social change. Many people, especially people with little cultural capital, have lost faith in established political parties and movements. We know that many of the old outlets for channeling socio-political discontent do not function as well as they once did (e.g., Lawson 1988), and many who possess little cultural capital have become increasingly pessimistic about the possibility of achieving social change within the established political institutions. With the two first options partly blocked, some will turn to the third alternative, that is, they try to change the established group classification scheme, or at least support political actors who claim that they will change it. One way of using the third strategy is by arguing that the established order of group classification is irrelevant and/or artificial (e.g., social class) and that there is an alternative order that is essential and of true relevance (e.g., ethnicity). Hence, those who find themselves in social decline may be more likely to support political programs that promise to redraw the boundaries of group classification. In the specific socio-historical context we cover in this book, we are mainly concerned with the increased salience of the socio-cultural cleavage dimension, and the corresponding decreased salience of the economic cleavage dimension. As a consequence of this partial realignment, many who previously defined themselves, their adversaries, and socio-political issues in terms of economic position, now define these in terms of ethnicity and nationality. By downplaying the existence of class stratification and by stressing the harmony and homogeneity of "the people," individuals in negatively evaluated groups may redraw, or at least support political actors who claim to redraw, the boundaries of classification, and thereby achieve higher self-esteem. Yet, at the same time a new out-group has to be identified (and partly constructed), in this case people of other ethnic origins, mainly "immigrants." In addition, since ethno-nationality is ascribed rather than achieved, which makes the impact of social competition less significant, a sense of positive distinction may be easier to sustain.

1 The populist right, the working class, and the changing face of class politics

Simon Bornschier and Hanspeter Kriesi

Introduction

To many, the transformation of West European party systems since the 1970s and 1980s was seen as evidence that the era of cleavage-based politics was over. The rise of identity politics was interpreted not only as a result of the waning of the traditional class and religious cleavages, but as evidence for a new era in which political preferences de-coupled from social structure began to shape voting behavior. It was assumed that voters were "beginning to choose" parties for their policy propositions, the quality of their personnel, or based on their value preferences. The more recent successes of the extreme populist right once again were taken to indicate that anti-establishment populist mobilization was cutting across class alignments. From this point of view, the by now well established finding that the working class is over-represented in the extreme populist right's electorate came unexpectedly.

While a host of hypotheses have been advanced to explain the propensity of parts of the working class to support the extreme right, the phenomenon still awaits a theoretical explanation and a systematic empirical test of the rival theses. In this chapter, we review the explanations that have been put forward and test whether economic grievances or cultural world-views are better in explaining the phenomenon. Both are related to the processes of modernization and globalization, which have a cultural as well as an economic component. We argue that the changing nature of conflicts in West European party systems is crucial in explaining the shift of the manual working class to the extreme right. In particular, the dual transformation of political space has resulted in a new cultural divide that plays a pivotal role in explaining the extreme populist right's appeal for the working class. Preferences along this divide are structured by education and by the experiences individuals undergo at their workplace, either making them more open to cultural liberalism, or leading them to endorse an anti-universalistic counter-model of community that is based on the exclusion of immigrants.

In conceptual terms, we make an innovative contribution by focusing both on the individual-level characteristics accounting for participation in elections as well as on those explaining the choice of extreme right-wing populist parties.

Using Heckman selection models, we show that the losers in economic modernization actually abstain from voting, while those uncomfortable with cultural modernity support the extreme populist right. Even if we control for political preferences and a number of other factors, however, the over-representation of blue-collar workers in the extreme right's electorate persists. The working class by now appears firmly rooted in this segment of the electorate. While not being the worst-off social segment in post-industrial society, this group has experienced a relative decline as compared to the postwar decades, making it receptive to the culturalist appeal of the extreme right.

These findings raise the question of how individuals with similar political preferences vote in countries where extreme right-wing populist parties are absent. In a final step, we tackle this question. We show that not voting is the preferred option of anti-universalistic or authoritarian segments of the working class where an extreme right option is missing. Thus, the capacity of the mainstream parties to rally this electorate appears limited even in those party systems not facing an extreme right challenger.

The analysis is based on survey data from thirteen West European countries, six of which feature sizable extreme right-wing populist parties, while these parties failed to achieve an electoral breakthrough in seven others, the Greek LAOS and the Swedish Democrats having been on the verge of breaking through. We start with the discussion of the continued relevance of social class in West European politics and lay out our account of the formation of a new cultural divide. We then discuss various explanations that may account for the propensity of the working class to support the extreme right, and include measures for these hypotheses in our statistical models. The empirical part of this chapter is structured as follows. In a first step, we look at the class basis of the extreme populist right and analyze to which degree the propensity of certain occupational classes to support these parties is explained by education and preferences along economic and cultural divides. We also take into account the factors explaining political participation. We then take a closer look at voting choices *within* the working class and try to discern the motives that push voters to vote for the extreme populist right, rather than other parties. Finally, we analyze the vote of those individuals within the working class that share the individual-level characteristics of those supporting populist right parties in the countries where these are present, but lack such an option in their own party system.

The transformation of cultural conflicts

In the aftermath of 1968, politics was shaken by new social movements that politicized issues relating to societal values and lifestyles, rather than the more traditional distributional or religious conflicts. As political parties responded to the progressive demands of these movements, a two-dimensional structure of conflicts became discernible in West European party systems (Kitschelt 1994). Cutting across the "old" distributional axis, a cultural line of conflict between libertarian and authoritarian values came to structure the attitudes of voters and the positions of parties. On the political left, the prominence of cultural liberalism gave rise to the establishment of Green parties and a transformation of social democratic parties early in the 1980s. These parties attracted an increasing number of voters from the middle class, especially among certain of its constituencies such as so-called social-cultural professionals. As a result, a new divide within the middle class emerged that was rooted in different work logics, the interpersonal logic resulting in the endorsement of libertarian or universalistic values, while employees in hierarchical settings developed or retained more authoritarian values (Kriesi 1989, 1993, 1998; see also Müller 1999). Thus, while some have taken the new saliency of cultural conflicts to mark the end of cleavage-based politics (e.g., Dalton *et al.* 1984; see also Franklin *et al.* 1992), these analyses showed that political conflict remained anchored in an evolving class structure.

While the counter-reaction against the New Left was delayed for at least a decade, new parties of the extreme populist right emerged in the 1980s and the 1990s in many West European countries (Ignazi 1992, 2003; see also Minkenberg 2000).[1] By developing their own traditional-communitarian conception of community, they came to challenge the New Left's universalistic values (Bornschier 2010a, 2010b). This novel ideology helped parties to foster the emergence of a collective identity among the losers of the processes of modernization and accelerating globalization. Consequently, they were able to mobilize what in the 1980s had still been a diffuse anti-universalistic potential, as shown by Sacchi (1998). The politicization of opposition against immigration and European integration, as well as the rejection of the cultural liberalism defended by the New Left, then, constituted the driving force of a second transformation of West European party systems in the late 1980s and in the 1990s (Kriesi *et al.* 2006, 2008b).

The populist anti-establishment character of the extreme right's mobilization at first appeared to support the more general claim that politics was losing its foundation in social class, as perhaps put most boldly by Kingston (2000), for whom a "classless society" had emerged. Early on, however, Betz (1994, 2004) assembled evidence for the "proletarianization" of the right-wing populist challengers' support base. Heavy reliance on blue-collar support was initially deemed characteristic only of certain exponents of this party family by Kitschelt and McGann (1995). By now, there is ample evidence to show that the working class has become the core clientele of parties such as the French Front National, the Austrian FPÖ, the Progress Party in Norway, the Danish People's Party, and the Belgian Vlaams Blok or Vlaams Belang (Betz 2001; see also Bornschier 2010a; Bjørklund and Andersen 2002; Mayer 2002; McGann and Kitschelt 2005; Minkenberg and Perrineau 2007; Oesch 2008; Oesch and Rennwald 2010; Perrineau 1997; Plasser and Ulram 2000; Swyngedouw 1998).

What accounts for the propensity of the manual working class to support the extreme populist right? In what follows, we review the hypotheses that have been advanced in the literature, related either to economic, or to cultural mechanisms. Our own work on the joint processes of modernization and globalization and the resulting new groups of "winners" and "losers" has highlighted both economic and cultural processes (Kriesi *et al.* 2006, 2008b). For the present purpose, we discuss the economic and cultural components separately. In addition, it is worth noting an indirect mechanism that tips the balance from economic in favor of cultural mechanisms: by de-politicizing economic policy-making at the national level, European integration and globalization have enhanced the saliency of the cultural dimension of conflict. By weakening alignments along the economic dimension, then, these processes have opened the way for political realignments.

The working class and the extreme populist right

Economic explanations

Economic modernization losers. In this perspective, the increasing competition engendered by processes of economic modernization and globalization result in new social divisions (Esping-Andersen 1999; see also Kriesi *et al.* 2006, 2008b). Economic marginalization makes voters opt for the extreme right to voice their discontent and to exclude immigrants, either as scapegoats or because they are blamed for this constituency's difficulties in the labor market (e.g., Betz 1994, 2004a; see also Lubbers *et al.* 2002). Furthermore, they rely on extreme right parties to voice their opposition to European integration. In a pioneering analysis, Mughan *et al.* (2003) show that job insecurity explained the vote for the Australian One Nation Party. Concerning the class correlates of the modernization loser hypothesis, low-skilled service workers are clearly the most disadvantaged class in terms of income and promotion chances (Oesch 2006b: 95–105). From an economic perspective, we would thus expect the service proletariat to constitute a core element of the populist right's electorate, together with the unskilled manual working class (or routine operatives). Members of the *skilled* manual working class, on the other hand, are not the most disadvantaged segment of post-industrial society, at least in terms of their absolute standard of living (Oesch 2006b: 95–105). Thus, the propensity of skilled workers to support the extreme populist right must be explained in terms of a *relative* decline of this class, making skilled manual workers a core segment of cultural modernization losers, as we argue below.

  Economic sector. Kitschelt (1994; see also Kitschelt and McGann 1995: 6) has argued that in post-industrial capitalism, employees in internationally competitive sectors are reluctant to endorse further redistributive measures and instead support market flexibility. If proved correct, this hypothesis would account for the over-representation of skilled workers, rather than routine operatives, in the extreme populist right's electorate. A division in economic preferences should thus be discernible, explaining why parts of the working class defect the left and support an extreme right party.[2] On the other hand, Walter (2010) argues that workers in more internationalized sectors are likely to opt for economic redistribution to reduce risk, making them more likely to support state interventionist policies and hence vote for leftist parties.

Cultural explanations

Cultural modernization losers. Individuals who disapprove of the universalistic norms that have become more widespread and also politically consequential in the past decades, have clearly lost in cultural terms. To a substantial degree, the new social movements have been successful in triggering social change, by advancing women's and gay rights, as well as the recognition of difference and the free choice of lifestyles. They have also introduced a global perspective in thinking about development and environmental protection. For those segments of society that shared the social conservatism characteristic of the immediate postwar decades, social change thus implied a fundamental loss of certainty and the withering of a "golden age", when their individual norms were in tune with those in society.

In part, the disenchantment of the working class with the left is triggered by those social democratic or socialist parties that underwent a New Left trans-formation. Certainly, due to the presence of more than one dimension of conflict, large parts of the working class had not voted for the left as early as the 1950s or 1960s, especially in continental Europe (Bartolini 2000: 497). However, the New Left's emphasis on universalistic values, along with its later emphasis on the constraints of globalization, and the fact that it no longer issues class-specific appeals (Goldthorpe 2002: 15–20), are likely to have eroded its support in the working class. Indeed, the cultural liberalism it advocates is diametrically opposed to the preferences of this constituency. The Social Democrats' new core constituency, the social-cultural professionals, have political preferences that differ starkly from those of the manual working class in cultural, although not in economic terms (Kriesi *et al.* 2008b; see also Oesch and Rennwald 2010).

To be sure, conservative parties have traditionally defended a more rigid social order, as well as national sovereignty and traditional moral values. Yet, not even Christian democracy has wholeheartedly opposed the societal trends of the past decades (Frey 2009). Thus, rallying the anti-universalistic potential present throughout the advanced industrial world (Sacchi 1998) required the emergence of a new actor with a novel political ideology. By adopting a discourse that meshes opposition against the diluting of the established national community due to immigration with resistance against cultural liberalism and European integration, the extreme populist right succeeded in seizing this potential. However, the saliency of the new cultural conflict for an individual voter will depend on how rooted he or she remains in established cleavages, which determine the space for the extreme right. We therefore test whether leftist economic preferences and religiosity dampen the propensity of individuals to support the extreme right.

In social structural terms, the cultural potential is shaped by a number of variables. While social class impinges both on cultural and economic preference formation, and will be discussed in more detail in the next section, we focus here on education and gender.

Education. The origins of the value change triggering the dual transformation of political space lie in the expansion of higher education and the subsequent diffusion of universalistic values (Allardt 1968; see also Kriesi 1999; Stubager 2008; Bornschier 2010a). Education has a "liberalizing effect" in contributing to cultural tolerance and openness, and it provides the cognitive and language skills that give access to other cultures. Individuals with low levels of education, on the other hand, are usually less tolerant and do not have the resources to communicate with foreigners or to "understand" other cultures (Lipset 1960; see also Grunberg and Schweisguth 1990: 54, 1997: 155–159, 168; Quillian 1995; Sniderman *et al.* 2000: 84; Kriesi *et al.* 2008b: 13). Stubager (2008) provides evidence for the socializing effect of education that instills universalistic values, and even shows that social groups defined by levels of education exhibit some degree of collective identity, perceiving an antagonism with one another in terms of interests (Stubager 2009). Education is also likely to influence attitudes regarding supra-national integration and political globalization: Early on, Inglehart (1977) conceived the ability to relate to a supra-national political community as conditional on a process of "cognitive mobilization". In short, education is strongly connected to some of the key issues relating to the new cultural conflict.

Gender. In a number of ways, men have lost their privileged societal role in the past decades. The women's movement has increased the autonomy of women, for example in terms of the liberalization of abortion and divorce. Furthermore, universalistic reforms in the welfare state have decoupled provisions from the male breadwinner (Häusermann 2010; see also Palier 2010). The rise of female employment and the advent of the service economy have led to a loss of prestige of male-dominated occupations, above all of the blue-collar working class. Thus, various authors have interpreted the over-representation of men in the extreme populist right's support base as an expression of a troubled male identity (Perrineau 1997: 105–107; see also Mayer 2002: 133–138; Betz 2004a: ch. 4).

Working-class culture and milieu

Finally, organizational penetration and socialization in the working-class milieu may play a role in explaining why certain members of the blue-collar working class support the extreme populist right, while others do not. The literature has tended to view individuals rooted in the working-class milieu as the core constituency of the left (e.g., Knutsen 2006) and to some degree insulated from the appeals of the extreme right. On the other hand, detailed analyses of the organizational networks of the Front National cast doubts on whether this is still the case. Perrineau shows that the Front National is firmly rooted in the working class by means of a number of sector-specific unions, which form part of a tightly knitted nationalist counter-culture reminiscent of the Communist party in its early years (Perrineau 1997: 46–47). Mayer (2002) provides evidence that workers with working-class parents and friends are especially prone to vote for the Front National.

The empirical analysis will focus on union membership, working-class family background and age. In terms of *union membership*, we expect the union movement to remain predominantly anchored on the left, thus containing the propensity of workers to vote for the extreme right. On the other hand, controlling for union membership, coming from a *working-class family* should no longer dampen support for the extreme right, given the popularity these parties have attained among the working class. Finally, if alignments between cleavage groups and political parties are to be altered primarily by generational replacement, rather than by shifts in party choice (Bornschier 2010a), then *age* should have an effect: younger working-class members should be more likely to opt for the extreme populist right than older members.

Data and operationalization

The analyses are based on the fourth round of the European Social Survey (ESS), with fieldwork being conducted between fall 2008 and spring 2009. Because our hypotheses are specific to countries that experienced the dual transformation of political space described above, the analysis is restricted to the fourteen West European countries covered by the survey. In a first step, we focus on those countries with successful extreme populist right parties. We use an inclusive definition and exclude from this group only those parties that Ignazi (2002, 2003) has labeled as proponents of the "old" or "traditional" extreme right, which adhere to overt racism and distrust democracy. Although there are differences within the resulting group of parties (Mudde 2007), most of them practice an "ethno-pluralist" discourse (Betz 2004a; see also Bornschier 2010a). The Swiss and the Danish People's Parties, the True Finns, the French Front National, the Belgian Vlaams Belang, Geert Wilders' Party for Freedom in the Netherlands, and the Norwegian Progress Party are the core exponents of this party family. We have also grouped some smaller formations in the same countries in this category in order to maximize the number of observations. If anything, using an inclusive definition of the extreme right amounts to a tougher test of our hypotheses than using narrower boundaries. We exclude Greece and Sweden from this group due to a limited number of members of the working class who voted for LAOS or the Swedish Democrats. Unfortunately, Austria is not featured in the fourth round of the ESS. The analysis of the countries lacking an extreme populist right party includes Germany, Great Britain, Greece, Ireland, Portugal, Spain and Sweden. To identify vote choice, we use the recall question pertaining to the last national election and combine it with the party preference of those who declare not having participated in the last elections. For the analyses pertaining to participation, both those who declare not having voted as well as those who could not recall their vote choice are considered to be non-voters.

Social class

To measure social class, we draw on the eight-class schema developed by Oesch (Oesch 2006b). The class schema has a vertical and a horizontal dimension. The vertical dimension of stratification focus on skills and income, whereas the horizontal differentiation captures different work logics that result in diverging political preferences (see also Oesch, Chapter 2 in this volume). More specific hypotheses regarding the preferences of social classes are presented below. Due to our specific interest in the working class, we also distinguish between skilled workers and routine operatives as the higher and the lower blue-collar segment, respectively, by drawing on the original sixteen-class variant of the schema. The operationalization follows Oesch (Oesch 2006b: 222–224). We thus distinguish the following nine classes, situated in four work-logics, as follows.

- *Self-employed:* (1) self-employed professionals and large employers; (2) small business owners.
- *Organizational work-logic:* (3) (associate) managers and administrators; (4) office clerks.
- *Technical work-logic:* (5) technical professionals and technicians; (6) skilled production workers; (7) routine operatives.
- *Interpersonal work-logic:* (8) socio-cultural (semi-)professionals; (9) service workers.

In making more specific predictions for the propensity of specific social groups to support the populist right, we focus on the lower segment within each work logic. Due to their underprivileged status, these groups are more likely than others to support the extreme populist right both for cultural and for economic reasons (due to low levels of education and income, respectively). The middle classes, on the other hand, represent the winners of modernization and globalization, and are thus not particularly likely to vote for the extreme right. We know, however, that socio-cultural specialists, the core electorate of the New Left, share a particularly strong aversion for the extreme right (see Oesch, Chapter 2 in this volume).

Among the classes most likely to support the extreme right, *small business owners* have long been considered potential supporters for these parties (Lipset 1960: ch. 5; see also Kitschelt and McGann 1995). Although perhaps not most touched by economic modernization and globalization, low levels of education make the so-called petty bourgeoisie particularly receptive for the particularistic and traditionalist stances of the populist right. Because their preferences are likely to be market-friendly, rather than state interventionist, they face no trade-off when it comes to voting for a right-wing party. Comparatively low levels of formal education characterize *routine operatives*, as well as large parts of the group comprising *skilled production workers*. This makes the manual working class as a whole relatively receptive to the traditionalist-communitarian ideology of the populist right. Furthermore, in terms of increasing competition, both groups are strongly affected by economic modernization and structural change. Although the skilled working class is not particularly badly off in terms of pay (Oesch 2006b), its members stand to lose compared to the golden age of industrial welfare capitalism, as we have argued. To the degree that their attachment to the left and to religious parties has weakened, members of the manual working class thus become a promising target for identity-based appeals. In fact, drawing on the Habermasian theory of modernization, Sacchi (1998) argues that this segment's early integration into market processes makes its members develop anti-statist attitudes, rather than hostility towards the market. In terms of pay, routine operatives could be considered the core potential for the extreme populist right, but on the other hand, low levels of education and political sophistication could also induce them to abstain from voting.

Service workers are most underprivileged in terms of pay (Oesch 2006b) and are characterized by low levels of education. This class constitutes a core potential for the populist right, but low levels of political interest might prevent its members from participating in politics. Finally, although *office clerks* represent the lower-class element within their organizational work logic, they are not badly off in terms of pay and education. We have no strong expectations regarding the political preferences of this group.

Other variables

Because we are interested in the effects of economic marginalization and poor educational skills, factors that might prevent individuals from participating in politics altogether rather than supporting the extreme populist right, we use Heckman probit selection models to explain the vote for these parties. In the first step, we use *political interest, income, education*, and *political support* to explain political participation. Our measure of political support combines assessments of support for the government and for democracy. Furthermore, we include *age* both in years and in squared form, as participation is known to rise over most of one's life-cycle, but to decline as one grows old. The coding of most of these variables is straightforward and does not require discussion. In terms of *education*, we use a distinction between low levels of education (elementary school and lower vocational training), medium levels (secondary education, vocational training), and higher education (undergraduate and graduate levels). Income, education, and satisfaction with democracy are also used to explain the vote for the extreme populist right.

Political preferences: to operationalize the *new cultural dimension*, we create indicators for the most important issues that have triggered the two transformations of political space since the 1960s. The concerns of the new social movements of the seventies and eighties are captured using five items pertaining to cultural liberalism (women's emancipation, rights of homosexuals, and the importance of authoritarian values in school and in criminal law). The issues relating to the second transformation are tapped using various items on immigration and European integration. Furthermore, the factor analyses reveal that welfare state misuse and welfare chauvinism empirically load on the cultural rather than the economic dimension. These categories are thus combined with the other cultural issues to form a single scale for the cultural dimension, again using factor analysis. *Economic preferences* are measured using indicators pertaining to redistribution, social insurance, and social investment. A detailed description of all items used to measure political preferences may be found in the Appendix.

Economic position: apart from absolute *income*, which is measured using ten categories, we have constructed an indicator for relative deprivation. *Relative income* identifies those individuals within the working class whose income is below the median of their class within the specific country. *Job insecurity* is measured by a factor based on items referring to whether respondents have been unemployed in the past five years and to how likely people think it is that they will become unemployed in the next twelve months. Finally, we use *trade openness* to tap the competitiveness of respondents' economic sector. We use Bürgisser's (2011) country-specific measure of the trade exposure of the sector in which respondents work (imports and exports relative to GDP), using information on the sixteen sectors listed in the ESS.

Working class culture and milieu: the variable *union membership* identifies all individuals who declare themselves to be current union members, or to have been so in the past. Analyses separating current and past union membership yield similar results, and are thus not reported. *Working class family background* is measured using two items asking respondents what their father's and mother's occupations were when they were fourteen. The variable scores 1 for respondents with at least one working-class parent and 0 for those with no working-class background.

The class basis of the extreme populist right vote

We begin with three Heckman probit selection models that explain electoral participation and the vote for an extreme right-wing populist party, including country dummies to account for country-specific factors in both steps (effects of the country dummies are omitted). The results are presented in Table 1.1. Starting with the factors that account for political participation, we see that, as expected, political interest, income, age and political support are related to participation in predictable ways. In terms of education, respondents with intermediate levels of education form the reference category, and those with low levels of education participate significantly less, while those with higher education vote significantly more than this group. In analyzing the vote for the extreme populist right, we follow the classical funnel of causality (Campbell *et al.* 1960), and introduce blocks of variables step-by-step.

For the explanation of the vote for the extreme right, Model 1 includes only social class and income. While income has no effect, three classes stand out in terms of their propensity to vote for the extreme right: both skilled and unskilled workers are over-represented in this electorate, while social-cultural specialists are significantly under-represented. Contrary to what earlier analyses revealed, small business owners no longer form a core constituency of the extreme right, and neither do any of the other lower classes. The inclusion of education in Model 2 clearly attests to the negative effect of higher education on the vote for

Table 1.1 Probit selection model explaining participation and the vote for the extreme populist right (table shows coefficients and z-values)

	Model 1 b/z	Model 2 b/z	Model 3 b/z
Vote for the extreme populist right			
Income	−0.01	0.00	0.01
	−1.30	−0.45	0.86
Self-employed	−0.08	−0.02	−0.08
	−0.66	−0.19	−0.58
Small business owners	0.05	−0.02	−0.12
	0.61	−0.32	−1.52
Office clerks	0.11	0.02	0.00
	1.35	0.30	0.01
Technical professionals	−0.04	−0.04	−0.05
	−0.51	−0.48	−0.50
Social-cultural specialists	−0.39***	−0.32***	−0.25**
	−4.73	−3.76	−2.70
Service workers	0.11	0.01	−0.02
	1.52	0.18	−0.21
Skilled production workers	0.44***	0.32***	0.19*
	6.01	4.09	2.30
Routine operatives	0.34***	0.25**	0.23**
	4.66	3.15	2.69
Low education		−0.07	−0.24***
		−1.15	−3.66
High education		−0.34***	−0.20***
		−5.89	−3.31
Economic dimension			0.11***
			3.44
Cultural dimension			−0.58***
			−17.30
Political support			−0.10***
			−3.64
Constant	−1.36***	−1.25***	−1.57***
	−14.74	−12.87	−14.82
Political participation			
Political interest	0.33***	0.33***	0.32***
	15.76	15.80	15.49
Income	0.02**	0.02**	0.02***
	2.92	3.07	3.33
Age	0.10***	0.10***	0.10***
	21.44	21.45	21.38
Age squared	−0.00***	−0.00***	−0.00***
	−15.99	−15.99	−15.85
Low education	−0.36***	−0.37***	−0.37***
	−8.67	−8.84	−8.94
High education	0.35***	0.32***	0.33***
	8.17	7.64	7.70
Support for democracy	0.13***	0.13***	0.11***
	6.60	6.52	5.64

Table 1.1 Continued

	Model 1 b/z	Model 2 b/z	Model 3 b/z
Constant	−2.23***	−2.23***	−2.24***
	−17.51	−17.53	−17.58
Athrho	0.70***	0.61***	0.54***
	4.17	3.89	3.52
Rho	0.60	0.54	0.49
N	10,404	10,404	10,392
Censored observations	1,904	1,904	1,904
Uncensored observations	8,500	8,500	8,488

Notes
Effect of country dummies not shown. Log likelihood of comparison between probit and selection models indicates that selection model is appropriate.
Significance levels: # $p \leq 0.10$ * $p \leq 0.05$ ** $p \leq 0.0.1$ *** $p \leq 0.001$.

the extreme right. While low levels of education reduce the propensity of individuals to turn out to vote, they have no effect on support for the extreme right: no difference is revealed between individuals with low and medium levels of education. Interestingly, however, introducing education into the model shows that the effects of class are not solely a function of education, as they are hardly reduced at all.

Thus, there is something specific to blue-collar working-class occupations not captured by formal education that impinges on their propensity to vote for the extreme right. Given that we have hypothesized cultural attitudes to be rooted in education, introducing them in a final model might nonetheless help us explain the class effect. Model 3 introduces positions on the economic and cultural dimensions as well as political support. The cultural dimension, indeed, exerts the strongest influence. Its highly significant negative effect implies that less universalistic attitudes make the vote for the extreme right much more likely. Market-liberal preferences also have a positive significant effect, while political support reduces the likelihood of voting for the extreme right. While these findings conform to expectations, the most significant result, from our perspective, is that the manual working class's affinity to the extreme right is not entirely explained by cultural preferences, contrary to what we had expected. The same goes for the socio-cultural specialists' aversion against the populist right. While the class effects are less clear-cut in the final model, they remain significant, at least at the 5 percent level.

Note that, when controlling for attitudes, the effect of lower education becomes significantly negative. Thus, if attitudes are taken into account, voters with medium levels of education stand out for supporting the extreme right most frequently. This is a first indication of a finding that emerges even more clearly in the subsequent analyses: it is not the least sophisticated and most economically deprived individuals who vote for the extreme right. Most importantly, however, Models 1 to 3 show that neither cultural world-views nor their educational antecedents are sufficient for explaining why the manual working class is over-represented in the extreme right's electorate.

What determines voting for the extreme populist right within the manual working class?

Given the roots the extreme populist right has formed in the working class, we now set out to determine whether some sub-segments of this class are particularly likely to support these parties. We thus restrict the sample to skilled production workers and routine operatives to study voting determinants *within* the manual working class. Table 1.2 shows the result of a Heckman probit selection model explaining participation and extreme right vote choice. The most important result is that a number of prominent hypotheses concerning the impact of economic insecurity and marginalization are in fact not confirmed. Contrary to the explanation suggested by the economic modernization loser hypothesis, job insecurity and low education actually prevent individuals in the manual working class from participating, rather than making them vote for the extreme right. The same tends to be true for low income, but the effect is not significant. Our measure of relative deprivation (low income as compared to the mean of the working class) fails to reach significance. Age and political interest have the hypothesized positive effect on participation.

Among working-class individuals, few factors distinguish those voting for the extreme right. By far the most powerful influence is exerted by anti-universalistic cultural preferences, while it is noteworthy that the extreme right does not attract working-class voters who are particularly market liberal. Trade exposure has no effect; nor is there an effect of skilled production workers, or union members. All in all, it is safe to say that skilled workers and routine operatives voting for the extreme populist right stand out predominantly for their position along the cultural dimension of conflict. With the exception of gender, working-class men having a higher propensity than women to vote for the extreme right, these preferences do not seem to be related in any clear way to social structural position. On the other hand, support for the government and for democracy tends to dampen support for the extreme right, and the same goes for religiosity.

Table 1.2 also provides evidence that working-class families are not immune to the appeal of the extreme right. Although the effect of having working-class parents is significant only at the 10 percent level, it is positive. Another way of looking at the rootedness of the extreme right in the working class is by using multinomial regression to determine what distinguishes those supporting the extreme right from those voting for the mainstream left within the manual working class (see Table A1.1 in the Appendix). This analysis shows us whether and how extreme right voters differ from the classical left-wing segment. Interestingly, the comparison shows that the classical agents of socialization in the left-wing milieu, labor unions, only immunize the core of the manual working class from voting for the extreme right: whereas skilled unionized workers are less likely to vote for the extreme right, no such effect is discernible for

Table 1.2 Probit selection model explaining participation and vote within the manual working class (table shows coefficients and z-values)

	Participation	Extreme right vote
Gender	0.02	−0.25*
	0.29	−2.20
Age	0.10***	−0.00
	10.11	−0.96
Age squared	−0.00***	
	−7.42	
Income	0.03#	0.03
	1.88	0.83
Relative income		0.05
		0.32
Political interest	0.32***	
	7.38	
Job insecurity	−0.12***	0.03
	−3.29	0.48
Low education	−0.35***	−0.19
	−4.4	−1.18
High education	0.15	−0.19
	0.92	−0.83
Political support	0.04	−0.09#
	0.95	−1.76
Skilled worker		0.29
		0.77
Union member		0.09
		0.61
Skilled × union		−0.31
		−1.58
Working-class family		0.24#
		1.86
Skilled × w-c family		0.11
		0.58
Trade exposure		0.01
		0.64
Church attendence		−0.07#
		−1.83
Economic dimension		0.05
		0.69
Cultural dimension		−0.60***
		−8.54
Constant	−2.17***	−1.10*
	−7.05	−2.03
Athrho	0.03	
	0.11	
N	2,020	
Censored observations	503	
Uncensored observations	1,517	

Notes
Effects of country dummies not shown.
Significance levels: # $p \leq 0.10$ * $p \leq 0.05$ ** $p \leq 0.01$ *** $p \leq 0.001$.

unionized routine operatives. The negative effect of age indicates that younger cohorts within the working class are less anchored in the left-wing milieu. Again, job insecurity has no influence, but workers in internationalized sectors are in fact more likely to vote for the extreme right rather than the left. In terms of political preferences, extreme right voters are also somewhat more market liberal, while anti-universalistic values are again of overpowering significance.

These findings are particularly interesting when contrasted to the mainstream right. While the effect of sector is similar to that for the extreme right, market liberalism pushes workers to support the mainstream right much more clearly than the extreme right. Anti-universalistic attitudes also exert a significant influence on the mainstream right vote, but the effect is weaker than for the extreme right. Furthermore, center-right parties attract working-class voters who are cross-pressured by religion, while church attendance does not set left-wing and extreme right workers apart. Thus, together with what we found in the previous model, this indicates that both left-wing and extreme right working class voters tend to be secular. Non voters and those not professing any party preference, on the other hand, have political preferences that are to some degree similar to those of center-right and extreme right voters, but the effect of the cultural dimension is much stronger for the latter. Non-voters are less politicized, and economically more marginal, however: they lack political interest, have low levels of education, and incomes below the median of the working class in their respective countries.

Anti-universalism and the working class in countries without extreme populist right parties

Given that the extreme right has broken into those segments of the working class that hold anti-universalistic preferences and rallies a particularly loyal following, as prior analyses have shown (Bornschier 2010a), the question arises as to which parties these segments vote for in countries that lack an extreme right-wing populist challenger. In a last set of analyses, we look at the party choice of working-class individuals with outlooks similar to those prevalent in the extreme right electorate in Belgium, Switzerland, Denmark, Finland, France, the Netherlands, and Norway. In order to identify potential extreme right voters and simulate their behavior in the seven countries—Germany, Great Britain, Greece, Ireland, Portugal, Spain, and Sweden, where parties of this type are not present—we must somehow take into account the context conditions that make for the differing levels of support for extreme right parties.

In the models above, these context conditions were captured by the country dummies (not shown in Tables 1.1 and 1.2 for reasons of space). The most favorable conditions for the extreme right are found in Switzerland, where the Swiss People's Party (SVP) faces little stigmatization due to its status as a long-established party, and due to the importance of the issue of European integration, which the SVP capitalizes on. We thus simulate a Swiss context to identify potential extreme right voters in the set of countries in which the

Table 1.3 Real vote of workers who have a low and a high potential for voting in favour of the extreme populist right, for countries without an extreme populist right

Vote	Britain		Germany		Greece		Ireland		Portugal		Spain		Sweden	
	low	high	low	high	low	high	low	high	low	high	low	high	low	high
Left	46.6	42.3	38.3	29.5	42.1	43.6	9.7	7.0	38.9	31.0	39.4	37.4	50.2	44.2
Right	14.7	17.1	29.9	23.8	22.7	26.7	59.5	42.1	10.8	7.1	20.3	17.1	23.3	17.4
Others/ethnic	4.0	3.3	0.3	1.3	4.0	4.0	7.8	**17.5**	0.6	0.0	7.8	3.3	2.0	**11.6**
Non-voter	34.7	**36.9**	31.5	**45.4**	30.3	25.7	23.0	**33.3**	49.7	**61.9**	32.5	**42.3**	24.5	**26.7**
Total	100	100	100	100	100	100	100	100	100	100	100	100	100	100
N	150	222	490	132	76	101	217	57	324	42	320	123	253	86
	G = 0.07		G = 0.22**		G = −0.06		G = 0.28*		G = 0.25		G = 0.10*		G = 0.12***	

extreme right has failed to make a breakthrough. We do so by predicting the probability of voting for the extreme right, based on the parameters presented in Table 1.2, including the Swiss country dummy for the voters from the seven countries without an extreme right party. Based on these predictions, we distinguish working-class voters with a high potential of voting for an extreme right party ($p > 0.5$) from those with a low potential of voting for such a party ($p < 0.5$). It turns out that, assuming the presence of a Swiss-style extreme right party, no less than 63 percent of the British working class has a high potential of voting for such a party. The corresponding shares for the other countries range from 57 percent (Greece) and 43 percent (Germany) to 28 percent (Spain), 25 percent (Sweden), 21 percent (Ireland) and a low of 11 percent (Portugal).

Table 1.3 shows, for each of these seven countries, the vote choice of working-class individuals with a low and those with a high potential of voting for the extreme right, based on the characteristics that we know to push voters to support the Swiss People's Party in Switzerland. The results tend to convey an impressive message: In the absence of a party that matches their profile, the most obvious choice for workers is to abstain from voting. In general, more than a third of this group does not vote, with rates of abstention climbing to 45 percent in Germany and 62 percent in Portugal. It is also interesting to note that the mainstream right is unable to capitalize substantially on the anti-universalistic potential in the working class. As is shown by Table 1.3, all but the British and Greek parties of the mainstream right obtain lower shares among the workers with a high potential for the extreme right than among those with a low potential for supporting such a party. Given the popular hypothesis that the mainstream right is able to close the political space to its right by taking tough stances on immigration—for example, in the case of Germany (e.g., van der Brug *et al.* 2005), this is a remarkable finding. In Ireland, Sinn Fein receives over-proportional support from this group; on the other hand, in Sweden it is the Swedish Democrats who score rather well in this group, although, overall, they only received 3 percent of the votes in the 2006 elections.

Conclusion

A voluminous literature has argued that extreme populist right parties thrive on the potential constituted by the economic and cultural processes of modernization of the past decades. Contrary to this assumption, we have shown that economic marginalization and job insecurity play no role in determining the vote for these parties. A first key finding of our analysis is that the worst off in society in terms of education and class status do not vote at all, and thus constitute a political potential not seized by any party. Nor do highly educated voters find the extreme right's anti-universalistic and exclusionist message particularly appealing. The typical extreme right voter disposes of an intermediate level of education, belongs to the manual working class, and is not disinterested in politics. A second key finding is that it is cultural world-views, over and above their educational antecedents, that play the most important role in determining the vote for these parties. Although extreme right voters constitute a sizable minority, and have their views politically represented by parties such as the Swiss and the Danish People's Parties or the French Front National, they distrust government and are not supportive of the way democracy works in their country.

Even controlling for political preferences and a host of other factors, the working class stands out for its support for the extreme right. How has the populist right achieved its status as the defender of the interests of this class? Our analysis shows that anti-universalism plays the most important role in explaining why some members vote for the extreme right, while others do not. Within the working class, market-liberal preferences play no role, and neither does job insecurity: culture clearly reigns supreme. While long considered a conservative force (Lipset 1960), our analysis shows that the classical agents of left-wing socialization in the blue-collar segment of society are weakening dramatically. Being the member of a labor union no longer immunizes workers from the appeal of the extreme right, and neither does coming from a working-class family. Again, the most economically insecure segments of this class abstain from voting rather than supporting the extreme right.

Cultural, not economic modernization losers support the extreme right. The only structural element shaping this world-view is gender. And indeed, the typical male blue-collar worker has most dramatically lost in terms of prestige with the advent of the service economy, as a consequence of the concomitant rise in female employment, as well as the gradual reform of welfare states centered on the single male breadwinner, and more equitable gender roles. The extreme populist right's traditionalist-communitarian ideology provides a dual remedy for this uncertainty. Not only do these movements champion the return to the orderly, culturally conservative society characteristic of the postwar decades, but in their demarcation from immigrants, they also contribute to an upgrading of this group's self-consciousness. It is a well known fact from social psychology that the construction of boundaries between in-groups and out-groups enhances individuals' self-esteem (Tajfel 1981; see also Monroe *et al.* 2000; Burke 2004).

Although we can thus partly explain the extreme right's appeal within the working class, we are left with the puzzle that these parties have not been successful throughout Western Europe. Our analysis clearly shows that this cannot be explained by differences in the size of country-specific potentials. While the anti-universalistic segment within the working class is small in Sweden, Portugal, and Ireland, it is sizable in the UK, Germany, and Spain—despite the fact that right-wing populist parties have not been successful in any of these countries. Rather than being rallied by the established parties, many voters that could be expected to support an extreme right party if the option were available simply choose not to vote. The only exception in this respect is the UK. Both in the UK and in Sweden, the left has avoided dividing the working-class electorate, possibly due to its lukewarm defense of universalistic values. Nonetheless, levels of abstention are high even in Sweden, as in many of the countries that lack an extreme right party, because the mainstream right is unable to rally the anti-universalistic potential. Were it not for the presence of the extreme populist right in various West European countries, then, our analysis would second Goldthorpe's (2002) hunch that the tensions produced by economic modernization and globalization do not necessarily result in a revival of class voting, but rather in a strengthening of the relationship between class and political participation.

Notes

1 We refer to these parties as extreme populist right (or extreme right for short) with reference to their extreme position along the new cultural dimension, following Ignazi's (1992, 2003) usage of the term. This does not imply that extreme right parties strive to overturn democracy. Furthermore, extreme populist right parties are characterized by an anti-establishment discourse and a hierarchical internal structure (for a more detailed discussion, see Bornschier 2010a: 33–36).
2 More recently, McGann and Kitschelt (2005) recognized that this mechanism may have worked only in the early phase of the rise of the extreme right, as most of these parties have watered down their neo-liberal credentials.

Appendix

Table A1.1 Multinomial logit model explaining participation and vote for the mainstream right, the extreme populist right, and lack of party preferences, as opposed to the mainstream left within the manual working class (table shows coefficients and z-values)

	Mainstream right	Extreme right	No vote or preference
	b/z	b/z	b/z
Age	−0.01**	−0.02**	−0.05***
	−2.63	−3.16	−10.74
Gender	−0.14	−0.55*	−0.07
	−0.86	−2.5	−0.45
Income	0.08	0.07	0.02
	1.39	0.93	0.37
Relative income	0.35	0.31	0.48*
	1.35	0.98	1.96
Skilled worker	0.55	1.21	0.67
	0.89	1.61	1.18
Union member	−0.42*	−0.02	−0.35#
	−1.96	−0.07	−1.7
Skilled x union	−0.39	−0.95*	−0.47
	−1.23	−2.43	−1.57
Working-class family	−0.31	0.32	−0.18
	−1.62	1.25	−0.98
Skilled x w-family	0.38	0.45	0.63*
	1.29	1.2	2.25
Trade openness	0.14*	0.13*	0.13*
	2.23	2.07	2.02
Job insecurity	−0.06	0.01	0.02
	−0.67	0.1	0.28
Church attendance	0.32***	0.04	0.06
	5.45	0.51	0.96
Low education	0.17	−0.21	0.74**
	0.67	−0.67	3.13
High education	0.38	−0.06	0.05
	1.13	−0.13	0.15
Economic dimension	0.50***	0.31*	0.31**
	4.44	2.23	2.86
Cultural dimension	−0.35**	−1.21***	−0.33**
	−3.17	−8.45	−3.12
Political support	0.12	−0.23*	−0.09
	1.32	−2.17	−1.06
Political interest	0.06	0.01	−0.61***
	0.65	0.06	−6.85
Constant	0.39	−0.31	3.26***
	0.5	−0.3	4.42
N	2,031		

Notes
Reference category: Mainstream left (excluding extreme left and Green parties).
Effect of country dummies not shown.
Significance levels: # $p \leq 0.10$ * $p \leq 0.05$ ** $p \leq 0.01$ *** $p \leq 0.001$.

Table A1.2 Survey items used for the construction of issue categories and dimensions

Item	Description	Issue category	Dimension
wmcpwrk	Women should be prepared to cut down on paid work for sake of their family	Cultural liberalism	Cultural dimension
mnrgtjb	Men should have more right to a job than women when jobs are scarce		
freehms	Gay men and lesbians should be free to live their own life as they wish		
schtaut	Schools must teach children to obey authority		
hrshsnt	People who break the law should be given much harsher sentences than they are these days		
imsmetn	Allow many/few immigrants of same race/ethnic group as majority	Immigration	
imdfetn	Allow many/few immigrants of different race/ethnic group from majority		
impcntr	Allow many/few immigrants from poorer countries outside Europe		
imbgeco	Immigration bad or good for country's economy		
imwbcn	Immigrants make country a worse or better place to live		
euftf	European Union: European unification should go further or has gone too far	Supra-national governance	
trstep	Trust in the European Parliament		
trstun	Trust in the United Nations		
uentrjb	Most unemployed people do not really try to find a job	Welfare abuse	
bennent	Many manage to obtain benefits/services they are not entitled to		
prtsick	Employees often pretend they are sick to stay at home		
imrccon	Immigrants receive more or less than they contribute to social security	Welfare chauvinism	Economic dimension
gvjbevn	Government's responsibility (scale 1–10): jobs for everyone	Government responsibility	
gvhlthc	Government's responsibility (scale 1–10): health care for the sick		
gvcldr	Government's responsibility (scale 1–10): child care services for working parents		
gvpdlwk	Government's responsibility (scale 1–10): paid leave from work to care for sick family		
gvslvol	Government's responsibility (scale 1–10): standard of living for the old		
gvslvue	Government's responsibility (scale 1–10): maintain standard of living for the unemployed		
dfincac	Large differences in income should be acceptable to reward talents and efforts	Income differences	
gincdif	Government should reduce differences in income levels	Redistribution	
smdfslv	For fair society, differences in standard of living should be small	Egalitarianism	

Imputations

Immigration, cultural liberalism, welfare abuse: constructed by factor analyses for the entire file, based on corresponding original ESS variables; missing variables on the original variables have been imputed based on the other original variables of the respective set.

Welfare chauvinism, supra-national governance, government responsibility, redistribution: transformed original variables; missing values on the original variables have been imputed based on related variables.

2 The class basis of the cleavage between the New Left and the radical right

An analysis for Austria, Denmark, Norway and Switzerland

Daniel Oesch

Introduction

The rise of the New Left in the 1980s and the radical right in the 1990s has been widely interpreted as the demise of class politics. Contrary to the established parties, these new movements were seen as no longer relying on particular social groups, but as attracting a broad range of citizens on the basis of their values and attitudes (e.g., Dalton 1996: 332). Taking up the issues of New Politics, these new parties exploit a conflict based on cultural values, which—unlike the material interests drawing the older political divides—were seen to be no longer rooted in different social positions. Likewise, the concept of cleavage—central to the understanding of Old Politics—no longer appeared to make sense with respect to these merely value-based parties.

This chapter fundamentally disagrees with this interpretation and argues that the New Left and the radical right form the opposite poles of a full-grown cleavage in Bartolini and Mair's (1990) sense. This means that their voters combine—alongside shared values and a common organization—a structural element, namely a common position within the employment structure. The constituencies of the New Left and the radical right thus not only disagree over issues of identity and community but they also feature very different socio-demographic profiles. This implies that voters' values are no more distributed randomly across the electorate in New Politics than they were in earlier times, but still remain firmly anchored in the social structure.

What has changed is that the rise of the New Left and—a decade later—the radical right triggered a process of electoral realignment where old ties between groups and parties became loose and were replaced by new ties. With respect to the New Left and the radical right, this means that their voters do not only take opposite stances over cultural issues, they also present the mirror image of each other in terms of class and education. The highly educated professionals and semi-professionals in health care, teaching, social welfare and the media disproportionately vote for the New Left, whereas the radical right receives disproportionate support from production workers, artisans and small business owners who rarely hold degrees beyond upper-secondary schooling.

Exclusively focusing on the demand side of politics, this chapter aims to unearth empirically the class pattern underlying the cultural conflict—and thus to analyze the micro-foundations of the cleavage between the New Left and the radical right. It does so for four small affluent West European countries where the New Left and the radical right have succeeded in the 1990s to establish themselves firmly in the party system: Austria, Denmark, Norway, and Switzerland. Our empirical analysis is based on individual-level data stemming from the first four rounds of the European Social Survey, covering the period between 2002/2003 and 2008/2009. The combination of four survey rounds affords us with large national samples of between 3,000 and 5,000 voters and permits us to go beyond simplistic (and outdated) class measures that just separate the working from the middle class.

Our chapter is structured as follows. Section two examines the critical juncture giving way to the new cultural cleavage and sketches out its underlying class pattern. Section three presents the data and discusses issues related to measuring class position and political preferences. Section four shows the empirical evidence on the ties between social structure and party choice. Section five then adds further results on the link between class position, economic and cultural preferences, and party vote. Section six concludes by putting the principal findings into a wider context.

The class pattern of the cultural cleavage

In political science and sociology, two misunderstandings about class voting stubbornly linger on. The first misunderstanding consists in reducing class voting to the phenomenon of industrial workers supporting leftist parties. As the link between the working class and labour parties has weakened in some countries (although not in others), some scholars announced the end of class voting (e.g., Franklin *et al.* 1992; see also Dalton 1996; Clark and Lipset 2001). However, workers' voting for the left is just one instance of class voting; it has—deservedly—received much attention because it overlaps with Europe's central political conflict of the last 120 years, the capital–labour cleavage. Yet several authors correctly pointed out that class voting simply implies the presence of systematic links between voters' class location and the parties they choose—which classes are linked with which parties is then an empirical question (Müller 1999; see also Evans 2000; Goldthorpe 2000).

A second misunderstanding is to limit the influence of a voter's class position to his or her *economic* preferences. As opposed to the approach suggested by a narrow Marxist interpretation of class, we argue that an individual's experience at work—insertion into the hierarchy, demand on skills, and interactions with colleagues, clients, and petitioners—contributes to shape his or her attitudes towards material *and* cultural issues, involving both questions of economy *and* identity. The idea is that voters generalize from one important sphere of life (work) to another (politics); they thus carry their occupational experiences—their experience of autonomy and control, of reasoning and routine—over from the job to the voting booth (Oesch 2006b: 267; see also Kitschelt 2010: 666; Kitschelt and Rehm 2011a: 6).

It is based on these two preliminary arguments that we expect occupational classes to diverge in their political preferences and party choice. This leads us back to our main argument that the divide between libertarian-universalistic voters of the New Left and traditionalist-communitarian voters of the radical right cannot be reduced to a mere conflict over values, but is also rooted in different positions within the social structure. This raises the question about the critical juncture of this cleavage: what evolution in the market, state or society brought it about? In our view, affluent democracies began to witness in the 1960s and, above all, the 1970s three socio-economic trends that created the potential for a new cultural divide within the electorate: (1) de-industrialization and service sector growth; (2) educational expansion; and (3) occupational upgrading (Kriesi 1999: 400; see also Bornschier 2010a: 63).

The first and possibly decisive change was the onset of de-industrialization in the 1970s, leading to a continuous decline in the proportion of industrial workers relative to the expanding private service personnel. Creation of service jobs was particularly pronounced in the public sector, where the massive expansion of the welfare state—in health care, education and social services—also provided a substantial boost to female labour market participation. Over the same period, the democratization of access to higher education led to a gradual increase in new cohorts' educational attainment. The steady growth among graduates with at least upper-secondary and then increasingly tertiary education was itself influenced by de-industrialization: as demand for semi-skilled industrial labor dried up, young people reacted by staying on at school. Finally, the joint impact of educational growth and service sector expansion, decisively pushed by technological change, led to the gradual upgrading of Western Europe's occupational structure: the share of highly skilled jobs in the professions and management strongly increased at the expense of less qualified jobs in manufacturing, the crafts, and agriculture (Tåhlin 2007; see also Oesch and Rodriguez 2011). Above all in the large European countries, the flip side of the rapid transformation of manufacturing was mass unemployment.

Tertiarization, educational expansion, and occupational upgrading stand for the transition from high industrialism to the service society. This transition has improved the life chances of some categories of the population, while making the prospects more sombre for others. Among the *winners* are the highly educated employees who took on the growing number of service jobs requiring specialized skills and expertise. This is particularly true for professionals and semi-professionals in social and cultural services: they benefited both from the opening up of higher education to new social categories (and new professional fields) and from the growth of the public sector (Kriesi 1998; see also Müller 1999). The expanding (semi-)professions in health care, teaching and welfare services proved a particularly effective channel of upward social mobility for women. The transition from an industrial to a service society afforded these occupational groups with relatively comfortable positions within the salaried middle class.

In contrast, the *losers* of the transition are primarily concentrated among production workers and small business owners. These mainly masculine categories have lost out from educational growth and occupational upgrading and find themselves at the gradually less populated lower end of the class structure. Subsequent structural changes in the economy—automation of manufacturing, lean production, outsourcing of routine activities—clearly undermined their position in the labor market: the evolution towards a more skill-intensive, rational and competitive service economy worsened their job prospects and reduced demand for their skills (Kitschelt 2007: 1181; see also Kriesi *et al.* 2008b: 4).

Although rooted in the employment structure, this divide between winners and losers of post-industrialization is not primarily about the economy and the just distribution of resources, but about culture and the definition of identity (Bornschier 2010a). Hence, winners and losers do not chiefly disagree over distributive concerns but over cultural issues: the political regulation of lifestyles (Herbert Kitschelt's *grid* dimension) and the acceptable extent of cultural diversity (Herbert Kitschelt's *group* dimension; see Kitschelt 2007: 1179).

Why culture and not economics? Professionals in social and cultural services are wage earners without major managerial responsibilities. As they mostly work in the public sector, they are unlikely to take great concern over the market-liberal interests of capital owners and their delegates, managers. In contrast, they have clearly defined cultural preferences: in their daily face-to-face interaction with patients, students, migrants, or the elderly, they constantly deal with human individuality. Their work process thus mainly consists of social interactions—teaching, nursing, counseling—which are interpersonally negotiated and require tolerance for cultural diversity. These communicative experiences are likely to give forth to a libertarian-universalistic outlook. This outlook is further enhanced by the fact that they mostly work outside clear-cut authority relations and enjoy considerable autonomy—an experience they are likely to generalize to other spheres of life (Kitschelt 1994: 17; see also Kriesi 1999: 169; Müller 1999: 143–144; Kitschelt and Rehm 2011a: 6–7).

The spearheads of libertarian-universalistic values should thus be found among (semi-)professionals engaged in an interpersonal work logic: medical doctors and nurses in health care; social workers and counselors in welfare; professors and teachers in education; journalists and artists in the media and entertainment. These members of the helping, teaching, caring, and entertaining occupations had already dominated the new social movements that crystallized in the 1970s and 1980s. By mobilizing for individual autonomy and the recognition of difference in terms of lifestyle, gender, or sexuality, they had set the foundation for the New Left and notably the Green parties (Kriesi 1989: 1096; see also Bornschier 2010a: 19).

The reaction to the rise of the New Left came with a delay of almost a decade, when radical right populist parties began to surface at the end of the 1980s. In our view, the emergence of the radical right is best understood as the communitarian counter-offensive to the universalistic values promoted by the New Left—as a backlash against post-industrial society and the ideas of 1968 (Ignazi

1992; see also Minkenberg 2001; Bornschier 2010a). Yet contrary to the offensive claims put on the agenda by the New Left, the radical right found its ideological niche in rearguard action: upholding national demarcation against disappearing borders, defending cultural homogeneity against increasing multiculturalism, salvaging traditional authority against individualistic choice. The contrast is not limited to ideology, but also spans different organizational logics. While the New Left had unfolded in a bottom-up process, where citizen groups mobilized around specific claims that were then adopted by parties, the mobilization of the radical right strongly depended on the deliberate molding of a collective identity by political entrepreneurs—on the presence of the charismatic leader typical of populist parties (Bornschier 2010a: 35–36).

In their rejection of cultural diversity, the radical right encountered the largest resonance among the main groups left out from the transition to the service society: production workers. The radical right's irate resistance to elitist libertarianism and its pointed defense of national traditions received as much support from no other class. The radical right's authoritarian discourse probably proved all the more successful among production workers as their daily job routine of close supervision has been shown to incline them to favor close conformity with rules and to be distrustful of brusque change (Kohn and Schooler 1969: 671). In parallel, rapid educational expansion had boosted the population's libertarian preferences through education's "liberalizing effect" (Kohn and Schooler 1969: 676). This meant that those left out from educational upgrading did not only face decreasing labor demand for their qualifications; they were also likely to find themselves at odds with growing segments of the increasingly well educated and libertarian citizenry, most notably with the elites in politics and the media.

In the end, the radical right's mobilization of production workers could only meet with large success because other collective identities rooted in working-class culture or religion had become less relevant (Andersen and Bjørklund 1990: 214). As working-class organizations were weakened by de-industrialization and mass unemployment—union membership declining in most affluent countries after 1990 (Bryson *et al.* 2011: 99)—other collective identities such as belonging to the national community could become salient among workers. In other words, the political potential of the new cultural conflict could only unfold where the established cleavage structure left the space and did not succeed in organizing these new issues (Bornschier 2010a: 4).

In any case, the new identity conflict does not unfold in a political vacuum, but coexists with older distributive and religious cleavages. A production worker may thus be torn between his economic identity as a member of the working class (and vote social democratic), his religious identity as a Catholic churchgoer (and vote Christian democratic), or his cultural identity as a proud member of the national community (and vote for the radical right). Party choice is then determined by the identity that is most salient—and the salience of identities in turn strongly depends on parties' efforts to articulate conflicts and thus to mobilize voters' identities (Bornschier 2010a: 58–59). This context of cross-cutting cleavages also explains why class voting always contains an indeterminate element: whether production workers vote for Labour or the radical right, both choices constitute articulate expressions of class-based preferences, where the former choice is based on economic and the latter on cultural preferences.

Strategy of analysis, data and measurement of key concepts

Our central argument is that the electoral competition between the New Left and the radical right is best understood as a cultural conflict entrenched in different class positions and based on opposing values. The New Left is expected to receive disproportionate support from (semi-)professionals in social and cultural services who hold libertarian-universalistic attitudes, whereas the New Right should primarily draw its strength from the working class—notably production workers—which defends traditionalist-communitarian attitudes. In order to substantiate these claims, our empirical analysis needs to establish the following three elements:

1   the electorates of the New Left and the radical right differ systematically in terms of their *class constituencies*;
2   these class differences in parties' electorate go along with different *cultural preferences*;
3   these cultural preferences account to a large extent for the reason why voters from a given class choose either the New Left or the radical right.

These three elements will be analyzed in a comparative perspective. As our focus lies on the demand side of electoral politics—voters' choices—we reduce variation on the supply side of party politics by selecting four small and affluent West European democracies where sizable parties of the New Left and the radical right have established themselves since the 1990s: Austria, Denmark, Norway, and Switzerland. While the New Left in Austria and Switzerland is represented by the Green Party, the major party of the New Left in Denmark and Norway features "Socialist" in its name. Yet both Denmark's Socialist People's Party and Norway's Socialist Left Party are affiliated to the Nordic Green Left Alliance and occupy a similar position in the party space as the Greens in Continental Europe. Table 2.1 gives an overview of the countries' main New Left and radical right parties and averages their electoral share over the national parliamentary elections held between 2000 and 2008. In all four countries, radical right parties obtained somewhat higher electoral scores than the New Left. While the latter's electoral share oscillated everywhere around 10 percent, the radical right obtained between 13 percent (Austria and Denmark), 16 percent (Norway), and almost 30 percent (Switzerland) of the national votes—with sometimes large movements from one election to another, notably in Austria.

Our analysis of class voting is set at the individual level and based on data stemming from the European Social Survey (ESS). By aggregating the four available rounds of the ESS (collected in 2002/2003, 2004/2005, 2006/2007, and 2008/2009),[1] we obtain large national samples of between 3,000 and 5,000 voters and thus cover party choice over the last decade. When comparing in Table 2.1 the parties' electoral share in our sample with their effective score, we find radical right voters to be under-represented and New Left voters to be over-represented in the ESS. Under-representation of Radical Right supporters is a common feature of electoral surveys and has been explained both by these citizens' lower response rates and socially conformist behaviour—people avoid admitting that they have voted for the Radical Right (Ivaldi 2001: 55–56).

In the ESS, respondents are asked what party they voted for in the last parliamentary election. This question provides us with the dependent variable, party choice. Our key independent variable is voters' class position. Drawing on a series of conceptual contributions (Kriesi 1989; see also Erikson and Goldthorpe 1992; Esping-Andersen 1993; Kitschelt 1994), we try to capture the increased heterogeneity in the employment structure by resorting to a detailed class schema based on two dimensions. A first dimension distinguishes *hierarchically* between more or less advantageous employment relationships based on people's marketable skills. A second dimension discriminates *horizontally* between four different work logics; it thus distinguishes different occupational experiences of otherwise similarly (dis-)advantaged classes (Oesch 2006b). When combining the two dimensions, we obtain the eight-class schema shown in Table 2.2. In order to convey an idea about the characteristics of different classes, we list for each class a few illustrative occupations and note the share of each class within

Table 2.1 Countries, parties, electoral scores and observations in the ESS

	Main party[1]	Electoral share, averaged for National elections 2001–2008[2,3]	Electoral share in ESS Sample 2002–2008	N voters aggregated in ESS sample 2002–2008
Austria	NL: Green Party	10.3	16.0	5,875
	RR: FPÖ (+BZÖ)	12.6	6.9	
Denmark	NL: SF (+EL)	10.3	12.0	5,685
	RR: DF	13.2	8.5	
Norway	NL: SV (+RV)	11.9	13.8	6,472
	RR: FrP	18.4	16.2	
Switzerland	NL: Green Party	8.5	10.7	6,390
	RR: SVP	29.7	26.6	

Notes
1 NL = New Left, RR = radical right.
2 Data for Austria are only available for the three first rounds (ESS02–ESS06). Accordingly, the effective electoral share has been calculated on the basis of the parliamentary elections 2002 and 2006 only (without 2008).
3 Source: own calculations based on European Election Database (http://eed.nsd.uib.no).
Abbreviations
Austria—FPÖ: Austrian Freedom Party; BZÖ: Alliance for the Future of Austria.
Denmark—SF: Socialist People's Party; EL: Red-Green Alliance.
Norway—SV: Socialist Left Party; RV: Red Electoral Alliance; FrP: Progress Party.
Switzerland—SVP: Swiss People's Party.

Table 2.2 The eight-class schema—with typical occupations and the size of each class within the electorate

Interpersonal service logic	Technical work logic	Organizational work logic	Independent work logic
Socio-cultural (semi-) professionals	Technical (semi-) professionals/ specialists	(Associate) managers	Liberal professionals and large employers
Medical doctors Teachers Social workers	Engineers Architects IT specialists	Administrators Consultants Accountants	Entrepreneurs Lawyers Dentists
AT 13 CH 14 DK 16 NO 14	AT 6 CH 8 DK 7 NO 8	AT 10 CH 17 DK 16 NO 16	AT 2 CH 3 DK 3 NO 1
Service workers	Production workers	Office clerks	Small business owners and farmers
Waiters Nursing aides Shop assistants	Mechanics Carpenters Assemblers	Secretaries Receptionists Mail clerks	Shop owners Independent artisans Farmers
AT 21 CH 17 DK 20 NO 25	AT 16 CH 15 DK 21 NO 19	AT 22 CH 13 DK 10 NO 9	AT 11 CH 13 DK 7 NO 7

Notes
The values below the country abbreviations indicate the proportion of countries' electorate (citizenry) set in each of the eight classes, based on pooled data from ESS 2002, 2004, 2006, and 2008 (2002, 2004, and 2006 for Austria).
N: AT (Austria): 5,875; CH (Switzerland): 6,390; DK (Denmark): 5,685; NO (Norway): 6,472.

the four countries' electorate in the 2000s, restricting our sample to national citizens.

Class location is measured on the basis of the respondents' current or past employment. If respondents do not mention any occupation, their class location is derived from their partner's present or past employment. Once we have determined the relevant source of their employment, respondents are then allocated to classes based (1) on their employment status, separating employers and the self-employed from the much larger category of employees, and (2) on their (past or present) occupation, as measured by the over 400 occupational codes in the ESS (ISCO-88 at 4-digit). The process followed to allocate occupations to different classes is described in more detail elsewhere (Oesch 2006b: 270–272).

Alongside the class variable, we construct two composite indices to capture citizens' preferences on an economic-distributive and a cultural-identitarian axis. For each of the two axes, we select four questions that seem, from a theoretical point of view, well suited to translate the underlying attitudes towards economic redistribution and cultural diversity. We then run first a factor analysis on economic attitudes by using the following four items (factor loadings decreasing in this order): (1) standard of living for the unemployed is government's responsibility; (2) Standard of living for the old is government's responsibility; (3) a job for everyone is government's responsibility; (4) government should reduce differences in income levels. This index gives us a measure for an economic axis going from a socialist to a capitalist pole.

We then run a second factor analysis on cultural attitudes by using another four items (factor loadings again decreasing in this order): (1) a country's cultural life is undermined or enriched by immigrants; (2) immigrants make a country a worse or better place to live in; (3) gays and lesbians should be free to live as they wish; (4) European unification has gone too far or should go further. This measure gives us a proxy for the cultural dimension underlying the politics of identity and community, which stretches from a libertarian-universalistic to an authoritarian-communitarian pole. By combining the attitudes on the two axes, we are able to determine voters' position in a two-dimensional political space as sketched out, among others, by Herbert Kitschelt (Kitschelt 1994: 27). The factor loadings of these two composite indices countries are shown in Tables A2.1 and A2.2 in the Appendix. Note that in both cases, one single factor explains over 90 percent of the variance in the items.[2]

Results for class voting

Our analysis starts with a look at the class basis of the New Left and the radical right in the four countries under study. Figure 2.1 presents the proportion in each class voting for either the New Left or the radical right, where horizontal bars to the left imply less-than-average support and bars to the right more-than-average support (blank bars mean not significantly different from the average). Only one class stands out as lending disproportionate support to the New Left: socio-cultural (semi-)professionals. Would the electorate entirely consist of this new and still growing class, the New Left would obtain between 22 percent and 33 percent of all votes in the four countries under study—at least twice its effective electoral score. In contrast, production workers are very unlikely to support the New Left: among production workers, the New Left receives one out ten votes at best (Denmark), and one out of twenty-five votes at worst (Switzerland). In Denmark, Norway, and Switzerland, production workers are joined by small business owners and clerks, who also manifest very little sympathy for the New Left.

When turning to the radical right, we find production workers to be its strongest supporters in all four countries: 30 percent among them vote for Norway's Progress Party and even 40 percent for the Swiss People's Party. In Denmark, Norway, and Switzerland, the radical right is also particularly successful in obtaining the support of service workers—the newer and more feminine component of the working classes. On the contrary, the radical right does not hold much appeal for socio-cultural (semi-)professionals. Were it only for this class, the radical right parties under study would be condemned to an insignificant minority status. Quite generally, the radical right receives lower-than-average support from the (upper)-middle classes, be they salaried (socio-cultural and technical professionals as well as managers) or self-employed (liberal professionals and large employers).

In sum, Figure 2.1 shows the class constituencies of the New Left and the radical right to present the almost exact mirror image of each other. Moreover, there is a striking similarity in the class pattern across countries: despite differences in their institutions, party systems, and political culture, we find in all four countries the same classes to rally behind the radical right and avoid the New Left (production workers and small business owners), as to support the New Left and to shun the radical right (socio-cultural professionals).

That these differences in electoral shares are not irrelevant becomes clear when we adopt a compositional perspective and disaggregate each camp's electorate according to class. Figure 2.2 shows that the New Left depends much more than the radical right on the votes of professionals: in all four countries, socio-cultural, technical, and liberal (semi-)professionals represent at least 40 percent of the New Left's voters, but 18 percent at most of those of the radical right. In contrast, clerks, production, and service workers—three categories without secure middle-class status—make up two-thirds of the radical right's electorate as compared to only 40 percent of the New Left in Austria, Denmark, and Norway. In Switzerland, the electoral relevance of the working classes is much smaller than in the other three countries because of a disproportionate share of—disenfranchised—immigrant workers. Yet the differences in the party constituencies are no less striking: the Swiss People's Party receives 44 percent of its votes from production workers, service workers, and clerks, as compared to only 18 percent from (semi-)professionals. The opposite is true for the New Left: 51 percent of its electorate are (semi-)professionals, but only 17 percent are production workers, service workers, and clerks. The New Left thus relies in all four countries on the middle classes, whereas the radical right is clearly dominated by the working classes.

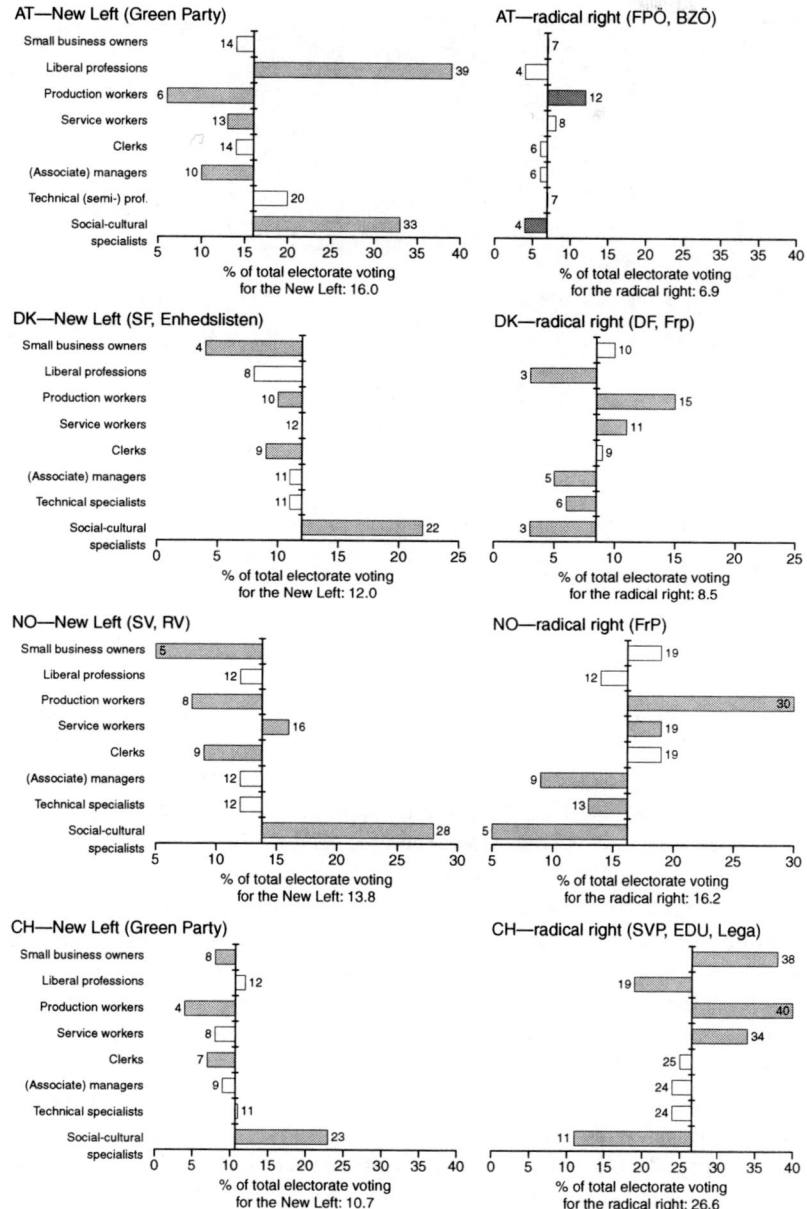

Figure 2.1 The electoral score of the New Left and the radical right by class in the 2000s.

Notes
Blank columns signify that the electoral scores of these classes are not statistically different from the party's total score in the electorate. Statistical significance is based on t-tests and $p < 0.05$.
N: Austria: 3,458; Denmark: 4,848; Norway: 5,074; Switzerland: 3,202.

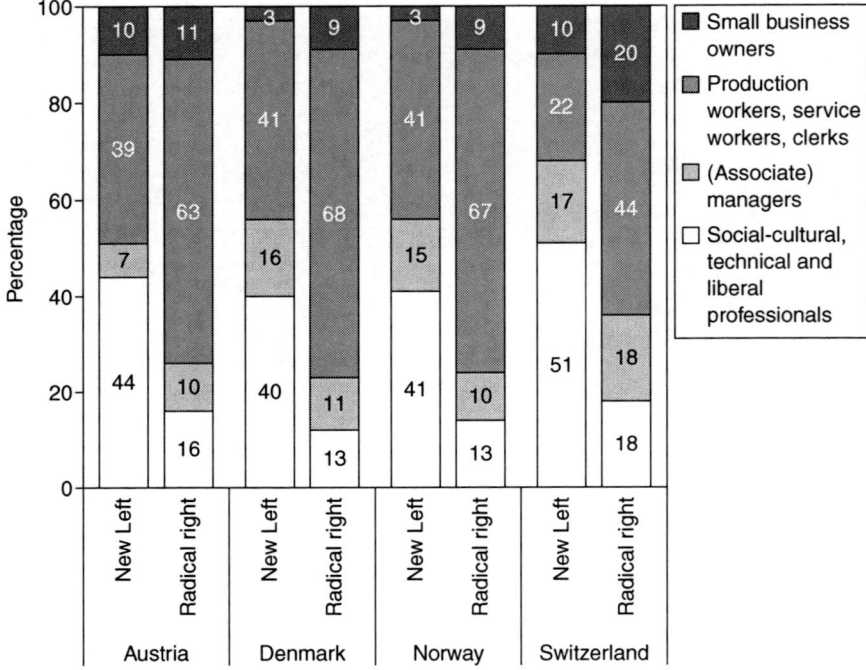

Figure 2.2 The class composition of the electorate of the New Left and the radical right.

An open question is whether the relationship between particular classes and political parties still holds once we take into account other individual character-istics such as gender, age or education. The electorates of the New Left and the radical right diverge much more in terms of gender than do those of the old left and the center right. In all four countries, the New Left attracts significantly more support from women than men, whereas the radical right is everywhere more successful among men than women. The gaps are particularly marked for Norway's Socialist Left Party at the one extreme (obtaining 10 percent of male and 18 percent of female votes) and the Austrian Freedom Party at the other (9 percent of male and 5 percent of female votes); but gender differences are by no means limited to these two parties—quite to the contrary. Again, the parallels between countries are remarkable.[3]

The two party families also diverge with respect to age. The New Left presents everywhere the youngest electorate, whereas the radical right has, on average, the oldest voters of all parties in Austria and Denmark and the second oldest in Norway and Switzerland. However, more relevant for the understand-ing of the new cultural conflict than age is education. Figure 2.3 shows that the relationships between educational attainment and party choice go into opposite directions for the New Left and the radical right. While support for the New Left rises steeply with increasing education, endorsement of the radical right drops

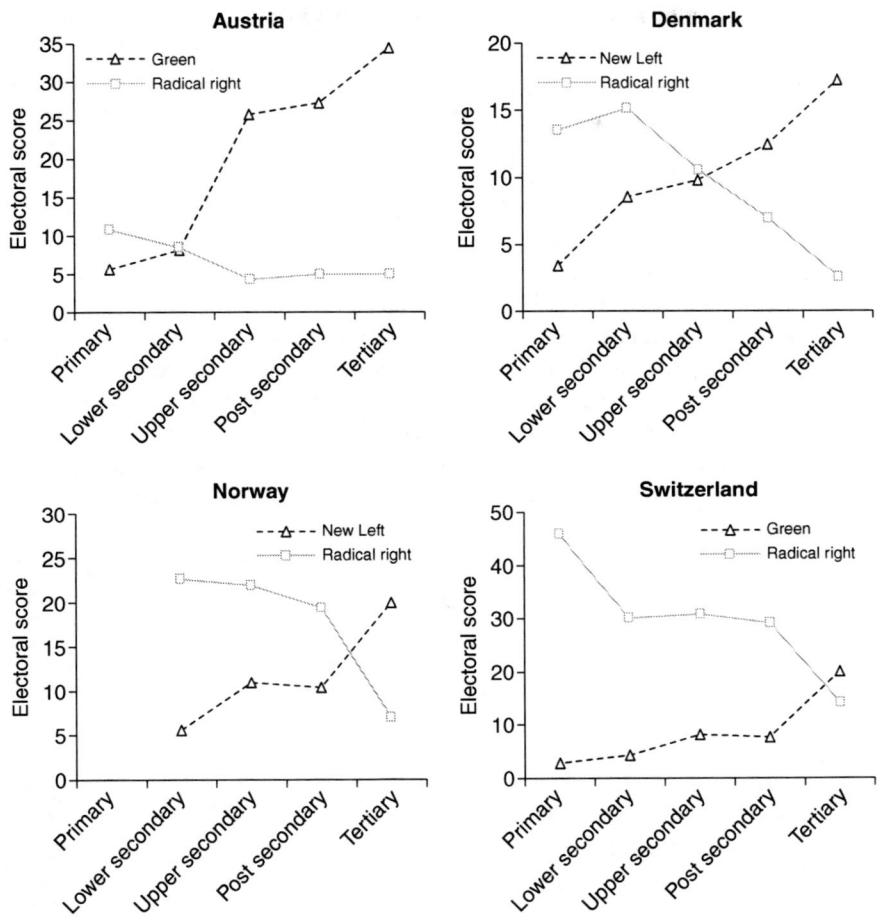

Figure 2.3 The electoral score of the New Left and the radical right by educational level in the 2000s (in %).

Notes
N: Austria: 2,381; Denmark: 4,960; Norway: 5,226; Switzerland: 3,320.

with rising education. As a result, citizens with no more than lower-secondary schooling are more likely to vote for the radical right than the New Left in all four countries, whereas holders of tertiary degrees give everywhere stronger support to the New Left than the radical right. These different propensities to vote for either party are also reflected in the composition of the respective electorates. In Denmark, Norway, and Switzerland, over 40 percent of the New Left's voters went to university or technical college as compared to less than 16 percent among radical right voters.

What happens to class once we control for differences in gender, age, and education? The results of multinomial regressions on party choice suggest that in all four countries, the class effect on party choice becomes weaker once we account for years of education (and the somewhat less consequential variables of gender and age). Yet in all four countries socio-cultural professionals remain nonetheless significantly more likely to vote for the New Left—as do production workers, together with service workers in Austria, Denmark, and Norway, to vote for the radical right than the reference category of (associate) managers.[4] Hence, although every additional year of education tips the balance away from the radical right toward the New Left, voters' class position continues to play a central role. Managers and socio-cultural professionals may have similar levels of education; their diverse occupational experiences still set them apart in terms of economic and cultural preferences. In any case, the temptation to play off class against education is somewhat academic as the two concepts are closely linked: access to several classes such as the socio-cultural and technical professions depends upon the successful completion of higher education: being a medical doctor, a lecturer or an engineer presupposes the existence of a tertiary degree. In contrast, class positions in routine production or service work make the possession of advanced education unlikely, as it is neither requested nor put to effective use in the job.

We try to make the results from multinomial regression accessible by calculating the predicted probabilities to support either the New Left or the radical right for the average voter: a man aged forty-five years, who either works as a socio-cultural professional or a production worker. Figure 2.4 shows that even when age and gender are held constant, the two classes strongly diverge in their

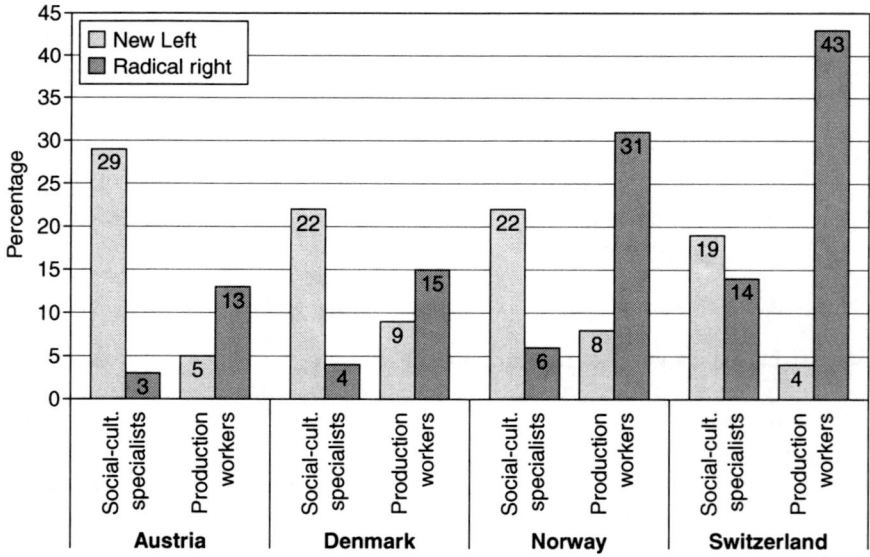

Figure 2.4 Predicted electoral share for the New Left and the radical right among forty-five-year-old men, working either as socio-cultural specialists or production workers (in %).

party choice. Among middle-aged male socio-cultural professionals, between 19 percent (Switzerland) and 29 percent (Austria) vote for the New Left, but only between 3 percent (Austria) and 14 percent (Switzerland) for the radical right. In contrast, middle-aged men employed as production workers are much less likely to support the New Left than the radical right. Differences are largest in Norway and Switzerland, where only 8 percent and 4 percent respectively vote for the New Left, but 31 percent and 43 percent vote for the radical right. The large differences between these two classes are not trivial, as socio-cultural professionals account for about 15 percent (tendency rising) and production workers for about 20 percent (tendency falling) of the electorate.

The cultural and economic preferences linking classes and parties

So far, our analysis has been limited to structural determinants of voting for the New Left or the radical right. However, the concept of cleavage implies the existence of a shared normative element—a common set of values—which provides a sense of identity to citizens' socio-structural position and thus converts it into voting (Bartolini and Mair 1990: 199). In other words, values and attitudes should pick up the class effect and translate it into party choice. Accordingly, we integrate voters' economic and cultural preferences into our analysis of the link between class location and party choice. We do so by constructing a two-dimensional political space, as sketched out, among others, by Kitschelt (Kitschelt 1994: 27; see also Kriesi *et al.* 2008b: 13). The horizontal axis distinguishes voters' attitudes towards the economy, going from a redistributive socialist pole to a free-market capitalist pole. The vertical axis separates voters according to their attitudes towards the political regulation of lifestyles and cultural diversity, going from a libertarian-universalistic to an authoritarian-communitarian pole.

Based on the factor analyses discussed above, we plot voters' preferences on the economic and cultural axes into the two-dimensional political space shown in Figure 2.5. While we calculate voters' mean preferences at the level of both occupational classes and party families, it is important to note that our analysis only carries on the electoral demand side: we depict parties' positions on the basis of their mean voter's economic and cultural preferences, and not on the basis of parties' programmes or stances over specific issues. Three findings in Figure 2.5 are noteworthy.

First, at the *party level*, we find voters of the radical right to occupy in all four countries the authoritarian-communitarian extreme of the cultural preference axis. While they differ very little from center-right voters in terms of economic preferences, sharing the same (Austria and Denmark) or almost the same (Norway and Switzerland) position on the state-market axis, they take a markedly more authoritarian stance over cultural issues. In consequence, they are at greatest variance with the New Left's electorate, which clusters at the libertarian-universalistic end of the cultural preference axis. While voters of the New Left are as strongly in favor of

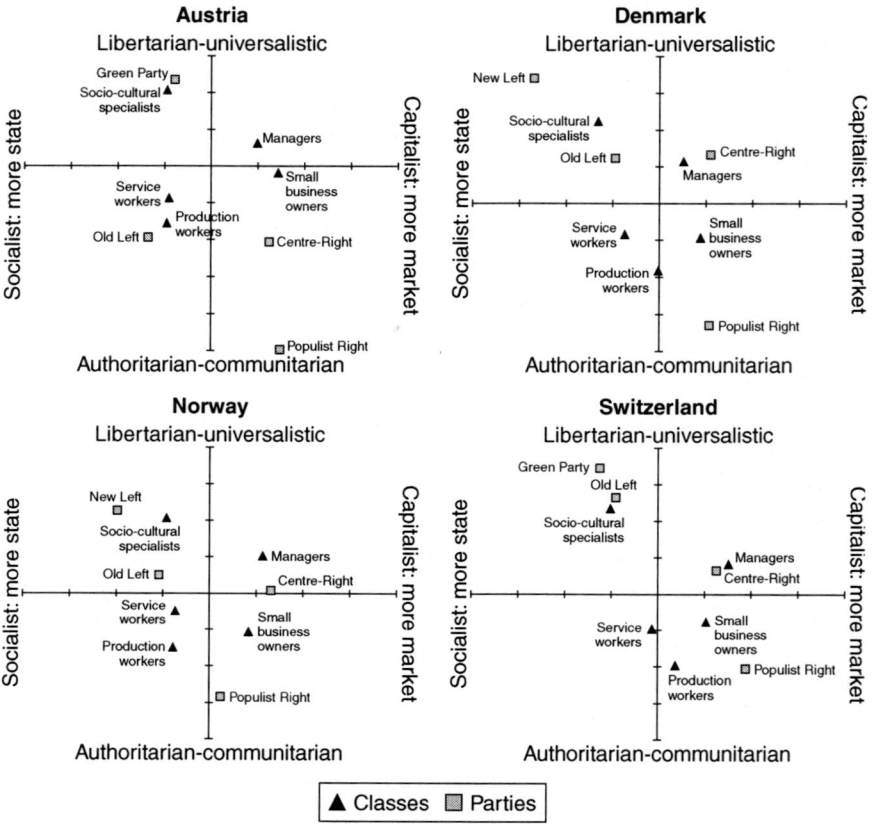

Figure 2.5 Voters' mean position on the economic (state-market) and cultural (integra-
tion-demarcation) preference axis, aggregated by class and party choice.

Note
See Tables A2.1 and A2.2 in the Appendix for the questions used to construct the factors underlying
the two axes. Three relatively small classes have not been included into the graphs: clerks, technical
specialists, and liberal professionals/large employers.

economic redistribution as the old left's electorate, they occupy culturally a much
more libertarian position everywhere, except in Switzerland where the Social
Democratic Party also adopted the claims of the new social movements. In the
other three countries, the electorates of the two dominant party families, the old
left and the center right, only disagree over economic issues, but share a similarly
centrist position on cultural issues related to immigration, homosexuality, and
European integration. This suggests that the two old party families mainly oppose
each other over an economic conflict ('Old politics'), whereas the two new party
families collide over a cultural divide ('New Politics').

Second, at the *class* level, socio-cultural professionals stand out as being particularly libertarian. In all four countries, they occupy the libertarian-universalistic end

of the cultural axis, and are thus a good distance away from the other large category of the salaried middle class: (associate) managers. While socio-cultural
professionals also take a more leftist stance over economic issues, what sets
them apart is their cultural libertarianism. The opposite—authoritarian—end of
the cultural axis is occupied by small business owners, service workers, and,
above all, production workers. No other class has preferences so traditionalist-
communitarian as production workers in our four countries. Interestingly, production and service workers are close to the old left in terms of economic
attitudes. What moves them into the vicinity of the radical right are their cultural
preferences. The radical right thus seems to secure the support of large working-
class segments *not thanks* to its market-liberal program, but *despite* it (Ivarsflaten 2005; see also Oesch 2008). Depending on whether economic or cultural
issues are more salient, production and service workers are likely to vote either
for the old left or the radical right.

Third, it is remarkable how much alike the political space looks in the four
countries under study. Even though we run a separate factor analysis for each
country, we obtain striking cross-country similarities in both economic and cultural preferences of party families and occupational classes. We find it difficult to
attribute these parallels to a different explanation than to political conflicts rooted
in the social structure—to cleavages. If attitudes were distributed randomly across
the electorate, we would certainly not expect such large commonalities in the cultural and economic preferences of occupational classes across countries. Note also
that individual-level analyses based on different data (and somewhat different class
measures) report very similar spatial configurations of the electorate in Denmark
(Harrits *et al.* 2009) and Switzerland (Oesch and Rennwald 2010).

In a last set of analyses, we estimate nested multinomial regressions on the
determinants of choosing the radical right over the New Left. The objective is to
determine the extent to which economic and cultural preferences account for the
class differences in party choice. We examine four different models: Model 1
only includes the socio-demographic variables of gender, age, education, and
class. Model 2 adds (and then removes) economic preferences, whereas Model 3
adds (and then removes) cultural preferences. Finally, Model 4 includes both
economic and preferences together with socio-demographic determinants. Since
we only dispose of all these measures in ESS round 4 (2008/2009), these analyses are run on a restricted sample and do not include Austria. The results are
shown in Table A2.3 in the Appendix. While they provide us with a load of
information on the determinants of voting behavior, we only discuss a few findings that seem particularly notable in the context of our study.

To begin with, socio-cultural professionals are everywhere systematically less
prone to vote for the radical right as compared to the New Left than all other
classes—except liberal and technical professionals—even accounting for differences in gender, age, and education (see Model 1). Holding preferences for economic redistribution clearly increases support for the New Left. Yet economic
attitudes do not explain why socio-cultural professionals are more likely to
favour the New Left over the radical right than other classes (see Model 2).

In comparison, cultural attitudes seem to be much more relevant for understanding why some classes rally behind the New Left and other classes behind the radical right: the coefficients for cultural preferences are in all three countries larger than those for economic preferences, most notably so in Switzerland (see Model 3). Once we account for voters' cultural preferences, socio-cultural professionals and service workers no longer differ significantly in their party choice and also the differences between socio-cultural professionals and production workers decline substantially in the three countries under study.

Likewise, the effect of higher education on preferring the New Left over the radical right seems to be channeled through cultural preferences. Hence, once we control for differences in voters' cultural attitudes, the effect of education shrinks, and becomes even non-significant in Switzerland—yet obviously, education determines cultural preferences, and not the other way round. These results suggest that the effect of class and education on the new cultural conflict is mediated through citizens' cultural preferences: their attitudes towards immigration, supranational integration, and different lifestyles. But of course, our imperfectly measured attitudes do not entirely explain why highly educated socio-cultural professionals are particularly likely to vote for the New Left and less qualified production workers (as well as clerks) particularly likely to support the radical right.

Conclusion

This chapter has argued that the electoral competition between the New Left and the radical right is best understood as a cultural divide that is firmly anchored in different class constituencies. The argument has then been subjected to an empirical analysis based on individual-level data stemming from four rounds of the European Social Survey. In a nutshell, our major findings can be summed up as follows.

We clearly find that party choice is not distributed randomly across the electorates in Austria, Denmark, Norway, and Switzerland. On the contrary, the New Left attracts disproportionate support from socio-cultural professionals and presents a clear-cut middle-class profile, where younger voters with tertiary education are strongly over-represented, while workers, clerks, and small business owners are under-represented. The radical right's constituency presents the mirror image of the New Left. In all four countries, the radical right is most successful among production and service workers and receives least support from socio-cultural professionals. More generally, the radical right strongly depends on the votes of less educated men and older citizens. Radical right parties have thus turned into a new type of working-class party, as two-thirds of their voters in Austria, Denmark and Norway do not have middle-class status.

However, the analysis of voters' preferences suggests that the radical right's success within the working class is due not to economic but to cultural issues. The New Left and the radical right thus collide over a cultural conflict of identity and community—and not over questions of market regulation and state redistribution. Economically, the voters of the New Left hold similar preferences as those of the old left. Likewise, attitudes toward the economy do not differ significantly between the electorates of the radical right and the center right. Yet in cultural terms, the New Left is much more libertarian and the radical right much more authoritarian than the constituencies of the two established parties. The New Left and the radical right thus primarily compete along the cultural dimension of politics. However different these two camps are, both lose out—to the old left or the center right respectively—if distributive issues linked to the economy are more salient in electoral campaigns. Likewise, they both flourish where questions related to immigration and cultural diversity appear more relevant to voters (Bornschier 2010a: 6). In other words, the success of the New Left and the radical right depends on the salience of the cultural as compared to the economic conflict.

In short, our analysis thus suggests that a full-grown cleavage has emerged in the four small and affluent European countries under study, separating a libertarian-universalistic pole from an authoritarian-communitarian pole. The emergence of this new divide has been accompanied by a process of class realignment: the beneficiaries of educational expansion and occupational upgrading—notably socio-cultural professionals—have decisively contributed to the growth of the New Left. In contrast, those left out from the transition toward the knowledge and service society—notably production workers—were successfully recruited by the radical right.

Appendix

Table A2.1 Factor analysis for the economic preference axis

Variable	Factor 1
Standard of living for the unemployed, government responsibility	0.74
Standard of living for the old, government responsibility	0.66
Job for everyone, government responsibility	0.59
Government should reduce differences in income levels	0.32
Eigenvalue	1.43
Proportion variance explained by factor	0.91

Note
N (based on ESS 2008 for CH, DK, NO): 4,820.

Table A2.2 Factor analysis for the socio cultural preferences axis

Variable	Factor 1
Country's cultural life undermined or enriched by immigrants	0.82
Immigrants make country worse or better place to live	0.82
Gays and lesbians free to live life as they wish	0.29
European unification should go further or gone too far	0.47
Eigenvalue	1.65
Proportion variance explained by factor	0.95

Note
N (based on ESS 2004, 2006, 2008 for AT, CH, DK, NO): 18,366.

Table A2.3 The determinants of voting for the Radical Right as compared to the New Left

	Denmark				Norway				Switzerland			
	(1)	(2)	(3)	(4)	(1)	(2)	(3)	(4)	(1)	(2)	(3)	(4)
Men					*Reference category*							
Women	0.03	0.07	−0.04	−0.01	−0.43	−0.37	−0.37	−0.32	**−0.63**	−0.61	−0.58	−0.55
Age	**0.02**	**0.02**	0.01	0.01	−0.01	−0.01	0.00	−0.01	**0.03**	**0.03**	**0.03**	0.03
Education	**−0.12**	**−0.10**	**−0.07**	−0.07	**−0.25**	**−0.26**	**−0.26**	**−0.20**	**−0.15**	**−0.15**	−0.08	−0.09
Socio-cult.					*Reference category*							
Technical	**1.92**	**1.64**	**1.66**	**1.47**	0.77	0.59	0.73	0.58	**1.33**	0.93	0.96	0.69
Managers	**1.11**	0.84	**1.12**	0.89	**1.27**	**1.01**	**1.28**	**1.05**	**1.32**	0.92	**1.40**	**1.07**
Clerks	**2.01**	**1.77**	**1.74**	**1.57**	**1.49**	**1.34**	**1.08**	0.94	**1.64**	**1.48**	**1.65**	**1.49**
Service w.	**1.17**	**1.14**	0.77	0.78	**1.15**	**1.13**	0.81	0.79	**1.46**	**1.33**	**1.13**	**1.06**
Product w.	**1.91**	**1.77**	**1.15**	**1.13**	**2.36**	**2.38**	**1.99**	**2.04**	**1.55**	**1.45**	**1.09**	**1.08**
Liberal pr.	1.26	0.86	1.04	0.77	0.26	0.34	0.07	0.08	0.61	0.09	0.46	0.01
Small bus.	**2.10**	**1.86**	**1.59**	**1.44**	**1.64**	**1.32**	**1.29**	**1.01**	0.82	0.51	0.88	0.62
Economic		**−1.18**		**−0.94**		**−0.95**		**−0.85**		−0.95		**−0.81**
Cultural			**−1.38**	**−1.18**			**−1.40**	**−1.33**			**−1.90**	**−1.79**
Constant	−1.33	−1.32	−1.14	−1.13	3.75	3.82	3.17	3.29	0.88	1.10	0.27	0.41
Pseudo R2	0.051	0.092	0.081	0.114	0.076	0.109	0.112	0.141	0.069	0.101	0.168	0.186
N	1,210	1,210	1,210	1,210	1,076	1,076	1,076	1,076	671	671	671	671

Notes

Figures show the coefficients of multinomial regressions on voting for the Radical Right as compared to the New Left (reference category). Results for the two other categories—Old Left and Centre Right—are not shown.

Bold figures imply coefficients that are statistically significant at $p < 0.05$.

Notes

1 Note that Austria was only included in the first three survey rounds of the ESS, but not in ESS 2008/2009.

2 In order to allow for country differences in attitudes, our analyses below rely on factor analyses run separately by country. The attitudinal factors thus vary across countries—although surprisingly little. Since the questions used to construct the economic axis were only included in the ESS 2008/09 and thus not available for Austria, Austria's economic factor is based on three other questions, included in ESS2002/03: (1) government should reduce differences in income levels; (2) the less government intervenes in the economy, the better for the country; (3) employees need strong trade unions to protect work conditions.

3 The differences in electoral scores by gender are the following.

   AT—New Left: 14 percent male, 18 percent female; radical right: 9 percent male, 5 percent female.

   DK—New Left: 9 percent male, 13 percent female; radical right: 10 percent male, 7 percent female.

   NO—New Left: 10 percent male, 18 percent female; radical right: 19 percent male, 13 percent female.

   CH—New Left: 9 percent male, 13 percent female; radical right: 30 percent male, 24 percent female.

4 The reference category is constituted of (associate) managers who vote for the center right. Significance levels correspond to $p < 0.01$. Detailed results are available from the author. See also Table A2.3 in the Appendix, discussed below.

3 Radical right parties

Their voters and their electoral competitors

Wouter van der Brug, Meindert Fennema,
Sarah de Lange and Inger Baller

Introduction

Since the late 1980s, Western Europe has experienced the rise of a large number of radical right parties.[1] At the moment there are ten radical right parties represented in nine West European national parliaments, with vote shares ranging from 5.7 percent in Sweden to 29.0 percent in Switzerland. As a result of their electoral success, several West European radical right parties have assumed office in recent years, such as the Bündnis Zukunft Österreich (BZÖ) and Freiheitliche Partei Österreichs (FPÖ) in Austria, the Lega Nord (LN) in Italy and the Lijst Pim Fortuyn (LPF) in the Netherlands. In recent years, radical right parties have also emerged in Central and Eastern Europe, where they have successfully contested elections in Bulgaria, Hungary, Slovakia, and Slovenia.

Since the emergence of radical right parties in the late 1980s, scholars have attempted to explain their electoral success. Much of the early research focused on the class basis of support for radical right parties and showed that less-educated male blue-collar workers were over-represented in the electorate of these parties. Betz (1994), for example, described the supporters of radical right parties as the "losers of modernity", arguing that they were less-educated men who had to compete with immigrants for low-skilled jobs and social housing. According to Betz, voting for the radical right could be seen as an expression of resentment against immigrants and against political elites, which is why he perceived of a vote for these parties as a "protest vote". More recently Ford and Goodwin (2010) and Kriesi *et al.* (2006) have used similar terms to describe the supports of radical right parties, calling them "angry white men" and the "losers of globalisation".

Irrespective of the appropriateness of these somewhat normatively loaded terms, there appears to be agreement that less-educated male blue-collar workers are over-represented among the supporters of radical right parties. We have been critical, however, of research that focuses predominantly on the class basis of the support for the radical right to explain its rise. We have emphasized that socio-demographic variables explain only a few percent of the variance in support for radical right parties (e.g., van der Brug *et al.* 2000) and have demonstrated that socio-demographic variables cannot explain cross-country differences in the aggregate success of these parties (e.g., van der Brug *et al.* 2005). Moreover, we have shown that voters for the radical right are just as much motivated by policy as voters for other parties and have therefore stressed that they should not be described as protest voters, but rather as rational voters (van der Brug and Fennema 2003).

To explain the rise of radical right parties, models need to include a combination of demand-side and supply-side factors: that is, including the attitudes and background characteristics of voters, as well as the agency of these parties and the competition they face from other parties (Eatwell 2003; see also Kitschelt 1995; Mudde 2007). Recent studies reveal that both types of factors play an important role in explaining the success of radical right parties (Arzheimer 2009a; see also Arzheimer and Carter 2006; Lubbers *et al.* 2002; Norris 2005; van der Brug *et al.* 2005). Moreover, these studies underline that concerns over the influx and integration of immigrants especially explain why voters support the radical right (Ivarsflaten 2008; see also van der Brug and Fennema 2003).

In this chapter we build upon these insights and address two questions that are relevant in the context of an edited volume on "class politics and the radical right." First, we examine which individual-level variables predict support for radical right parties. We explore the explanatory power of three models (the socio-structural model, the protest vote model, and the policy voting model), because the explanatory power of "social class" can only be evaluated when compared to that of other factors. Second, we study the degree to which radical right parties compete with other parties for electoral support. If "class politics" explains electoral behavior, we would expect social democratic and socialist parties to be the most important competitors of radical right parties, because they would also vie for the support of less-educated male blue-collar workers. Yet, class divisions may have been replaced by new cleavages, which give rise to other patterns of competition. So in the second empirical section of this chapter we explore these patterns of party competition.

This chapter contributes to the literature on the electoral support of the radical right in a number of ways. First of all, we test three models to explain the support for twenty radical right parties, in a comparative research design. Previous studies have included a much smaller number of radical right parties, except for Arzheimer (2009a). However, in the latter study the policy voting model could not be tested, because the data set did not include attitudes toward immigrants and left–right distance. Second, the present study includes a large number of radical right parties for which the support base has never been analyzed in a comparative study, such as the Bündnis Zukunft Österreich (BZÖ), the Partij voor de Vrijheid (PVV), and the Sverigedemokraterna (SD). Moreover, we provide updated analyses for parties that have been studied before, such as the Freiheitliche Partei Österreichs (FPÖ), the Front National (FN), and the Vlaams Belang (VB). These updates are needed, because previous studies have shown that there have been large changes in the support bases of radical right parties (van der Brug and Fennema 2003). Third, previous studies have mainly concentrated on the competition radical right parties face from the largest mainstream party of the right, even though some scholars see radical right parties as important competitors to social democratic parties (e.g., Bale *et al.* 2010). In this chapter we examine which parties are the radical right's main electoral competitors in the twenty-first century.

Explanations for the electoral success of the radical right

Various theories have been put forward to explain why voters support radical right parties, some derived from the rational choice literature and others originating from the (psycho-)sociological tradition. However, irrespective of their origins most theories assume that voters express some form of grievance by casting a ballot for the radical right. The grievances cited most often in the literature on the radical right are: economic grievances; grievances related to the functioning of democracy and political institutions, such as governments and political parties; and grievances caused by mass immigration, especially from Muslim countries (e.g., Ivarsflaten 2008).

A first group of scholars has focused first and foremost on the economic grievances certain groups of voters have developed as a result of the globalization process. They argue that support for radical right parties comes from those citizens who feel threatened by the rapid changes that have taken place in post-industrial societies. Blue-collar workers with low levels of education feel especially insecure, because they risk losing their jobs as a result of changes in modes of production and growing competition from low-wage countries (Kitschelt 1995; see also Kriesi *et al.* 2006). Moreover, they increasingly have to compete with immigrant groups for scarce resources such as jobs and houses, a phenomenon also known as ethnic competition (Lubbers 2001). Recent research has demonstrated, however, that there is no economic realignment fueling the success of radical right parties (Ivarsflaten 2005).

A second group of scholars believes that the support for radical right parties is driven by discontent with politics (Belanger and Aarts 2006; see also Bergh 2004; Swyngedouw 2001). They contend that the vote for the radical right is best described as a protest vote. In the literature, the concept of the "protest vote" consists of two elements. The first element that distinguishes a protest vote from other types of vote is that discontent with politics, which manifests itself as political cynicism or distrust, should have a strong effect on support for a radical right party (e.g., Belanger and Aarts 2006; see also van der Brug 2003). The second element is, in the words of Lubbers and Scheepers (2000: 69), that "political attitudes [...] are expected to be of minor importance" when explaining the vote for the radical right. The main motivation behind a protest vote is, after all, not to affect public policies, but to express discontent. On the basis of these considerations van der Brug *et al.* (2000) and van der Brug and Fennema (2003) conceptualize protest voters as voters who support a party out of discontent and for whom policy considerations are relatively unimportant. Since they find that most voters for radical right parties vote on the basis of policy considerations, they conclude that these voters cannot be qualified as protest voters (Ivarsflaten 2008).

A third group of scholars believes that policy voting largely explains the support for radical right parties. In the policy voting model voters are considered to be rational consumers of policy programs and political parties as providers of such programs. In elections several parties provide their policy programs and voters choose from these alternatives. Of course, voters do not know the content of all these programs. To be able to choose with restricted information on these programs, voters rely on other indications of the party programs. They tend to rely on general information and images that refer to the ideological profile of the parties. The policy voting model predicts, therefore, that even with limited information the voters' decisions in the ballot box are based on the content of the party programs (i.e., on issues and ideological positions). Electoral research has shown that votes for many radical right parties—particularly the more successful ones—are predominantly based on policy orientations, which are expressed in left–right positions and attitudes toward immigrants and immigration (Kitschelt 1995; see also Lubbers *et al.* 2002; Mughan and Paxton 2003; van der Brug and Fennema 2003; van der Brug *et al.* 2000).

Several researchers have argued that explanations of radical right parties' electoral fortunes need to include both demand-side and supply-side factors (e.g., Eatwell 2003; Kitschelt 1995; Mudde 2007), but causal models including both types of factors have only been tested empirically in recent years (Arzheimer 2009a; Arzheimer and Carter 2006; Lubbers *et al.* 2002; Norris 2005; van der Brug *et al.* 2005). These models explain more of the variance in the electoral success of radical right parties than models that only include demand-side factors.[2] However, most studies that test causal models including demand-side and supply-side factors assume the electoral space in West European countries to be one-dimensional—with Green and social democratic parties being on the left, and Christian democratic, conservative, liberal, and radical right parties being on the right—and therefore identify right-wing parties as the most important competitors of radical right parties. Since it has been argued that radical right parties do not compete primarily along the left–right dimension (e.g., Kriesi *et al.* 2008b), we have to consider the possibility that they compete with other parties as well.

This idea has its origins in the work of Ignazi (1992, 2003), who claims that radical right parties emerged in the 1980s in reaction to the rise of Green parties a decade earlier. Following Inglehart (1977), he considers the rise of Green parties to be a consequence of the fact that non-materialist issues have become more important in post-industrial societies. Ignazi (1992, 2003) argues, however, that only a small group of voters has developed post-materialist values and approves of libertarian policies. Other voters are disturbed by the decline of traditional norms and values, the erosion of social structures such as the family, the loss of national identity and sovereignty, and the weakening of authority, and they therefore support authoritarian policies.

As the protagonists of non-material politics, Green and radical right parties have introduced a new dimension to European politics, usually referred to as the libertarian–authoritarian dimension, which is orthogonal to the left–right or socio-economic dimension on which established parties traditionally compete.[3] On this new dimension Green parties take a libertarian position, favoring open borders, participatory democracy, libertarian values, and sustainable development, while radical right parties take an authoritarian position, campaigning for a sharp reduction in the influx of immigrants, obligatory integration programs, nationalist values and tougher punishment of criminals (Kitschelt 1995). Scholars agree that socio-cultural issues have become more prominent in West European politics in recent decades, partially as a result of the rise of Green and anti-immigration parties. Yet, scholars disagree on the extent to which the party systems in Western Europe are now two-dimensional, as has been argued by Kriesi *et al.* (2008b).

Others have argued, however, that the emergence of Green and radical right parties did not fundamentally change the dynamics of competition in European party systems. Despite the new dimension of competition, a clear distinction could still be drawn between left-libertarian parties (e.g., communist, Green, and social democratic parties) and right-authoritarian parties (e.g., Christian democratic, conservative, and radical right parties). However, in reaction to the success of Green and radical right parties, established parties have adjusted their positions on the libertarian–authoritarian dimension, with most established parties moving in the direction of the authoritarian pole of this dimension (Bale 2008; see also Bale *et al.* 2010; Carter 2005; Meguid 2005; Norris 2005; van Spanje 2010). This process of "contagion of the right" has caused a rotation of the main axis of competition, with the main opposition now being between Green and left-libertarian parties on the one hand and radical right parties on the other hand (Kitschelt 2003; van der Brug and van Spanje 2009). Established parties take a variety of positions in between these parties. So, the relevant literature yields different predictions about the structures of electoral competition. When the electoral spaces are largely uni-dimensional, their main competitors will be other parties from the right. However, if they compete along two axes of competition, they will compete with the traditional parties from the left *and* the right.

Below, we will first analyze the explanatory power of the three models of support for radical right parties: the socio-structural model, the protest vote model, and the policy voting model. Then, we will turn to our second research question, focusing on the structure of electoral competition.

Method

To answer our research questions we employ the European Elections Studies (EES), which is a survey conducted among a representative sample of approximately 1,000 citizens from each of the twenty-seven member states of the European Union right after the elections to the European Parliament, which were held in June 2009. The advantage of using this data set is that it provides us with comparable data across a large number of countries and with the appropriate measures of electoral support for various types of parties, including radical right parties.[4]

To measure electoral support we use a set of questions included in the 2009 EES, which asks respondents how likely it is that they will ever vote for a particular party. Respondents answer this question by placing themselves on an eleven-point scale, where 0 is labeled "I will certainly never vote for this party" and 10 "I will almost certainly vote for this party sometime in the future." It has been demonstrated by Tillie (1995) that the "propensity to support" question is almost perfectly linked to voting behavior, because respondents normally give the highest score to the party they intend to vote for in a national election. In addition, the propensity to support question provides information about the attractiveness of all parties for each respondent, including those the respondent does not intend to vote for. By analyzing this question, we thus arrive at valid estimate of the determinants of party choice (e.g., van der Eijk *et al.* 2006). The variable is therefore also used in a series of regression analyses that estimate how well the three main explanations for the electoral success of radical right parties described in this chapter perform.

To test the first model (the socio-structural model), we analyze the effect of a number of relevant demographic and socio-economic variables, such as age, education, gender, occupation, religion, social class, and standard of living, on the support for these parties. To test the second model (the protest vote model), we include four measures of discontent: "approval of government record"; "trust in the institutions of the EU"; "responsiveness of national parliament"; and "satisfaction with democracy." The measures are based on respondents' agreement or disagreement with four statements included in the EES (see Appendix). To test the third model (the policy voting model), we add three types of variables. First, we measure the distance between the respondent's own position on the left–right scale and the position of the radical right party on this scale. We also measure the distance between the respondent and the radical right party on a scale that measures positions on European unification. Second, we include four measures of issue salience. Issue salience is measured by the question, "what is the most important problem facing the country?" As a follow up, respondents are asked whether there is a second or a third important problem facing the country. We focus on four issues that may have been relevant for choosing a radical right party: crime fighting; environmental issues; opposition to the EU; and opposition to immigration. Third, we add attitudes toward other issues, such as abortion, gay marriage, integration policy, and redistribution of wealth. These attitudes were measured using a number of statements included in the EES with which respondents could agree or disagree (see Appendix).

The questions that measure the dependent and independent variables were asked in each of the twenty-seven member states of the European Union. However, in ten of these member states radical right parties did not compete in elections at the time of the survey. These countries were therefore excluded from our analysis. In the remaining seventeen member states, twenty radical right parties competed in elections and were therefore included in the analysis. Of these twenty radical right parties, fourteen are from Western Europe and six from Central and Eastern Europe (see Table 3.1). Their success in recent

Table 3.1 Most recent election results of radical right parties

Country	Party	Abbreviation	Election year	Election result (%)
Western Europe				
Austria	Freiheitliche Partei Österreichs	FPÖ	2008	17.5
	Bündnis Zukunft Österreich	BZÖ	2008	10.7
Belgium	Vlaams Belang	VB	2010	7.7
Denmark	Dansk Folkeparti	DF	2007	13.9
Finland	Perussuomalaiset	PS	2011	19.0
France	Front National**	FN	2007	2.4
Greece	Laikós Orthódoxos Synagermós	LAOS	2009	5.6
Italy	Lega Nord	LN	2008	8.3
Malta	Azzjoni Nazzjonali**	AN	2008	0.5
Netherlands	Partij Voor de Vrijheid	PVV	2010	15.5
	Trots op Nederland**	TON	2010	0.6
Norway*	Fremskrittspartiet	FrP	2009	22.9
Sweden	Sverigedemokraterna	SD	2010	5.7
Switzerland*	Schweizerische Volkspartei	SVP	2007	29.0
United Kingdom	British National Party**	BNP	2010	1.9
	United Kingdom Independence Party**	UKIP	2010	3.1
Central Eastern Europe				
Bulgaria	Ataka	Ataka	2009	9.4
Hungary	Jobbik	Jobbik	2010	16.7
Lithuania	Tvarka ir teisingumas	TT	2008	10.6
Romania	Partidul România Mare**	PRM	2008	3.2
Slovakia	Slovenská Národná Strana	SNS	2010	5.1
Slovenia	Slovenska Nacionalna Stranka	SMS	2008	5.4

Notes
* Country not a member state of the European Union and therefore not included in the European Election Study.
** Party currently not represented in parliament.

elections varies greatly, from 0.5 percent for the Azzjoni Nazzjonali (AN) in Malta to 17.5 percent for the Austrian FPÖ.

What explains support for radical right parties?

To assess to what extent the three models can explain support for radical right parties, we conduct a series of regression analyses in which we estimate the proportions of explained variance (adjusted R^2) for each of the models. To assess the extent to which the socio-structural model explains support for radical right parties, we estimate the effects of nine groups of demographic and socio-economic variables (see Table 3.2). As was expected, in most countries the various demographic and socio-economic variables explain only a small portion of the variation in support for radical right parties. Age, gender, religion, socio-economic status, and standard of living play hardly any role when explaining the

Table 3.2 Explanatory power of the socio-structural model

Country	Party	Age	Female	Education	SES	Standard of living	Religious (dummy)	Religious denomination	Church going	Occupation	Total
Austria	FPÖ	0.00	0.00	0.05	0.02	0.00	0.00	0.00	0.01	0.03	0.09
	BZÖ	0.01	0.01	0.04	0.01	0.00	0.00	0.00	0.00	0.05	0.11
Belgium	VB	0.00	0.01	0.02	0.00	0.00	0.02	0.00	0.00	0.03	0.05
Bulgaria	Ataka	0.03	0.02	0.02	0.00	0.00	0.00	0.03	0.01	0.02	0.11
Denmark	DF	0.01	0.00	0.05	0.02	0.00	0.00	0.00	0.00	0.03	0.19
Finland	PS	0.01	0.02	0.06	0.03	0.02	0.01	0.02	0.02	0.08	0.19
France	FN	0.04	0.00	0.14	0.00	0.00	0.02	0.01	0.01	0.07	0.26
Greece	LAOS	0.00	0.00	0.01	0.00	0.00	0.02	0.02	0.02	0.01	0.06
Hungary	Jobbik	0.09	0.02	0.01	0.01	0.00	0.03	0.02	0.01	0.02	0.18
Italy	LN	0.00	0.01	0.02	0.00	0.01	0.03	0.01	0.04	0.02	0.08
Lithuania	TT	0.00	0.00	0.10	0.01	0.00	0.00	0.04	0.01	0.09	0.23
Malta	AN	0.02	0.00	0.03	0.00	0.01	0.00	0.02	0.00	0.00	0.07
Netherlands	PVV	0.00	0.02	0.05	0.02	0.01	0.00	0.00	0.01	0.04	0.11
	TON	0.01	0.01	0.02	0.00	0.00	0.00	0.00	0.00	0.05	0.08
Romania	PRM	0.00	0.00	0.02	0.00	0.01	0.00	0.03	0.00	0.02	0.07
Slovakia	SNS	0.02	0.00	0.06	0.03	0.02	0.00	0.00	0.00	0.04	0.14
Slovenia	SMS	0.03	0.00	0.06	0.00	0.01	0.02	0.00	0.02	0.04	0.13
Sweden	SD	0.00	0.00	0.01	0.00	0.00	0.00	0.01	0.00	0.01	0.04
UK	BNP	0.00	0.00	0.04	0.03	0.00	0.00	0.01	0.01	0.03	0.11
	UKIP	0.00	0.00	0.04	0.01	0.00	0.00	0.03	0.01	0.11	0.14
Average		0.01	0.01	0.04	0.01	0.00	0.01	0.01	0.01	0.04	0.13

support for these parties, with levels of explained variance of 0 to 4 percent. Stronger effects are found for education (between 1 percent and 14 percent explained variance) and occupation (between 1 percent and 11 percent explained variance), but the average amount of variance explained by the nine groups of demographic and socio-economic variables is only 13 percent.

Important cross-national differences exist though, with the total amount of variance explained ranging between 5 percent and 27 percent. In countries like Belgium, Austria, and the Netherlands, the electorate of radical right parties does not have a clearly defined demographic or socio-economic profile. The radical right parties in these countries seem to attract support across all social strata in society. In France, Hungary, Denmark, and Lithuania, on the other hand, supporters of the radical right have a much more distinct sociological profile. In these countries the socio-structural model has substantial explanatory power. This finding is quite surprising, given that van der Brug and Fennema (2003) concluded that demographic and socio-economic variables only accounted for a minor portion of variance in the support for radical right parties in the 1999 and 2004 EES. Moreover, they note that the effect of these variables declined over time. It seems that this trend has came to a halt, or has even been reversed in recent years, perhaps as a result of the changing socio-economic position of radical right parties.

To assess the extent to which the protest voting model explains support for radical right parties, we estimate the effects of five measures of discontent (see Table 3.3). The explanatory power of this model varies between countries. In Denmark, France, Hungary, Italy, Lithuania, and the Netherlands, the measures of discontent explain more than 15 percent of the variance in support for radical right parties.[5] In other countries, however, the percentages are considerably lower. Consequentially, the protest voting model on average explains 9 percent of the variance in the support for European radical right parties, leaving 91 percent of the variance unaccounted for. Hence, political grievances do not seem to be the main driver for the success of radical right parties, even though this is an important factor in some countries.

To assess the extent to which the policy voting model explains support for radical right parties, the explanatory power of both general and specific policy preferences is examined (see Table 3.4). In most countries, the distance between the radical right and voters on the left–right dimension as well as issue positions and issue salience explain variance in the support for radical right parties fairly well. The first variable explains on average 17 percent of this variance, while the second group of variables explains up to 34 percent. Even though some variation exists between countries in the extent to which the policy voting model manages to explain differences in the level of support for the radical right, the model explains these differences much better than the socio-structural or the protest vote model. This is especially true for the West European countries, where policy voting explains more than a third of the variance. The results suggest that, especially in Western Europe, support for radical right parties is guided more by policy considerations than by group solidarity or protest voting.

Table 3.3 Explanatory power of the protest vote model

Country	Party	Trust in institutions of the EU	National parliament is responsive	Satisfaction with democracy	Government approval	Total
Austria	FPÖ	0.10	0.04	0.06	0.01	0.12
	BZÖ	0.03	0.01	0.02	0.01	0.04
Belgium	VB	0.01	0.03	0.03	0.00	0.05
Bulgaria	Ataka	0.01	0.02	0.02	0.04	0.05
Denmark	DF	0.03	0.00	0.00	0.15	0.19
Finland	PS	0.02	0.01	0.01	0.01	0.03
France	FN	0.10	0.01	0.04	0.08	0.25
Greece	LAOS	0.00	0.01	0.00	0.00	0.01
Hungary	Jobbik	0.03	0.06	0.03	0.15	0.17
Italy	LN	0.02	0.04	0.03	0.15	0.19
Lithuania	TT	0.08	0.01	0.05	0.11	0.18
Malta	AN	0.00	0.01	0.00	0.00	0.00
Netherlands	PVV	0.04	0.06	0.07	0.12	0.16
	TON	0.01	0.02	0.02	0.03	0.04
Romania	PRM	0.00	0.00	0.00	0.00	0.00
Slovakia	SNS	0.04	0.01	0.01	0.07	0.11
Slovenia	SMS	0.01	0.01	0.00	0.02	0.03
Sweden	SD	0.01	0.03	0.02	0.00	0.04
UK	BNP	0.04	0.01	0.03	0.01	0.05
	UKIP	0.11	0.04	0.02	0.07	0.14
Average		0.03	0.02	0.02	0.05	0.09

Table 3.4 Explanatory power of the policy voting model

Country	Party	Left–right distance	EU distance	Issue positions and salience	Total
Austria	FPÖ	0.20	0.09	0.29	0.37
	BZÖ	0.19	0.06	0.15	0.28
Belgium	VB	0.13	0.07	0.10	0.26
Bulgaria	Ataka	0.12	0.01	0.03	0.22
Denmark	DF	0.23	0.09	0.34	0.43
Finland	PS	0.12	0.11	0.16	0.28
France	FN	0.20	0.00	0.35	0.42
Greece	LAOS	0.19	0.02	0.09	0.22
Hungary	Jobbik	0.41	0.06	0.16	0.49
Italy	LN	0.36	0.12	0.20	0.43
Lithuania	TT	0.20	0.06	0.11	0.34
Malta	AN	0.06	0.02	0.04	0.17
Netherlands	PVV	0.24	0.03	0.30	0.44
	TON	0.15	0.05	0.13	0.24
Romania	PRM	0.13	0.06	0.07	0.24
Slovakia	SNS	0.03	0.08	0.10	0.15
Slovenia	SMS	0.10	0.03	0.08	0.16
Sweden	SD	0.07	0.04	0.13	0.18
UK	BNP	0.13	0.00	0.14	0.25
	UKIP	0.12	0.00	0.21	0.26
Average		*0.17*	*0.05*	*0.16*	*0.30*

So far, we have only examined how well the various models explain variance in the support for radical right parties. Yet, we are not only interested in the explanatory power of the three models, but also in the direction and strength of the effects of the independent variables. Table 3.2 demonstrates, for instance, that the variable "age" explains 1 percent of the variance in support for the Austrian BZÖ, but this percentage does not tell us whether younger or older voters are more supportive of this party. Examining these effects for each of the radical right parties under investigation in this study would be beyond the scope of this chapter. Therefore, Table 3.5 presents a "pooled" analysis across seventeen countries, including all variables from the three models previously discussed.[6] To account for differences in the aggregate level of popularity of radical right parties in the seventeen countries, we conduct a multi-level analysis with a random intercept at the country level.

Several of the demographic and socio-economic variables presented in Table 3.5 have a significant effect on the support for radical right parties. Radical right parties attract more support from younger than from older generations and they are more popular among men than among women. In addition to effects from age and gender, we find that voters that are church going and voters with lower levels of education are more likely to support radical right parties. We also find that farmers and skilled workers are more likely to support radical right parties than voters with other occupations. The variables "standard of living,"

Table 3.5 Multi-level model explaining support for radical right parties

	Effect	*se*	*Sig.*
Intercept	5.7769	0.4186	0.000
Background characteristics			
Age	−0.0175	0.0023	0.000
Female	−0.1527	0.0654	0.020
Subjective social class	−0.0572	0.0373	0.124
Standard of living	0.0432	0.0306	0.158
Religious (dummy yes/no)	−0.0942	0.0984	0.338
Church going	0.0648	0.0268	0.016
Age of leaving full time education[1]			
15	−0.2416	0.2041	0.237
16	−0.2060	0.1940	0.288
17	−0.2792	0.1974	0.157
18	−0.2069	0.1673	0.216
19	−0.1776	0.1839	0.334
20	−0.2946	0.1944	0.130
21	−0.4826	0.1997	0.016
22	−0.3291	0.2019	0.103
23 or older	−0.4962	0.1687	0.003
Still in education	−0.3370	0.2369	0.155
Religious denomination[2]			
Protestant	0.2135	0.1306	0.102
Orthodox	0.2030	0.1997	0.309
Jew	−0.3128	0.7518	0.677
Muslim	−0.3996	0.3629	0.271
Hindu	0.0112	1.2098	0.993
Buddhist	1.5140	0.7516	0.044
Church of England	−0.0196	0.2851	0.945
Presbyterian	−0.5319	0.8641	0.538
Methodist	−0.8993	0.8654	0.299
Baptist	−0.5724	1.3564	0.673
Other	0.0196	0.2014	0.922
Occupational category[3]			
Higher administrative	0.0024	0.1264	0.985
Clerical	0.0601	0.1054	0.568
Sales	0.0394	0.1350	0.771
Service	0.0258	0.1112	0.817
Skilled worker	0.4032	0.1139	0.000
Semi-skilled worker	0.0933	0.1529	0.542
Unskilled worker	0.1386	0.1663	0.405
Farm worker	0.3270	0.2413	0.175
Farm proprietor, farm manager	0.6454	0.2635	0.014
Still in education	0.0868	0.2089	0.678
Never had a job	0.0311	0.2728	0.909

continued

Table 3.5 Continued

	Effect	se	Sig.
Discontent			
Trust institutions of EU	0.1671	0.0310	0.000
National parliament is responsive	0.0090	0.0301	0.765
Satisfaction with democracy	0.1581	0.0445	0.000
Government approval	−0.0129	0.0706	0.855
Distance to party			
On left–right dimension	−0.3500	0.0120	0.000
On EU dimension	−0.0878	0.0112	0.000
Issue salience			
Crime	0.1670	0.1157	0.149
Environment	−0.1985	0.1117	0.076
EU	−0.0016	0.1771	0.993
Immigration	0.3282	0.0845	0.000
Issue positions[4]			
Harsher sentences	0.0369	0.0327	0.259
Children should obey authority	0.0493	0.0328	0.133
Private enterprise solves problems	−0.0341	0.0286	0.232
More state ownership	0.0148	0.0263	0.574
No government intervention	−0.0437	0.0263	0.097
Redistribute wealth	0.0790	0.0291	0.007
Prohibit same-sex marriage	0.0577	0.0262	0.028
Pro-choice on abortion	−0.1179	0.0332	0.000
Women should stay at home	0.0130	0.0277	0.639
EU matters decided by referendum	0.1336	0.0289	0.000
Immigrants should assimilate	0.2040	0.0328	0.000
Decrease immigration	0.3522	0.0310	0.000
Random Effects			
$\sqrt{\psi}$	0.7500		
$\sqrt{\theta}$	2.6854		
Rho	0.0724		
N	7,765		
Groups	17		

Notes
1 14 or younger.
2 Roman Catholic serves as the base category.
3 "Professional and technical" serves as the base category.
4 A higher score means more agreement with the statement.

"socio-economic status," "religious," and "religious denomination" do not influence the support for radical right parties.

Several of the variables measuring discontent with democracy and politics also have a significant effect on the support for radical right parties. Voters who consider supporting radical right parties express little trust in the institutions of the European Union and are rather dissatisfied with the way democracy functions. However, voters who do not approve of the government and voters who feel that the national parliament is unresponsive are *not* more likely to support radical right parties than voters who do not feel that way.

In addition to the effects of a number of demographic and socio-economic variables and various measures of discontent, we also find strong effects from general policy preferences, such as distance to the radical right on the EU and left–right dimension. The effects of these two variables are negative, indicating that the smaller the distance between the position of these parties and the respondent on these dimensions, the more likely the respondent is to support the radical right. When interpreting these finding it is important to realize that the left–right dimension does not necessarily measure parties' and respondents' positions on socio-economic issues. There is some evidence that voters associate the right with, for example, stricter immigration legislation and tougher punishment of crime, and the left with environmental protection (Knutsen 1995). This interpretation of the findings is supported by the fact that our analyses show that immigration is the main issue voters of radical right parties are concerned about and that attitudes on issues that belong to the libertarian-authoritarian dimension, such as abortion, immigration, and same-sex marriages, exert the strongest effects on preferences for these parties. Voters for radical right parties tend to be pro-life on the question of abortion and tend to think that immigration should be reduced and that immigrants should assimilate. Moreover, they believe that there ought to be a referendum on new EU treaties and that same-sex marriages should be prohibited. Attitudes towards socio-economic issues do not influence the support for radical right parties, with the exception of respondents' attitudes towards the distribution of wealth.

Who are the main competitors of the radical right?

Given the fact that voters vote largely on the basis of policy preferences, the question arises where parties and voters are located on the main policy dimensions. As we outlined above, we expect two dimensions to be particularly important in structuring conflicts on contemporary issues: a socio-economic dimension and a libertarian–authoritarian dimension. We will now explore the positions of voters and parties on these policy dimensions.

To assess where voters position themselves, we focus on two questions in the EES that accurately measure voters' positions on the two dimensions that structure competition in Europe. As an indicator of positions on the socio-economic dimension, we employ responses to the question of whether income differences should be decreased or not. As an indicator of positions on the libertarian–authoritarian dimension, we employ responses to the question of whether the number of immigrants should be decreased. Tables 3.6 and 3.7 show how voters' preferences on these two issues are distributed in Western and Central and Eastern Europe. For the sake of clarity we do not present the percentages of the neutral category "neither agree nor disagree," which explains why the percentages do not add up to 100 percent.

The percentages presented in Tables 3.6 and 3.7 show that the largest group of voters in both parts of Europe takes a left-wing position on the issue of

Table 3.6 Distribution of voters on two dimensions in Western Europe (%)

		Redistribution of income	
		Agree	*Disagree*
Decrease immigration	Agree	41	12
	Disagree	16	8

Table 3.7 Distribution of voters on two dimensions in Central and Eastern Europe (%)

		Redistribution of income	
		Agree	*Disagree*
Decrease immigration	Agree	38	12
	Disagree	9	7

income differences and an authoritarian position on the immigration issue. This goes for 41 percent of voters in Western Europe and 38 percent of voters in Central and Eastern Europe. When using other indicators of positions on the socio-economic and authoritarian–libertarian dimension, the percentages are of course slightly different but the general pattern remains the same. The largest group of voters leans toward the left on the socio-economic dimension and toward the authoritarian pole of the libertarian–authoritarian dimension. In both parts of Europe, the smallest group of voters occupies a position in the opposite quadrant (7 percent in Central and Eastern Europe and 8 percent in Western Europe), combining a libertarian position with a right-wing position in the socio-economic scale. The main difference between Western Europe and Central and Eastern Europe concerns the size of the group of voters that can be qualified as left-wing and libertarian. In Western Europe, 16 percent of the respondents can be qualified as such, whereas in Central and Eastern Europe only 9 percent of voters have left-wing and libertarian views.

Now that we have seen how the voters are distributed on the two main axes of conflict, the question arises as to where parties situate themselves. To measure party positions, we employ a data set from an expert survey among political scientists, who were asked to indicate where parties from their country position themselves on a number of policy dimensions (Hooghe *et al.* 2010). The scales are somewhat different from the items that we used to measure voters' positions, but they are functionally equivalent to those in voter surveys. Figure 3.1 presents the positions of ninety-one West European political parties on two policy scales: the socio-economic dimension and the libertarian–authoritarian dimension. Inspection of Figure 3.1 shows that most Green, social democratic, and social populist parties take left-libertarian positions, whereas most Christian democratic, conservative, and liberal parties take a right-authoritarian position.[7] Radical right parties also position themselves in the right-authoritarian quadrant, but their authoritarian profile is much more outspoken than their right-wing

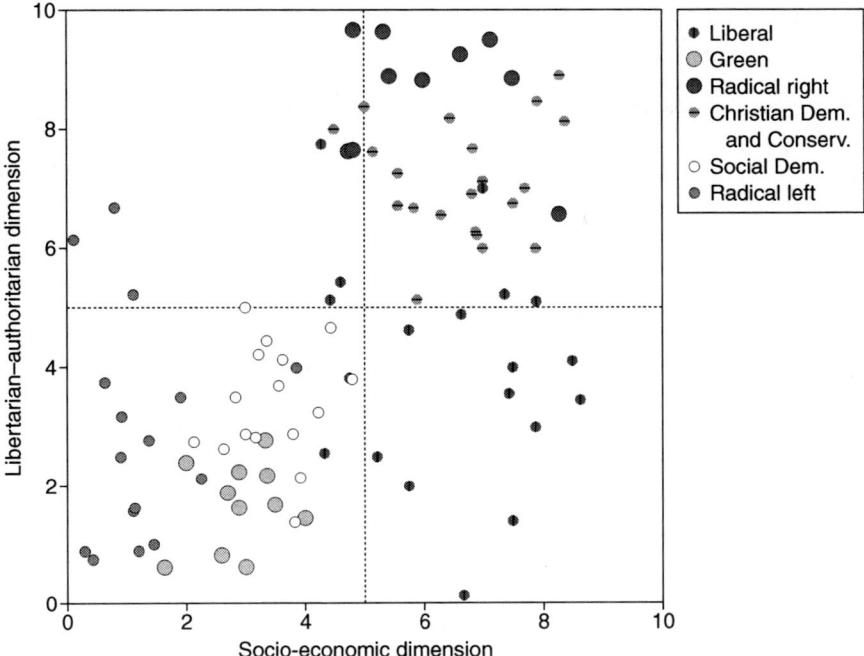

Figure 3.1 Party positions in Western Europe.

profile. As a result, the correlation between the two dimensions is strong. However, the most striking aspect of Figure 3.1 is that hardly any parties take a clear left-authoritarian position. The emptiness of this quadrant is quite amazing, because this is where the largest group of Western European voters is located.

Figure 3.2 shows the positions of fifty-seven parties from Central and East European countries on the socio-economic dimension and the libertarian–authoritarian dimension. The first thing that stands out is that all four quadrants are filled with parties, as a result of which the two dimensions are weakly correlated.[8] Another important observation is that the members of Central and East European party families do not cluster together as much as the members of West European party families. This indicates that Central and East European party families are less ideologically coherent than their West European counterparts. This is also the case for radical right parties. As expected, these parties have a clear authoritarian profile, but most of them lean to the left rather than to the right on socio-economic issues. Based on our analysis of the distribution of voters, these parties are in a very advantageous position to attract electoral support.

On the basis of these analyses it can be concluded that in Western Europe, Christian democratic, conservative, and liberal parties are ideologically much closer to the radical right than Green, radical left, and social democratic parties.

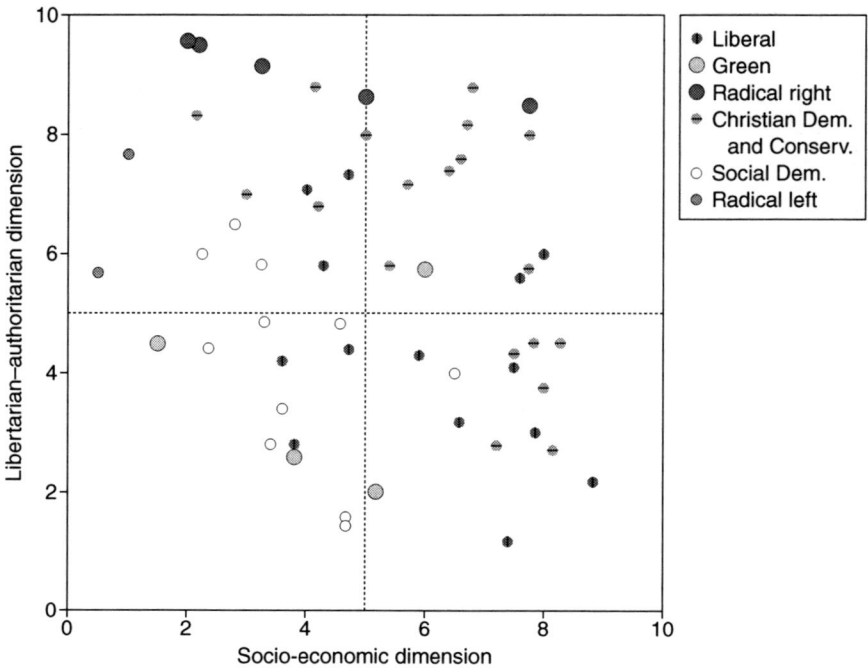

Figure 3.2 Party positions in Central and Eastern Europe.

We would therefore expect the former group of parties to be the main competitors of the radical right. Yet, there may also be a lot of competition for the large group of left-authoritarian voters, whose ideological positions are not represented by any party. These voters may consider supporting both left-wing and right-wing parties.

To study electoral competition between parties we need to look at groups of voters with high preferences for more than one party. If a voter gives a high preference score to two parties, he or she could cast a vote for both of them and thus belongs to the potential electorate of both parties. In order to measure electoral competition, we first have to define the group of potential supporters of a party. We define the electoral potential of each party to consist of those voters who give a probability to vote score of 7 or higher to a party. Voters who give a score of 7 or higher to a party indicate that they consider this party a serious candidate for their vote. However, parties cannot expect to mobilize their full electoral potential, because voters might consider other parties worthy of their vote as well. So, in order to assess which other parties radical right parties compete with, we look at the extent to which their electoral potential overlaps with that of other parties. Large overlaps of electoral potential indicate strong competition between the parties that have overlapping support. In order to establish to what extent radical right parties compete with other parties, Table 3.8 presents the size of the potential electorate of each of the radical right parties included in this study.

Table 3.8 The electoral potential of the radical right

Country	Party	Electoral potential	Overlap with the left			Overlap with the right			
			Greens	Social Democrats	Other left	Christian Democrats	Conservatives	Liberals	Other right
Austria	FPÖ	19.0	7.4	23.2	1.1	27.9	–	2.1	41.6
	BZÖ	11.0	8.2	19.1	1.8	39.1	–	2.8	71.8
Belgium	VB	12.7	11.8	18.9	10.2	23.6	35.4	26.2	–
Bulgaria	Ataka	13.9	–	12.3	–	–	14.5	2.2	–
Denmark	DF	19.1	11.6	13.6	–	–	36.1	1.6	–
Finland	PS	19.1	46.6	41.9	11.0	51.8	58.1	49.2	–
France	FN	6.0	9.3	11.1	0.0	–	36.4	7.3	–
Greece	LAOS	13.0	31.5	25.4	16.9	–	45.4	–	–
Hungary	Jobbik	30.2	–	2.3	1.3	80.1	5.0	0.7	–
Italy	LN	24.0	–	7.5	2.1	8.8	34.6	–	–
Lithuania	TT	23.0	–	35.2	–	14.8	18.3	11.7	–
Malta	AN	2.1	57.1	52.4	–	66.7	–	–	–
Netherlands	PVV	17.5	8.0	9.7	9.7	25.0	–	43.2	26.1
	TON	4.9	10.2	22.4	0.0	32.7	–	64.6	93.9
Romania	PRM	15.7	–	41.4	–	10.8	16.6	37.6	–
Slovakia	SNS	15.6	–	75.5	12.0	8.2	27.7	12.7	–
Slovenia	SMS	14.4	27.8	37.8	–	27.3	54.5	24.5	–
Sweden	SD	1.6	31.3	25.0	17.6	18.8	31.3	0.0	–
UK	BNP	7.5	26.7	8.0	–	–	56.6	21.3	57.3
	UKIP	18.9	23.8	10.1	–	–	52.4	34.9	22.8
Average		14.5	22.2	24.6	7.0	31.1	34.9	20.2	52.3

Table 3.8 shows that the electoral potential for radical right parties ranges from 1.6 percent in Sweden to 30.2 percent in Hungary, with an average of 14.5 percent of voters indicating that they would consider radical right parties a serious candidate for their vote. Interestingly, the extent to which radical right parties can still grow in future elections varies greatly across countries. While the Austrian BZÖ and FPÖ, the Dutch PVV, and the Finish PS seem to have realized most of their electoral potential in recent elections, many other radical right parties could double or triple their vote share by realizing their full electoral potential.[9]

Table 3.8 shows the complexity of the patterns of electoral competition. In West European countries the largest competitors of the radical right are always either the conservatives or the Christian democrats. However, in most of these countries a small group of potential supporters of the radical right considers voting for the social democrats a viable option. Even the Greens are not ruled out by many of them, despite the fact that they are ideologically at opposite ends of the spectrum. In Central and Eastern Europe, things are different. In Slovakia, Romania, and Lithuania, the social democrats are the main competitors of the radical right, whereas in Hungary hardly any voters can be found with high preferences for the radical right and the social democrats.

Conclusion

Although radical right parties have been on the rise in Central, Eastern, and Western Europe for quite some years, comprehensive and systematic tests of explanations for their electoral success are still lacking. In this chapter we have put various explanations advanced in the literature on the radical right to the test. Moreover, we have investigated to what extent these parties face competition from other parties, in an attempt to understand who votes for the radical right. Our findings contradict conventional wisdom and highlight a number of developments that have taken place in recent years.

First, demographic and socio-economic variables explain only a small portion of variance in voters' preference for the radical right. Yet, these sociological background characteristics of voters still account for 13 percent of the variance in the vote for radical right parties, which is a higher percentage than that found in 1999 or 2004. This is partly due, however, to the inclusion of Central and East European radical right parties in the analysis, which tend to receive more support from the working class than radical right parties in Western Europe. Shortly after the fall of communism, class divisions were not very important in explaining political preferences and voting behavior (Tworzecki 2003; see also Kitschelt 1992; Kitschelt *et al.* 1999). However, as a result of the introduction of a market economy, class interests developed, followed by party mobilization aligned with these interests. Some authors have predicted that the role of social class in structuring party preferences will increase in Central and Eastern Europe (Szelényi *et al.* 1996, 1997; see also Evans 1997; Jasiewicz 2009). Our results appear to be in line with these predictions.

Contrary to what we expected, socio-structural factors have become more rather than less important in the explanation of the radical right vote in Western Europe. On the one hand, it may well be that after 9/11 European societies have become more polarized, because the less-educated blue-collar workers have moved toward the radical right, and the well educated professionals have moved away from these parties. Perhaps even more important, however, are developments at the supply side. Kitschelt (1995) argued that the "winning formula" for radical right parties was an ideological position that combines an authoritarian position on the socio-cultural dimension with a free market position on the socio-economic dimension. Van der Brug and van Spanje (2009) argue, however, that the winning formula is a combination of an authoritarian position on socio-cultural issues with a left-wing position on socio-economic issues. Several authors have noted that radical right parties have recently adjusted their positions on the socio-economic dimension away from their free market orientation. Their more centrist or perhaps even "left-wing" orientation, which has been described as welfare chauvinism (e.g., Bastow 1997; De Lange 2007; Mudde 2007), might have made these parties increasingly attractive to "authoritarian workers."[10]

Voting for radical right parties is only for a small part an expression of political discontent. Less than 10 percent of the probability to vote for the radical right can be explained by political discontent. This is not to say that there is no political discontent in the countries we included in this study. Rather, the discontent is spread fairly evenly among the voters for different parties.

Voters for radical right parties are—just like voters for other parties—policy oriented. They tend to vote for these parties because of their opposition to immigration and multiculturalism. They also reject further political integration of the European Union, even though in terms of issue salience the preoccupation with the European Union is clearly secondary to the preoccupation of the radical right voters with immigration and integration. Policy considerations account for 30 percent of the variance in the probability to vote for the radical right. This percentage increases substantially if a number of Central and East European countries (e.g., Slovakia and Slovenia), as well as Greece and Sweden, are excluded from the analysis. All in all, policy considerations account for a third of the variance in the support for radical right parties, while socio-structural factors account for a little more than 10 percent and political discontent for even less.

We have also shown in this chapter that the ideological profile of radical right parties in Western Europe is more similar and coherent than that of the radical right parties in Eastern Europe. The radical right in Western Europe clearly is a party family; the radical right parties in Eastern Europe are still more of a mixed bag. A second but related conclusion is that the radical right parties in Western Europe tend to have a right-wing position on both the cultural left–right dimension and—though less so—on the socio-economic left–right dimension. Most voters, however, are to be found in the quadrant defined by a left position on the socio-economic dimension and a very right position on the cultural left–right dimension. Only some Central and East European parties maintain a position that is left leaning on socio-economic issues and radical right on cultural issues. These are therefore most likely to attract more voters. But then we also find in East European countries more parties that are positioned in the same quadrant. In Western Europe the main competitors of the radical right are the conservative parties, be they Christian democratic, conservative, or liberal. In the peripheral EU countries (Malta, Romania, Slovakia, Slovenia, Lithuania, and Finland), the social democrats have more to fear from radical right parties.

A decade ago, van der Brug *et al.* (2000) concluded on the basis of 1994 data that it was not the position one occupies in society that determines one's preference for a radical right party, but one's attitudes and ideological positions. At the end of the day, the radical right parties tend to attract rational voters, who want to change immigration and integration policies and maintain national sovereignty. While this conclusion still holds in 2009, things have changed somewhat since then. On the basis of 1999 survey data, van der Brug and Fennema (2003) concluded that the basic conclusion was still only valid for the large and successful radical right parties. Yet, the most recent results presented in this chapter mark some changes among these larger radical right parties, such as the DF, FN, FPÖ, and PVV. Even though their support is grounded mainly in policy preferences, their supporters have a more clearly demarcated sociological background now than fifteen years ago. Moreover, discontent plays a more important role now. A possible implication of the fact that radical right supporters stand out most clearly in terms of (lower) education and occupational status, in combination with possessing stronger feelings of discontent, is that European societies become more deeply divided between supporters and opponents of these parties. It is therefore important that research on the support base of radical right parties continues.

Our results also point toward another direction of future research. We noted quite substantial differences between radical right parties in Central or East Europe, and Western Europe. As a result of European integration, we would expect these parties to become more similar, which is something that needs to be explored in future research.

Appendix

In the European Election Study 2009, respondents were asked to indicate to what extent they agreed or disagreed with the statements in Table A3.1, which were included as items in the multiple regression analysis.

One of the items, distance to party on EU dimension, is not based on the reaction to a statement, but on the difference between the answers to the two following questions.

> Some say European unification should be pushed further. Others say it has already gone too far. What is your opinion? Please indicate your views using a scale from 0 to 10.
> And about where would you place the following parties on this scale?

Table A3.1 Statements in the EES

Items	Statement
Harsher sentences	People who break the law should be given much harsher sentences than they are these days
Children should obey authority	Schools must teach children to obey authority
Private enterprise	Private enterprise is the best way to solve (country's) economic problems
More state ownership	Major public services and industries ought to be in state ownership
No government intervention	Politics should abstain from intervening in the economy
Redistribute wealth	Income and wealth should be redistributed toward ordinary people
Prohibit same-sex marriage	Same-sex marriages should be prohibited by law
Pro-choice on abortion	Women should be free to decide on matters of abortion
Women stay at home	A woman should be prepared to cut down on her paid work for the sake of her family
EU matters decided by referendum	EU treaty changes should be decided by referendum
Immigrants should assimilate	Immigrants should be required to adapt to the customs of (country)
Decrease immigration	Immigration to (country) should be decreased significantly
Trust institutions of EU	You trust the institutions of the European Union
National parliament is responsive	The national parliament takes the concerns of the citizens into consideration
Satisfaction with democracy	On the whole, how satisfied are you with the way democracy works in your country?
Government approval	Do you approve of the government's record to date?

Notes

1 We have argued elsewhere (Fennema 1997; van der Brug *et al.* 2005) that West European radical right parties are better labeled 'anti-immigrant' or 'anti-immigration' parties, because their anti-immigrant stance is their unique selling point. However, this argument pertains to West European radical right parties only. In Central and Eastern Europe the rhetoric of radical parties is primarily against ethnic minorities, like indigenous minorities, Jews, or Roma. In this chapter we will therefore use the more inclusive term radical right.
2 The model developed by van der Brug *et al.* (2005), for example, explains 83 percent of the variance in the electoral success of thirteen West European radical right parties.

3 This dimension is sometimes also referred to as the GAL–TAN dimension (Hooghe *et al.* 2002, Marks *et al.* 2006) or the socio-cultural dimension (Kriesi *et al.* 2006).

4 We weighted the data by a weight variable (V131) that calibrates the voting distribution based on the real distribution in the entire electorate (including non-voters). This variable is not available for Greece, so that all Greek respondents were given a weight of 1.

5 It should be noted, however, that the number of FN supporters in the EES 2009 is extremely low, which makes it difficult to make any claims about the electorate of this party.

6 In the countries where two radical right parties compete for support, we included the most prominent radical right party. Hence, the BNP, FPÖ, and PVV are included in the pooled analysis, while the BZÖ, TON, and UKIP are excluded from it.

7 The only exceptions to this rule are the social liberal parties, which can be found in the right-libertarian quadrant.

8 This finding is consistent with previous research on Central and Eastern Europe, which demonstrates that some party families in this region, such as radical right parties, take different positions on the socio-economic dimension than their West European counterparts (Hooghe *et al.* 2002; Marks *et al.* 2006).

9 We should be cautious about the results for the FN in France, because their electorate is grossly under-represented in the sample.

10 The term "authoritarian workers" was coined by Lipset (1960).

4 Working-class parties 2.0?

Competition between centre-left and extreme right parties

Kai Arzheimer

Introduction: the rise of the extreme right and the transformation of West European policy spaces

Over the last three decades, parties of the "radical", "populist" or "extreme" right have become an almost ubiquitous feature of West European party systems. During this "third wave" (Beyme 1988) of radical right mobilisation, preexisting parties modified their ideological profiles (e.g. the Austrian Freedom Party, the Swiss People's Party, the Scandinavian Progress Parties), and many more completely new parties emerged. While some of them were nothing more than a flash in the pan (e.g. New Democracy in Sweden, see Taggart 1996), others found more durable electoral support. As of today, almost all West European political systems had to adjust (at least for a couple of years) to sustained extreme right mobilisation.

Initially, many observers interpreted these developments as a throwback to the extreme right's interwar onslaught on democracy (e.g. Prowe 1994). But soon it became clear that the more successful among these parties departed in a crucial way from the political stances of the interwar extreme right movements and parties. Following the highly successful strategy of the French National Front (Rydgren 2005), they abandoned biological racism, hyper-nationalism, and open hostility towards liberal democracy and instead made immigration (or more specifically the influx of non-West Europeans into Europe) their main issue. For that reason, some authors branded the emerging new party family simply as "anti-immigrant" (e.g. Fennema 1997; Fennema and Pollmann 1998; van der Brug *et al.* 2000; Bjørklund and Andersen 2002; Gibson 2002; Boomgaarden and Vliegenthart 2007; Art 2011), whereas others disputed the "single-issue thesis" (Mitra 1988; Mudde 1999) or argued for a more nuanced classification of subtypes (e.g. Kitschelt 1995; Fennema 1997; Mudde 2007).

This is certainly not the right space to reopen the (largely fruitless) "war of words" (Mudde 1996) that dominated the scholarly debate in the 1990s. Today, most scholars working in the field agree on a set of stylised facts that can be summarised as follows.

- While there are important differences among the "new" parties on the right in terms of their political traditions, policy positions, and general political style, these parties also display important similarities that set them apart from the centre right. Therefore, they should be grouped into a single (if very heterogeneous) party family.

- While some of these parties harbour extremists and many of them are highly critical of single aspects of liberal democracy (most prominently minority protection), very few of them pursue a transition to authoritarian rule.
- Therefore, "radical" or "extreme" (as opposed to extremist) right are convenient shorthands for this party family.[1]
- Immigration of non-West European people into Western Europe is not the only but is the single most important issue for all members of this party family. Mobilisation against immigrants and immigration is crucial for their electoral success.

Moreover, there is broad agreement that the rise of the extreme right presents politicians in Western Europe with a set of formidable challenges. First and foremost, their electoral success raised important questions of legitimacy. Did a vote for the extreme right indicate a more general lack of trust in the elites, or even a rejection of the democratic system? Was there reason to fear new "shadows over Europe" (Schain *et al.* 2002), i.e. a return to the confrontational and often violent politics of the 1920s and 1930s? Should the existing parties engage in a dialogue with their challengers or just ignore them?

Second, like the emergence of Green and left-libertarian parties, the rise of the New Right signalled a fundamental change in the patterns of party competition and cooperation in most West European countries. For much of the postwar period, party competition in Western Europe was chiefly organised along a single left–right axis that largely reflected conflicts about economic redistribution (Fuchs and Klingemann 1989; van der Brug 1999). However, both issues of the "New Politics" and matters of citizenship and immigration were not primarily perceived as economic problems and were therefore not easily aligned with the old left–right conflict. Consequently, two or three dimensions are required to reconstruct the policy spaces of most West European democracies (Kitschelt 1994, 1995; Warwick 2002; Cole 2005; Bornschier 2010a), making party competition more complex and equilibria less likely.[2]

Third, and perhaps closest to the hearts of politicians, the zero-sum nature of electoral competition implies that the emergence of a new party family will bring about losses for existing parties in terms of votes, seats and eventually even ministerial portfolios. But which parties would suffer most?

Competition between centre-left and extreme right parties

From the party family's moniker, one might be tempted to assume that the centre right had most to lose from the emergence of the extreme right, at least if voters care primarily about issues: in a classical Downsian (1957) perspective, demand for right-wing policies is fixed at least in the short and medium term, and— depending on party positions and voters' ideal points—the entry of a new competitor would significantly reduce the vote share of the centre-right parties. If voters behave in line with a directional model (Merrill and Grofman 1999), the outlook for the centre right is even starker, as voters who disagree with their radical policies may still vote for the extreme right for tactical reasons.

Aggregate trends of electoral support of electorate support in sixteen West European countries from the six decades since the end of World War II seem to corroborate these arguments: while support for the right as a whole[3] has been largely stable, Christian democratic parties have on average lost about five percentage points of their electorate support, while the far right could increase their share of the vote by almost seven points (Gallagher *et al.* 2011: 301).

Accordingly, much of the political and academic debate has focused on the negative implications that the rise of these parties has had for conservative, Christian democratic, liberal, and agrarian/centre parties (e.g. Mair 2001: 71).[4] But Green/New Left parties are perhaps the only ones *not* affected by the extreme right's ascendancy, as these party families appeal to very different demographics and occupy diametrically opposed positions in West European policy spaces.[5]

Taking a more analytical approach, Kitschelt (1994, 1995) argued almost twenty years ago that a shift of the "main axis of partisan competition" was under way that would pit the New Left against the extreme right and present the social democratic/centre-left parties with a conundrum: they would lose many of their more liberal voters to the parties of the New Left because they did not adequately represent the issues of the "New Politics" (Flanagan and Lee 2003). At the same time, the extreme right would seize a sizable fraction of the working-class vote, because the centre left had allegedly lost touch with its traditional voter base (Bale 2003: 70–74).

But why would working-class voters turn to the extreme right? Historically, support for the postwar extreme right had chiefly come from the "petty bourgeoisie" of artisans, small shopkeepers and farmers that made up the lower strata of the middle classes. This constituency was authoritarian and staunchly anti-communist/anti-socialist.

Working-class voters, on the other hand, were often embedded in a network of trade unions and similar intermediate organisations, held strong preferences for redistribution, and were firmly attached to traditional left parties. Even if many voters (and some of the rank-and-file members) of these parties expressed a healthy degree of working-class authoritarianism (Lipset 1959), elites and opinion leaders within the traditional working classes were firmly committed to principles of equality and international solidarity. Therefore, the idea of a large-scale swing from the centre left to the extreme right would have looked rather far-fetched three or four decades ago.

Through twin processes of de-alignment (Dalton *et al.* 1984) and social change (Crouch 1999), however, swathes of the (non-traditional) working class have become available for other parties than the traditional left. Moreover, the extreme right has modified its programmatic appeal considerably over the six decades since the end of World War II, thereby becoming more palatable for members of the working class.

Perhaps the most radical interpretation of these programmatic changes was developed by Herbert Kitschelt in a highly influential monograph (Kitschelt 1995). Kitschelt argued that under conditions of economic globalisation, workers outside the public sector would develop a taste for free market policies. At the same time, they would remain authoritarian with respect to their socio-cultural attitudes. According to Kitschelt, catering for these twin demands was the electoral "winning formula" that fuelled the unprecedented successes of the French National Front and the Austrian Freedom Party during the 1980s and early 1990s. A similar argument was developed by Betz in his seminal monograph (Betz 1994). Figure 4.1, which slightly simplifies the presentation in Kitschelt (1995), shows the respective policy positions of social democratic, old-style "welfare chauvinist" and more modern "radical right" parties.

In hindsight, however, the extreme right's flirtation with "neoliberalism"—presumably not a very serious affair in the first place—proved short-lived and inconsequential (de Lange 2007). Within a few years after the publication of Kitschelt's book, many extreme right parties had gone all the way from being vocal champions of neo-liberalism to globalisation critics, and the allegedly outdated "welfare chauvinist" strategy that campaigns for a strong but ethnically exclusionary welfare state had gained a lot of currency in far-right circles. Consequentially, Betz (2003) has altoghether abandoned the idea that the extreme right does seriously pursue a "neo-liberal" agenda or has done so in the past, while Kitschelt has modified his original ideas considerably (McGann and Kitschelt 2005).

Moreover, more recent research (Arzheimer 2009b) demonstrates that there is no working-class demand for "neo-liberal" policies. Where both members of the

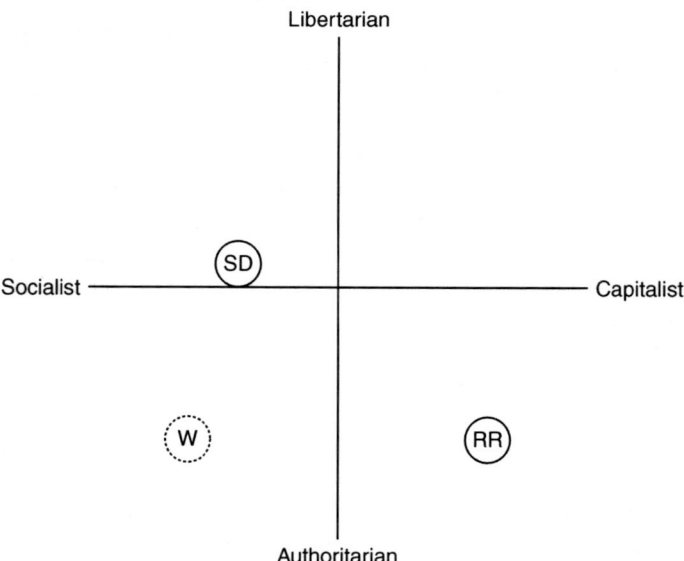

Figure 4.1 Kitschelt's 1995 view of West European party systems.

working class and the petty bourgeoisie support the extreme right, they tend to *disagree* on economic policies and cast their vote because the salience of economic issues is low (Ivarsflaten 2005).

But even if the mid-1990s accounts by Betz and Kitschelt were wrong in their diagnoses, they clearly identified a very important symptom: since the early 1980s, the extreme right has undergone a process of "proletarization and (uneven) radicalization" (Ignazi 2003: 216). At least for the relatively successful parties (e.g. the Austrian Freedom Party, the Norwegian Progress Party and the French National Front), there is some evidence for a trend from electorates that were heterogeneous or centred around a core of voters from the petty bourgeoisie towards more working-class-dominated constituencies (Beirich and Woods 2000; Betz 2002b; Bjørklund and Andersen 2002; Mayer 1998, 2002; Riedlsperger 1998; Rydgren 2003; see Oesch 2008 for a comparative cross-sectional analysis of Austria, Belgium, France, Norway and Switzerland).

This new pattern of class voting in Western Europe is not based on long-standing party loyalties but rather on group- and policy-related attitudes: public opinion data consistently shows that the extreme right vote is driven by intense worries about immigrants and immigration,[6] which are most prevalent among voters with low levels of educational attainment who are either unemployed or holding blue-collar jobs.[7]

While many authors frame these worries as "resentment" and interpret the underlying policy dimension primarily in terms of "culture" and "identity", one should not ignore the fact that concerns about immigrants and immigration have clear economic underpinnings: the vast majority of immigrants in Western Europe are unskilled or semi-skilled workers. Obviously, members of the working class are much more likely to perceive these persons as an economic threat than middle-class voters, who might actually benefit from the additional supply of cheap labour.

On the whole, research since the mid-1990s suggests that patterns of party competition and class voting have indeed changed, although in a way that is quite different from Kitschelt's original reading of the situation (see Figure 4.2). Instead of converging on the "radical right" strategy, parties of the extreme right are looking for a (not very) "new winning formula" (de Lange, 2007) and have incorporated elements of "welfare chauvinism" into their manifestos, although to a varying degree. Social democratic parties, on the other hand, have cautiously moved to more economically centrist (and arguably more socially liberal) positions in a bid to respond to the new challenges of the twenty-first century and to become more attractive for middle-class voters (see Keman 2011 for a comprehensive analysis that outlines the extent of this shift in nineteen polities). This programmatic change opened up additional space for the extreme right and made it even easier for them to poach working-class voters from the centre left. That raises the question of whether there is anything the centre left can do about this development.

The remainder of this chapter is organised as follows. Section 2 gives a brief overview of the data base and the statistical models and methods used for its

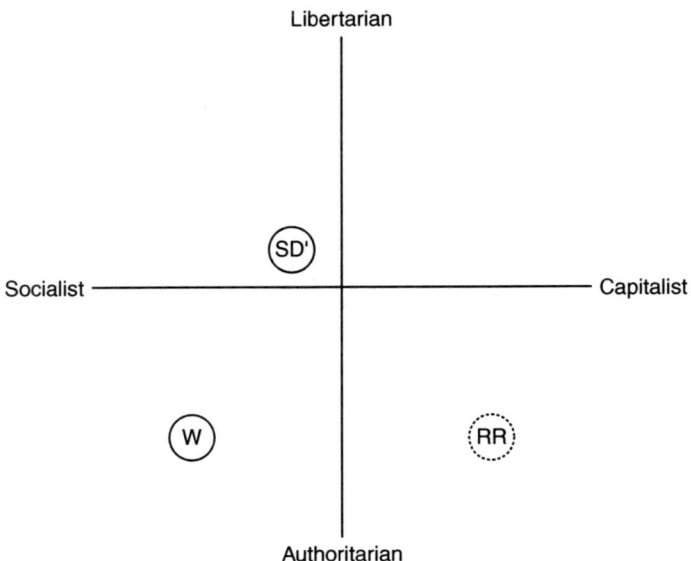

Figure 4.2 An updated perspective on West European party systems.

analysis. Section 3 presents a comparative longitudinal analysis of the "proletari-sation" of the West European extreme right vote since 1980. Section 4 looks directly at the competition between extreme right and centre-left parties for the working-class vote. Finally, section 5 briefly summarises the findings.

Data, model, method

The analyses presented in the following sections cover the member states of the European Union (EU) as it existed before the Eastern enlargement rounds, plus Norway. Survey data come from the Mannheim Eurobarometer Trend File (Schmitt *et al.* 2009), a partial cumulation of the bi-annual series of Eurobarom-eter surveys that greatly facilitates cross-national and longitudinal analyses. The temporal coverage of these data spans the whole period of the extreme right's electoral ascendancy during the 1980s and 1990s, as well as a few years of the new millenium.

There are, however, a few gaps: data for Austria, Finland, Sweden and Norway are not available for the whole period. Moreover, surveys without any supporters of the extreme right had to be excluded, which removed the United Kingdom and the Republic of Ireland from the analysis.[8] Figure 4.3 gives a graphical overview of the spatial and temporal coverage.

Information on social class in the Eurobarometer series is effectively restricted to present occupation. To simplify the presentation, respondents were coded as holding blue-collar jobs ("workers"), belonging to the petty bourgeoisie

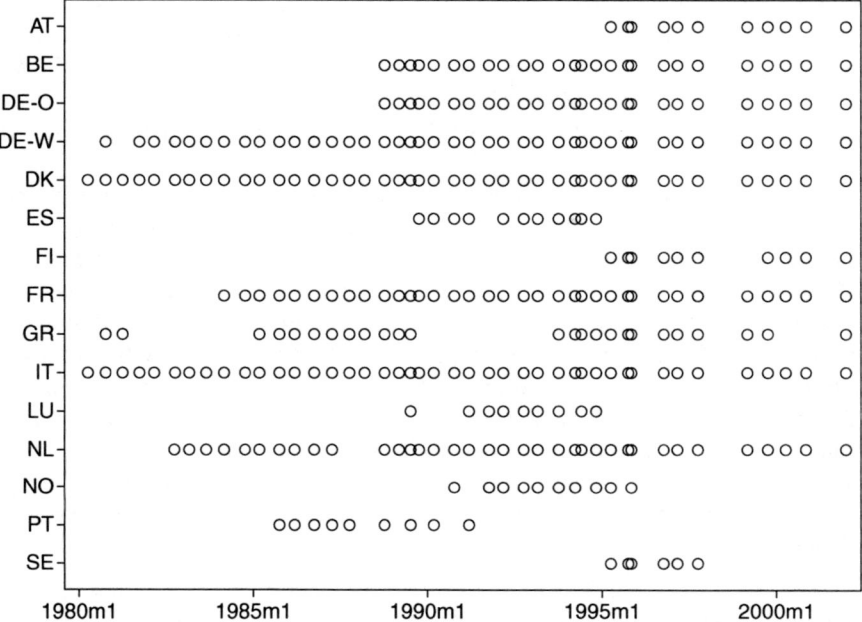

Figure 4.3 The spacing of relevant Eurobarometer surveys in time and across countries.

("farmers and owners"), holding any other occupation ("other"), being unemployed, or being retired.[9]

In order to model contextual effects on right-wing voting, the Eurobarometer surveys were augmented with macro data. Information on unemployment rates and unemployment benefits comes from the OECD (2002, 2003, 2004), while data on new asylum applications—in the West European context, a very useful proxy for actual immigration figures—were taken from reports compiled by the OECD and the Office of the United Nations High Commissioner for Refugees (OECD 1992; UNHCR 2002).

Finally, the Comparative Manifesto Project database was used to construct a series of five variables that capture the positions of mainstream parties with respect to the issues of the extreme right, i.e. "internationalism", "multiculturalism", "national lifestyle" and "law and order" (for a more detailed discussion of the rationale behind these measures, see Arzheimer and Carter 2006; Arzheimer 2009a). These variables pertain to the position of the respective social democratic party, the most extreme position taken by any other mainstream party, the salience of these issues for the social democrats, the salience for all other mainstream parties and the variation in policy positions across all other mainstream parties.[10]

To account for the hierarchical nature of the data (respondents are nested within 336 survey waves that were conducted in fifteen polities), binary logistic multi-level models are specified. Because the extreme right is persistently stronger in some countries (e.g. Belgium and France) than in others (say, Spain and Germany), stable unit (country) effects are represented by a series of dummies.[11] These dummies are also required to control for changes in the national composition of the sample over time. Specifying country effects leaves just two levels of analysis: voters, and the particular contexts in which they were interviewed.

Even when controlling for unit effects and contextual information, it makes sense to assume that people who are interviewed in the same survey wave are subject to common random political shocks that affect their voting behaviour. These shocks are modelled as draws from a Gaussian distribution with standard deviation σ_u, which estimated from the data in addition to the usual parameters. As a result of these shocks, respondents in the same context will give more similar answers than one would expect by chance alone. The intraclass correlation coefficient ρ that ranges from 0 to 1 is a measure for this similarity, with values closer to unity indicating greater alikeness within a context.[12]

All models were estimated using the xtlogit procedure in Stata 11.2. Checks indicate that the number of quadrature points used was sufficient to guarantee stable estimates.

The proletarisation of the West European extreme right vote, 1980–2002

The idea of a "proletarisation" (Ignazi 2003) of the West European extreme right features prominently in the literature, but very little comparative cross-temporal empirical evidence for this alleged development has been presented so far. With the Eurobarometer Trend File, however, it is possible to trace the purported trajectory of the extreme right's electorate.

As can be seen from the coefficients, being unemployed or belonging to the working class or the petty bourgeoisie considerably increases the chances of an extreme right vote, compared to the "other" category. Either factor increases the logit of an extreme right vote by 0.4 to 0.5 points. Being retired, on the other hand, does not make an appreciable difference.

The exact impact of this increase depends on the fixed country effects but is roughly proportional to a 50 per cent change in the probability of the extreme right vote. In Austria, for instance, members of the "other" group have an estimated probability of just under 15 per cent of voting for the Freedom Party. For workers, the estimated probability is almost 22 per cent.

The term proletarisation, however, implies change over time. In the right column (2) of Table 4.1, the membership indicators were interacted with an additional variable that represents the time (in months) at which the survey was taken. In order to minimise collinearity, the variable was centred so that it takes a value of zero for March 1991, which is the midpoint of the period under observation. Given the huge range of the time variable (see Table 4.2), it is not surprising that the estimated coefficients are very small. Nonetheless, the picture

Table 4.1 Socio-demographic factors and the extreme right vote, 1980–2002/2003

XR vote	(1)	(2)
Worker	0.483***	0.441***
	(0.0277)	(0.0307)
Farmer/owner	0.438***	0.478***
	(0.0347)	(0.0363)
Retired	0.0546	0.0563
	(0.0282)	(0.0318)
Unemployed	0.555***	0.552***
	(0.0410)	(0.0455)
time		0.00593***
		(0.000666)
Worker X time		0.00176***
		(0.000433)
Farmer/owner X time		−0.00207***
		(0.000512)
Retired X time		−0.0000549
		(0.000442)
Unemployed X time		0.000120
		(0.000665)
Observations	254,726	254,726
σ_u	0.720	0.621
ρ	0.136	0.105
N	336	336

Notes
Fixed country effects omitted.
Standard errors in parentheses.
* $p<0.05$, ** $p<0.01$, *** $p<0.001$.
The left column (1) of Table 4.1 shows the estimates from a simple socio-demographic multi-level model of extreme right voting in Western Europe. The model is based on just under 255,000 interviews.

that emerges is remarkably clear. The effect of being a pensioner is essentially stable, while the effect of being unemployed increases only very slightly over time. The effect of being a member of the working class, on the other hand, becomes considerably stronger with time, while the effect of belonging to the petty bourgeoisie becomes *weaker* at roughly the same rate.

Taken together, these results show that the extreme right electorates indeed underwent a process of proletarisation between 1980 and the early 2000s. Moreover, these findings cannot be ascribed to changes in the composition of the sample (i.e. the accession of Greece, Spain and Portugal to the European Union during the 1980s and the 1995 enlargement), because fixed country effects are controlled for. Therefore, the interaction effects represent common trends across all fifteen polities. This constitutes the first truly comparative and longitudinal evidence for a general proletarisation of the extreme right vote in Western Europe.

Table 4.2 Socio-demographic model: summary statistics

	Min.	p25	Mean	p75	Max.
XR vote	0.00	0.00	0.04	0.00	1.00
Worker	0.00	0.00	0.18	0.00	1.00
Farmer/owner	0.00	0.00	0.10	0.00	1.00
Retired	0.00	0.00	0.22	0.00	1.00
Unemployed	0.00	0.00	0.06	0.00	1.00
Time	−131.00	−36.00	10.22	56.00	130.00
AT	0.00	0.00	0.03	0.00	1.00
BE	0.00	0.00	0.07	0.00	1.00
DE-E	0.00	0.00	0.06	0.00	1.00
DE-W	0.00	0.00	0.14	0.00	1.00
DK	0.00	0.00	0.14	0.00	1.00
ES	0.00	0.00	0.03	0.00	1.00
FI	0.00	0.00	0.03	0.00	1.00
FR	0.00	0.00	0.11	0.00	1.00
GR	0.00	0.00	0.06	0.00	1.00
IT	0.00	0.00	0.12	0.00	1.00
LU	0.00	0.00	0.01	0.00	1.00
NL	0.00	0.00	0.13	0.00	1.00
NO	0.00	0.00	0.03	0.00	1.00
PT	0.00	0.00	0.02	0.00	1.00
SE	0.00	0.00	0.02	0.00	1.00
N	254,726				

Note
4 Left or (Extreme) Right? The Western European Working Class Vote, 1980–2002.

But how important are these trends in substantive terms (i.e. votes and seats)? Again, the exact size is context-dependent and most easily illustrated by calculating estimates for an arbitrary country. The estimated vote share of the Danish extreme right among workers in 1980, for instance, was just under 2 per cent, while the respective figure for members of the Danish petty bourgeoisie was about 3 per cent. In 2002, the estimate for the petty bourgeoisie was 8 per cent, while the figure for the working class has risen to almost 13 per cent. Although the extreme right has made considerable inroads into both groups, the ratio of the respective propensities to vote for the extreme right has been reversed. Therefore, it does indeed make sense to talk about a proletarisation of the extreme right vote. This trend is further amplified by the fact that the petty bourgeoisie is shrinking even faster than the working class.

One should not, however, throw out the baby with the bath water: Precisely because the working class is in decline, there is a natural limit to this process. Moreover, while social class has obviously lost some of its previous importance (Clark *et al.* 1993; Nieuwbeerta and Graaf 2001), its effect on the probability of voting for the traditional left has by no means disappeared completely (Evans 2001). Thus, the next section section will look specifically at the competition between extreme right and social democratic parties over the working-class vote.

In their recent analysis of social democratic reactions to the rise of the extreme right, Bale *et al.* (2010) have usefully identified three elements of this challenge, and three strategies available to the centre left: the presence of extreme right parties will heighten the salience of "right" issues in general, can increase the number of potential coalition partners for the centre right and may lure working-class voters away from the left. Social democratic parties can respond by holding on to their traditional relatively tolerant position towards immigrants, by trying to "defuse" the immigration issue, or by shifting their position (Bale *et al.* 2010: 412).

As Bale *et al.* (2010: 413–414) point out, the effectiveness of the "defuse" strategy is very limited, making the first strategy the default, as social democratic party elites are normally committed to values of tolerance and international solidarity. Therefore, they will find it difficult to abandon their support for relatively liberal immigration policies to avoid political losses. Such normative convictions seriously restrain the centre left's room for manoeuvre.

Nonetheless, the qualitative analysis of developments in Austria, Denmark, the Netherlands and Norway by Bale *et al.* shows that social democratic parties have sometimes modified their positions on the immigration dimension (for an overview, see Bale *et al.* 2010: 421). A quantitative analysis (see Figure 4.4) of the CMP Data provides further evidence for such programmatic shifts: although there is considerable national variation, social democratic parties in many countries, including Germany, Denmark, Finland, France, Italy, and the Netherlands, have taken consistently tougher stands on issues of migration and national identity over the years.

But how do working-class voters respond to this repositioning of the centre left? The left column (1) in Table 4.4 gives the estimates for the coefficients of a very simple baseline model. The sample is restricted to working-class respondents who intend to vote either for a social democratic party (0) or an extreme right party (1). The model features a single socio-demographic control to account for the well known gender gap, and a linear (in the logits) trend factor. Like the models in the previous section, the model also contains fixed country effects to account for stable differences between polities. Estimates for these effects (not tabulated) are very low in countries as diverse as Germany (–3.3), Spain (–6.3), Finland (–4), Luxembourg (–4.6), Portugal (–5.7) or Sweden (–5.2), which implies that in these countries, the odds of a social democratic vote are between 27 (exp(3.3)) and 545 (exp(6.3)) times higher than the odds of an extreme right vote.

There is, however, a set of countries including Austria (–1.7), Belgium (–2), Denmark (–2.2), France (–2.4) and particularly Italy (–.65), where the odds of an extreme right vote are much higher in comparison. While the result for Italy might be due to the fact that the AN as the largest relevant party in the country has become relatively moderate since the 1990s, the findings for the other countries are striking: across the board, a social democratic vote is only between 5.5 and eleven times more likely than an extreme right vote in this core constituency of the centre left.

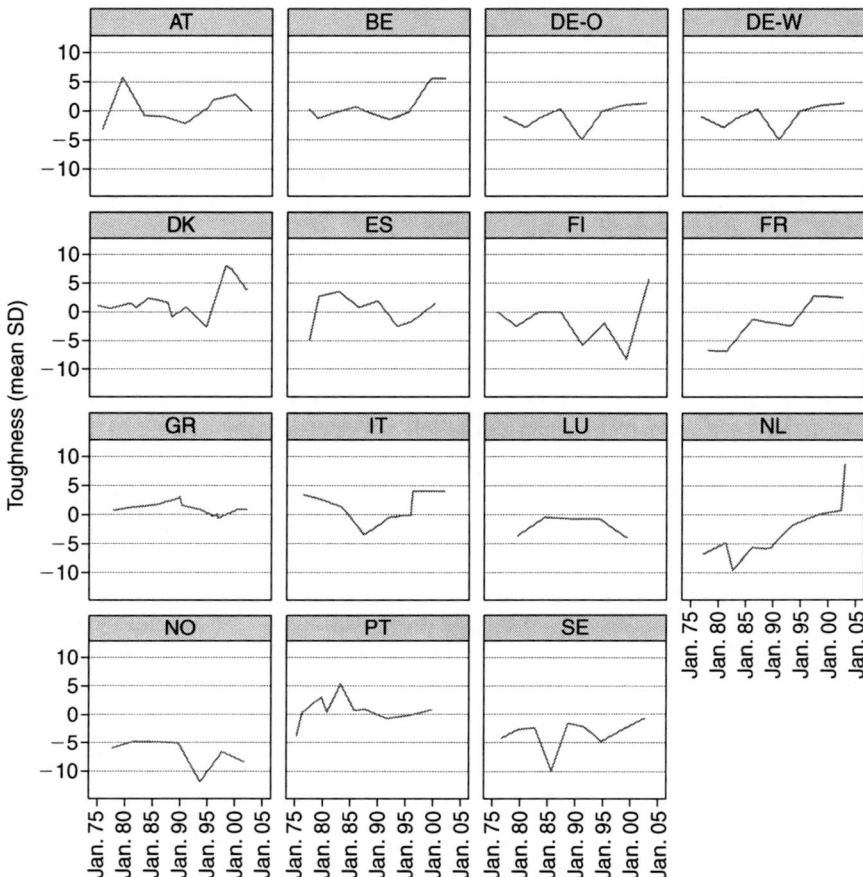

Figure 4.4 Ideological movement of social democratic parties over time.

Moreover, the trend factor indicates that the odds of an extreme right vote have risen considerably over time: if one is prepared to take the model estimates at face value, the odds of a working-class respondent voting for the extreme right increase by a factor of almost 13 (exp(0.0098 × 261)) between the first and the last survey wave. Even if one takes potential deficiencies of the data and model specification into account, this clearly demonstrates that social democratic parties are losing support among working-class voters.

While this is certainly an interesting finding in itself, time is chiefly used as a control in a second series of models (columns (2) and (3)) that build on Arzheimer's (2009a) contextual model of extreme right voting.[13] This amended model allows for a direct test of the viability of two of the strategies outlined by Bale *et al.* (2010), as well as for an indirect test of the third.

Since some elections were contested by two or more parties that were classified as social democratic by the CMP, social democratic ideology was

Table 4.3 Full model: XR vs Social Democratic vote amongst working-class respondents

	(1)	(2)	(3)
Male	0.445***	0.449***	0.448***
	(0.0515)	(0.0517)	(0.0517)
Time	0.00982***	0.00692***	0.00651***
	(0.000874)	(0.00121)	(0.00127)
Toughness (max. SD)		0.0327	
		(0.0270)	
Toughness (mean SD)			0.0296
			(0.0309)
Ideology salience (SD)		−0.0437	−0.0383
		(0.0257)	(0.0247)
Toughness (other)		−0.00246	0.00360
		(0.0255)	(0.0242)
Ideological variance (other)		−0.0131**	−0.0137**
		(0.00437)	(0.00429)
Ideology salience (other)		0.119***	0.116***
		(0.0291)	(0.0288)
New asylum applications		0.0386	0.0326
		(0.0667)	(0.0663)
Unemployment		0.0999**	0.106**
		(0.0374)	(0.0388)
Replacement rate		0.0515***	0.0520***
		(0.0138)	(0.0138)
Observations	19,858	19,663	19,663
σ_u	0.733	0.645	0.646
ρ	0.140	0.112	0.113
N	336	327	327

Notes
Fixed country effects omitted.
Standard errors in parentheses.
* $p<0.05$, ** $p<0.01$, *** $p<0.001$.

operationalised in two variants: "toughness" refers either to the most right-leaning party (column (2)) or to the average of all social democratic party positions, weighted by the respective party's share of the vote (column (3)).[14] However, the way social democratic ideology is measured makes virtually no difference.

According to this second set of estimates, the trend towards more extreme right voting is slightly less pronounced[15] once the additional contextual variables are taken into consideration. Nonetheless, given its wide range, time still has the strongest effect among all covariates.

The level of welfare state protection as measured by the OECD's standard-ised wage replacement rate for the unemployed also has a strong positive effect on the probability of an extreme right vote. Raising the standards from the first to the third quartile of its empirical distribution (see Table 4.4) will almost quadruple the odds of a right-wing vote. Given the extreme right's rediscovery of centre-left-leaning policies, this could be interpreted as a result of "welfare chauvinism" and (perceived) ethnic competition (Bélanger and Pinard 1991) over a resource that is still plentiful. However, an alternative explanation is at least as plausible: only if the welfare state is seen as safe and taken for granted will workers turn from social democratic parties towards the extreme right.

Another factor that has a strong effect on the electoral prospects of the extreme right is the *salience of their issues* for other parties (excluding the social democrats). The more statements other parties make on questions of immigration, national identity and the like, the better the extreme right does in the polls, *irrespective of the direction of these statements.* Since objective factors such as unemployment and new asylum applications (which have weak or insignificant effects) are statistically controlled for, this finding can be interpreted as evidence for an agenda-setting effect (Arzheimer 2009a).

Table 4.4 Full model: summary statistics

	Min.	p25	Mean	p75	Max.
XR vote	0.00	0.00	0.12	0.00	1.00
Male	0.00	0.00	0.60	1.00	1.00
Time	−131.00	−47.00	1.99	55.00	130.00
Toughness (max. SD)	−11.71	−2.01	−0.12	1.51	13.68
Toughness (mean SD)	−11.71	−2.37	−1.02	1.12	7.45
Ideology salience (SD)	0.00	3.45	6.83	9.19	16.08
Toughness (other)	−4.54	0.59	4.84	7.92	27.54
Ideological variance (other)	0.00	1.87	17.18	16.50	244.60
Ideology salience (other)	0.50	5.08	8.95	12.41	31.25
New asylum applications	−0.98	−0.61	0.16	0.58	4.46
Unemployment	−4.91	−1.31	0.35	1.69	12.29
Replacement rate	−31.62	−4.19	4.07	18.48	32.96
AT	0.00	0.00	0.05	0.00	1.00
BE	0.00	0.00	0.06	0.00	1.00
DE-E	0.00	0.00	0.06	0.00	1.00
DE-W	0.00	0.00	0.19	0.00	1.00
DK	0.00	0.00	0.17	0.00	1.00
ES	0.00	0.00	0.03	0.00	1.00
FI	0.00	0.00	0.02	0.00	1.00
FR	0.00	0.00	0.12	0.00	1.00
GR	0.00	0.00	0.04	0.00	1.00
IT	0.00	0.00	0.05	0.00	1.00
LU	0.00	0.00	0.00	0.00	0.00
NL	0.00	0.00	0.10	0.00	1.00
NO	0.00	0.00	0.05	0.00	1.00
PT	0.00	0.00	0.04	0.00	1.00
SE	0.00	0.00	0.01	0.00	1.00
N	19,663				

Ideological variation in the manifestos of other parties has a moderate negative effect on right-wing voting, whereas ideological "toughness" (i.e. attempts by mainstream parties to steal the immigration issue) does not shift the balance between the extreme right and the social democrats.

Taken together, the effects of salience and ideological variation indicate that a strategy of issue diffusion could be viable in principle, if (and only if, as the social democrats can hardly shape political discourse single-handedly) the other mainstream parties cooperate.

While this test of the "defuse" strategy might be somewhat indirect, the efficiency of the "hold" and "adopt" strategies can be more readily assessed by looking at the estimates for the "toughness" and salience variables that refer to social democratic parties. Neither of them has a significant effect on the odds of voting for the extreme right. Put differently, in this core constituency of the centre left, it does not make a difference whether the social democrats stick to their traditional positions on immigration or whether they try to toughen up their policies. Either way, their fortunes vis-à-vis the extreme right are largely determined by external factors and an overall negative trend.

The null effect of salience provides an interesting correlate. This variable takes a value of zero if social democrats completely ignore the issues of the extreme right, which is equivalent to a very radical "defuse" strategy, whereas positive values represent attempts to engage with the issue by making affirmative and/or critical statements. The insignificance of the coefficient provides further evidence for the assertion that a "defuse" strategy is only viable if pursued in concert.

Conclusion

After World War II, parties and movements of the extreme right were most closely associated with the petty bourgeoisie. Over the last three decades, however, the propensity of workers to vote for the extreme right has risen significantly. This "proletarisation" is the result of the interplay between a long-term dealignment process and increasing worries among the European working classes about the immigration of cheap labour. As a result, West European centre-left parties may find themselves squeezed between the New Right on the one hand and the New Left on the other.

The analyses in the previous section have shown that there is no obvious strategy for dealing with this dilemma. Staying put will not win working-class defectors back. Toughening up immigration policies is unpalatable for many party members, does not seem to make social democrats more attractive for working-class voters, and might eventually alienate other social groups.

That leaves what Bale *et al.* (2010) have called the "defuse" option, i.e. efforts to downgrade the immigration issue. In democracies, however, a single party cannot normally sustain control over the political agenda. Any attempt to de-politicise immigration would therefore require some sort of agreement among mainstream parties. Given that centre-right (Bale, 2003) and (for completely opposite reasons) even New Left parties might have a strategic interest to keep the debate on immigration alive, this is not a very likely outcome. In all probability, the working-class parties "of a new type" will continue to poach voters from the social democrats.

Notes

1　I will treat these two terms as interchangeable through the remainder of this chapter.
2　For a slightly different account of these developments, see van der Brug and van Spanje (2009), who claim that European parties' actual policy proposal can still be arranged on a single vector even though parties and voters operate in a two-dimensional space.
3　Gallagher *et al.* subsume five party families under this label: Christian democrats, conservatives, liberals, agrarian and centre parties, and the far right.
4　Other authors, however, have highlighted the strategic opportunities that the rise of the new party family may present for the right as a whole if and when the extreme right can be brought into a coalition (Bale 2003).
5　Consequently, the rise of the extreme right has sometimes been framed as a "silent counter-revolution" (Ignazi 1992) against the growing influence of the New Left and its post-materialist electoral base.
6　These feelings are related to, but not identical with, xenophobia and racism (Rydgren 2008).
7　See, for example, van der Brug, Fennema and Tillie (2000) and Arzheimer (2009b) for reviews of the importance of ideology, and Arzheimer and Carter (2009) for the nexus between class and attitudes.
8　The OECD does not provide standardised unemployment rates for Luxembourg. Thus, the country had to be excluded from the series of models presented in section 4.
9　Homemakers were coded according to the occupation of the householder, if available.
10　For the construction of the two latter variables, positions were weighted with the parties' shares of the vote. In some cases, elections were contested by two or more parties coded as social democratic by the CMP. See section 4 for details.
11　East and West Germany are treated as two separate polities.
12　Equals the proportion of total variance contributed by σ_u.
13　To ease the estimation and interpretation, a number of interaction effects and relatively stable macro variables were dropped. Moreover, all attitudinal and most sociodemographic variables were dropped, since they do not vary much in this subset of working-class voters. The findings for many variables are somewhat different from those reported in Arzheimer (2009a) because they apply to a more limited choice set and a sub-sample of the original data.
14　The salience variable was always constructed as a weighted average over all social democratic party positions in the respective election (if applicable).
15　The estimated factor change in the odds is $\exp(0.007 \times 261) = y6$.

5 In or out of proportion?

Labour and social democratic parties' responses to the radical right

Tim Bale, Dan Hough, and Stijn van Kessel

Introduction

Given the media's tendency to stereotype those voters most tempted by radical right-wing populist parties as poorly educated, working-class men, it is easy to see why Europe's centre-left parties are worried. These, after all, are the people they traditionally relied upon—their core vote, if you like. These are also the people, the narrative runs, who never consented to the immigration, the multiculturalism, the permissive society that political progressives helped usher in, and are now exacting their revenge. As a result, Labour and social democratic parties all over Europe are wondering what they should do (see the various contributions in Policy Network 2011). This chapter looks at three centre-left parties, each operating in a very different institutional environment but each of which has had to consider in recent years the damage or potential damage done to it by the radical right. They are the Dutch Labour Party (working with a pure PR electoral system and facing a very successful radical right opponent), the German SPD (working in a mixed electoral system and facing a radical right that still finds it hard to gain legitimacy), and the British Labour Party (working in a plurality system where the radical right has some localised support and earns plenty of publicity but has virtually no chance of breaking through). Are these parties right to worry or is there any sense in which, either by overreacting or picking the wrong counter-strategy, they might be getting things badly wrong?

Dealing with the far right: opportunities and risks for the centre left

Political structures (in whatever form) shape the opportunities open to parties in articulating their demands and subsequently in the fight for votes (Tarrow 1998; Koopmans and Statham 2000; Boswell and Hough 2008). These opportunity structures can be constraining or enhancing, and they tend to play out in one of three ways. First, parties may see vacant ideological, programmatic, or strategic terrain and look to make the most of it. Second, a party may wish to adopt sets of new policy preferences but finds that another competitor has long since mobilised on this particular territory. It may either choose to embrace the policy prescriptions anyway (as it happens to believe in them or think it electorally dis-advantageous not to), or it may look for other potentially more lucrative vote-winning options. Third, a party may realise that it could be politically and elec-torally expedient to adopt particular positions, but that doing so would bring with it considerable risks; parties have histories and bring with them "baggage", and playing down—or just ignoring—these can be more harmful than adopting policies for short-term electoral or political gain.

Social democratic parties, then, face both costs and benefits in changing their policy and strategic approaches on the basis of a perceived electoral threat from a populist radical right keen to steal their voters—often, it has been said, their male working-class voters—on the basis of a shared hostility to immigration. A number of parties, including centre-left parties, subsequently began to think about adjusting their programmes and rhetoric accordingly (Bale *et al.* 2010). However, attempts to mobilise support by tightening up stances on issues associ-ated with the far right carries with it two obvious risks. For one thing, tightening immigration policy can bolster support for precisely the parties that one is trying to fight by increasing the salience of the issues in question and rendering restric-tive positions more credible (Bale 2003). For another, it can lead a social demo-cratic party to undermine: (1) the legitimacy of its own (internationalist and humanitarian) values; (2) the coherence of a programme aimed, for example, at protecting and promoting the interests of all (not just some) working people, and/or encouraging economic growth by facilitating the entry (perhaps via the EU) of skilled and flexible labour; and (3) the party's practical credibility by, for instance, opening up too big a gap between its tough new rhetoric and policies that cannot simply be done away with in an instant (Hansen 2000).

Given the complexity of the cost–benefit calculations involved in responding to the radical right, it seems legitimate to ask not only whether the centre left is getting those calculations right but also whether they are worth the bother. Is it really the case that social democratic and labour parties stand to lose as many voters to radical right-wing populists as some of their leaders and members think? Or are they getting things out of proportion, worrying more about a rela-tively marginal threat when the real challenge on an issue like immigration comes from more mainstream competitors on the centre right (Bale 2008)? The answer, we suggest, varies according to the institutional environment in which they operate, influenced most obviously by the electoral system. But it also depends on the type of far-right threat that they face. In polities with permissive electoral systems and far-right competitors who are treated by other parties as players rather than pariahs, social democratic and labour parties are right to worry, although, as the case of the Netherlands shows, this doesn't necessarily mean they take effective action. In polities where either the electoral system and/or the characteristics of the far-right parties involved mean the latter are periph-eral pariahs, social democrats have much less to worry about. However, as the contrast between the relatively relaxed attitude of the German SPD and the near-paranoia of the British Labour Party clearly demonstrates, a similar opportunity structure need not prompt an identical response.

The Dutch Labour Party and its far-right competitors

For a long time Dutch politics has been dominated by three large party families: the Christian democrats, the liberals and the social democrats, whereas the radical right has played only a marginal role. Issues related to ethnic minorities and immigration only became salient among a substantial share of the electorate from the 1990s onwards (Aarts and Thomassen 2008). The most notable radical right parties active at this time, the Centre Party and Centre Democrats, were unable to present themselves as appealing alternatives to the established parties and were also widely considered to be "beyond the pale" (Lucardie 1998). Furthermore, the opportunity structure for the radical right remained unfavourable due to the hard line on immigration taken by Liberal Party leader, Frits Bolkestein, in the 1990s. In spite of the "pure" proportional electoral system—which, in theory, is conducive to the entrance of small newcomers—no radical right party was able to make much of an electoral impact.

By the time of the 2002 election, however, the Liberals had moderated their position on issues related to immigration and minorities. Prior to this election, Pim Fortuyn had entered the political fray. Fortuyn was a maverick politician who made fierce criticisms of the incumbent government and held outspoken views on immigration, social integration, and, most notably, the Muslim minority population. Although (and partly perhaps because) Fortuyn was assassinated just days prior to the election, his party List Pim Fortuyn (LPF) managed to win no less than 17 per cent of the vote. The party suffered from numerous internal conflicts, and the coalition government in which it took part broke down after just eighty-seven days. At the 2006 election the LPF disappeared from parliament but was replaced by a radical right newcomer, the Freedom Party of former Liberal MP Geert Wilders, which received just under 6 per cent of the vote. With his harsh Islamophobic and populist anti-establishment rhetoric, Wilders came, in the years that followed, to dominate Dutch political debate. The Freedom Party successfully managed to dissociate itself from political extremism and, unlike the Fortuyn's party, remained united under Wilders' undisputed leadership (van Kessel 2011b, 2011c). Wilders' popularity was evident in the general election of 2010, at which the Freedom Party won over 15 per cent of the vote. After the election the Freedom Party agreed to support a minority coalition formed by the Christian Democrats and the Liberal Party.

The PvdA in and out of government

The Dutch Labour Party (*Partij van de Arbeid*, PvdA), meanwhile, has struggled in the electoral arena over the last decade. The party, which formed part of the two coalition governments that governed the Netherlands between 1994 and 2002, was hit hard by the Fortuyn "revolution" in 2002. It won just 15.1 per cent of the vote, meaning that its vote share almost halved. Under the leadership of Wouter Bos the party recovered remarkably in the next parliamentary election (of 2003), taking over 27 per cent of the vote. In 2006, however, the party suffered another defeat (with a vote share of 21.1 per cent) and in 2010, under the new leader Job Cohen, the party received just below 20 per cent.

How did the Dutch Labour Party react to the new challenge of the radical right? With the rise of Pim Fortuyn, issues related to immigration and integration suddenly became politicised and mainstream parties generally took on more restrictive positions (Oosterwaal and Torenvlied 2010). Indeed, a closer look at its short manifesto for the 2003 parliamentary election indicates that the Labour Party prioritised the issue of social integration of ethnic minorities to a greater extent than in previous programmes. The party may already have taken a more restrictive stance with regard to immigration policies while in government in the 1990s, but this move was never very publicly pronounced (Bale *et al.* 2010: 416). In the Labour Party's programme of 2006 the issue receded to the middle of the document. The party again stressed the need for ethnic minorities to participate and integrate in Dutch society and argued in favour of a "selective" immigration policy. But it came nowhere near adopting the harsh, confrontational language of the radical right. The PvdA instead spoke of the dialogue required in order for cultural cleavages to be bridged and explicitly claimed that Islam had become over time a common element of Dutch society (PvdA 2006: 36, 39).

Despite Geert Wilders' popularity growing markedly after the election of 2006, the Labour Party's manifesto of 2010 did not choose to emphasise immigration and integration issues. They were briefly raised in the manifesto's introduction, but were only discussed in a little more depth towards the end of the document, the party wanting to acknowledge their increased salience at the same time as retaining both internal programmatic coherence and remaining true to its more liberal values. Changes in both language and substance were therefore carefully managed with a view to taking account of the "new reality". However, the relatively low priority given to immigration and integration by the party and its "middle of the road" approach suggest that the PvdA was aiming, above all, to play down those issues. In any case, it would also have been almost impossible for the Labour Party credibly to copy the policy positions of Fortuyn and Wilders, not least because both men made much of the PvdA's supposed responsibility for the problems caused by the lack of social integration of Muslims.

This does not mean that a discussion *within* the party was absent. Broadly speaking, the party has been divided between members with a more liberal outlook on immigration and multiculturalism, and members more inclined to push for the assimilation of ethnic minorities in Dutch society. Questions of value legitimacy were subsequently important for a significant portion of the membership. In an internal report on the reasons why the party did badly in the 2002 election, diverging opinions within the PvdA with regard to immigration and integration were mentioned, as was the party's general disregard of those issues in the previous years (PvdA 2002: 26–28). There were subsequently discussions about the need to move to where the voters were, while both maintaining programmatic coherence and remaining true to long-held values. The party published another report in 2004 that was to function as a starting point for a new debate about immigration and integration. It was, however, a more recent resolution from 2009, entitled "Divided Past, Shared Future" ("Verdeeld verleden, gedeelde toekomst") that demonstrated the divisions within the party most clearly. A first version of the document was criticised for conveying a message that was too nationalistic and intolerant (see Schuyt *et al.* 2009). Former PvdA Integration Minister Ella Vogelaar, for instance, criticised some of the "Rambolike" rhetoric in the report (Vogelaar 2009). The final version of the resolution, accepted in March 2009, touched on the heated intra-party debate in its introduction (PvdA 2009: 3). At the same time, some of the strongest assimilation-oriented rhetoric was toned down and more sentences were included condemning right-wing extremism and discrimination against ethnic minorities.

Although the debate predominantly remained an internal affair, the disunity showed in some of the more high-profile decisions made by the party leadership. Towards the end of 2008, Wouter Bos, for instance, dismissed Vogelaar, who was well known as a supporter of "multiculturalism". However, in April 2010 after Bos had resigned, the party chose as his successor the mayor of Amsterdam Job Cohen, who took a "soft" stance on, say, the social integration of the Muslim minority. All this arguably illustrated the "irresolution" of the party with regard to the integration issue (van Kessel 2011a).

Should the PvdA be worried?

The Dutch Labour Party remains divided on issues related to immigration and the integration of ethnic minorities, although the debate predominantly remains an intra-party affair. Especially with Job Cohen as party leader, the social democrats have not conveyed an assimilation-oriented message to the outside world. Does the PvdA have to worry that many of its potential voters are attracted by the harsh anti-Islam rhetoric of Geert Wilders' Freedom Party? As van der Brug *et al.* find (chapter 3, this volume), the main competitors of the radical right in Western Europe remain the conservatives and Christian democrats, but there is also some overlap between preferences for the radical right and social democratic parties. Indeed, a post-2010 election survey by the research institute Synovate (2010) suggested that the Freedom Party managed to win a few seats at the cost of the PvdA. In addition, data from the Dutch Parliamentary Election Study indicates that there were former PvdA supporters among the voters who opted for the Freedom Party (CBS *et al.* 2012). Judging from the data, the Freedom Party also drew support from former supporters of the Socialist Party, a party to the socio-economic left of the PvdA.

The fact that some presumably "left-wing" voters opted for the radical right may well have to do with the Freedom Party's shift towards the left in 2010 on some socio-economic issues. Considering that a plurality of voters in Western Europe combine a left-wing stance on such issues with a right-wing position on cultural issues like immigration (see van der Brug *et al.*, Chapter 3, this volume), the PvdA may be right to worry about losing its "authoritarian working-class" support base to the Freedom Party. At the same time, the PvdA runs the risk of losing votes to the benefit of the aforementioned Socialist Party, which has taken a more pronounced left-wing stance on socio-economic issues. If the PvdA chooses to appeal more clearly to the authoritarian left, however, it might suffer from the competition of the parties—notably GreenLeft (GroenLinks) and the Democrats '66 (D66)—with a more "cosmopolitan" message and an outspoken liberal position on cultural issues.

In the Dutch multiparty environment with a large floating vote, the Dutch Labour Party would appear to face serious competition from parties on both sides of the cultural divide. Moreover, the threat to the Labour Party will only be greater if it fails to position itself clearly on issues that have recently become salient to the electorate. In light of the financial and economic crisis, European integration might well become such an issue: the PvdA faces competition from staunchly Eurosceptic parties like the Freedom Party and the Socialist Party, but could lose votes to more Europhile parties like D66 and the GreenLeft if it takes on a more sceptical stance as a consequence. Several prominent party members, among them Chairwoman Lilianne Ploumen, voiced concerns about the lack of vision and visibility of the party in opposition, and the performance of party leader Job Cohen.

The UK Labour Party and the far-right "threat"

From the mid-1940s to the mid-1970s, politics in the UK was dominated by the Conservative and Labour Parties. From the two general elections of 1974 onwards, British voters have proved increasingly inclined to support so-called "minor parties". The biggest of these is the Liberal Democrats, although the nationalist parties in Scotland and Wales have also been an important factor in the erosion of the two-party vote. Voters across the UK have also been able to support parties on the far left (most recently the Respect Coalition), and on the environmental left (the Greens). To the right of the Conservatives, the choice has been between the extremist British National Party (BNP), whose origins lie in the neo-Nazi nationalist politics of the 1970s, and the more mainstream, but equally populist and proudly Eurosceptic, UK Independence Party (UKIP)— sometimes referred to by its opponents as "the BNP in blazers" and, as such, seen to be more of a threat to the Conservatives than Labour (John and Margetts 2009: 508–510).

Because the UK retains its first-past-the-post plurality electoral system, Labour and the Conservatives continue to share between them the bulk of the seats in parliament, with the Liberal Democrats trailing a distant third and the nationalist parties picking up seats in their respective bailiwicks. The Greens picked up their first ever seat at Westminster at the general election of 2010, but representation in the House of Commons has so far eluded both the BNP and UKIP. At the 2010 general election, the BNP won just over half a million votes, but its average vote share in the seats in which it stood was just 3.8 per cent— and 1.9 per cent across Great Britain as a whole. UKIP, which on the whole gets less attention from journalists, garnered just over 900,000 votes and an average share across Great Britain of 3.1 per cent, although its average share in the constituencies it contested was, at 3.5 per cent of the vote, a little lower than the BNP's. That said, actual electoral performance is not the same as potential and a breakthrough cannot be completely discounted, since research suggests that latent support for both UKIP and the BNP is considerably higher than that which has so far manifested itself at general elections (John and Margetts 2009; see also Ford 2010). Moreover, both parties have been able to win seats in the European Parliament, elections for which are fought on a proportional basis, using regional lists: in 2009 the BNP won just over 6 per cent of the vote nationwide, while UKIP won just over 16 per cent, sensationally knocking Labour into third place. The BNP has also been able to win some seats on local authorities.

The BNP continues, in spite of attempts in recent years to shift "from boots to suits", to provide a home for voters with strikingly xenophobic and racist views (YouGov 2009a). One could argue that UKIP has more in common with most of the radical right-wing populist parties of continental Western Europe: it was UKIP, after all, who famously invited Geert Wilders to show his film, *Fitna*, in the House of Lords. However, it is the BNP that is most often evoked in media stories comparing the threat to mainstream politics elsewhere with the threat which supposedly faces Britain too—in part because that threat is now so closely associated with the Islamophobia which, for the BNP at least, has become such an integral part of its brand. The media is also convinced that the BNP poses a far greater problem for Labour than it does for the Conservatives, largely on the basis that its supporters are, it would seem, precisely those uneducated working-class men living in run-down parts of big cities and industrial towns who traditionally, it is assumed, would have turned out to vote Labour. Moreover, it is well known that Labour retains the support (worth less than it might be because of their greater propensity not to turn out) of Britain's black and minority ethnic (BME) voters, prompting obvious questions about whether it can continue to please both audiences simultaneously.

New Labour in government—tough on asylum, soft on immigration

This media analysis seems to have been largely accepted by Labour politicians. This, it is thought, is because a number of high-profile members of the parliamentary party have seen wards in their constituencies elect BNP rather than Labour candidates at local elections and therefore fear, if not for their seats, then for their majorities. This then feeds into a wider anxiety within the Party that the modernisation associated with Tony Blair and "New Labour" may have alienated some of its more traditional working-class (and often, therefore, authoritarian) supporters. It also resonates with a belief, prevalent since it was first made explicit by Labour (and Conservative) politicians back in the 1960s, that good race relations ultimately depend on being able to demonstrate to the native population that the numbers of migrants arriving in Britain is subject to the strictest possible control. It was precisely this, some Labour politicians argue, that the party failed to do in government. This failure, they claimed, had opened up space that the far right (which was able to capitalise on media stories about supposedly special treatment handed out to migrants when it came to welfare benefits and public housing) was more than happy to fill. According to this line of reasoning, the Labour Party will continue to see its vote eaten into unless and until it commits itself to limiting immigration and asylum and promoting assimilation or else undertakes the more demanding (and therefore more unlikely) task of engaging with people and persuading them that immigration and a multiethnic, multi-faith UK is inevitable.

Academic experts on migration see all this as rather ironic, even laughable, given that Labour spent much of the thirteen years it was in government after 1997 doing its utmost, if not to advertise quite how many people were arriving in Britain, then at least to demonstrate the economic benefits of immigration and, above all, to convince voters that it was anything but a soft touch when it came to asylum seekers (for example, Blunkett 2002). Life for the latter was made increasingly unpleasant by a raft of rule changes and primary legislation, as well as rhetoric, which made it clear that asylum seekers (at least the majority, whose claims were thought to be "bogus") were unwelcome (for details, see Mulvey 2010). But while the emphasis on detention, deportation and limited eligibility (or none at all) for work and welfare benefits attracted outrage and scorn from NGOs and liberal commentators, it seemed to do the government very little good. Indeed, if anything, it was counterproductive: the tougher rhetoric used by ministers simply legitimated and then ratcheted up the hostility and suspicion on which tabloid newspapers and opposition parties on the right thrived. This was because it became clear that, although numbers of asylum applications were falling after the turn of the century, the state was losing track of those claiming and failing to deport those whose claims had been turned down; this then encouraged the government into still stricter measures (Mulvey 2010; see also Squire 2008: 254–255). In any case, there was a glaring mismatch between the Labour government's antipathy to asylum seekers and illegal immigrants (the two were one and the same thing, some suggested) and the red carpet it seemed to be rolling out to those migrants coming to the country to work legally, either on one of the newly expanded, fast-tracked work permit programmes or as a consequence of the decision to allow unconditional entry to workers from the eight countries that joined the EU in 2005 (Balch 2009; see also Flynn 2005). By the time Labour left office, annual net migration had more than trebled.

But if policy makers were convinced that this was the right thing to do, the general public remained stubbornly sceptical (Ford 2010). Growth was duly delivered, but with it came more competition for jobs at the lower end of the labour market as well as greater pressure on public services, particularly in the wake of the EU accession in 2005. Moreover, a series of high-profile failures in systems of control, some of which cost ministers their jobs, only heightened concerns, while the move (in March 2008) towards an "Australian-style" points-based system for those migrants wanting to live and work long term in Britain—a system that embodied the distinction between more and less deserving cases—left the public cold even if, polls suggested, it made sense to most people (Allen 2011: 20). And a promise in 2007 by Gordon Brown, who finally took over from Blair that year, to secure "British jobs for British workers" provoked, from most voters, nothing more than a hollow laugh: polling showed that immigration was one of their top two or three concerns, but they also showed that Labour was far from being the party most trusted to deal with it. A poll in August 2008, for example, found that only 5 per cent of respondents mentioning the issue as important rated Labour as the "best party" on immigration, while 46 per cent named the Conservatives—figures that remained almost exactly the same when the question was next asked in March 2010 (Ipsos/Mori n.d.)

Should Labour be worried?

A decade of eye-catching initiatives, international and domestic, aimed at showing that Labour understood public concerns and was urgently acting to address them—promoted not just by a succession of Labour home secretaries and immigration ministers, but by two Labour prime ministers (Somerville 2007: 119–129)—had, then, apparently failed to convince voters. But if Labour lost out, then who gained? Undoubtedly, the biggest beneficiary of Labour's woes was the Conservative Party—not surprisingly perhaps, because its leader since 2005, David Cameron, steered a skilful course between the need, on the one hand, to reassure well heeled and well educated voters that his party was no longer as "nasty" on asylum as it had been under his predecessors and, on the other, to convince everyone else that it was as robust as ever (and certainly more competent than Labour) on immigration (Bale *et al.* 2011). The down-side risk of this double game was a loss of support at the margins to UKIP, whom Cameron (in his earlier, arch-modernising phase) had dismissed in early 2006 as "a bunch of fruitcakes and loonies and closet racists". But Cameron reasoned, quite correctly, that, as long as he kept up the pressure on Labour (and indeed the Lib Dems) on immigration and asylum (which was exactly what he did in the run-up to the election and in the campaign itself), then any such loss would be marginal compared to the gains that would be made as a result of the Tories being seen once again to occupy the centre ground more generally. As for the BNP, they were seen as largely Labour's problem.

The numbers suggest that the actual picture was (and is) rather more complex. Of one thing there can be little doubt, and it is worth stressing again and again: the vast bulk of any loss in support experienced by Labour on immigration and asylum at the general election in 2010 went to the Conservatives. The perceptions of the two main parties' stances on such issues are poles apart. In a YouGov poll taken just after the election, some 44 per cent of respondents included "immigrants and non-white Britons" in the two or three groups they thought Labour most wanted to help, making those people—at least in voters' eyes—the party's most important client group (single-parent families on 35 per cent and ordinary working people on 24 per cent came next). Only 8 per cent included such people in the two or three groups that the Tories most wanted to help (Kavanagh and Cowley 2010: 342).

As for support for the radical right, it seems probable, first, that the common wisdom that UKIP is more likely to "steal" votes from the Conservatives than from Labour is correct. In 2010 UKIP did best in well-to-do constituencies containing a relatively large number of older (even elderly) voters on (or near) the South and East coasts of England (Curtice *et al.* 2010: 404). Those areas are far from fertile territory for Labour. As for the BNP, we need to be careful not to assume—as many Labour politicians seem to assume—that just because research (Goodwin 2011: 97–119; see also Cutts *et al.* 2011) suggests that the profile of its supporters is a better match with those of Labour than any of the other parties (at least insofar as social class, lack of education, and property ownership goes) then this automatically means that the two parties are fishing in the same pool. For one thing, there are differences: Labour gains a slightly disproportionate share of women voters (although this is offset by the fact that it fares worse among older voters, more and more of whom are female), whereas around two-thirds of BNP voters are male; traditionally, Labour also does slightly better among younger voters than its opponents, whereas BNP voters are "greying" as the result of the party's lack of appeal to younger voters who are generally (and increasingly) tolerant of ethnic minorities and the "multicultural" ethic. For another, the same research concludes as follows: (1) that "the BNP is not over-whelmingly more likely than other parties to recruit ex-Labour voters"; (2) that BNP supporters identify themselves as right-wing; (3) that they are "profoundly hostile toward Labour"; and (4) that, possibly because they tend to read the most virulently anti-immigration tabloid newspapers, they are almost obsessively concerned with immigration and asylum. Nine out of ten BNP supporters identify these as the most important issues for the country and six out of ten as the most important to themselves and their families—figures that suggest they are unlikely to respond to Labour's appealing to them on other issues, especially when those that resonate most with them (e.g. law and order) are "owned" by the Conservatives, whereas issues owned by Labour (welfare and health) do not concern them anywhere near as much. It is worth adding that, according to a YouGov poll conducted in October 2009, the BNP is still seen as a pariah party by most voters and there is no evidence that the BNP's "toxic brand" is any less toxic to Labour's than to other parties' voters (YouGov 2009b).

In other words, when we consider the populist radical right in the UK we are talking about two parties that are unlikely to appeal that much to those who might otherwise vote Labour—and certainly far less likely to appeal to them than are the Conservatives or the Liberal Democrats (or indeed the Scottish and Welsh Nationalists). And when it comes to those who already vote for those parties, we may well be talking (particularly in the case of BNP supporters) about people who, however much they look like Labour voters at first glance, are currently beyond Labour's reach. Whether, of course, that should be the case is—actively—a matter for debate. There are some Labour Party thinkers, the most high profile being Lord Glasman, a sociologist with links to Ed Miliband, the current Labour leader, whose "Blue Labour" ideas about reconnecting with the party's traditions and traditional communities controversially (not least among those who count themselves as believers) involve stepping away from the common sense that immigration is a good (and anyway inevitable) thing (see Stears 2011). It may even become easier to argue this without losing "progressive" voters to the Liberal Democrats now that that party (which many had thought of as lying to the left of Labour, and which had campaigned, for instance, for an amnesty for illegal immigrants) has formed a coalition government with the Conservatives, committed, among other things, to substantially lowering immigration.

The German SPD and a far right that doesn't bark

The position of the German SPD is altogether different to both that of Labour in the UK and the PvdA in the Netherlands. Even though the far right, in the shape of the German People's Union (DVU) and National Democratic Party (NPD), gets plenty of attention in the German media, it has not—as yet—posed a significant electoral threat to either of the catch-all parties. Both the DVU and NPD have had sporadic successes in regional elections (mirroring in a way the successes of UKIP and the BNP in second-order elections), but neither has come anywhere near making a breakthrough at the federal level (Heinrich and Schoon 2007; see also Kintz 2010).

This is particularly interesting as in recent times Germany's cosy two-and-a-half party system has come under sustained threat from small parties of different persuasions (Blondel 1968; see also Hough 2011; Jun 2011). The left-libertarian Greens have pushed the economically liberal FDP ever more into the arms of the CDU/CSU, as two blocs of parties have established themselves either side of the political centre. The rise of the Left Party (LP) since 1990 has further complicated the coalition arithmetic. The Left Party grew out of the primarily East German PDS—which itself grew out of the former ruling party of the GDR, the Socialist Unity Party—as it attempted to make its socialist platform more marketable in West Germany (Olsen 2007). The 2009 election saw the LP improve its standing still further, registering 11.9 per cent nationwide—which, given that both the Greens and the FDP each polled over 10 per cent as well, illustrates how smaller parties have risen to challenge the long-held dominance of the catch-all actors.

The increasing diversity in Germany's party system has not shaken the anti-totalitarian consensus that has long underpinned it. However, the incorporation of seventeen million East Germans with (much) weaker ties to (the ostensibly West German) parties prompted, unsurprisingly, a more diversified form of political competition to take hold; both in the Eastern Länder *but also, as a knock on effect, in a number of the Western states too*. And, as the Left Party has become ever more accepted as a political actor (even if it still remains beyond the coalition pale at the federal level), and its function as a genuine protest party has receded, parties of the far right have occasionally risen to fill the "protest party" role.

The right-wing populist DVU was the first, in the late 1990s, to make an impact in regional elections. The DVU was founded by a Munich-based publisher, Gerhard Frey, as an informal association in 1971 and established as a party in 1987. It remains staunchly conservative, and proudly nationalist, but in essence it is a protest party without any real programmatic core. Indeed, at times it appears to be more like a phantom party, disappearing from public life for long periods before popping up again at election time. In late 2010 it had around 3,000 members. Financially, it is dependent on Frey and he is the pivotal figure in directing its activities—so much so that, once represented in parliament, the DVU has often been crippled by the inexperience and naivety of its politicians.

The DVU's intermittent successes have been overshadowed by a potentially more dangerous competitor as a rejuvenated National Democratic Party (NPD) has risen to prominence. The NPD is the largest, and frequently the most militant, of the far-right parties, and it is currently represented in three (of the six) East German regional parliaments. Even before the recent upsurge in support— in December 2010 it had around 6,600 members—the federal government attempted (ultimately unsuccessfully) to set a process in motion that would lead to it being banned on account of the anti-constitutional activities of some of its members. Many members hold attitudes similar to those in the British BNP, with xenophobia, racism, and anti-Islamicism much to the fore. The NPD and DVU have recently tried to join forces with the aim of uniting the far right under one banner. Indeed, in December 2010 the parties declared that they were going to fuse their organisations, only for a Munich court to rule the merger illegitimate in January 2011. The ruling was, however, based on procedural mistakes, since rectified, making it almost certain that the far right will be represented by a single party at the next federal election

The SPD in government

On returning to government after a sixteen-year hiatus in 1998, the Social Democrats gave themselves a long to-do list. The majority of the new government's aims surrounded socio-economic reform proposals directed largely, although by no means exclusively, at rejuvenating the (East) German economy and dealing with the continuing fallout from unification. However, one key aim of the red-Green government was explicitly to "modernise" both immigration and citizenship policy (Green 2007). Pre-1998 governments had maintained time and again (and in manifest opposition to reality on the ground) that "Germany is not a country of immigration". By this, right-wing politicians in particular were claiming that the vast majority of non-nationals who worked, and therefore by definition tended to live, in the FRG, were only there temporarily. The so-called *Anwerbestopp* of 1973 (preventing further guest workers from abroad from being recruited) was supposed to halt the increase, and then lead to a periodic reduction in the number of, low-skilled non-nationals in the country. Yet the numbers kept on rising, mainly as a result of many of the migrants' families moving to Germany to be with them. This, coupled both with an influx (post-1990) of ethnic Germans (who often spoke poor German and struggled to integrate well) and—between 1990 and 1993—over 1.2 million asylum claims, saw immigration bubbling up into a politically contentious issue (Green 2007: 98). This provided far-right politicians with plenty of ammunition with which to attack Gerhard Schröder's red-Green administration.

Schröder's government subsequently had to deal more or less immediately with issues that the far right were attempting to mobilise on (immigration, citizenship); and in many ways the government did not shirk the challenge. The SPD/Green administration did make good on its promise to update Germany's citizenship law (which dated from 1913) to reflect more adequately the reality explained above (see Hogwood 2000). The red-Green administration certainly adapted policies here that were much more in line with the values of the moderate centre left than anything parties of the far—and even centre—right were likely to have proposed. For the most part (there were exceptions: the CDU in the state of Hesse was quick to campaign openly, and nastily, on an anti-reform platform in 1999—see Broughton 2000), the centre right was careful in shaping its criticisms so as not to appear too intolerant; however, a whole raft of objections were certainly registered when it came to details, such as on whether dual citizenship should be allowed and what the specific criteria for becoming German should be (Green 2004: 79–109). In essence, the CDU/CSU sought to stress that immigrants needed to illustrate that they had integrated into German society before citizenship was granted—something that the SPD felt was a smoke screen for simply refusing many potential immigrants the right to become German. The SPD, however, was also acutely aware that "new Germans" tended overwhelmingly to vote Social Democrat (or at least to vote for parties of the left); the only immigrants who consistently voted CDU/CSU in any number were ethnic Germans who had been granted citizenship on the basis that an (often distant) relative had had German citizenship in the past (Wüst 2004). It was no surprise that the CDU/CSU, through the language of cultural identity, was much less quick to criticise the methods by which this group gained citizenship.

Although the citizenship law was ultimately passed, there was much public discussion not just about the details but also about exactly what the aim of Germany's citizenship policy should be. Indeed, the new law is clearly more in tune with Germany as it is today (in particular through the partial introduction of *ius soli*), but its overall impact has not been anywhere near as dramatic as had been expected. The debates surrounding who should be granted citizenship also show that, much as is the case in the UK, it is the centre right that poses by far the biggest threat to the social democrats on these issues. The voices of the DVU and particularly the more hardline NPD are rarely heard; they predictably call for a narrow, frequently racial, understanding of who Germans are, and all but the lunatic fringe ignores them. It is the CDU/CSU that the SPD worries about in this regard, not the far right.

A second key area of debate involved labour migration; another area where the far right has traditionally tried to make an impact. The SPD (and Greens) were certainly keen to promote Germany as a country that welcomes highly skilled migrants. Indeed, Germany's demographic challenge and its skills gap in areas such as information technology ensured that it desperately needed to attract highly skilled foreigners. And, much like New Labour in the UK, it passed legislation to try to do this. In February 2000, Chancellor Schröder announced a so-called "Green card" scheme, whereby up to 20,000 foreign IT specialists would be allowed to work in Germany for up to five years. The business lobby heartily approved, and the CDU/CSU was pushed onto the back foot. Arguably, for the first time in thirty years the case was being made that inward migration could be good for Germany, and even though the scope of this project was limited it sent out a strong signal. It fitted with the SPD's new pro-business agenda (and therefore had programmatic consistency with the SPD's 1998 election campaign) and it also struck a chord with the values of internationalism and openness to which the left has traditionally signed up. Just as importantly, it was eminently doable.

The logic of this policy was carried on through into what would have been a first in German history: a comprehensive law on immigration policy. Indeed, a commission (led, curiously, by CDU grandee Rita Süssmuth) was set up to make recommendations on what such a law should look like. The far right's voice here was effectively non-existent, the major points of criticism coming (not unsurprisingly) from the CDU/CSU. And the rush of enthusiasm for liberalising Germany's laws in this area began to wane, not least among the wider public at large, as unemployment continued to bite and Germany's economy bumped along. An immigration law was nonetheless passed, coming in to force on 1 January 2005, but in reality it failed to go beyond providing only very limited opportunities for non-EU labour to come and work in the FRG (Green 2007: 105). Indeed, by this time the much-heralded Green card scheme was being questioned, as even the (rather modest) original quotas were shown not to have been filled.

Should the SPD be worried?

In recent times, the SPD has struggled in national elections. Following seven years of governing with the Greens and then four as a junior partner in a grand coalition, it returned to the opposition benches in 2009 with its tail between its legs. Indeed, its 23.0 per cent of the vote was its worst performance on record. In the aftermath, the party conducted a series of internal reviews of what had gone wrong and why. In none of them did confronting issues that the far right were trying to make much of play a prominent role. Indeed, in the areas of multiculturalism, integration, citizenship, and national identity it is undoubtedly the CDU/CSU that poses the much greater threat. It is the CDU/CSU that is often more in tune with the conservative leanings of many Germans when it comes to immigration issues, and if any party gained from the "reform fatigue" that set in after the SPD/Green government launched (and largely completed) its citizenship and immigration reforms, then it was the CDU/CSU.

A look at the individual-level data on changing voting preferences illustrates clearly how (in)significant the far right was in all this. The SPD polled

6.2 million fewer votes in 2009 than it did in 2005. Of those, just over two million did not vote at all in 2009, while the party that benefited most from the SPD's troubles was the Left Party, gaining 1.1 million voters who had supported the Social Democrats in 2005. The CDU/CSU and Greens benefited almost identically: the CDU/CSU made a net gain of 880,000 (comprised of 1.3 million SPD voters opting for them in 2009, compared with 460,000 previous CDU/CSU voters moving to the SPD), and the Greens' gain was 870,000 (500,000 previous Green supporters moved to the SPD, but 1.37 million went the other way). Despite its programmatic distance from the SPD, the Free Democrats, a party that did very well in 2009, also gained significantly from the Social Democrats' woes (plus 530,000). All of the other parties together—and this includes the NPD and DVU, as well as new upstarts such as the Pirate Party (which won 2 per cent of the vote nationwide in 2009 but was not around to compete in 2005)—only managed to attract 320,000 former SPD voters: in other words, fewer combined votes than any of the major parties (Neu 2009: 95).

The evidence from 2009 therefore illustrates that politicians of the left in Germany almost certainly understand the threat posed by the NPD and DVU well enough. The SPD realises that, if only on account of Germany's history, it needs to be clear in articulating the dangers inherent in turning a blind eye to right-wing extremism. But all democratic politicians in Germany do this. The everyday political threat that the SPD faces from these groups is minimal. And it is for that reason that the SPD has to concentrate its efforts on competing with the CDU/CSU, and to an extent the Left Party. Indeed, it is the LP that successfully wrestled away much of the party's blue-collar support in 2009, and the SPD knows that winning it back is fundamental to winning national elections again.

Conclusion

Political opportunity structures matter, but parties' responses do not flow automatically from them. Because it operates in a complex multiparty system where far-right parties are no longer perceived as extreme, and are permitted by the electoral system to turn votes into seats, the Dutch PvdA has more to worry about, and is obliged to perform a more delicate balancing act, than Labour in the UK or the SPD in Germany. It is hard to tell whether the PvdA's recent difficulties indicate that it has not played the game well or whether they simply reflect the fact that, in the present climate, the game cannot be won. The game in the other countries looks, on the face of it, much easier. In Germany in particular, the threat from the radical right is currently negligible and the SPD's relative lack of concern over confronting it looks wholly rational. The UK, however, presents us with a paradox. Because of the electoral system and the fact that the radical right poses no particular threat to Labour, there would appear to be no more reason for the party to worry than the SPD. And yet it does worry, even if there is precious little evidence to suggest that such worrying has helped it electorally—probably because of a yawning gap between its rhetoric and the reality of the immigration (if not the asylum) policies the party pursued during thirteen years in government between 1997 and 2010.

The existence of that gap has undoubtedly helped the UK's radical right parties, although nowhere near enough to mean that they are capable of winning a seat in parliament. The biggest beneficiary, of course, has also helped Labour's only real opponent, the Conservatives, who have no intention of losing their reputation as being tough on immigration. Unless they are completely irrational, none of this can have escaped Labour politicians—which prompts an interesting question. Is fear of the BNP stealing some of its ordinary working-class voters the real reason why those politicians point to the necessity of talking tough on immigration? Or is stressing the supposed need to counter the BNP simply an easier way to persuade their more liberal supporters and colleagues to support policies and rhetoric which in actual fact are there to counter the more prosaic but much bigger threat posed on the issue by the Conservatives? If this is the case, then, perversely, the presence of the radical right in some polities is a boon rather than a burden—a phantom that can be conjured up to justify a competitive strategy that, given public opinion on the issue, would have to be adopted anyway.

6 Right-wing populist parties and the working-class vote

What have you done for us lately?

Hans-Georg Betz and Susi Meret

Introduction

Right-wing populist parties owe their electoral success to a significant extent to their ability to appeal to, mobilize, and seduce voters from among what in French is commonly known as the *couches populaires*—blue-collar workers and lower-level employees. Until well into the 1980s, these occupational groups represented the core constituency of the traditional left. Today, they constitute an increasingly important source of right-wing populist support. An example today is the Front National. In April 2011, *Le Monde* and other major French newspapers reported that opinion poll data showed that Marine Le Pen, the party's newly elected head, was the "preferred candidate of workers" for the presidential election of 2012. A few weeks later, a report by the socialist think tank Terra Nova (Terra Nova 2011) went so far as to suggest that if the left wanted to have any chance of realizing a progressive program, it would have to forge a new coalition of disparate social groups, such as the better educated, the young, women, and naturalized immigrants. Although the authors rejected accusations that their report suggested that the left abandon its pursuit of the *couches populaires*, commentators interpreted the strategy adopted in the report as a clear indication that the left had largely given up on them.[1] As the philosopher Michel Onfray, one of France's leading public intellectuals, somewhat sarcastically put it, the new strategy could be resumed in "two words"—bobos (bourgeois bohemians) against prolos (Onfray 2011: 78).

Right-wing populist parties are today's new working-class parties

This development, of course, is hardly new and not only restricted to the French case. Already in the 1990s, Austrian observers characterized the FPÖ as being a "new type of working-class party"; this was reflected in the fact that the party derived a disproportionate amount of electoral support from blue-collar workers. In 1995, about 24 percent of manual workers had cast their vote for the FPÖ (Plasser and Ulram 2000). At the same time, the support from the blue-collar workers' electorate to the Austrian Social Democratic Party (SPÖ) had declined from about 65 percent in the 1970s to 35 percent in the late 1990s (Plasser and Ulram 1999). Today, the working-class profile is valid for virtually all right-wing populist parties. To be sure, not all workers are the same. The Lega Nord, for instance, has traditionally derived much of its support among the working class, predominantly from workers employed in small- and medium-sized private companies in the most affluent regions of northern Italy. The "productivist ideology" of these groups of workers is substantially different from the ethos of blue-collar workers from Milan, Turin, or the industrial areas of Emilia Romagna (Beirich and Woods 2000: 137). However, quite significantly, the Lega Nord has in more recent years gained increasing support, for example among trade union members (e.g., Casellato and Zazzara 2010) and from areas of central Italy generally considered to be Italian "red" electoral strongholds, such as Emilia Romagna, Toscana, and Marche (Biorcio 2010; see also Stefanini 2010).

Even more significant are the high levels of working-class support to the populist right in the Nordic countries. Take Denmark, for example, where the Dansk Folkeparti has become the most clear-cut working-class party in Danish politics (Meret 2010: 226–229). More than half of the Dansk Folkeparti votes come today from skilled and unskilled manual workers, principally men with lower educational attainment. Also in this case, the support from the working-class profile was achieved at the expense of the traditional working-class parties of the past—in this case the Social Democrats—which in the past decades have lost considerable voting support among manual workers.

The Progress Party in Norway (FrP) shows a similar voter profile. The Norwegian party is over-represented among skilled and particularly unskilled manual workers (Bjørklund 2011: 285). In 2005 the FrP was the most popular party, electorally speaking, among unskilled workers (and, interestingly, particularly among women belonging to this group) and the second-most voted party among manual workers after the Labour Party (Bjørklund 2009: 15–18). The FrP achieved this profile despite the fact that the party strongly supports neo-liberal politics and positions, asking, for example, to abolish progressive taxation and to remove the inheritance tax. During the 1990s the party leadership became increasingly aware of the FrP role as the "new working-class party" and introduced ad hoc pro-welfare measures that appealed to this part of the electorate. One of the measures proposed by the party, for instance, was to "use oil reserves to benefit the common people", going to finance the building of infrastructures and the improvement of the social, health care, and schooling systems. However, the FrP still claims economic liberalism to be at the core of the party ideology and neo-liberal positions continue to characterize the party's approach to redistributive issues (Fremskrittspartiet, Prinsipp- og handlingsprogram 2005–2009: 5). Indeed, this makes it more problematic to understand the reasons behind the popularity of the FrP among the working class and among the less well off in Norwegian society. In relation to this, the scholars Andersen and Bjørklund observed that: "this unusual composition is perhaps the strongest indicator of a changing cleavage structure and of the classification of the Progress Parties as belonging to a genuinely new party type" (Andersen and Bjørklund 2000: 216).

The Progress Party and the Danish People's Party have thus succeeded to mobilize and—even more importantly—to maintain the working-class votes, by responding to the demands coming from these social groups and left unanswered by the other political parties and in particular by the left wing.

This seems also the case for Sverigedemokraterna, now with parliamentary representation. At the 2010 Swedish national elections the party doubled its votes and reached 5.7 percent of the consent. The extremist past of the Sverigedemokraterna (e.g., Lööw 2011) and the marginalization strategies used by the other parties and by the media to keep the Sverigedemokraterna out of political influence, did not prevent skilled and unskilled workers, the unemployed, and those who had retired early from the labor market from casting a vote for this party (Oscarsson and Holmberg 2008).

In Finland, a recent survey on party identification (Taloustutkimus Oy 2011) indicated that among manual workers about 40 percent identified with the Perussuomalaiset, or Sannfinländarna (True Finns). The party, led by Timo Soini, won more than 19 percent of the votes at the last Finnish general elections in 2011 and it is at present the third-largest political force in the Nordic country.

The strong working-class support for the populist right has given rise to different interpretations, often emphasizing the impact of the societal and economic consequences of globalization on social groups whose economic, social, and labor situation are more uncertain and at risk (e.g., Betz 1994). However, the image of the "losers of modernization," which has been used to account for the growing appeal of the populist right among working-class voters, seems hardly to fit reality, and little empirical evidence has been found for this explanation (Knigge 1998; see Swank and Betz 2003). The fact that right-wing populist parties have done particularly well in the Scandinavian countries and in prosperous areas such as northern Italy, the Flemish part of Belgium, and the cantons surrounding Zurich in Switzerland, to name only a few, raises further doubts about the explanatory power of this approach.

In this chapter, we propose an alternative explanation. It is inspired in part by an observation made in the Terra Nova report, which notes that under the new leadership of Marine Le Pen, "for the first time in more than thirty years," there is now a party [i.e., the Front National] in France that is once again in sync with the values and aspirations of the *"classes populaires."* In what follows we propose to examine the supply side of right-wing populist politics: i.e., what do these parties offer programmatically that might appeal particularly to blue-collar workers and more in general to lower-level employees.

Globalization, new social and political cleavages and the populist right electoral appeal

Our analysis is derived from established narratives about the transformation of the cleavage structure of contemporary capitalist democracies, brought about by the challenge of globalization and its impact on the logic of party competition (Kriesi *et al.* 2008b; see also Bornschier 2010a). According to this view, the emergence and implantation of right-wing populist parties in Western Europe's party systems are above all a function of the strategic moves that established left-wing parties made in response to the two major cultural-political revolutions that have marked the past four decades: on the one hand, the emergence of libertarian values in the wake of the anti-authoritarian revolt of the late 1960s, which gave rise to new parties on the left of the political spectrum directly competing with the established left; on the other hand, the loss of faith in socialism as a viable economic alternative, which robbed the established left of its ideological foundation, blunting its profile, and thus posing a serious challenge to its very identity. In response, the established left has generally adopted a dual strategy: in order to maximize its potential support base (i.e., appeal to highly educated professionals) and thus limit the gains of new left-libertarian parties, traditional left-wing parties moved toward left-libertarian positions (e.g., environmentalism, feminism, and multiculturalism). At the same time, they increasingly adopted neo-liberal positions under the guise of a "third way," aptly characterized by Michael Lind as "the reasonable mean between the welfare-state left and the economic libertarian right" (Lind 2007).[2] These strategic moves not only set in motion a reconfiguration of the political space, but also opened up opportunities for new parties to fill the ensuing programmatic void, both with respect to traditional authoritarian values and traditional left-wing economic positions. Recent studies on the response of various social groups toward globalization—and here particularly transnational migration, which "lies at the core of the ongoing process of globalization" (Kahanec and Zimmerman 2008: 2)—suggest that a programmatic mix combining authoritarian positions with traditional statist positions should be particularly appealing to the *couches populaires*. Existing literature suggests that attitudes toward globalization are informed primarily by anxieties with respect to the labor market, worries regarding repercussions on the welfare state, individual uncertainties about future economic perspectives, and concerns about cultural identity (see, for instance, Dustman and Preston 2007).

Globalization entails heightened competition in the labor market, both internal and global. Trade theory relying on factor endowment models suggests that attitudes toward globalization in advanced liberal capitalist economies are strongly correlated with a person's skill and educational level. Persons whose skill and educational levels are relatively low can be substituted relatively easily, be it by immigrant workers or, increasingly frequently, by workers in low(er)-wage countries, such as China or India. As a result, under the impact of globalization, these workers either see their wages—and standard of living—stagnate or, even worse, they face redundancy given dramatically shrinking job opportunities. A recent *Wall Street Journal* article illustrates the point: during the first decade of the new millennium, American multinational corporations—which traditionally have employed a fifth of the American labor force—cut their workforce in the United States by some 2.9 million, while concomitantly adding 2.4 million workers to their payrolls overseas (Wessel 2011). In response, workers and employees with potentially substitutable skills are expected to oppose both the

state discussed earlier, the perceived strain on social security systems caused by immigrants has a direct and easily understood impact on workers and employees who not only contribute to the funding of social services, but potentially have to compete with immigrants for increasingly scarce social provisions.

In Denmark, recent studies confirm the close relationship between negative views of the impact of non-Western immigration and attitudes toward wealth redistribution and welfare access (Larsen 2011). Actually this has not changed the general positive attitude toward public spending for traditional welfare sectors, but has rather introduced and widened the consent for "dualized" forms of access to welfare, supporting the introduction of restrictive politics lowering access to welfare benefits and services for non-Western immigrants considered to represent a socio-economic burden for society.

Unsurprisingly these arguments comprise exactly the position taken up today by virtually all anti-immigration parties in the Nordic countries, which thus respond in particular to the voters who are most concerned about the economic consequences of immigration and integration. This focus on the economic consequences of immigration seems also to be an approach that gains comparatively more consent in periods of economic crisis.

But attitudes toward globalization are also strongly shaped by concerns about culture and national identity. These, in turn, are linked to the problems of solidarity and trust, which in part at least inform the welfare state debate. Already in 1997, Francis Castells maintained that in "a world of global flows of wealth, power, and images, the search for identity, collective or individual, ascribed or constructed, becomes the fundamental source of social meaning." This was hardly a new phenomenon. However, in a "historical period characterized by widespread destructuring of organizations, delegitimation of institutions, fading away of major social movements, and ephemeral cultural expressions" identity was "becoming the main, and sometimes the only source of meaning" (Castells 1996: 3). At the same time, however, globalization threatens to destabilize national identity. As John Tomlinson has argued, this is not primarily a result of the spread of a uniform global consumer culture, but of the "proliferation of identity positions" that potentially challenge and perphaps even threaten "the dominance of national identity" (Tomlinson 2003: 274).

The point goes beyond the narrow question of the impact of ethnic diversity on interpersonal trust and reciprocity—itself a rather contentious issue among social scientists (see, for instance, Gesthuizen *et al.* 2008)—it is fundamentally about the challenge posed by the assertion of cultural distinctiveness by immigrant groups, advocated, supported, and sustained by official multicultural policies (such as one promoting "racial identity nurturing"), and increasingly seen by its critics as promoting cultural separatism (what in French is referred to as *communitarianisme*), societal fragmentation (with minority communities leading "parallel lives"), and eventually the breakdown of social cohesion (for a detailed analysis along those lines for France, see Guilluy 2010). The result is the emergence and strengthening of a new political cleavage pitting those who believe greater diversity represents an asset and a source of strength to society against those who hold that great diversity undermines national identity. A recent YouGov poll in the UK found roughly 20 percent of respondents agreeing with either position. A relative majority of 45 percent agreed with the moderate position that greater diversity "brings benefits to our society, but it's important to maintain a clear sense of British identity" (Darlington 2010). Poll results also suggest that hostility to multiculturalism and greater diversity is particularly pronounced among workers and those who come from lower social strata in general (Ipsos/Mori 2009).

When in March 2011, the newly appointed Danish integration minister and member of the Liberal Party Soeren Pind blatantly declared that he preferred a policy of assimilation to integration, as "Denmark only has room for foreigners that adopt and respect Danish values, norms and traditions" and "if they don't, they shouldn't be here at all," he responded in part to the overall negative opinion already existing among the population. Asked about their attitude to this issue, 58 percent agreed in fact with the wording that multiculturalism has ousted Danish culture, and the majority maintained that immigrants and their descendents must predominantly live according to Danish norms (TNS Gallup 2011). Also in this case, manual workers and private sector self-employed often show higher levels of concern (Frølund Thomsen 2006: 81–83).

The situation gets more complex when Islam is brought into the picture. In a recent French poll on the question of mosques and minarets, when asked whether they were in favor of, or opposed to, the construction of mosques (if requested by the country's Muslim community), 41 percent of respondents said they were opposed; among workers, however, almost two-thirds expressed hostility toward the idea. The result was similar with regard to a ban on the construction of minarets, which was favored by 46 percent of all respondents, but by 60 percent of workers (IFOP 2009).

The cultural protectionism of the populist right

The arguments developed so far suggest that a political party seeking to appeal to the *couches populaires* would have to adopt a program that offers a mixture of economic and cultural protectionism, supported by a firm commitment to a strong, comprehensive, if not authoritarian (welfare) state. Ironically enough, right-wing populist parties, although staunch promoters of cultural protectionism, have generally promoted the opposite with respect to the economy. The Norwegian Progress Party, for instance, has recently been characterized (in a leading magazine of the American neo-conservative right) as a "Reaganite, Thatcherite" party (Nordlinger 2010). Jean-Marie Le Pen himself boasted in an interview in the late 1980s that the Front National had adopted the principles underlying Reaganomics and Thatcherism way before neo-liberalism started to become fashionable (Le Pen 1989: 117–119). As recently as the 2007 presidential election, Jean-Marie Le Pen called for a drastic reduction of the tax level in France, which would have been of particular benefit to the rich. And in Austria, the dramatic gains of the FPÖ under the leadership of Jörg Haider occurred at a time when the party promoted itself as a revolutionary force intent on deconstructing the country's corporatist system. In fact, in 1994, the FPÖ defined itself as a party appealing "to people who attach value to personal achievement, who are willing to accept the responsibilities of freedom rather than sacrifice personal goals to apparent collective security" (Austria Documentation 1994: 19). Kitschelt was hardly wrong when he explained the populist right's success largely in terms of their adoption of a "winning formula" combining market liberalism with authoritarian positions with regard to immigration, internal security, and traditional values (especially on the position of women in society). It should not be forgotten that particularly in Scandinavian countries, but also in northern Italy and Austria, the populist right, at least initially, derived much of their appeal from their ability to promote themselves as the vanguard of a larger tax revolt.

This, however, is only half of the story. As Anthony Mughan *et al.* have pointed out, the populist right's promotion of laissez-faire liberalism has applied only to the domestic market. With regard to international trade, these parties have generally advocated economic nationalist positions supposed to counter and reverse the pernicious effects of globalization and thus allow the state to regain control over domestic economic and political choices. For Mughan *et al.* the basics of the populist right's economic program represent an "essential contradiction." For whereas neo-liberalism aims at weakening the state, economic nationalism presupposes a relatively strong state, if only to stand up to the forces of globalization (Mughan *et al.* 2003: 619).

This represents only an apparent contradiction, whose resolution lies in the parties' populist appeal. Like today's Tea Party wing of the Republicans in the United States, the populist right sees neo-liberalism primarily as a weapon to be used dramatically to curtail the scope of the state. In its view, the state has largely been captured by left-wing groups, collectively representing a "new class," which uses the state and its resources not only to impose their ideas on society but also to promote and financially support the sectoral interests and projects (particularly multiculturalism) of disparate clienteles (Betz and Johnson 2004). The same reasoning informs the populist right's economic nationalism. Here too, these parties attack the established economic, political, and cultural elites for having sold out to a "globalist economic philosophy and practice that erodes national economic independence and thereby necessarily undermines the nation's political and cultural sovereignty" (Mughan *et al.* 2003: 619). In both cases, the immediate goal is to undermine the legitimacy and appeal of the established elites as a first step toward a fundamental reconstruction of the role of the state, which, in turn, would put it in a position to recapture a measure of national economic and cultural autonomy and independence against the forces of globalization.

The same rationale lies behind the populist right's position on the social welfare state, which has increasingly become a central policy issue for these parties. Generally, the populist right staunchly supports a comprehensive system of social security, as long as there are guarantees and safeguards against abuse by work-shy welfare scroungers. At the same time, the populist right's conception of social security radically breaks with the notions of egalitarianism and universality, which informed the postwar West European welfare state. Instead, the populist right promotes what Cas Mudde has called a "nativist interpretation" of the welfare state, where benefits are restricted to the "native needy" while non-native residents without citizenhip—be they labor migrants or refugees—are systematically excluded (Mudde 2007: 132). This approach is then further justified by referring to the need of safeguarding the degree of solidarity and cohesion that is considered to constitute the "glue" for the survival of the welfare state. We find this nativist approach to welfare issues already clearly defined in the Dansk Folkeparti's early manifestos and later also taken on by other right-wing populist parties in Scandinavia, as for example the Sweden Democrats.

The populist right justifies its exclusionary position on welfare benefits, arguing that such as policy of "national preference" would serve to shut down, as the Front National program put it in 2007, the "*pompes aspirants*" sucking in new migrants, attracted by the prospect of being able to live on generous social welfare benefits. At the same time, the populist right's nativist conception of the welfare state serves as yet another means to undermine the established political and cultural elites and their multicultural agenda, which, for the populist right, represents a trojan horse of globalization since it must invariably lead to the destruction of national communities and identities. Finally, in terms of political strategy, the populist right's exclusionary conception of the welfare state has a strong appeal to lower-class voters. Lower-class voters are generally very much in favor in of redistributive policies; at the same time, however, they show considerable hostility to the idea that benefits should be extended to immigrants. In a recent article, Jeroen van der Waal *et al.* have shown that this attitude reflects these voters' relatively limited amount of cultural capital, which leads them to perceive immigrants as a source of threat to, rather than an enrichment of, society (van der Waal *et al.* 2010: 353).

From this perspective, it is hardly a coincidence that in recent years, virtually all electorally successful right-wing populist parties have adopted the question of Islam (or, more precisely, the specter of an alleged "Islamization" of Europe) as their central mobilizing issue (Betz and Meret 2009). In the populist right's view, Islam poses a fundamental threat to the values, identity, and way of life of Western Europe's liberal democracies; yet the promoters of multiculturalism ignore and play down the essential danger posed by the growing number of Muslim residents and migrants in Western Europe. At the same time, as Thilo Sarazzin has most famously put it, Muslim migrants are charged with falling signficantly short of the demands made upon them by sophisticated industries that rely on a highly skilled labor force in order to remain internationally competitive. As a result, Muslim migrants are said to be predisposed to be unemployed and to rely disporportionately on social services, thus representing a significant drain on welfare states that are already severely strained. Given this scenario, Western Europe's growing Muslim community represents an ideal target for a political strategy based on bundling and articulating popular fears, anxieties, and resentment (particularly given the dramatic fall in native birth rates). On the one hand, there are anxieties that the growth of a culturally alien, if not hostile, community threatens to undermine the sense of trust, reciprocity, and solidarity that are vital for the preservation of a comprehensive welfare state; on the other, there is the fear that the establishment of a growing alien underclass represents additional competition for increasingly scarce resources.

The Front National's latest turn toward social issues

The Front National's programmatic "recalibration" set in motion by Marine Le Pen in the run-up to the decisive party conference in January 2011, from which she emerged as the new leader of the Front National, is emblematic of the new direction the populist right in Western Europe has started to take in recent years. Central to this recalibration has been a strong emphasis on economic and social questions designed—according to the new leader of the Front National—to expand the party's agenda beyond the traditional issues of security and immigration and thus "bring coherence" to the party's political cause (Le Pen 2011e). Le Pen's programmatic "turnaround" has drawn considerable attention in the French media while provoking concern and anxiety, particularly on the traditionalist and extreme right. The main extreme right publications were quick to charge Marine Le Pen with having abandoned the party's traditional neo-liberal program in favor of a new left-wing agenda. She was attacked for seeking to claim France's jacobin tradition and, in the process, coming dangerously close to "walking in the footsteps" of Maurice Thorez, the leader of the Communist Party in the immediate postwar period (Letty 2011; see also Villedary 2011). For the traditionalist right, Marine Le Pen's aggressive adoption of the "social question" posed a serious threat to the established right, if only because of its likely appeal to lower-class voters disenchanted with Nicolas Sarkozy and the mainstream center right (Folch 2011).

These observations are well founded. As an analyst in *Alternatives Economiques* has noted, with regard to the Front National's new economic program, Marine Le Pen's rupture with the party headed by her father is "clear and profound" (Pech 2011: 43). Under Jean-Marie Le Pen, the Front National subscribed to a large degree to a "populist free-market capitalism," à la Thatcher and Reagan. The emphasis was, on the one hand, on lowering taxes for higher incomes, slimming the welfare system, and generally reducing the size and scope of the state; on the other hand, on ecouraging broad-based property ownership, which was supposed to promote individual initiative, responsibility, and self-reliance (Bastow 1997: 63).

This is strongly reminiscent of the Dansk Folkeparti programmatic turnover in the mid-1990s from the ultra-liberal and tax-protest orientation that had characterized the Progress Party ideology and program. However, in the Danish case this required a more radical break with the past, and the creation of a new party in order to complete the change. The launch of the Dansk Folkeparti in 1995 offered thus an unprecedented opportunity to disengage with too strong neo-liberal legacies and tax-protest issues, developing instead a pro-welfare profile with a strong emphasis on the sense of community and solidarity linked to the welfare state. Already in the mid-1990s, the Dansk Folkeparti defined welfare as a responsibility and natural solidarity felt by the Danish community toward the weakest of society, referring to specific groups represented by the elderly, early retirees, the sick, the handicapped, and the socially marginalized (Dansk Folkeparti 1997: 10–11). This automatically implied that welfare benefits were not for all; immigration was immediately portrayed as a most "serious threat to the survival of Denmark as a universal welfare state" (Dansk Folkeparti 1997: 6). On this point the party has always been very explicit: welfare must be limited to those who have paid for it with savings from their hard work, not a "free self-serve" for the many foreigners coming to the country. For Dansk Folkeparti, three main conditions sustain the redistribution principle to take from those with higher incomes to those with lower incomes: all have to work together for the same cause; those better off do not go away; and immigrants must not have the right to access social benefits and services as soon as they have come into the country (Dansk Folkeparti 2009).

At the same time, the Dansk Folkeparti criticized the irresponsible immigration policies approved by former governments. The critique was addressed in particular to the Social Democrats, who were considered to have repudiated their role as protectors of welfare values and principles in the name of libertarian stances—on immigration, for instance—undermining the welfare state present and future. In direct continuity with this, the Dansk Folkeparti leadership has in the last decade often profiled the party as the only credible and real inheritor of traditional social democratic values. This line of reasoning could effectively appeal to those workers feeling that levels of welfare were threatened by an increasingly globalized world, where growing immigration is among the consequences.

The new Front National and the construction of the concept of *demondialisation*

In recent days Marine Le Pen's economic and social program turns around a central notion—*demondialisation* (de-globalization)—an idea, to be sure, that resonates far beyond the circles of the populist right (Chavagneux 2011). *Demondialisation* refers to a political process of retreating from globalization if not reversing its course. The disagreement between its advocates is over the question of on what level *demondialisation* should take place—national or European.

Marine Le Pen's adoption of the idea of *demondialisation* fit perfectly with the party's carefully cultivated self-image as an uncompromising bulwark against the forces of globalization and an unrelenting critic of its ideological justifications, denounced as "*mondialisme.*" For the Front National, *mondialisme* represented a "monstrous totalitarian utopia" whose aim it was, as Jean-Marie Le Pen put it in 2000, to allow its promoters to "attain the complete domination of the planet" by destroying the nations and their identities ("Discours de Jean-Marie le Pen—1er mai 2000", cited in Betz 2002a). This position, albeit rich in rhetoric and pathos, fell considerably short in proposing concrete policy measures on how to counter effectively the process of globalization. It was left to Marine Le Pen to turn the party's anti-globalization rhetoric into a coherent and ideologically consistent political project, which is quite unique when considered in relation to other populist right-wing approaches.

Marine Le Pen too markets herself primarily as an advocate of ordinary people against the prevailing *mondialiste* discourse—a "totalitarian ideology," as she put it in a major programmatic speech, pursuing a "monstrous project" intent on subjugating humanity to "consumption and production for the benefit of a few big enterprises and banks which are the only ones to profit from it" (Le Pen 2011c). Central to Le Pen's anti-*mondialiste* counter-project is the demand that France abandon the euro—characterized as the most visible symbol of France's loss of sovereignty over its monetary policy—and reinstate the franc. For Marine Le Pen, the euro represents a "monetary corset," which prevents the members of the euro zone to respond to economic crises and thus leads them to economic ruin and social devastation (Le Pen 2011d). By exiting the euro zone—Marine Le Pen's promise—France will "rejoin the game of the nations," thanks to having regained its "monetary freedom" (Le Pen 2011a). Monetary freedom means above all to be able to devalue the currency to regain competitiveness. A relatively weak franc would allow French companies to increase their exports, which would provide the "oxygen" to the French economy that "today it cruelly lacks" (Front National 2011: 9). At the same time, Marine Le Pen's economic program envisions the installation of national protectionist measures (i.e., strict border controls, introduction of import quotas, tariffs, and strict health standards) targeted against low-cost imports from emerging countries such as China and India, which the party has frequently charged with engaging in "disloyal competition." These measures are supposed not only to stop the relocation of French companies to developing countries but also to promote the "re-industrialization" of France. As Marine Le Pen puts it, there is no reason why smartphones cannot be produced in France instead of in China.

Marine Le Pen's project of a "national economic patriotism" accords a key role to the state. As the new leader of the Front National put it during her first 1 May address, today, "more than ever, France and the French people" were in need "of a strong state." For, as she charged in her inaugural discourse of January 2011, when there is a need "to regulate, protect and innovate, it is toward the state that one naturally turns, because it is the state that is large enough to act, that has the necessary democratic legitimacy, and that is written into our national DNA" (Le Pen 2011a). In this context, the Front National economic program goes so far as to advocate the re-nationalization of certain "strategic" industries, such a transport and energy, as well as banks that are in trouble. As a result, for a number of French analysts, the Front National's new economic program represented a return to the dirigist, etatist policies of the past, a revival of "*colbertisme.*"

This is also true with respect to the social welfare state. Whereas the Front National under Jean-Marie Le Pen called for a drastic reduction of the public sector, the new party line accords it a central role. Public services are no longer seen as a provider of commodities, "which could be mechanically replaced by private suppliers" but as "a guarantee of the equality of the citizens" (Le Pen 2011b). For, as Marine Le Pen put it in a programmatic speech, for those who have nothing, social services are "the only right, the only good, and even a part of their dignity" (Le Pen 2011b). Therefore, she promised, the Front National would not only defend France's "*acquis sociaux*" but "in taking back the keys of our destiny" it would make sure that they continue to be guaranteed.

Social services can only be maintained, however, if France introduces a strict policy of national preference. Should France, instead, continue "to welcome all the misery of the world," it will invariably see its welfare system ruined. Only a policy of *preference nationale* that accords absolute priority to French citizens will put an end to "the globalization of welfare benefits, which destroy our social protection systems." This means, on the one hand, that certain benefits (such as the *revenu de solidarité active*) are limited to French citizens; on the other, that foreign residents are required to pay higher premiums for health and unemployment insurance than French citizens. At the same time, the Front National promotes itself as the only serious defender of French workers' salaries and standard of living, both undermined by globalization. For globalization not only inevitably leads to a lowering of social standards, but also to a constant downward "readjustment" of wages, particularly as a result of the pressures caused by transborder migrants, who constitute a modern "reserve army of capitalism." This means that there "is no social without the effective control of the migratory flows in our country." This implies, above all, stopping the inflow of migrants from Muslim countries. Like other right-wing populist parties, as for instance the Dansk Folkeparti, Marine Le Pen's Front National banks on the mobilizing power of Islamophobia, based on the notion that Islam is fundamentally incompatible with the values and principles that inform the French republic and its notion of secularism or *laicité*. And like Geert Wilders, Filip Dewinter and Heinz-Christian Strache, Marine Le Pen promotes herself and her party as fighting against the "Islamisation" of her country and Europe in general, going so far as to compare the visible presence of Muslims in France with the Nazi occupation during World War II.

Conclusions

In this chapter we have argued that right-wing populist parties owe their success at the poll to a large extent to their ability to appeal to lower-class voters, and in particular to manual workers. It is generally assumed that lower-class voters are particularly attracted to these parties' restrictive position on immigration and their opposition to multiculturalism. Against that, we have tried to demonstrate that right-wing populist parties have increasingly advanced socio-economic policy propositions traditionally associated with the left, which jibe with the political expectations of lower-class voters. This is clearly the case for the Dansk Folkeparti, for instance, which was among the first right-wing populist parties consciously to choose and promote this programmatic strategy. Quite significantly, this direction has later been followed by several other parties and most recently by the French Front National, whose programmatic turnaround suggests that also in this case we are in front of a deliberate and well considered strategy on the part of the populist right, designed to shape a new cleavage that has opened up with the acceleration of the process of globalization and the current economic crisis.

Critics might charge that projects that aim at decoupling the nation from the process of globalization amount to nothing but "a political form of resistance to change" that is bound to fail (Reynié 2011: 134). And in fact, the policies advanced by Marine Le Pen do seem to seek to revive the golden days of the *trente glorieuses*, while ignoring and/or dismissing the disastrous results of the country's history of competitive devaluations. At the same time, however, the Front National's project has to be seen within a larger, serious discussion on de-globalization, which extends far beyond the confines of the populist right. As one prominent figure in the debate has put it, the exit from globalization is "on top of every realistic agenda for the next five years" (Juvin 2010: 225). In the face of the current financial, economic, and social crisis, in France—but not only there—pro-tectionist measures are increasingly seen as a viable solution. Under these cir-cumstances, the way the populist right deals with globalization by suggesting protectionist solutions, and the way these parties defend the welfare state by claiming that only a nativist approach can guarantee its survival, are propositions that cannot be easily dismissed as irrational or completely unrealistic. Neither can the parties' self-promotion as defenders of the interests of the "common people" be ignored by the political establishment, both right and left. In this respect, the outcome of the upcoming French presidential election in 2012 is likely to deter-mine not only whether or not the programmatic union of economic populism and cultural nativism into a coherent political project proves attractive to mobilize lower-class voters against globalization, but also whether or not the European populist right will adopt such as project as a common platform. This has proven to be the case at the national level in several other European countries. If this happens, the populist right can be expected to pose an even more serious chal-lenge to the established left than it has already done hitherto.

Notes

1 See particularly Amable (2011) and Sawicki (2011), who express their shock with respect to the "incomprehension" and "contempt" (Sawicki 2011) toward the *couches populaires* revealed in the report.
2 Anthony Giddens' recent observations about New Labour are rather telling. Although he still maintains Labour was right to become "more business friendly," he faults Labour for allowing

> the prawn cocktail offensive to evolve into fawning dependence, with the result that the UK was transformed into a kind of gigantic tax haven. The idea that Labour should be "intensely relaxed about people getting filthy rich" not only exacerbated inequalities, but also helped to create a culture of irresponsibility. Bosses protected themselves from the risks they asked their employees to bear.
> (Giddens 2010: 26)

As a result, by the end of the Brown government, inequality in Great Britain was at a level not seen since the end of World War I (Dorling 2010).

7 Voting for the populist radical right in Western Europe

The role of education

Elisabeth Ivarsflaten and Rune Stubager

Introduction

In this chapter we show that voters with lower education are more likely to vote for the populist radical right in Western Europe than voters with higher education. Furthermore, we show that while education is strongly related to occupational class, an education effect on the populist radical right vote exists that does not operate through occupational class. Additionally, we show that occupational class and education are to differing degrees associated with key issues in the two-dimensional political space of contemporary Western Europe (Kitschelt 1994, 1995; Kriesi *et al.* 2008b; Kriesi 2010). Class is most strongly related to the economic left–right dimension, while education is more strongly related to the libertarian–authoritarian dimension.

As is previously well documented, and replicated in our analysis, populist radical right parties mobilize voters primarily along the second political dimension (Ivarsflaten 2008; Bornschier 2010a; Mudde 2007). Based on our analysis, we therefore advance an issue explanation for the education effect on populist right voting. It holds that the educational profile of populist radical right parties is caused by these parties' focus on second-dimension issues. These second-dimension issues are more strongly related to education than are issues along the economic left–right dimension, and the socio-demographic pattern of the populist radical right vote reflects this.

Our analysis is based on well known and much used comparative survey data from the European Social Survey (2002/2003, first round). In the discussion following the main analysis, we engage the question of why there is a stronger education effect on the second political dimension than on the first. In particular, we address the ethnic competition hypothesis, which suggests that support for strict immigration and integration policies among those with lower education is a result of material position or economic vulnerability rather than ideational differences related to norms, values, and cognitive capacity. The data we have used for this study does not allow firm conclusions in this important debate. By documenting a strong connection between education and a tendency to view immigration and immigrants as a social ill across a number of issues, however, the chapter challenges any straightforward conclusions about the material foundations of the populist radical right vote.

Populist radical right parties in the two-dimensional political space

In his book on social democracy in Western Europe, Kitschelt introduced an influential two-dimensional map of European political space. It included an economic left–right dimension consisting of issues of taxation and redistribution and a libertarian–authoritarian dimension consisting of issues such as immigration, law and order, and traditional family values (Kitschelt 1994). Kitschelt subsequently used this two-dimensional map in collaboration with McGann to explain the rise of radical right parties in Western Europe in the late 1980s and early 1990s (Kitschelt and McGann 1995). By now several refinements to this analytical framework have been suggested and more recent empirical trends and examples have been included, but the fundamental insight about the structure of European politics as two dimensional, where the content of the two dimensions is roughly as outlined by Kitschelt, has if anything been strengthened in recent research (Kriesi *et al.* 2008b; Bornschier 2010a).

While building on the Kitschelt framework in this way, more recent research on the populist radical right has in other respects departed clearly from McGann and Kitschelt's analysis of the early manifestations of radical right parties. In the initial McGann and Kitschelt formulation, the "winning formula" of the populist radical right was seen to be neo-liberal on the first dimension and authoritarian on the second dimension. More recent research, however, emphasizes the importance of the second dimension much more strongly (de Lange 2007; Ivarsflaten 2008; Bornschier 2010a). Electorally successful populist radical right parties are either argued to be centrist or divided on the first dimension (Ivarsflaten 2005b), or to subordinate or link economic issues to their main ethno-nationalist (Rydgren 2005) or nativist (Mudde 2007) frames. This latter political framing of economic issues in nativist terms has also been referred to as welfare chauvinism (Goul Andersen 1992).

The scholarly debate about which issues the populist radical right parties mobilize has thus contributed to a reappraisal of the importance of the second dimension for populist radical right electoral success. However, the implications of this reappraisal for the socio-demographic structure of the populist radical right vote have not been fully examined. In the following, we therefore analyze how the social structure of the second dimension differs from that of the economic left–right. Our main finding is that education plays a more prominent role for attitudes on the second dimension and that this prominence of education for libertarian–authoritarian positions explains the under-representation of the highly educated among the populist radical right's voters.

Country selection, data and analytical procedure

For the mechanisms underlying our hypotheses about populist radical right (PRR) voting to manifest themselves clearly in relation to a given PRR party, it needs to attain a sizable number of votes. To ensure this we have decided to focus on PRR parties that have attained at least 5 percent of the popular vote in the national elections prior to the collection of our survey data in 2002/2003. This narrows the field to PRR parties in seven countries: the *Freiheitlichen Partei Österreichs* in Austria; *Vlaams Blok* in Belgium;[1] *Schweitzerische Volkspartei* in Switzerland; *Dansk Folkeparti* in Denmark; *Front National* in France; *Lijst Pim Fortuyn* (LPF) in the Netherlands; and *Fremskrittspartiet* in Norway.

For the analyses, we rely on data from the first round of the European Social Survey, which is a data set of high quality containing measures of the core variables of the analysis (see below) in all seven countries. The data was collected in 2002/2003, and includes the parties running for election at that time. In the meantime, some parties have changed or disappeared (most notably the LPF in the Netherlands). However, the mechanisms examined are expected to generalize to present day PRR parties. Indeed, most of the parties analyzed are still vibrant political forces today. We pool the data across the seven countries in the analysis.[2] We present our operationalizations of the measures in the analyses below.

Operationalization

The dependent variable takes two values: 1 for respondents who voted for a PRR party; and 0 for those who voted for another party (non-voters, refusals, etc. are excluded from the analysis).

Education: The educational measure available in the data for all seven countries distinguishes between five levels of education: less than secondary education (i.e., less than seven years of schooling); lower secondary education (i.e., up to ten years of schooling); upper secondary education (e.g., high school and vocational educations); post-secondary non-tertiary education; and tertiary education (i.e., BA level and above). Since there are very few cases in the first and fourth categories they have been combined with the second and third, respectively.

Social class: Class is measured by means of the Erickson, Goldthorpe, Pontocarero (EGP) scheme which contains eleven categories.[3] In order to avoid too many small categories in the analysis, however, we have combined them into the following seven categories (Roman numerals refer to the EGP scheme): I higher controllers; II lower controllers; IIIa routine non-manual; IIIb lower sales-service; IV self-employed, including farmers; VI skilled workers, including manual supervisors; and VII unskilled workers, including farm laborers. Due to errors in the data collection process, the self-employed category is missing in France and Norway.

The two attitudinal dimensions are based on two items each. Immigration attitudes are made up of the following Likert scale items: (a) "refugees whose applications are granted should be entitled to bring in their close family members"; and (b) "if people who have come to live here commit a serious crime, they should be made to leave." Economic attitudes, for their part, are made up of the following items: (a) "the government should take measures to reduce differences in income levels"; and (b) "employees need strong trade unions to protect their working conditions and wages."

Each item has five response categories ranging from "agree strongly" to "disagree strongly" and they correlate at 0.26 and 0.31 for immigration attitudes and economic attitudes, respectively. The combined scales are coded to run from 0 to 1 with 1 being the most right-wing position. While it would have been preferable to include more items in the scales, and while this is possible for the immigration dimension, we are limited by the availability of items on the economic dimension. With respect to the former, previous research has found similar patterns using both short and long versions of the immigration scale (Ivarsflaten 2008, 2005a). Further, it has been documented in previous research that asylum, refugee, and immigration questions load on the same dimension in this survey and that questions related to asylum and immigration therefore may be grouped together (Ivarsflaten 2005a).

In addition we include gender and age as control variables. To be able to control for the common perception that PRR parties attract particular support from either the youngest and/or the oldest voters, we have categorized the age variable in three categories: up to twenty-five years; twenty-six to sixty years; and sixty-one years and above.

The analyses are carried out by means of least squares as well as logistic regressions. The first step in the analyses consists in investigating the socio-structural anchoring of the two attitudinal dimensions by means of ordianry least squares (OLS). Thereafter, we analyse PRR voting in four steps using logistic regression. In the first step, age, gender and education are entered (Model I) to examine our proposition that PRR parties are more popular among voters with lower rather than higher education. In the second model we include class instead of education in order to gauge its independent effect before entering education and class together in Model III. In Model IV, finally, immigration and economic attitudes are added to the model to complete the test. Below we show both the regression coefficients, tests of the significance of each variable and predicted probabilities of voting for the PRR for each level of education and class. The predicted probabilities are calculated for males, aged between twenty-six and sixty years, with general upper-secondary education, and a lower sales-service occupation.

Results

The structural roots of attitudes to immigration and economic distribution

In accordance with the considerations set out above, we first investigate the structural roots of voters' attitudes on the two core ideological dimensions in West European countries—i.e., attitudes related to immigration and immigrants and the distributional conflict from the economic domain. The main question in this context is whether and to what extent education and class (controlled for gender and age) explain individuals' positions on the attitudinal dimensions. The analysis of this question is presented in Table 7.1.

Table 7.1 The generation of immigrant and economic attitudes in Western Europe (OLS regression coefficients, standard errors, and model fit).

	Immigrant attitudes		Economic attitudes	
	Coef.	SE	Coef.	SE
Intercept	0.65***	0.02	0.39***	0.02
Age	***			
26–60 years	0.03*	0.01	0.01	0.01
61+ years	0.07***	0.01	0.00	0.01
Gender	−0.01	0.01	−0.03***	0.01
Education	***		***	
Upper-secondary education	−0.06***	0.01	0.03***	0.01
Tertiary education	−0.14***	0.01	0.05***	0.01
Class	***		***	
II Lower controllers	0.01	0.01	−0.05***	0.01
IIIa Routine non-manual	0.01	0.01	−0.07***	0.01
IIIb Lower sales-service	0.03*	0.01	−0.07***	0.01
IV Self-empl. incl. farmers	0.05***	0.01	0.03*	0.01
VI Skilled workers	0.05***	0.01	−0.09***	0.01
VII Unskilled workers	0.04***	0.01	−0.10***	0.01
Adjusted R^2	0.092		0.054	

Notes
* Significant at the 0.05 level; ** Significant at the 0.01 level; *** Significant at the 0.001 level. $N=6,880$. Reference categories are males, up to 25 years, lower-secondary education, and higher controllers. The dependent variables range for 0 to 1 with 1 being the most right-wing position. Asterisks for entire categorical variables indicate significance in F-tests of the block of coefficients associated with a given variable.

The table reveals an interesting pattern. Education plays a much larger role in relation to immigrant attitudes than class, but for economic attitudes the situation is the reverse. While on immigrant attitudes voters holding tertiary education are predicted to be almost 0.14 scale points to the left of those with lower-secondary education, the difference between the two groups is less than half (0.05) on economic attitudes, and that even in the opposite direction (i.e., voters with tertiary education are placed farther to the right than those with lower-secondary education). For class, the largest difference on immigrant attitudes appears between higher controllers and the self-employed, with the latter taking the most rightist position, but only by 0.05 scale points. On economic attitudes, the self-employed again come out in the right-most position, with unskilled workers constituting the left extreme situated some 0.13 scale points away. Among the control variables, gender is significant for economic attitudes and insignificant in relation to immigrant attitudes, while the opposite is the case for age. Of these effects, only that for age in relation to immigrant attitudes is worth mentioning. With the oldest group placed 0.07 points farther to the right than the youngest, this effect actually surpasses the maximum effect of class.

Since we find that education is more closely related to the core second-dimension issue of immigration than is occupational class, we may expect that the social structure of the PRR vote is more strongly marked by education than by occupational class—at least insofar as recent research is correct in arguing that PRR parties are mainly concerned with second-dimension issues. We therefore now turn to an investigation of the social structure and attitudinal roots of the PRR vote.

The structural and attitudinal roots of PRR voting

Table 7.2 contains the results of the test of the influence of education, class, and the attitudinal dimensions on PRR voting. Looking at the results for Model I, we find that, as expected, education has a clear effect on PRR voting. Thus, the education variable is overall significant and, as expected, people with higher levels of education vote less for PRR parties than people with lower levels of education. The first column of Table A7.1 shows the predicted probabilities of a PRR vote for the three educational levels based on Model I in Table 7.2. The predictions show the strength of the relationship in the sense that there is a difference of 12 percentage points in the probability of a PRR vote between the highest and the lowest educational category. The table also shows that the difference mostly exists between the highest and the two lower categories, since the upper-secondary category shows only 3 percentage points fewer PRR votes than the lower-secondary category.[4]

Of the two control variables in the model, only gender comes out significant with women being less likely to vote for the PRR than men. As for the suspected age effect, Table 7.2 makes clear that there are only very minor (indeed, insignificant) differences in the propensity to vote PRR across the different age categories.[5] In sum, the results of Model I lend support to our issue-based expectation about the popularity of PRR parties among less-educated voters.

However, as noted above, education and class are not independent of each other. This means that the education effect in Model I could potentially be due to education's relationship with class rather than a genuine education effect. Model II gives some credence to this point. Thus, when we include occupational class instead of education in the model we also find significant results. And just as one might expect based on previous work, the highest probability of a vote for radical right parties is found among such economically vulnerable groups as (particularly unskilled) workers and the self-employed, while the lowest probability is found among economically more secure higher controllers and routine non-manuals. Also, column two in Table A7.1 shows that with 11 percentage points, the differences in predicted probabilities between the extreme categories is about as large for class as for education. It should, though, finally be noted that the explained variance of Model II is slightly smaller than that for Model I, which included education.

A more direct test of the relative strength of the two variables is contained in Model III, which includes both education and class. The first thing to note about the results is that both education and class attain significance in the model. Neither explanation can stand alone, it thus seems. However, the table also shows that education retains most of its effect. This means that the education

Table 7.2 Voting for the radical right in Western Europe (logistic regression coefficients, standard errors, and model fit).

	Model I		Model II		Model III		Model IV	
	Coef.	SE	Coef.	SE	Coef.	SE	Coef.	SE
Intercept	-1.05***	0.19	-2.35***	0.17	-1.80***	0.20	-4.31***	0.27
Age								
26–60 years	-0.16	0.14	-0.11	0.14	-0.12	0.15	-0.22	0.15
61+ years	-0.22	0.16	-0.06	0.16	-0.18	0.16	-0.37*	0.17
Gender	-0.32***	0.08	-0.23**	0.08	-0.25**	0.08	-0.23**	0.09
Education	***				***			
Upper-secondary education	-0.25**	0.09			-0.15	0.09	-0.01	0.10
Tertiary education	-1.17***	0.12			-0.93***	0.13	-0.61***	0.14
Class			***		***			
II Lower controllers			0.32*	0.13	0.19	0.13	0.24	0.13
IIIa Routine non-manual			0.32	0.17	0.08	0.18	0.15	0.18
IIIb Lower sales-service			0.56***	0.16	0.22	0.17	0.26	0.17
IV Self-employed incl. farmers			0.75***	0.16	0.41*	0.17	0.26	0.18
VI Skilled workers			0.84***	0.14	0.45**	0.15	0.43**	0.16
VII Unskilled workers			1.02***	0.13	0.61***	0.14	0.63***	0.15
Economic attitudes							0.82***	0.18
Immigrant attitudes							3.15***	0.21
Nagelkerke's R^2	0.038		0.028		0.044		0.120	
Log likelihood	-2,367.59		-2,402.47		-2,355.89		-2,219.02	

Notes
*: Significant at the 0.05 level; **: Significant at the 0.01 level; ***: Significant at the 0.001 level. N=6,880. Reference categories are males, up to 25 years, lower-secondary education, and higher controllers. The dependent variable takes the value of 1 for a radical right vote and 0 for a vote for all other parties. Asterisks for entire categorical variables indicate significance in χ^2-tests of the block of coefficients associated with a given variable.

effect found in Model I is not mediated to any large extent by class. It is not so, that is, that the differences between the educational groups exist because of the class implications of having a particular level of education. Rather, education has an effect in its own right separate from the effect of occupational class. In accordance with this interpretation, column three in Table A7.1 reveals that the span between the predicted probability of a PRR vote from members of the extreme education categories drops by only 0.04 from Model I to Model III (see also the comparable drop in the logistic regression coefficients in Table 7.2).

Likewise, the tables show a genuine class effect. Net of the effect of education we find a clear difference in the propensity to vote for the PRR across individuals with differing class positions—again with unskilled workers and higher control-lers in the extreme positions. The difference in predicted probabilities between the two extremes is at 0.08 comparable to that for the education categories (see Table A7.1). In other words, it seems that at the structural level, both of the two explanations of radical right voting discussed above have something to recom-mend them and that therefore, analyses that focus exclusively on either may be missing the point, since both variables influence voters' behavior. Before drawing this conclusion, however, we need to take the analyses a step further.

It is one thing to find an association between socio-structural variables like education and class and electoral behavior; it is quite another to explain such an association. Thus, while the results found for the structural variables have indi-cated that both education and class may influence PRR voters we cannot know why these relationships arise. That is, socio-structural categories like educational groups and classes do not, in themselves, contain explanations. Therefore, it is necessary to include the two attitudinal dimensions in the analysis as well. This is done in Model IV.

Two things stand out immediately. First and foremost, immigrant attitudes are clearly strongly related to PRR voting, and while economic attitudes also attain significance, the effect appears much weaker. Just how much weaker can be ascertained from Figure 7.1, which shows the predicted probabilities of voting for PPR parties at different levels of both immigrant and economic attitudes. While PRR parties attain only few votes (less than 2 percent) among those favo-rable toward immigration and immigrants, the share rises sharply to a level of almost 30 percent as we move to the right end of the scale. For economic atti-tudes the change from one end of the scale to the other is only about one-third of this (9 percentage points), thus demonstrating the relative strength of immigrant attitudes. Further, we can note that PRR parties are most popular among voters at the right end of the economic dimension. This speaks rather strongly against the economic explanation of PRR voting, which maintains that the parties are attractive to economically vulnerable, and thus presumably more left-wing, voters. It does, on the other hand, lend some support to Kitschelt's (1995) original proposition that PRR parties attract voters on a neo-liberal position.[6] We shall return to this point in the discussion below.

Going back to Table 7.2, the other noteworthy point is that the direct effect of both education and class is weakened, even if both variables are still significant.

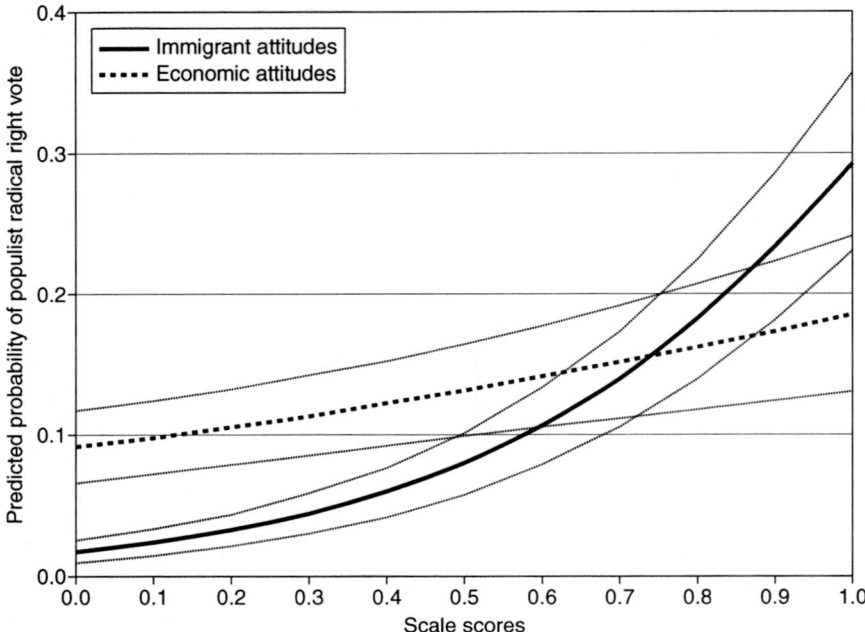

Figure 7.1 Predicted probability of voting for the radical right in Western Europe for varying levels of immigration and economic attitudes.

Note
Predictions are based on Model IV in Table 7.2. The non-varying independent variables have been kept at the following values: male, 25–60 years, upper-secondary education, lower sales-service occupation; immigration and economic attitudes are held at their means. Dotted lines indicate 95 percent confidence intervals.

In other words, part of the effect of both structural variables on PRR voting is mediated by the attitudinal dimensions—immigration attitudes in particular. When these results are considered in connection with those in Table 7.1, a pattern seems to emerge. Thus, although class and economic attitudes are significant aspects of the populist radical right vote, education and immigrant attitudes appear to be important variables in their own right. Still, it might be questioned if the difference between, on the one hand, education and immigrant attitudes and, on the other, class and economic attitudes can be drawn as clearly as the analyses so far suggest. We deal with this question in the discussion below.

Discussion: why is education more strongly connected to opposition to immigration than class?

The idea that education influences political preferences and in turn voting behavior is as old as the field of voting behavior itself. A vast literature has proposed a multitude of potential effects and causal paths (e.g., Stubager 2006, 2008, 2010;

Van de Werfhorst and de Graaf 2004; Nie and Stehlik-Barry 1996; Lipset 196(
Some emphasize the association between education and certain political value,
such as tolerance or more general libertarian values. Others emphasize that lack
of education is associated with specific material constraints, since opportunities
in the labor market and society more generally depend to a large extent on education. This discussion is highly relevant for how we interpret our education
findings above.

Those who argue for a link between education and certain political values,
such as tolerance, do not agree on the nature of this connection. Some focus on
the cognitive development that can be encouraged by education (e.g., Nunn *et al.*
1978; Lipset 1960). Such cognitive development can prevent mistaken or simplistic conclusions about the causes of negative societal outcomes (i.e., "immigrants cause unemployment"), and thus dampen scapegoating of out-groups.
Others note the communicative interaction skills learnt through higher education
(e.g., Altemeyer 1988). Such communicative interaction skills can make a more
heterogeneous society less threatening. Yet others focus on the socialization into
specific social norms and beliefs that occurs at universities and other institutions
of higher education (e.g., McClosky and Brill 1983). The imperative not to be
prejudiced against individuals because of their gender, race, ethnicity, and religion is one example of a highly relevant social norm, which is more strongly
held among those with higher education (Ivarsflaten *et al.* 2010).

Those who argue that education affects political preferences mainly because
it is connected to material positions in society are more inclined to see education
as one of a cluster of variables perpetuating and regenerating persistent inequality between social classes and groups within society. This argument also appears
in various other forms. Inglehart (e.g., 1977) states that political preferences are
shaped early in life, in the family and local communities, alongside preferences
for education, and that education is simply one of a number of variables that
along with affluence go together to make people less concerned about their own
material well-being. Kitschelt (1994, 1995) emphasizes the market situation of
individuals and how these could reinforce skills and values learned through
education.

In the limited populist radical right voting literature concerned with education, arguments usually emphasize how the processes of de-industrialization or
internationalization differently affect those with and without education (Betz
1994; Kitschelt 1995; Lubbers 2001; Carter 2005). Our finding that education is
weakly associated with positions along the traditional economic dimension of
politics, and furthermore that this economic axis is only weakly related to the
likelihood of voting for the populist radical right, does not generally support an
economic deprivation explanation of the radical right vote. As seen also in previous work, it appears that voters concerned with issues along the economic axis
prefer to vote for other parties than the populist radical right (Kitschelt 1995; de
Lange 2007; Ivarsflaten 2008).

The ethnic competition thesis is an alternative, but still fundamentally materi-
ally based hypothesis, about the link between education and anti-immigration

attitudes. According to this hypothesis, "voters turn to the new radical right because they want to reduce competition from immigrants over scarce resources such as the labor market, housing, welfare state benefits, or even the marriage market" (Rydgren 2007: 250). While studies on ethnic heterogeneity in neighborhoods and populist radical right voting are needed to examine this hypothesis in full, our analysis can shed some light on this discussion because the ESS survey includes questions that ask about perceived ethnic competition.

We should be careful, however, not to view ethnic competition survey measures as objective sources of information about the degree of competition actually confronted by respondents. As Sniderman *et al.* (2004) pointed out, we do not know what these measures mean if studied on their own. They could reflect a preference for cultural homogeneity that leads respondents to perceive outgroups as a threat independent of their own economic vulnerability. In this case the economic competition attitudes would align clearly with other attitudes toward immigration that are not connected to economic vulnerability. Or they could reflect a preference for protecting material goods and positions, which would lead respondents to view immigrants as a threat only insofar as they compete for the same jobs and benefits. In the latter case, the ethnic competition measure ought to align less strongly with other anti-immigration measures and more strongly with general economic outlook.

To investigate this empirically we constructed a measure of ethnic competition based on six items tapping into the perceived effect of immigration on society[7] and included it in the analysis in Model IV in Table 7.2. The results (not shown) lend some support to the ethnic competition perspective. Thus, the new scale is clearly significant, and its coefficient is 2.98, about three times the size of that for immigrant attitudes (0.94, still significant at the 0.001 level) when the two measures are included in the same model.[8]

But how should one interpret this result? The caveat raised by Sniderman *et al.* (2004; see above) warns us that it might not be justified to see a high level of perceived ethnic competition as a pure reflection of economic vulnerability and concerns about increased competition over scarce resources; a preference for restrictive immigration policies arising for other reasons (values, for example) may lead to the same type of answers. A way to gauge which type of effects are driving answers to the ethnic competition scale is to compare its socio-structural anchoring to those of immigrant and economic attitudes (cf. Table 7.1). To the extent that our new measure is actually driven by an economically based rather than a value-based or culture-based rejection of immigration, we should expect occupational class and the economic concerns reflected herein to be a stronger predictor than education. Vice versa, to the extent that value considerations dominate we should expect to see a pattern like that found for immigration attitudes in Table 7.1—i.e., a dominance of education over class.

In Table 7.3 we have reproduced the results for economic and immigrant attitudes from Table 7.1 and added two new measures: ethnic competition and strain on personal economy (to which we return below). The results for ethnic competition come out very clearly: as is the case for immigrant attitudes, education is by far the strongest predictor of positions on this variable. Although class also has significant effects, with the self-employed and workers perceiving more competition than the salaried, these effects are not even half as strong as the 0.1 point difference on the 0–1 scale that is found between the two extreme educational categories, where the most-educated group perceives least competition. Furthermore, the pattern of results (including that for age, where the oldest category perceives more competition than the youngest) is even very close to that for immigrant attitudes in the first column, and thereby also distinctly different from the results for economic attitudes in the second column.

The results indicate that our worry about the drivers of perceptions of ethnic competition is justified. The results suggest that ethnic competition (at least as measured on the basis of the data at hand) is driven rather more by an underlying preference for ethnic homogeneity than by economic considerations. In other words, ethnic competition should be considered as another reflection of the same values that are tapped by our measure of immigrant attitudes. This interpretation is further strengthened when inspecting the intercorrelations between the attitudinal measures that are presented in Table A7.2. Thus, while ethnic competition is correlated at 0.00 with economic attitudes, the correlation between ethnic competition and immigrant attitudes is as high as 0.51. With individual-level data, correlations of this size indicate a very high level of covariation.

Clear as the results presented so far would seem, they do leave one problem unanswered: even if (the available measure of) ethnic competition is based more on value considerations than on economic vulnerability, a purer measure of perceived economic vulnerability might be the real driver of both immigration attitudes, ethnic competition and, in the final instance, PRR-voting. Fortunately, we are also able to address this concern with the data set that contains an item measuring respondents' perception of the strain on their personal economy.[9] An inclusion of this item in the final voting model in Table 7.2 does not change much, however. While the variable itself attains a significant (at the 0.05 level) coefficient of 0.31, immigrant attitudes retain a coefficient of 3.05 (significant at 0.001). This does not suggest any pivotal role for perceived personal economic grievances.

This interpretation is further reinforced in Table A7.2, which shows that perceived strain on the personal economy correlates at only 0.07 and 0.13 with, respectively, immigrant attitudes and ethnic competition. Again, this suggests that neither of the two latter variables are driven to any major extent by personal economic vulnerability. Finally, the fourth column of Table 7.3 also indicates a clear division between perceived personal, economic strain and the two immigration-related measures. Thus, although there is a significant education effect on the perception of personal, economic strain (with the higher educated perceiving less strain), there is also a large class effect where several groups find their personal economies more strained than do higher controllers. The finding of such large class and education effects sets the results for the economic strain variable apart from the three other variables in the table and places it, so to speak, in between the two immigration-related measures and economic attitudes.

Table 7.3 The generation of immigrant and economic attitudes in Western Europe (OLS regression coefficients, standard errors, and model fit)

	Immigrant attitudes		Economic attitudes		Ethnic competition		Strain on personal economy	
	Coef.	SE	Coef.	SE	Coef.	SE	Coef.	SE
Intercept	0.65***	0.02	0.39***	0.02	0.50***	0.01	0.27***	0.02
Age	***				***			
26–60 years	0.03*	0.01	0.01	0.01	0.01	0.01	−0.03	0.02
61+ years	0.07***	0.01	0.00	0.01	0.04***	0.01	−0.04	0.02
Gender	−0.01	0.01	−0.03***	0.01	0.01*	0.00	0.03***	0.01
Education	***		***		***		***	
Upper-secondary education	−0.06***	0.01	0.03***	0.01	−0.04***	0.00	−0.06***	0.01
Tertiary education	−0.14***	0.01	0.05***	0.01	−0.10***	0.01	−0.16***	0.01
Class	***		***		***		***	
II Lower controllers	0.01	0.01	−0.05***	0.01	0.01	0.01	0.04***	0.01
IIIa Routine non-manual	0.01	0.01	−0.07***	0.01	0.00	0.01	0.08***	0.02
IIIb Lower sales-service	0.03*	0.01	−0.07***	0.01	0.02*	0.01	0.10***	0.02
IV Self-empl. incl. farmers	0.05***	0.01	0.03*	0.01	0.04***	0.01	0.13***	0.02
VI Skilled workers	0.05***	0.01	−0.09***	0.01	0.03***	0.01	0.09***	0.02
VII Unskilled workers	0.04***	0.01	−0.10***	0.01	0.02**	0.01	0.11***	0.02
Adjusted R^2	0.092		0.054		0.098		0.072	

Notes
* significant at the 0.05 level; ** significant at the 0.01 level; *** significant at the 0.001 level. $N=6,880$ (6,147 for strain on personal economy). Reference categories are males, up to 25 years, lower-secondary education, and higher controllers. The dependent variables range for 0 to 1, with 1 being the most right-wing position. Asterisks for entire categorical variables indicate significance in F-tests of the block of coefficients associated with a given variable.

What should be clear, however, is that economic vulnerability as reflected in this very direct and "immigration-free" measure does not seem to play a major role in explaining either immigrant attitudes, perceptions of ethnic competition, or PRR voting.

Conclusion

This chapter demonstrates that the relative importance of education and occupational class as predictors of the populist radical right vote is strongly influenced by the parties' support profiles along the two core dimensions of political competition in West European countries. The more strongly these parties attract voters on the basis of their preferences along the libertarian–authoritarian dimension of politics, the stronger is the education profile of the parties' electorates. In our empirical analysis of the most successful populist radical right parties in the early 2000s, we found clear evidence that their support profiles are most strongly associated with preferences along the second, libertarian–authoritarian, dimension of politics. And this strong connection between the second dimension of politics and the populist radical right vote is reflected in the socio-demographic composition of these parties' electorates, which is marked by a distinct and non-class-based education profile: the least educated are three times as likely as the most educated to vote for PRR parties.

In an extended and detailed discussion of this finding, we examine to what extent it is possible to separate concerns over immigration from economic vulnerability. It is of course possible to take the position that those with lower education are more vulnerable to competition from immigrants, and therefore no further evidence is needed. Based on a broader literature on the connection between education and voting, however, we suggest that the connection between education and populist radical right support may not primarily be about material concerns, but that it could be more ideational in nature. Higher education is found, not only in our study, to decrease the likelihood of viewing immigration and ethnic heterogeneity as a social ill. The analysis in the discussion section of this chapter supported this interpretation by showing that perceived ethnic competition is much more closely aligned with general preferences toward immigration than with general preferences for redistribution or perceived economic vulnerability.

Above all, our analysis suggests that education and occupational class effects should not be seen as necessarily pointing in the same direction in explanations of the populist radical right vote. Clearly both people with low levels of education and members of the working class (and to some extent the self-employed) are economically vulnerable, but our analysis suggested that education makes a much larger difference than does occupational class for the likelihood of viewing immigration as a social ill. The larger debate about the social structure of the populist radical right vote would in our view benefit from incorporating this chapter's insight about the independent education effect, which we primarily found on preferences along the libertarian–authoritarian dimension of politics.

Appendix

Table A7.1 Predicted probabilities of voting for the radical right in Western Europe

	Model I		Model II		Model III	
	Predicted probability	Confidence interval	Predicted probability	Confidence interval	Predicted probability	Confidence interval
Education						
Lower-secondary education	0.18	(0.15; 0.20)			0.15	(0.12; 0.19)
Upper-secondary education	0.15	(0.13; 0.16)			0.14	(0.10; 0.17)
Tertiary education	0.06	(0.05; 0.08)			0.07	(0.05; 0.09)
Class						
I Higher controllers			0.08	(0.06; 0.09)	0.11	(0.09; 0.14)
II Lower controllers			0.11	(0.09; 0.12)	0.13	(0.11; 0.15)
IIIa Routine non-manual			0.10	(0.08; 0.13)	0.12	(0.09; 0.15)
IIIb Lower sales-service			0.13	(0.10; 0.16)	0.14	(0.10; 0.17)
IV Self-employed incl. farmers			0.15	(0.12; 0.19)	0.16	(0.12; 0.20)
VI Skilled workers			0.16	(0.14; 0.19)	0.16	(0.14; 0.19)
VII Unskilled workers			0.19	(0.16; 0.22)	0.19	(0.16; 0.22)

Notes
Predictions are based on the models estimated in Table 7.1. The non-varying independent variables have been kept at the following values: male, 25–60 years, upper-secondary education, lower sales-service occupation.

Table A7.2 Correlations among immigrant attitudes, economic attitudes, ethnic competition, and strain on personal economy (Pearson's r)

	Immigrant attitudes	Economic attitudes	Ethnic competition
Economic attitudes	0.08***		
Ethnic competition	0.51***	0.00	
Strain on personal economy	0.07***	–0.15***	0.13***

Notes

1 Since Vlaams Blok is only of importance in Flanders we shall focus on this region in the analyses below. Vlaams Blok has now changed its name to Vlaams Belang, but was still called Vlaams Blok at the time of the survey.
2 Similar patterns can, however, be observed in the individual countries.
3 The coding is based on the ISCO-88 scheme, using the so-called Ganzeboom (see Ganzeboom and Treiman 1996) syntax as adapted to ESS1 by Ivano Bison (see www.svt. ntnu.no/iss/ClassSyntaxes.html).
4 This difference between the first and second level of education may have been stronger if we had been able to separate vocational from non-vocational upper-secondary schooling. Regrettably this was not possible with the data at hand.
5 Similar results are obtained if age is included as a continuous variable.
6 Analyses that use a more fine-grained dependent variable on the same data find that while populist radical right voters are clearly to the right of voters of mainstream parties of the left, they are to the left of or indistinguishable from voters of mainstream parties of the right (Ivarsflaten 2008).
7 "The items were the following: "Average wages and salaries are generally brought down by people coming to live and work here.", "People who come to live and work here generally harm the economic prospects of the poor more than the rich.", "If people who have come to live and work here are unemployed for a long period, they should be made to leave.", "Using this card, would you say that people who come to live here generally take jobs away from workers in [country], or generally help to create new jobs?", "Most people who come to live here work and pay taxes. They also use health and welfare services. On balance, do you think people who come here take out more than they put in or put in more than they take out?", and "Would you say it is generally bad or good for [country]'s economy that people come to live here from other countries?". The three former items have a 5-point Likert response scale ranging from "Agree strongly" to "Disagree strongly". The three latter have 0-10-scales with labeled endpoints. The combined scale runs from 0 to 1 with 1 being the highest level of perceived ethnic competition. Cronbach's Alpha for the scale is .74."
8 Note that the ethnic competition and the immigration preference measures are not balanced. Since many more items make up the ethnic competition measure we would expect it to explain more variance than the immigration measure. This is, however, not a problem for the analysis of the social structure of the attitudes which follows below.
9 "Which of the descriptions on this card comes closest to how you feel about your household's income nowadays? Living comfortably on present income; coping on present income; finding it difficult on present income; finding it very difficult on present income." In the analyses the item is coded 0–1, with "living comfortably" as 0, "coping" as 0.5, and the two remaining categories as 1. Similar results are obtained if the analyses are run with a standard sociotropic, retrospective measure of the development in the national economy.

8   Gender, class, and radical right voting*

Hilde Coffé

Introduction

Previous research on radical right voting in Western Europe has suggested that people from lower social classes are over-represented in the radical right electorate. Betz (1994) even speaks of a *proletarization* of the radical right electoral base. The disproportionate amount of workers from the lower classes among radical right voters has been explained by economic, cultural, and political grievances (Ivarsflaten 2008; see also Oesch 2008). Briefly, the economic explanations refer to people of the lower classes as being in competition with immigrants over scare resources (including housing, jobs, and social welfare benefits) and as the main victims of economic globalization and dislocation, which leads them to be more likely to agree with radical right parties' ideas about the restriction of immigration and rejection of economic modernization (Oesch 2008). The cultural explanation contends that people from the lower social classes, who generally have lower cognitive skills, feel more threatened by different social and cultural changes, including the move toward a multicultural society and the presence of foreign cultures and immigration. Hence, they are inclined to turn to radical right parties, which represent the authoritarian response to the dominance of libertarian values and multicultural society (Ignazi 2003). Finally, the political grievance explanation argues that being confronted with unemployment and stagnating income, and dissatisfaction with the way traditional (left-wing) parties have handled the weakening economic position of workers, people from the lower classes are anticipated to be attracted by radical right parties' rhetoric against mainstream politics and politicians (Betz 1993).

Besides the over-representation of lower-class voters, men's disproportionately high presence has also been a consistent finding in research on the radical right electorate. Gender is indeed considered to be one of the main predictors of radical right voting and some research has focused on explaining this gender gap (Fontana *et al.* 2006; see also Gidengil *et al.* 2005; Givens 2004; Johns *et al.* 2011; Rippeyoung 2007). Most of these studies found that, although women are less likely to work (full time) outside the home and to have a blue-collar working-class status, these gender differences in class positions and patterns of employment fail to account for the gender gap in radical right voting. Thus, women and men do not seem to have different radical right voting behavior because of gender differences in class positions. Yet most studies have taken for granted that men and women support the radical right for the same reasons, and little is known about the interaction between gender and social class. Therefore, this chapter will explore to what extent and how class is related to radical right voting among men and women. This leads us to the following research question: *to what extent does class position affect radical right voting behavior among male and female voters?* Moreover, we will test to what extent the effects of class on radical right voting are explained in the same way among men and women. In particular, we will investigate to what extent class differences may be explained by negative attitudes towards immigrants, political dissatisfaction, and economic grievances, as suggested by previous research (Ivarsflaten 2008; see also Oesch 2008). Hence, our second research question reads: *to what extent is the influence of class on radical right voting behavior explained by economic, cultural, and political grievances among male and female voters?*

By answering these research questions, we aim to move beyond the gender gap in radical right voting and find out what motivates women and men to vote for the radical right. If there is a significant gender gap in radical right voting, there may also be substantial variation in what motivates women and men to vote for the radical right. Investigating such differences is relevant for studies on both radical right and class voting, and a failure to recognize the possible differences between the two gender groups in radical right class voting patterns would mean that empirical results reveal findings for a single homogeneous group of voters that in fact does not exist. Should class have a different effect on radical right voting for men and women, future research would have to acknowledge such gender differences.

To answer our research questions, we will perform logistic regression analyses and utilize data from the 2008 European Social Survey (ESS) and include eight West European countries that have (at least one) meaningful radical right party: Belgium, Denmark, Finland, France, Greece, the Netherlands, Norway, and Switzerland. Before turning to a description of the data and measurements, we introduce relevant theories and develop our expectations.

Theory

Time and again, it has been found that radical right parties tend to draw a large proportion of their votes from the lower social classes (e.g., Ivarsflaten 2005; see also Oesch 2008). Scholars such as Ivarsflaten (2008) and Oesch (2008) have suggested several explanations—economic, political, and cultural—for this difference in voting pattern. The economic explanation refers to the concept of *modernization losers*, among which people from lower classes are overrepresented (Betz 1994). As the numbers of industrial jobs have declined, workers from the lower strata of the economic ladder have been hit hardest by the globalizing economy and their market position has been weakened due to the spread of new information technologies and economic dislocations (Minkenberg 2000). Moreover, these so-called *modernization losers* are more likely to be in competition with immigrants over limited resources such as housing, jobs and social welfare benefits, resulting in more unfavorable attitudes towards the presences of immigrants (Coenders and Scheepers 2003). In line with this *ethnic competition* argument and considering their vulnerable and precarious economic position, people from the lower classes are attracted by the radical right parties that reject economic modernization, take a protectionist stance toward international competition, and defend the "own people first" principle (Oesch 2008).

Another explanation for the over-representation of people from the lower classes starts from *theories of politics of resentment* and *theories of protest politics*. These theories contend that some lower-class voters facing a weakening economic position are disillusioned by traditional left-wing parties, traditionally the political *Heimat* of lower-class voters, and by their elites' incapability to secure jobs and unresponsiveness to the increased economic inequality and social insecurity, in combination with the development of the multicultural society (Betz 1998; see also Norris 2005). More generally, people from the lower classes are assumed to have less political skills and a more distant relationship to politics, resulting in higher levels of political distrust (Bovens and Wille 2010). As a consequence of their dissatisfaction with politics and the traditional (left-wing) parties, they turn to the radical right and its anti-establishment and anti-politics discourse (Betz 1993; see also Norris 2005; Oesch 2008).

Besides economic and political grievances, cultural grievances have been presented as important factors leading to radical right voting among lower-class people. Indeed, both Oesch (2008) and Ivarsflaten (2005) show empirically that cultural attitudes related to issues of migration and identity are crucial explanations for the likelihood of lower-class voters being attracted by the radical right. Being less educated and having lower cognitive skills, people from the lower classes are more likely to perceive multicultural society as a threat to their way of life and are less equipped to deal with different cultural and social changes, including the shifts toward a multicultural society (Sniderman and Hagendoorn 2007). This makes them more likely to scapegoat immigrants, to have more outgroup hostility, and to use exclusive group claims compared to voters from the upper classes, who are on average more positive toward multiculturalism and who demonstrate greater cultural openness (Coenders and Scheepers 2003; see also Derks 2004). As a consequence, people from the lower classes are more inclined to turn to radical right parties, which share an emphasis on ethno-nationalism and xenophobia (Rydgren 2007) or what Mudde (2007) refers to as *nativism*: a combination of nationalism and xenophobia.

All previous studies investigating the relation between class and radical right voting have taken for granted that male and female radical right voters are similar. Indeed, whereas radical right research has shown a substantial gender gap in radical right voting, with women being substantially less likely to vote for the radical right compared to men, little focus has been given to possible gender differences in socio-economic and attitudinal characteristics that lead to a radical right preference (notable exceptions include Fontana *et al.* 2006; Gidengil *et al.* 2005), and no research has specifically assessed the impact of class on radical right voting among male and female voters. Here, we aim to fill this gap and explore how class may relate differently to radical right voting among men and women. Our general starting point is the idea that although women have made great progress during the last decades in their participation on the labor market, they are often assumed to have less strong ideas about their class and to have looser attachments to the labor market given their relatively recent arrival in the workforce (Clarke *et al.* 2005). Moreover, there is a strong tradition of basing women's class on their husband's position (Erikson 1984; see also Simpson *et al.* 1988; Sørensen 1994). As a consequence, the expectation put forward is that class will be less salient when explaining voting behavior, and radical right voting—which has been found to be class related (e.g., Ivarsflaten 2008; see also Oesch 2008)—in particular.

Besides exploring the relevance of class to radical right voting among women and men, below we will also empirically test whether different explanations for the possible class patterns are relevant for women compared to men. The notions of *economic man* and *social woman* (Gidengil 1995) lead us to expect that voting behavior will be more likely to be explained by economic attitudes and grievances among men than among women. Indeed, these concepts are based on the idea that men and women have different values and concerns, with men's policy opinions being more likely to be influenced by economic concerns compared to women. In addition, lower-class men are more likely to be working in industries that are generally hit harder by globalization compared to industries in which mainly lower-class women are present, such as the social service and health sector. Hence, economic grievances may be greater among men compared to women and also be more salient in their party choice. The finding that *pocketbook* voting is more apparent among male than female voters (Welch and Hibbing 1992) may also indicate that personal economic grievances will be a greater driving force for voting behavior among men compared to women. All this leads us to anticipate that radical right voting behavior and a possible class pattern therein is more likely to be explained by economic grievances, and in particular personal ones, among men compared to women.

In comparison to men, women tend to work in the social service and health sector, which is a sector in expansion and tends to have fewer immigrants (Givens 2004). If women, even those from the lower classes, do not feel that they are in direct competition with immigrants over a limited (or decreasing) number of jobs, women may not only have more positive attitudes toward immigrants, but immigration may also be less of a salient issue for them (Givens 2004). Hence, we expect cultural grievances, and in particular attitudes toward immigrants, to be more relevant for men compared to women when explaining radical right voting and a possible class pattern therein.

Finally, previous studies revealed that women generally have less trust in political institutions and feel politically less efficacious (Coffé and Bolzendahl 2010). Although these attitudes are reflected in the discourse of radical right parties, we also know that women are less interested in politics (Coffé and Bolzendahl 2010). This may incline that political attitudes and grievances are less relevant and salient when explaining radical right voting and the class pattern therein among women compared with men (Gidengil *et al.* 2005).

Below, we will investigate class patterns in radical right voting among men and women and empirically explore our (tentative) expectations for possible gender differences to the extent that cultural, political, and economic grievances explain the class pattern in radical right voting. We turn first to a detailed description of our data and measurements.

Data and measurements

To answer our research question and investigate the link between social class and radical right voting among men and women, we utilize data from the 2008 European Social Survey (ESS). The ESS is a cross-national collaboration of standardized surveys of the adult non-institutionalized population across European countries. More detailed information about the survey, including sampling procedures and any deviations, is available on the ESS website (http://ess.nsd. uib.no). We look at eight West European countries that have a substantial number of radical right voters, making a meaningful analysis possible: Belgium, Switzerland, Denmark, Finland, the Netherlands, France, Greece, and Norway. Listwise deletion of observations with missing data was employed (Allison 2002). The final sample size is 8,984 and includes only those respondents who were eligible to vote and who said they had voted at the last elections. Moreover, it includes only those who voted for a particular party (thus excluding those who submitted blank or invalid votes).[1] Before turning to the analyses, in the next sections we discuss the dependent, explanatory, and control variables. Descriptive statistics broken down by gender are available in Table A8.1 in Appendix.

Dependent variable

Our dependent variable relies on the question about the respondents' party choice at the last national elections and is coded into two categories: (1) voting for a radical right party; (2) voting for any other party.

Table A8.2 in the Appendix offers an overview of the parties considered as radical right in the various nations included in our study, and is based on previous radical right studies by Mudde (2007) and Norris (2005).

Independent variables

Social class

Our main explanatory variable, *social class*, has been operationalized in EGP (Erikson, Goldthorpe, and Portocarero) classes on the basis of the 1988 International Standard Classification of Occupation (ISCO88) (Ganzeboom and Treiman 1996). The EGP class schema aims to group occupations with similarities in requirements of specific human capital and with similar monitoring problems (Goldthorpe 2000). Our EGP class measurement represents eight categories and refers to the respondent's current or last job if the respondent is currently not working.[2] First, we distinguish five groups of employees (the Roman numerals refer to the categories as presented by Ganzeboom and Treiman 1996) with different responsibilities and required skills: (1) I high service; (2) II low service; (3) III routine non-manual and sales; (4) V and VI manual supervisors and skilled manual workers; (5) VII unskilled manual workers. We further introduce: (6) IVa self-employed with employees; and (7) IVb self-employed without employees. These are relevant categories for research on radical right voting behavior as some research has argued that the old middle class of self-employed craftsmen and small shop-owners have been threatened by the growth of large-scale and centralized industry (Rydgren and Ruth 2011). Some empirical tests have indeed found that radical right parties gather disproportional support from small business owners—in addition to disproportional support from people from the lower classes (e.g., Ivarsflaten 2005; see also McGann and Kitschelt 2005; Lubbers *et al.* 2002). Finally, we include a separate category (8) for those who have never been active in the labor force. The latter is a particular relevant category given our focus on gender differences and since women have a greater likelihood of never having participated in the labor market. The higher service professionals and managers are the reference category in the analyses below.

Attitudes

To measure *cultural grievances*, we include attitudes towards migration. The scale adds three similarly scaled items (0–10) measuring to what extent "people coming to live here from other countries is good for [country]'s economy," "[country]'s cultural life is undermined or enriched by people coming to live here from other countries," and "people coming to live here from other countries made [country] a worse or better place to live" ($\alpha=0.86$). Hence, the scale measures attitudes toward immigrants both from an economic and cultural perspective. Each item was reverse coded, so that higher scores refer to a more negative attitude towards immigrants.

To measure economic grievances and the more vulnerable economic position of the lower classes that may explain their greater likelihood of considering voting for the radical right, we use two indicators. One indicator refers to *general economic grievances* and is measured by one item: "On the whole how satisfied are you with the present state of the economy in [country]?" The possible answers range from (0) "extremely dissatisfied" to (10) "extremely satisfied." Answers have been reversed so that higher values refer to more dissatisfaction with the country's economy. The second indicator of economic grievances is a measurement referring to an evaluation of one's own economic situation. In particular, we introduce a statement on how the respondent feels about his/her household's income nowadays. Answer categories range from (1) "living comfortably on present income" to (4) "finding it very difficult on present income."

Finally, the measure of *political grievances* is based on two items referring to "satisfaction with the job the [country] government is doing" and "satisfaction with the way democracy works in [country]" (correlation = 0.629). Each item has answer categories ranging from (0) "extremely dissatisfied" to (10) "extremely satisfied." The answer categories were recoded so that higher scores on our sum scale refer to more dissatisfaction and thus more political grievances.

Control variables

Furthermore, we control for a number of characteristics that are known to be related to radical right voting or which may further explain class differences (and gender differences therein) in radical right voting behavior. Since women are typically more likely to work in the welfare and social services, an area that is generally more left-wing oriented (Kitschelt 1994), we include a dichotomous variable that measures the *employment in the social sector* (1), indicating that the respondent is working in the social, health or educational sector, and (0) when the respondent is working in another sector.[3] Furthermore, different socio-economic groups are controlled for. *Age* is a continuous control variable. *Educational level* is represented by three categories: less than secondary school; secondary school; and higher than secondary education. The latter category is the reference category and includes those who have achieved post-secondary and tertiary education. *Religious denomination* is a dichotomous variable with the value (0) for religious and (1) for no religious denomination. In addition, we introduce *religious attendance*, which is a continuous variable ranging from (1) "every day" to (7) "never". The answers have been reversed so that higher values refer to more frequent attendance at religious services, and recoded to start at zero. *Marital status* is coded in two categories distinguishing (1) respondents who are married or in a civil partnership from (0) those who are not. All variables and attitudinal sum scales have been recoded to range between zero and one.

Analytical strategy

Given that our dependent variable is a dichotomous variable (voting for a radical right party vs voting for a non-radical-right party), we performed logistic regression analyses. To investigate gender differences in the effect of class for radical right voting, we divide the sample by gender and test separate models for women and men. A comparison of the logistic regressions allows us to observe the different weights each gender group employs in the voting decision. For tests of significant differences between men and women, we performed analyses with gender and class, and gender and attitudes interaction terms. The significant interaction effects are marked in shaded cells in Tables 8.1 and 8.2 below.

Two multivariate models will be presented for males and females. The base model only includes the class characteristics and control variables. A second model adds political, cultural, and economic attitudes. This allows us to investigate to what extent class differences may be explained by these attitudes and to what extent these explanations are similar for women and men.

All models include country dummy variables. As a further control for country-specific influences, all standard errors are robust and clustered according to nation.[4]

Results

The results of the logistic regressions of the base model for men and women are given in Table 8.1. In addition to the unstandardized coefficients and their associated standard errors, the table reports how variation in each independent variable is estimated to change the predicted probability of radical right voting, with the other independent variables set to their means.

Focusing first on the male respondents, we find routine non-manual workers and all manual workers to be significantly more likely to vote for a radical right party than for any other party compared to high service managers and professionals, all else held constant. There seems to be a clear distinction between the service group and the routine non-manual and manual (both skilled and unskilled) groups. The probability of casting a radical right vote is 7 to 8 points higher for skilled and unskilled workers than for service managers and professionals, *ceteris paribus*. Furthermore, those who are self-employed and have no employees are slightly more inclined to vote for a radical right party (Δ prob. = 0.04) than are those with high service occupations.

The story is different for women. Although radical right voting is least common among women in high service occupations compared to the rest, the only contrast that reaches statistical significance involves women holding unskilled manual jobs. The probability of a radical right vote is 4.5 points higher among this group of women compared to those holding professional or high service managerial posts. Thus, while we find for men and women alike that unskilled work increases the likelihood of casting a radical right vote, there seems to be—as anticipated—more numerous and clearer distinctions between the different social classes among men than among women. In particular, the effect of unskilled work is less significant among women compared to men, and among men we see a greater gap between professionals and higher service managers and those who do not have a service-related job. Also interesting to note is that while neither the self-employed with employees nor those who have never been employed differ significantly from the higher service group for both women or men, additional models including interactions between female and the EGP classes indicate that the effect of both classes is significantly (at $p < 0.05$) different for men and women. In comparison to male, female self-employed with employees and those who have never been employed are substantially more likely to vote for the radical right than female higher service managers and professionals.

Looking briefly at the control variables, our results reveal that, as one would expect, working in the social and health sector modestly—but significantly

Table 8.1 Base logistic regressions radical right party choice in eight West European countries (men N=4,370; women N=4,614)

	Men			Women		
	B	SE	Δ Prob[a]	B	SE	Δ Prob[a]
Class (ref. high service)						
Low service	0.147	0.141	0.010	0.193	0.321	0.008
Routine non-manual and sales	0.507***	0.131	0.039	0.404	0.320	0.017
Supervisor and skilled manual	0.930***	0.131	0.080	0.132	0.296	0.005
Unskilled manual	0.817***	0.173	0.068	0.842**	0.320	0.045
Self-employed with employees	−0.390	0.371	−0.022	0.499	0.421	0.024
Self-employed without employees	0.541*	0.240	0.042	0.192	0.463	0.008
Never employed	−1.235	0.731	−0.049	0.507	0.322	0.024
Control variables						
Social sector employment	−0.388	0.263	−0.022	−0.629***	0.146	−0.023
Age	−1.988*	0.939	−0.121	−0.116	1.264	−0.005
Age squared	2.251*	0.928	–	−0.812	1.174	–
Educational level (ref. tertiary education)						
Lower education	0.312	0.387	0.022	0.722*	0.349	0.037
Secondary education	0.459*	0.210	0.029	0.816**	0.266	0.032
No religion	0.011	0.131	0.001	−0.135	0.101	−0.005
Religious attendance	−1.184**	0.387	−0.058	−0.648 *	0.294	−0.022
Married	−0.059	0.107	−0.004	0.010	0.144	0.000
Constant	−2.342***	0.166		−3.384***	0.371	
Pseudo R^2	0.140			0.128		

Source: European Social Survey, 2008.

Notes
*** $p < 0.001$; ** $p < 0.01$; * $p < 0.05$ (two tailed). All models include country fixed effects. Shaded cells refer to significant ($p < 0.05$) differences between males and females (based on analyses including interaction terms between female and classes).

a This column shows how the probability of a radical right party vote is estimated to change as the independent variable goes from 0 (minimum) to 1 (maximum), with all other independent variables set to their means.

(at $p<0.001$)—decreases the likelihood of voting for a radical right party, at least among women (Δ prob. $=-0.02$). Hence, women working in the *soft* sector are less likely to vote for the radical right compared to women working in other sectors. A similar, albeit less reliably estimated and non-significant, pattern is seen for men.[5] Furthermore, both men and women with a low or medium level of education are more likely to choose a radical right party than any other party compared to the more highly educated. Regular churchgoers, men and women alike, are also less likely to vote for the radical right. Finally, age has a negative effect on the likelihood to vote for a radical right party instead of any other party among men, though it increases at higher ages as demonstrated by the significant and positive effect of age squared.

Table 8.2 presents the results of the analyses, including attitudes related to political, economic, and cultural grievances, which are expected to explain (part of) the class effects. Starting our discussion with the effects of class character-istics on radical right preferences among men, we still find that those not belong-ing to the service sector differ substantially from those belonging to the high service occupational group. Indeed, routine non-manual workers and sales people, as well as skilled and unskilled manual workers, are substantially more likely to vote for the radical right compared to high service voters, net of polit-ical, economic, and cultural grievances: their probability of casting a radical right vote is 3 to 4 points higher. Yet compared to the base model (Table 8.1), the coefficients and calculated changes in probabilities decrease somewhat, indi-cating that at least some part of the effect of class may be explained by these grievances. These grievances also explain why male self-employed without employees are more inclined to vote for a radical right party. Indeed, those who are self-employed without employees no longer differ significantly from higher service voters once different attitudes are controlled for. In particular, negative attitudes toward immigrants have a major impact on the likelihood to vote in favor of a radical right party. The probability of voting for the radical right increases about one-third of a point (Δ prob. $=0.35$) as our scale of negative atti-tudes towards immigrants goes from its minimum (0) to its maximum (1). Dis-satisfaction with government and democracy also has a negative effect on the preference for another party than a radical right party. Thus in line with what one would expect based on theories of resentment and protest politics, dissatisfaction with politics is more prevalent among male radical right voters compared to men voting for another party. More precisely, the probability of a radical right vote increases by 7.4 points as our political grievances scale travels from its minimum (0) to its maximum (1). Furthermore, whereas general grievances about the nation's economy do not seem to influence men's preference for a radical right party, evaluations of the personal economic situation do matter, though mod-estly. A change from the lowest (0) to the highest (1) level on our scale of per-sonal economic grievances increases the likelihood of voting for the radical right by almost three points. Thus, the harder men find it to live on their current household income, the more likely they are to vote for another party than those of the radical right. If men feel insecure about their own household finances,

Table 8.2 Attitudinal logistic regressions for radical right party choice in eight West European countries (men N=4,370, women N=4,614)

	Men			Women		
	B	SE	ΔProb.[a]	B	SE	ΔProb.[a]
Class (ref. high service)						
Low service	0.139	0.105	0.007	0.211	0.348	0.006
Routine non-manual and sales	0.464**	0.143	0.028	0.325	0.298	0.010
Supervisor and skilled manual	0.646***	0.168	0.041	0.003	0.260	0.000
Unskilled manual	0.610***	.137	0.038	0.561*	0.269	0.020
Self-employed with employees	−0.465	0.392	0.020	0.353	0.451	0.012
Self-employed without employees	0.429	0.299	0.026	0.013	0.451	0.000
Never employed	−1.094	0.686	−0.036	0.407	0.273	0.014
Attitudes						
Neg. att. toward immigrants	4.210***	0.427	0.345	4.469***	0.321	0.242
General economic grievances	−0.411	0.412	−0.021	−0.073	0.378	−0.002
Personal economic grievances	−0.658*	0.305	−0.029	0.045	0.272	0.001
Political grievances	1.306*	0.636	0.074	1.599*	0.675	0.052
Control variables						
Social sector employment	−0.124	0.248	−0.006	−0.613***	0.168	−0.016
Age	−1.604	1.135	−0.078	−0.794	1.274	−0.022
Age squared	1.497	1.147	–	−0.565	1.319	–

Educational level (ref. tertiary education)						
Lower education	0.111	0.308	0.006	0.188	0.304	0.006
Secondary education	0.276	0.180	0.014	0.475*	0.240	0.014
No religion	0.102	0.111	0.005	−0.221*	0.110	−0.006
Religious attendance	−1.062**	0.397	−0.042	−0.537*	0.271	−0.014
Married	−0.039	0.100	−0.002	0.026	0.145	0.001
Constant	−4.777***	0.358		−6.233***	0.449	
Pseudo R^2	0.220			0.217		

Source: European Social Survey, 2008.

Notes
*** $p < 0.001$, ** $p < 0.01$, * $p < 0.05$ (two tailed). All models include country fixed effects. Shaded cells refer to significant ($p < 0.05$) differences between males and females (based on analyses including interaction terms between gender and class, and gender and attitude).
a This column shows how the probability of a radical right party vote is estimated to change as the independent variable goes from 0 (minimum) to 1 (maximum), with all other independent variables set to their means.

they seem to prefer to support another party than a radical right outsider. In other words, and in contrast to what would be expected from the losers of modernization theory, the success of radical right parties among men does not seem to be fueled by feelings of personal economic insecurity. On the contrary, personal economic grievances increase the likelihood of voting for a party other than the radical right.

Switching to the analyses for women, we still find a negative and weakly significant effect of being an unskilled worker. Unskilled female workers are about two points more likely to cast a radical right vote than female professionals and managers. Thus, even taking economic, political, and cultural grievances into account, female unskilled workers are slightly more likely to vote for the radical right compared to high service voters. Yet, the effect is modest and—compared to our base model—we do see some decline in the coefficient, indicating that at least some part of the class effect may be explained by different attitudes between the classes. In particular and similar to men, negative attitudes toward immigrants carry great weight in the explanation of radical right voting. The probability of casting a vote for a radical right party increases by about one quarter (Δ prob. = 0.24) with an increase from the lowest (0) to the highest (0) score on our scale of negative attitudes toward immigrants. Similarly, dissatisfaction with the government and the way democracy works fuels radical right voting. A change of our scale measuring political grievances from lowest to highest will increase of the probability of a radical right vote by 5 points. Thus in contrast to what we had expected, we do not find any substantial gender differences in the effect of cultural and political grievances on radical right support.[6] Both seem to matter equally for men and women when explaining radical right voting. However, whereas personal economic grievances do negatively affect men's likelihood to be favorable toward the radical right, such grievances do not seem to influence the probability to support the radical right among women. Thus, economic grievances play a more substantial role among men compared to women, which is in line with our expectation and confirms previous research by Welch and Hibbing (1992) and Clarke *et al.* (2005) that suggests that men are more likely to rely on *pocketbook* evaluations. As additional interaction models have shown (indicated by the shaded cells in Table 8.2), this effect of personal economic grievances is substantially different between women and men.

To further illustrate gender differences in class patterns of radical right voting, we calculated predicted values based on the attitudinal models for each class (other classes at 0 and all other variables held at their mean). These calculations are based on the separate male/female attitudinal models and thus take the different effects and mean levels of class and other characteristics into account.

As can be seen from Figure 8.1, in each EGP class except those who have never been employed and the self-employed with employees, men are on average more likely to vote for the radical right compared to women. The gender difference is largest among manual supervisors and skilled manuals. Male skilled

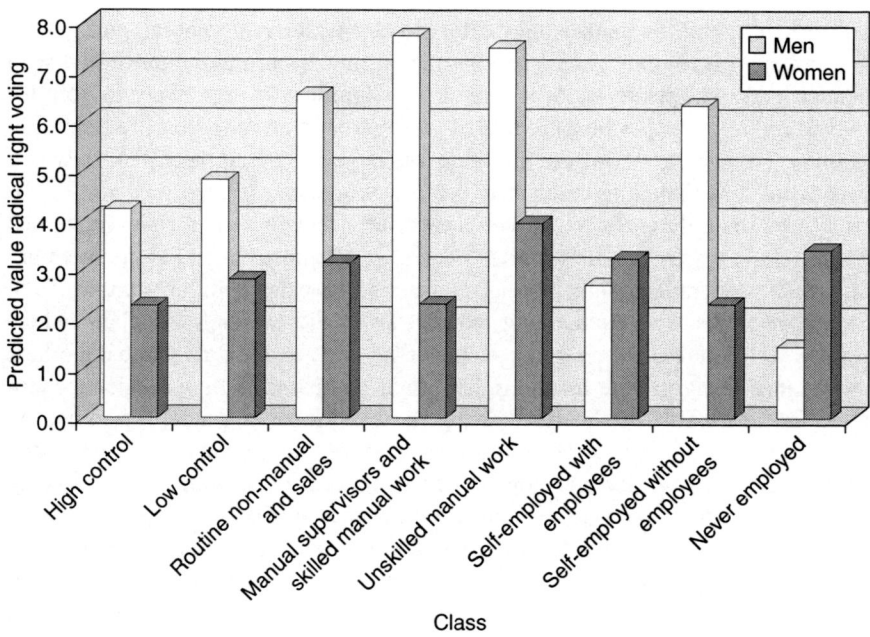

Figure 8.1 Predicted values (in percentages) for radical right voting per EGP class (based on separate male/female attitudinal models).

manuals have a predicted probability of scoring 0.077 (out of 1) or a likelihood of 7.7 percent to support the radical right. By contrast, female skilled manual workers have a likelihood of 2.2 percent. The figure also illustrates nicely how the difference in likelihood to prefer a radical right party between the EGP classes is smaller among women than among men. It is indeed particularly among men that radical right parties do not seem to appeal equally across all social classes. Leaving aside those who have never been active in the labor force and the self-employed, the predicted values among women range between 2.3 and 3.9, those among men between 4.2 and 7.7. There is also a clearer pattern in radical right voting among men than among women. Whereas the likelihood to favor the radical right increases with moving from high service manager and professional to unskilled worker (though with a small decrease again in the last category of unskilled workers), there is no such pattern among female voters. Finally, it is interesting to note the gender pattern of radical right voting among the self-employed. We find self-employed women with employees being more likely to vote for the radical right compared to self-employed men. By contrast, among self-employed without employees, men have on average a slightly higher probability to vote for the radical right than women.

Conclusion

Hitherto, the bulk of gender and party choice literature in general, and gender and radical right voting research in particular, has been mainly concerned with gender gaps. The tendency of women to be significantly less likely to vote for radical right parties has become part of the conventional wisdom of radical right politics. To date, however, the literature has largely ignored the extent to which party choice explanations differ between the two gender groups. The aim of our study was to explore to what extent class affects female radical right voters differently than it affects male voters. As such, we attempted to add to the literature on gender and radical right voting, and aimed to paint a fuller picture of the radical right voter by challenging the portrait of the *unisex* lower-class radical right voter. Whereas we do find both unskilled male and female manual workers to be more likely to vote for the radical right compared to high service technocrats and specialists, our analyses demonstrate evidence of gender differences in the effect of class on radical right voting. Among men, a clear and robust distinction between service and non-service workers occurs, with the latter being substantially more likely to vote for the radical right than for any other party. We do not find such pattern among women. Our analyses among women only reveal a minor positive effect of unskilled manual work, net of economic, cultural, and political grievances. In particular, cultural grievances, measured as negative attitudes towards immigrants, lead to greater support for radical right parties and seem to explain some part of the class differences in radical right voting for men and women alike (though these class differences are smaller among women compared to men from the start). Radical right voting is also fostered by political dissatisfaction. Radical right voting does not seem to be mobilized by general economic grievance. Yet men who feel uncertain about the economic situation of their household tend to be more likely to turn to another party than the radical right. They seem to prefer to *play safe* rather than to vote for a political outsider. We do not find such an effect among women.

Given the relatively small differences in coefficients (as also indicated by additional interaction models), it may be an exaggeration to say that there is a consistent and different male or female radical right voter. Yet, on balance, some gender differences do occur in the radical right voting class pattern, and in line with what we had anticipated, class seems a more salient force driving radical right voting behavior among men compared to women. The calculation of predicted values for the different social classes, taking all gender differences (both in effect and means) in socio-economic and attitudinal characteristics into account, indeed illustrate how class differences are more substantial among men compared to women. This is a relevant finding and emphasizes the importance of challenging the assumption of similarity between male and female voters that has informed most previous research on radical right voting. Our focus on the interaction between class and gender is particularly interesting given the ongoing changes in the status of women in the economic order, and future research may study these gender differences in greater detail. At the end, EGP class is a general measurement of class position, lacking detailed information about job content and environment. For example, women in manual jobs are more likely to be involved in the service sector, which faces less competition from foreign workers and is less likely to be dislocated. Although we controlled for working in the social, health, or educational sector in our analyses, future research investigating interactions between class, sector, and gender in greater detail is certainly warranted, in particular given our finding that employment in the social, health, or educational sector negatively influences women's likelihood to vote for the radical right, whereas it does not affect men's probability of choosing a radical right option.

Furthermore, whereas our focus was on exploring differences in the effect of class on radical right voting between men and women regardless of nation, further work can usefully take a cross-national perspective and explore the influence of national context. For example, the effect of class on radical right voting, for men and women alike, may be strongly influenced by the ideological discourse of the radical right parties and their competitors. To give an example, research on the radical right in Belgium (Coffé 2008) shows how the Social Democratic Party in the French-speaking region of Wallonia has been more successful in holding its traditional electorate of lower-class people by keeping traditional economic themes high on the political agenda in comparison with the Social Democratic Party in Flanders, which lost a substantial part of its electorate to the radical right party Vlaams Belang (previously Vlaams Blok). In addition, cross-national differences in gender diversity in the relation between class and radical right voting may be related to differences in women's position in the labor force. Indeed, it seems possible that in those countries where men and women have a more similar economic position, the effect of class on radical right voting may be less different between the two gender groups compared to countries where gender differences in economic position are stronger.

Appendix

Table A8.1 Means for all variables (standard deviations in parentheses) across eight West European countries (men *N*=4,370, women *N*=4,614)

	Range	Men		Women	
		Mean	St. Dev.	Mean	St. Dev.
Radical right voting	0/1	0.10	0.30	0.06	0.24
Class (ref. high service)					
Low service	0/1	0.24	0.43	0.30	0.46
Routine non-manual and sales	0/1	0.07	0.26	0.29	0.45
Supervisor and skilled manual	0/1	0.15	0.36	0.03	0.18
Unskilled manual	0/1	0.15	0.36	0.11	0.32
Self-employed with employees	0/1	0.05	0.21	0.02	0.13
Self-employed without employees	0/1	0.09	0.29	0.06	0.24
Never employed	0/1	0.01	0.12	0.08	0.27
Attitudes					
Negative att. toward immigrants	0–1	0.46	0.20	0.47	0.20
General economic grievances	0–1	0.49	0.25	0.52	0.24
Personal economic grievances	0–1	0.24	0.26	0.27	0.27
Political grievances	0–1	0.45	0.22	0.47	0.21
Control Variables					
Social sector employment	0/1	0.12	0.32	0.34	0.47
Age	0–1	0.41	0.21	0.41	0.21
Educational level (ref. tertiary education)					
Lower education	0/1	0.10	0.29	0.11	0.32
Secondary education	0/1	0.53	0.50	0.50	0.50
No religion	0/1	0.45	0.50	0.36	0.48
Religious attendance	0–1	0.20	0.21	0.25	0.23
Married	0/1	0.63	0.48	0.56	0.50

Source: European Social Survey, 2008.

Note
All variables have been recoded to range between 0 and 1.

Table A8.2 Radical right parties

Country	Radical right parties
Belgium	Vlaams Belang, Front National
Denmark	Danish People's Party
Finland	True Finns
France	Front National
Greece	The People's Orthodox Rally (LAOS)
The Netherlands	List Pim Fortuyn, Liveable Netherlands, Party of Freedom
Norway	Progress Party
Switzerland	Swiss People's Party, Swiss Democrats, Lega dei Ticinesi

Notes

* The author gratefully acknowledges the valuable feedback from Tim Immerzeel on an earlier version of this chapter. She would also like to thank Laura Stoker for her methodological suggestions.
1 Originally, the data set included 14,856 respondents, of which 2,195 did not turn out to vote and 1,329 were not eligible to vote.
2 We also included a dichotomous variable measuring whether the respondent was currently unemployed, since that might have affected the influence of class and since some previous research found unemployment to boost radical right voting (Lubbers *et al.* 2002). Yet the effect of being currently unemployed was not significant and inclusion of the variable did yield similar results as those presented below.
3 Since previous research (e.g., Knutsen 2005) found stronger support for radical right parties among private employees compared to public employees, we also included a variable distinguishing those who work in the public sector from those who do not. Yet the effect was not significant and did not influence our main findings.
4 The inclusion of country dummy variables is similar to creating a fixed-effects model in multilevel analyses, and controls for differences that are not independent within nations. Thus we do not focus on explaining differences between countries, but rather gender and class patterns that have emerged regardless of nation.
5 This may be because there are fewer male than female respondents working in the social, health, and occupational sector.
6 We also ran our attitudinal models including the three items of our scale measuring negative attitudes towards immigrants separately to test whether they were related similarly to radical right voting and whether they had the same effect among male and female voters. All items had a positive effect on radical right voting and our main conclusions related to the effect of class remained. Yet, the issue of whether the presence of people coming from other countries to live in the country is good for the country's economy was significantly related to radical right voting only among men. It does not affect radical right voting among their female counterparts. This supports our presumption that economic issues are more likely to be salient among men compared to women.

9 The class basis of extreme right voting in France

Generational replacement and the rise of new cultural issues (1984–2007)

Florent Gougou and Nonna Mayer

Introduction

Yesterday, the working class was the core clientele of the left. Today, all over Europe, it is increasingly giving support to the radical right. The political impact of this shift is considerable, because manual workers still represent at least a quarter of the electorate. The trend has already been documented by a host of studies (Betz 1994, 2004b; see also Kitschelt and McGann 1995; Lubbers *et al.* 2002; Ivarsflaten 2005; Oesch 2008; Spies 2010). But they do not agree on the explanatory variables, they rarely cover a long span of time and their methodologies, especially in terms of key indicators of social class and vote choice, are seldom identical.

To assess more thoroughly the extent of working-class support for the radical right and its causes, we build on the French case. The French National Front was one of the first of the new European extreme rights to develop a significant constituency, as early as 1984, and it is still considered as a model for many others. Its attraction among blue collars and the emergence of a "*gaucho-lepénisme*" or Lepenism of the Left, started to be discussed in the 1990s (Perrineau 1995, 1997; see also Mayer 2002 (1999); Evans 2000). Although the electoral base of the party shrank in the presidential election of 2007 to 10.4 percent of the valid votes (Mayer 2007),[1] a new dynamic seems to have started after the European elections of 2009 and the regional elections of 2010 (Gougou and Labouret 2010). In the local (cantonal) elections of 2011, the score of the FN rose above 15 percent. Opinion polls even give Marine Le Pen, who succeeded to her father at the head of the party in January 2011, some 20 percent of the voting intentions for the coming presidential election of 2012, and up to 36 percent among working-class voters.[2] The working-class vote is more than ever a topical issue, and the report of the socialist think tank Terra Nova, "Left: Which Electoral Majority in 2012?" (Terra Nova 2011), questioning whether the socialists would ever regain the favor of the popular classes, has sparked a heated debate.

This chapter puts these shifts in a long-term perspective, taking into account the transformation of cleavage structures and voters' alignments since the beginning of the Fifth Republic. We argue that the increasing support of the working class for the extreme right stems from three distinctive but complementary processes. The first one is a gradual dealignment of manual workers from the left, between the end of the 1970s and the end of the 1990s. It reflects the transformation of the working class (declining numbers, fragmentation, individualization, and pauperization). The second is the repolarization of the political debate along cultural lines, around the issues of immigration and law and order, instead of the economic ones that dominated in the 1960s and the 1970s (anticommunism, nationalizations, pro- and anti-welfare state), until the neo-liberal turn taken by the left after it came into office. The 1981–1984 realignment era, which led to the national electoral emergence of the National Front, marks a turning point (Martin 2000). The third process is generational. Gradually the generations born between the two world wars, who experienced the politicization of the class cleavage and the rise of the Communist Party, and the baby boomers, who were socialized at a time of economic growth and class polarization, were replaced by new cohorts of workers, who were hit by the economic recession and lacked political marks, making them more receptive to the National Front's ideas.

Data and methods

We draw from an exceptional pooled data set, gathering 25,880 observations coming from eight election studies (post-electoral) and covering more than forty years of the French electoral history, from 1962 to 2007 (Appendix I). Our dependent variable is declared vote choice in the first round of the election, which we consider a more reliable indicator than party proximity or voting intentions.[3]

Our class variable is derived from the French coding of socio-professional groups (CSP/PCS). Despite important differences in the logic of classification,[4] it is possible to recode these groups into the EGP class schema (see Table 9.1): (I) upper service class; (II) lower service class; (III) routine non-manual employees; (IV) petty bourgeoisie; and (V) manual workers.[5] Respondents were coded according to their present occupation and those who were not currently working (mainly retired and unemployed people) were assigned to their last occupation. People who had never had a job were assigned to their husband or wife's occupation; when information was unavailable regarding both husband

Table 9.1 Correspondence between the Erikson/Goldthorpe class schema and the French code of socio-professional groups and categories

Erikson, Goldthorpe (1992)	*Insee (1982)*
EGP class schema	Socio-professional categories and groups
I Upper service class	*Cadres, professions intellectuelles supérieures* (+ *chefs d'entreprise*)
II Lower service class	*Professions intermédiaires*
III Routine non-manual employees	*Employés*
IV Petty bourgeoisie (self-employed)	*Agriculteurs, commerçants, artisans*
V Working class (skilled and unskilled)	*Ouvriers*

and wife we chose the head of the household's occupation. Students and people who could not be categorized were excluded from the analysis. The other socio-demographic control variables are detailed in Appendix I, as well as our attitudinal variables of economic liberalism and ethnocentrism-authoritarianism (Appendix II).

The first section of this chapter models the global effect of class versus other socio-demographic variables (education, age, and gender) on the one hand, versus economic and cultural attitudes on the other, on the whole sample. The second one focuses on the electoral evolution of the working class. It shows its progressive dealignment from the left, especially among the younger cohorts, making it available for realignment toward the radical right, and the emergence of a new cleavage, mostly on immigration and law-and-order issues. A conclusive section analyzes the continuation of these trends, with the growing support of the working class for Marine Le Pen, at the eve of the 2012 presidential election.

Class politics, value conflicts, and radical right

To assess the class basis of extreme right voting in France, we fit a logistic regression model into our data set, focusing on the first round of the four presidential elections from 1988 to 2007 in which the National Front candidate gained a sizable share of the valid votes, which had not been the case in the previous elections studied.[6] Our dependent variable is support for the extreme right, a dummy variable, contrasting the vote for the radical right with all other votes. Our main independent variable is social class, the effect of which on support for the extreme right we test in four successive models.

The first model (1a) enters social class alone. It shows that the class variable has a statistically significant effect on support for the extreme right, which mostly appeals to the lower classes and the petty bourgeoisie. Taking upper service class as the baseline modality, all the other classes, with the exception of the lower service class, give more support to the extreme right throughout the period, but manual workers more than any other (Table 9.2).

The second model (1b) introduces basic socio-demographic control variables: generation, education, income, and gender. As a result, the effect of social class completely disappears, except for the group of routine non-manual employees where it persists, but to a weakened extent. Income, often used as a surrogate for class, has no effect either. The three other variables make all the difference. Men give more support than women to the extreme right, an established finding for which several explanations have been put forward (Betz 1994; see also Gidengil and Hennigar 2005; Akkermann and Hagelund 2007). Elderly women are more religious and therefore more conservative, prone to support the old-style right-wing parties.[7] Younger women reject the traditional conception of gender relations defended by these parties, which conversely appeal to men resisting women's emancipation (Mayer 2002: chapter 6; see also Perrineau 1997: 105–107). Women in general are repelled by the aura of violence and

Table 9.2 Logistic regression models predicting extreme right voting behavior (1988–2007)

	Extreme right vs non-extreme-right voting			
	Model 1a	*Model 1b*	*Model 1c*	*Model 1d*
Constant	–3.369**	–2.975**	–3.224**	–4.310**
Social class				
Working class	0.956**	0.277	0.417**	0.056
Petty bourgeoisie	0.707**	0.225	0.140	–0.077
Routine non-manual	0.775**	0.461**	0.562**	0.312
Lower service class	0.134	0.087	0.180	0.203
Upper service class	Ref.	Ref.	Ref.	Ref.
Birth cohort				
...– 1913		–0.241	–0.246	–0.218*
1914–1928		Ref.	Ref.	Ref.
1929–1945		0.203	0.196	0.276**
1946–1960		0.366**	0.410**	0.748**
1961–1977		0.632**	0.663**	1.157**
1978 –...		0.689**	0.807**	1.494**
Education				
University		–0.990**	–1.050**	–0.185
Secondary		–0.456**	–0.486**	–0.062
Technical, commercial		–0.028	–0.048	0.130
Primary		Ref.	Ref.	Ref.
Income				
0–20		0.148	0.285*	0.119
21–50		–0.048	0.073	–0.055
50–75		–0.020	0.073	0.045
76–90		–0.029	–0.009	–0.064
91–100		Ref.	Ref.	Ref.
Gender				
Women		–0.551**	–0.513**	–0.600**
Men		Ref.	Ref.	Ref.
Economic liberalism			0.341**	0.177**
Ethnocentrism				1.428**
N	9,934	9,934	9,934	9,934
Surveys	4	4	4	4
R² Nagelkerke	0.037	0.067	0.086	0.268

Notes
Levels of significance: * <0.05; ** <0.01. All models include a term for each year.

aggressiveness attached to these parties (Mossuz-Lavau 1997). The second key variable is education. The higher the level of education, the smaller the likelihood of supporting extreme right parties, because education opens up to other cultures, conveys the democratic norms, and protects against prejudice. Conversely, in post-industrial societies where skills and information are essential, a low level of education leads to precarious jobs and unemployment, breeding resentment that feeds support for the extreme right. For authors like Stubager (2009), education today, as class yesterday, generates group identities and awareness, as well as group conflicts. Last, generational belonging appears decisive. Compared to the baby boomers born between 1946 and 1960, who benefited from the "Thirty Glorious" years of postwar prosperity and were socialized at a time when the class cleavages and left–right polarization were strong and meaningful, the cohorts that came after are far more likely to support the FN. They are the generations of the recession, confronted with a mass unemployment that no government, whatever its political orientation, seems able to beat. And several episodes of "cohabitation" between a socialist president and a right-wing prime minister (1986–1988 and 1993–1995) or vice versa (1997–2002) have blurred the very distinction between left and right.

On the whole this model explains why manual workers appear in Model 1a to be the most supportive of the extreme right: they concentrate all the factors that account for such a vote. Manual workers are mostly men (over 80 percent), with the lowest level of education of all groups, and the cohorts coming of age to vote after the baby boomers were the most exposed to unemployment and precariousness (Mayer 2002; see also Gougou 2011).

The third model (1c) introduces attitudes toward the economy and government spending. The degree of economic liberalism is measured by questions about the welfare state, social inequalities, the weight of public services, the image of profit, stock exchange, socialism, etc., on the base of a specific multiple correspondence analysis performed in each survey (Appendix II). The impact of this attitude is significant: a higher degree of economic liberalism slightly increases the probability of voting for Le Pen.[8] But gender, education, and birth cohort remain significant predictors; their effects are even enhanced by the introduction of the economic dimension. And social class becomes significant again, the lower classes (manual workers and routine non-manual employees) supporting Le Pen more than any other group, all things being equal.

The last model (1d) includes attitudes towards "others": immigrants, but also foreigners, Muslims, Jews. These ethno-cultural attitudes are tightly correlated with a demand for law and order: restoring the death penalty, more discipline in schools, harsher sentencing, etc. Another specific multiple correspondence analysis was used, on the model of the one used for the economic attitudes, revealing an ethno-authoritarian latent dimension, in the line of Adorno's pioneer study (Adorno *et al.* 1950). The results are impressive: this attitude considerably reduces the impact of the economic dimension, and cancels out the effect of all the socio-demographic variables, with the exception of gender and generation. Education is significant in the previous models mainly because it commands the level of ethnocentrism and xenophobia. The introduction of the ethno-authoritarian attitude enhances considerably the effects of gender and, above all, generation. Each new cohort displays a higher propensity to vote for Le Pen, reaching a peak among those born between 1961 and 1977. And those born afterwards seem to be taking the same path. The global explanatory power of the model reaches its highest level.

This model shows clearly how the French extreme right benefited from two factors: the growing importance of the cultural dimension at the expense of the economic one in the political competition space, and the mechanism of generational replacement. We shall use this model to analyze more thoroughly the electoral realignment of the working class toward the extreme right.

The realignment of the working class

The fact that blue collars have become the core clientele of the extreme right appears as a paradox, especially in a country like France, where the Communist Party has long been the "working-class party" *par excellence.* At the end of the 1960s, the more working-class attributes a person had (being working class herself or himself, having a working-class father, having a working-class spouse), the higher the chance that he or she would support the Communist Party. The proportion of declared votes for the Communist Party was 43 percent among male workers combining this objective class belonging with subjective class awareness, and over 50 percent if they also were detached from the Catholic religion (Michelat and Simon 1977: 247, 443; see also Michelat and Simon 2004).[9] In the legislative elections from 1973 to 1981 some 70 percent of the workers supported the candidates of the socialist or communist left (Gougou 2011). Yet since the presidential election of 1995, when a Sofres survey showed that 30 percent of the workers had voted for Le Pen, giving more voices than to any other candidate, the FN has often been presented as "the first working-class party of France".

How could this happen? It results, as we will show, from a double process, a dealignment of the working class from the left, making this electorate available for a new political offer, and a realignment towards the extreme right, sustained by generational replacement. From our initial data base covering eight elections from 1962 to 2007, we extracted the sub-sample of 4,461 manual workers, to which we fitted a multinomial logistic regression. The dependent variable is vote in the first round of each election, in four categories (left, moderate right, extreme right, others), with votes for the moderate right as the reference category. The independent variables are birth cohort, size of agglomeration, income, gender (Table 9.3).

The predicted probabilities for workers' birth cohorts to vote for the left (Figure 9.1) show a contrasted pattern. There are movements that affect all cohorts at the same time. Thus support for the left rose slowly after the first years of the Fifth Republic, with a first peak in the 1967 legislative elections. This trend came to a stop in the aftermath of the May '68 social movement. In the June 1968 legislative elections support for the left in all cohorts declined sharply in favor of the Gaullist right, which had meanwhile negotiated the Grenelle Agreements allowing for a general increase of wages. Then the electoral dynamic of the United Left started again capturing a growing share of the working-class votes, until its victory in 1981. And after two years in office, disappointment settled in. But each cohort has a different history reflecting the moment it enters the electorate and its previous socialization (Beck 1974). The chances to vote for the left are higher among the cohorts born between the two

Table 9.3 Multinomial regression models predicting working-class voting behavior (1962–2007)

	Left vs moderate right		Extreme vs moderate right	
	β	*Stand. error*	*β*	*Stand. error*
Constant	0.528*	0.223	−0.257	0.322
Birth cohort				
…—1913	−0.915**	0.141	−1.466**	0.545
1914–1928	−0.510**	0.121	−1.000**	0.261
1929–1945	−0.577**	0.108	−0.469**	0.182
1946–1960	Ref.	Ref.	Ref.	Ref.
1961–1977	−0.224	0.125	0.075	0.170
1978 –…	−0.110	0.269	0.092	0.379
Agglomeration				
Rural	−0.596**	0.090	−0.648**	0.158
Less than 20,000 inhab.	−0.356**	0.099	−0.441*	0.178
20,000–100,000	−0.098	0.113	−0.215	0.200
More than 100,000	Ref.	Ref.	Ref.	Ref.
Income				
0–20	0.654**	0.199	−0.087	0.285
21–50	0.582**	0.196	−0.322	0.286
50–75	0.494*	0.197	−0.445	0.290
76–90	0.511*	0.219	−0.296	0.333
91–100	Ref.	Ref.	Ref.	Ref.
Gender				
Women	−0.295**	0.072	−0.677**	0.145
Men	Ref.	Ref.	Ref.	Ref.
N	4,461			
Surveys	8			
R² Nagelkerke	0.234			

Notes
Levels of significance: * <0.05; ** <0.01. All models include a term for each year.

wars or just after World War II than among those born before 1913, socialized when the class cleavage had not yet asserted itself and when politics were dominated by the opposition between republicans and monarchists. The vote of the working class for the left reaches a peak in the 1970s, when the baby boomer cohort reaches voting age, and this group remains the most faithful to the left in the 1980s and 1990s. While the two cohorts born after 1960, voting for the first time when the left is already in office, when mass unemployment has settled in and when the issue of immigration has started to loom, have systematically less chances to vote for the left than the previous ones.

The dealignment of the working class from the left profited the right in general. Since 1995, the right has been systematically drawing a majority of working-class votes in the first round of the presidential election. And the odds ratio for workers voting for the left instead of the right compared to the national

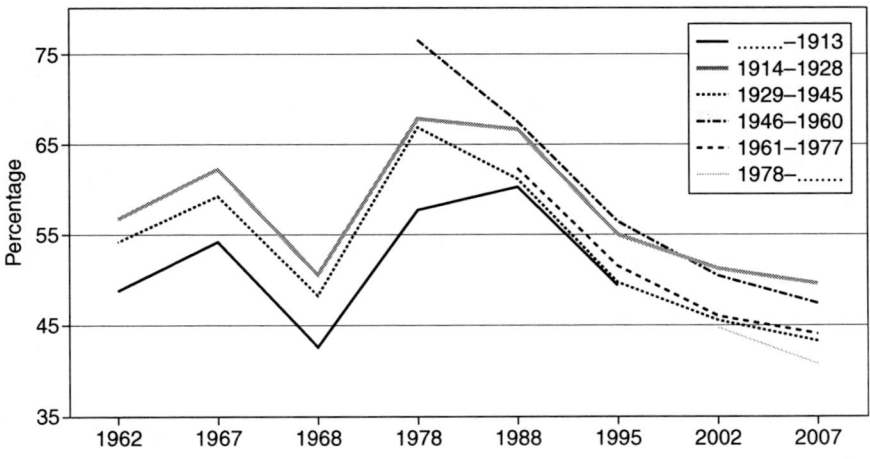

Figure 9.1 Workers' "class vote" and generational replacement (1962–2007).

Note
This figure represents the average probability of workers to vote for the left by birth cohort. These pre-dicted probabilities were computed on the base of the logistic regression model presented in Table 9.3.

average has fallen from 2.5 in the 1970s to 1 or less by the end of the 1990s (Gougou 2011). But a dynamic of realignment is also going on, that profits more to the extreme right than to the moderate right: since the first round of the 1988 presidential election, the manual workers are about twice as likely to prefer an extreme right candidate to a moderate right candidate than the average French person (Gougou 2011). This realignment is driven by the demographic renewal of the electorate: it is the new working-class cohorts that proportionately give more support to Le Pen and his party (Figure 9.2).

At first sight there is a paradox: these younger generations have the same economic attitudes as the older ones, and they are far less ethnocentric and less authoritarian (Gougou 2011). However, the paradox is solved when one looks at the respective impact of these two attitudes on the vote, by cohort and by election (Table 9.4). The older cohorts more likely to vote for the left attach more importance to economic issues, while among the post-baby-boomers, the cultural dimension outweighs the economic one. The younger workers are more tolerant and more permissive than the elder, but far more polarized on cultural issues.

From Jean-Marie to Marine Le Pen

These trends should amplify at the eve of the 2012 presidential election. The Front National is doing well in the polls and the voting intentions for its new leader, Le Pen's daughter, are taking off. Rising from 13 percent in July 2010 to 20 percent on average in May 2011,[10] for a while they even surpassed the voting intentions in favor of Nicolas Sarkozy.[11] A year away from the presidential race,

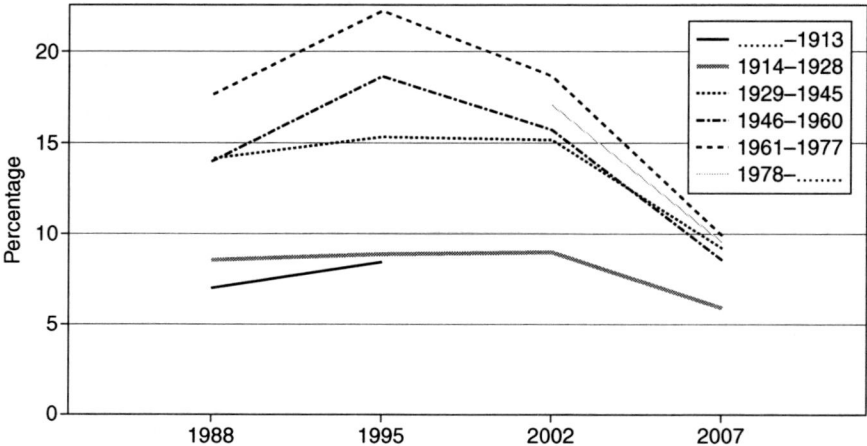

Figure 9.2 Workers' extreme right vote and generational replacement (1988–2007).

Note
This figure represents the average probability of workers to vote for the extreme right by birth cohort. These predicted probabilities were computed on the base of the logistic regression model presented in Table 9.3.

Table 9.4 The relative impact of economic and ethno-cultural attitudes on manual workers' voting behavior by birth cohort (1988–2007)

	Left voting				Extreme right voting			
	1988	*1995*	*2002*	*2007*	*1988*	*1995*	*2002*	*2007*
Workers	2.31	0.78	0.86	1.37	0.86	0.26	0.42	0.21
...–1913	1.86	–	–	–	0.75	–	–	–
1914–1928	2.35	1.11	1.03	–	0.90	0.53	1.02	–
1929–1945	2.16	0.73	0.90	1.37	0.61	0.34	0.49	0.32
1946–1960	2.06	0.73	0.84	1.26	0.88	0.32	0.43	0.30
1961–1977	1.92	0.66	0.82	1.25	0.70	0.26	0.43	0.22
1978–...	–	–	0.81	1.26	–	–	0.50	0.33

Notes
The index reported in this table measures the relative weight of economic and ethno-cultural attitudes on manual workers' voting behavior. It results from the predicted probabilities derived from four multinomial regression models (one model was performed for each election, with voting choice as dependent variable, and birth cohort and the two attitudinal dimensions as independent variables). It is computed as the ratio of the standard deviation of the probabilities predicted by the socio-economic dimension by the standard deviation of the probabilities predicted by the ethno-cultural dimension. Thus it measures which attitudinal dimension causes the more dispersion between individuals, and therefore weighs more on voting behavior.

not yet knowing for sure who will be candidate, one must be cautious with such polls. Yet they show the undeniable dynamism of the FN and its president. The political and economic context plays in favor of Marine Le Pen. Nicolas Sarkozy was elected on the promise, "Work more, to gain more." The recession shattered the dream, bringing about unemployment and precariousness. Besides the impact of the global financial crisis, the very policies adopted by his government have fueled discontent, such as the "fiscal shield" reducing the income tax of the rich (no one has to pay more than 50 percent of his or her annual income in tax) or the pension reform bill, seen as unfair for the working classes and for women, which sent millions of demonstrators to the streets (September–October 2010). Several "affairs" of embezzlement and favoritism have tarnished the image of the political class and President Sarkozy's unpopularity has reached record levels. Of the French population, 76 percent do not want him to run for a second mandate, and only 20 percent say they trust him. The Socialist Party could have benefited from this discontent, but it seems too absorbed in its divisions and quarrels about the choice of its presidential candidate. On the extreme left, the New Anticapitalist Party (NPA) is in crisis and hindered by the new party of the left, launched by the socialist Jean-Luc Mélenchon (2010). This opens a political space for an anti-system movement such as the FN that rejects both the left and the right.

Meanwhile, the revolutions in the Arab world since December 2010 are kindling fears of immigration and of Islamic fundamentalism. The annual Barometer survey on racism, anti-Semitism, and xenophobia for the National Commission for Human Right (CNCDH), conducted in January 2011, shows that intolerance toward immigrants, foreigners, and Muslims, which had been declining steadily since 1990 (Mayer *et al.* 2010), has seen all its indicators go up again since the last wave (October 2009).[12] Added together, these elements offer an exceptionally favorable context of opportunities for the FN, from which Marine Le Pen could easily profit. She has developed social issues in the direction of the lower classes, pleading for a strong state and a vibrant public service, while using the global recession to rationalize her nationalist stance (quit the eurozone, restore the French franc, close the borders, stop helping Greece, etc.).

As for the workers, their support for her and her ideas is higher than in any other occupational group. An IFOP poll in April 2011 evaluated the proportion of workers intending to vote for Marine Le Pen in the 2012 presidential election at a record level of 36 percent, 17 percentage points above the national average, the leader of the FN alone drawing more of their votes than the socialist and the UMP candidates together. More significantly, these voters agree passionately with the FN's ideas on ethno-cultural issues even more than on the economic issue of national preference for jobs (Table 9.5).

Table 9.5 Opinions about the Front National and ethnocentrism by occupation (%)

	Too many immigrants	Too many rights for Muslims	Not feeling at home	Restore death penalty	Agree with FN's ideas	National preference for jobs
Average	53	53	43	30	22	20
Petty bourgeoisie	67	62	43	27	34	17
Upper service class	31	38	22	15	8	9
Lower service class	44	47	30	20	18	12
Routine non-manual	56	55	48	35	22	20
Working class	70	68	60	42	34	30
Difference WC–Av.	+16	+15	+17	+12	+12	+10

Notes
Survey TNS-Sofres/*Le Monde*, Canal +, France Inter, face to face, 3–4 January 2011 (N=1,000, not weighted).

Conclusion

France appeared for a long time as an exception in Europe, because of the endur-
ing effect of class, as well as religion, on vote choice. Analyzing the presidential
election of 1995, Michael Lewis Beck could conclude:

> In terms of the social dimension, these 1995 results indicate that the French
> electorate remains "stalled". [...] In other nations of Western Europe these
> old cleavages have ceased to exercise their pull. But in France they still con-
> tribute reliably to the left-right political division the country has known for
> two hundred years
>
> (Lewis-Beck 1998: 51)

A closer look shows that this is not the case, and was not the case long
before 1995. As in other democracies, the class cleavage has lost its grip,
manual workers having turned away from the left and given a growing
support to the radical right represented by the Front National. Yet as van der
Waal *et al.* (2007) remind us, "Class is not Dead – It Has Been Buried Alive"
(Houtman *et al.* 2008; see also Bornschier 2010a). Economically, workers
still lean toward the left. But cross-cutting cultural issues (immigration, identity,
Islam), rooted in educational differences, have become more important, so
that ethnocentric cultural values are prevailing over redistributive economic
values.

Appendix I

Academic French post-electoral surveys

Data

This chapter mobilizes the French academic studies conducted by Cevipof (and
sometimes other partners) at each presidential election since 1988. This collection also includes a study for the 1978 legislative elections. For the 1960s, we
use academic studies achieved through the efforts of French and American
scholars: the 1962 Michelat–Dupeux study, the 1967 Converse–Pierce study,
and the 1968 Inglehart study.[13] If France does not have a tradition comparable to
the *American National Election Studies* or the *British National Election Studies*
in terms of the replication of indicators and variables, these surveys nevertheless
form a fairly long series covering the entire Fifth Republic.

Only the post-electoral surveys have been selected. Among the ten available,
two were excluded: the 1958 study, which lacked certain variables; and the 1997
study, in order to maintain the homogeneity of the data for the two main periods
of the French electoral history since 1958 (legislative elections for the period
1962–1981, presidential for the period 1984–2007). The main characteristics of
the eight surveys we use here are detailed in the following table.

Table A9.1 Academic French post-electoral surveys

	N	First investigators	Institute
L1962	1.511	G. Dupeux, G. Michelat	IFOP
L1967	2.046	P. E. Converse, G. Dupeux, R. Pierce	SOFRES
L1968	1.902	R. Inglehart	IFOP
L1978	4.507	CEVIPOF	SOFRES
P1988	4.032	CEVIPOF	SOFRES
P1995	4.078	CEVIPOF	SOFRES
P2002	4.017	CEVIPOF—CIDSP—CECOP	SOFRES
P2007	4.006	CEVIPOF	IFOP

Control variables

Our control variables are gender, birth cohort (before 1913, 1914–1928, 1929–1945, 1946–1960, 1961–1977, after 1978), city size, education, and income. Despite evolutions in the structure of the French education system, we could distinguish four levels of education: primary, technical, secondary, and university. Regarding income, we had to face two problems, since income figures are categorical and refer to the household rather than to each individual. We decided to follow recent developments in the French literature (Le Hay and Sineau 2010; see also Capdevielle and Dupoirier 1981) and divide the household income figure (the mean of the category) by the number of individuals living in the household (the first adult counting for 1 and each other person for 0.5; each child under fourteen counting for 0.3 if the question is asked). As our concern is in relative levels rather than in absolute levels of income, we could then build a five-category income variable, going from the very poor to the very rich (0–20, 21–50, 51–75, 76–90, 91–100).

Appendix II

Attitudinal dimensions

Construction

The two attitudinal variables used in this chapter, measuring the degree of economic liberalism and of ethno-authoritarianism, were constructed on the base of the data available in the abovementioned academic electoral studies (Appendix I).

The small number of questions common to all the post-electoral surveys mobilized excludes the possibility of directly comparable measures throughout the period. To bypass this difficulty we elaborated an alternative strategy, based on the idea of latent dimensions: for each survey, we assume that voters can be singled out according to their degree of agreement with economic liberalism and ethno-authoritarianism, and that these two dimensions can be indirectly approached by survey questions related to them.

The statistical technique we chose is specific multiple correspondence analysis (MCA). This technique allows us to build axes on the base of the questions integrated in the analysis, axes which display a latent dimension of the data. This method also allows us to establish a hierarchy between the axes, according to their weight in the structuration of the data, but it does not give any definite indication about their substantive content. Axes must be interpreted from the cloud of modalities and this requires us first to decide which axis captures best the attitudinal dimension we are looking for.

This method is particularly well adapted to the exploration of the answering modalities to opinion questions asked in French academic surveys: specific MCA implies nominal variables and allows us to include individuals who haven't answered a question without affecting the definition of the axes (modalities of non-interest do not take part in the computation of the distances between individuals and in the construction of the clouds of individuals).

In this method, each individual is defined by his or her factor scores on the different axes constructed. Each axis selected to measure an attitudinal dimension takes the shape of a continuous variable. However, an axis computed in one survey is not directly comparable with an axis defined in another survey, for their boundaries are not the same. To solve this problem, each axis can be transformed and standardized in standard deviation units in the survey from which it originates. Therefore in each study all the individuals have a position computed in relation to the average point of the sample from which they are extracted. By definition, this average point is zero. Thus, if the standardization of the axes does not give the possibility to follow the evolution of the average point of each sample through time (and consequently to know if endorsement of economic liberalism is increasing or declining, for instance), it enables us to evaluate the evolution of the relative position of voters depending on their social or political characteristics, which is precisely the aim of our study.

Economic liberalism

Hereafter are listed all the opinion questions that contributed to the construction of the measure of agreement with economic liberalism. In all the surveys examined, this attitudinal dimension was captured by the first axis of the specific MCA performed.

> 1978. Suppress the advantages of a good many in order to reduce social inequalities (t26). Enlarge and develop the nationalized sector (t27). Redundancies should be banned as long as a new job has not been found (t30). We live in a society characterized by class struggle (t68).

1988. If everybody earned the same salary people would have no incentive to work (q1a6). When you hear that someone has made his fortune over the course of a few years what do you feel (q3). The way the state should handle business (q4). What suggests the word socialism (q8a1). What suggests the word profit (q8a2). What suggests the word stock exchange (q8a3). What suggests the word nationalizations (q8a4)]. What suggests the word business (q8a4). What suggests the word privatizations (q8a6). The state should ensure every household a minimum income (q31a2). The surtax on the rich should be reintroduced (q31a9).

1995. What suggests the word competition (q21a4). What suggests the word profit (q21a5). What suggests the word privatizations (q21a12). Priority to the improvement of the wage earners situation or to the competitiveness of French economy (q36).

2002. Companies should not have the right to lay staff off (xq237). The way the state should handle business (xq239). The number of civil servants should be cut down (xq39p2_0). What's important is to reduce the gap between the rich and the poor (xq238_4).

2007. One should raise the taxes of people who earn more than €4,000 monthly (Q64SC). One should take from the rich to give to the poor (Q64SD). What suggests the word privatizations (Q138S1). What suggests the word profit (Q138S2). Globalization is a danger or an opportunity (Q320). The guaranteed minimum wage is a necessary helping hand or risks to incite people to make do with it (Q321). Bosses should have the right to lay staff off more easily (Q322S2). The number of civil servants should be cut down (Q322S5). The way the state should handle business (Q323). Priority to the improvement of the wage earners' situation or to the competitiveness of the French economy (Q136).

Ethno-authoritarianism

Hereafter are listed all the opinion questions that contributed to the construction of the measure of agreement of ethno-authoritarianism for each year. Here too this attitudinal dimension was systematically captured by axis 1 of the specific MCA performed.

1978. The strictness of courts towards juvenile delinquents (t74). School should primarily develop a sense of discipline or form sharp-minded people (t77).

1988. I am proud to be French (q1a4). There are too many immigrants in France (q1a9). School should primarily develop a sense of discipline or form sharp-minded people (q10). Nowadays one does not feel as at home as we used to (q31a3). Jews have too much power in France (q31a5). In a society we need a hierarchy and leaders (q31a7). It is only fair for Muslims living in France to have mosques (q31a8). The death penalty should be reintroduced (q31a10).

1995. There are too many immigrants in France (q7a1). The death penalty should be reintroduced (q7a4). It is only fair for Muslims living in France to have mosques (q7a5). Nowadays one does not feel as at home as one used to (q7a6). What suggests the word authority (q21a8). What suggests the word Islam (q21a13). School should primarily develop a sense of discipline or form sharp-minded people (q22a1).

2002. There are too many immigrants in France (xq39p2_1). The death penalty should be reintroduced (xq39p2_2). Jews have too much power in France (xq39p2_4). School should primarily develop a sense of discipline or form sharp-minded people (xq58). The importance of law and order (xq238_2).

2007. The death penalty should be reintroduced (Q64S5). There are too many immigrants in France (Q64S6). Nowadays one does not feel as at home as one used to (Q64S7). As far as jobs are concerned, priority should be given to the French (Q64SH). School should primarily develop a sense of discipline or form sharp-minded people (Q135). What suggests the word Islam (Q138S3). What suggests the word national identity (Q138S8).

Notes

1 The sudden fall of the National Front was confirmed in the 2007 legislative elections: Jean-Marie Le Pen's party did not manage to reach 5 percent of the valid votes, preventing it from getting refunded for its campaign expenses. The consequences were dramatic: the FN suffered from huge financial problems and could only present a list in fewer than half of the largest cities in the 2008 municipal elections (Gougou 2008).

2 IFOP/Europe 1, *Paris Match*, 20–21 April 2011, CAPI survey, quota sample, $N=917$ registered voters.

3 Vote choice is computed on the base of the valid votes, so that abstention is not taken into account; for details on working-class abstention, see Gougou and Roux 2011. Data are not weighted, so that the declared votes for Le Pen are slightly lower than his actual results in the four elections, owing to the moral reprobation still attached to the FN and his leader. Before the 2007 presidential election, Jean-Marie Le Pen was still considered as a danger for democracy by more than two-thirds of the French voters and was placed on the extreme right of the left–right scale by three out of four.

4 The French classification of social class does not explicitly refer to any sociological theory and does not take into account any type of employment contract (worker or service contract).

5 We excluded of the analysis the category "foremen and supervisors" because of its social heterogeneity and the contrasted support for the extreme right of the two groups it comprises. The category "workers" includes skilled and unskilled manual workers, in manufacturing and production but also storage, transportation, construction, restaurants, and crafts.

6 For the legislative elections of 1978, six years after the creation of the FN, there were only twenty-four extreme right voters remaining once missing data for the key variables of our model had been excluded.

7 Women are more abiding by the rules of the Church, which has repeatedly condemned Le Pen and his message of intolerance as being in opposition to the Evangelists. As a result of this religious practice, women vote less often for the leader of the FN than men (Sineau 2004).

8 One must remember though that votes for the extreme right are opposed to all others, and that actually Le Pen voters in our four surveys appear somewhere in the middle on economic issues: more interventionist than moderate right voters and less so than the left-wing voters. This is partly because among Le Pen voters one finds two contrasted groups, self-employed, who tend to be very liberal, and blue-collar workers, who tend to be very interventionist (see Ivarsflaten 2005; Mayer 2002: chapter 12).

9 IFOP national survey ($N=1,780$), December 1966, on "The Political Universe of the French and the Image of the Communist Party".

10 Survey TNS-Sofres/*Nouvel Observateur*/I-Télé, "Présidentielle 2012: Intentions de vote", 4 waves (20–21 August and 19–20 November 2010, 18–19 February and 20–21 May 2011), national samples representative of the French population of voting age ($N=1,000$), quotas sampling. We computed the average of the voting intentions tested with different lists of candidates.

11 With 23 percent of voting intentions versus 21 percent for Martine Aubry and Nicolas Sarkozy according to the online survey by Harris Interactive for *Le Parisien/Aujourd'hui en France*, 5–6 March 2011 (sample of 1,347 individuals drawn from the *access panel* Harris Interactive, representative of the French population of voting age, quotas sampling).

12 This was confirmed by another survey conducted at the same moment (TNS-Sofres/*Le Monde*, Canal +, France Inter, 3–4 January 2011, $N=1,000$).

13 All data are available either at the Centre for Socio-Political Data at Sciences Po (CDSP) or at the Inter-University Consortium for Political and Social Research at the University of Michigan (ICPSR), except the 1962 study. We are grateful to Guy Michelat, who could provide us with the 1962 study and made painstaking efforts to reconstruct the data set.

10 Another kind of class voting

The working-class sympathy for Sweden Democrats

Maria Oskarson and Marie Demker

Introduction[1]

In the Swedish 2010 national election campaign one of the slogans presented by the Liberal Party was "Yes to Europe".[2] The party's idea was probably not to wish for Sweden to become like the rest of Europe in terms of having a populist right party in parliament, but that is what happened. After the election in 2002, when the populist/nationalist party Sweden Democrats gained representation in many municipalities, opinion polls had shown an increasing support for the party; and in the election of 2010, the Sweden Democrats entered the Swedish parliament, the Riksdag, for the first time, with 5.7 per cent of the votes.[3] With the election of 2010 it was proved that the Swedish voters, at last, were willing to give a party with a populist xenophobic and/or nationalist political programme type a place in the highest legislative institution in Sweden, the Riksdag. As in most other European countries, support for the Sweden Democrats is comparatively strong from the working class—a phenomenon that might be seen as something of a paradox. Sweden has for many years been known as a society with solid class voting, a uni-polar ideological conflict pattern organized around economic left and right, a non-polarized political climate and also a social democracy tightly connected to the welfare state. The conditions were therefore not the most favourable for an anti-establishment, populist or right-wing party to make a sizable footprint in the Swedish working class. Nevertheless, it happened. This chapter is an attempt to explain how this could be understood. The explanation is framed in a discussion of previous research on social cleavages and political alignments, and more specifically of the importance of incorporating both the citizens' side (demand) and the party side (support). After a presentation of the general theoretical framework we proceed with a discussion of the decreasing class voting in Sweden as well as the decreasing left–right polarization between the main parties in the Swedish party system. In light of this opportunity structure we employ an individual-level regression analysis, decomposing the correlation between working-class position and sympathy for the Sweden Democrats into class-related factors, taking into account attitudes to politics as well as position along economic left–right and authoritarian–libertarian ideological dimensions.

Data

The analysis will mainly be based on a specialized national SOM survey performed in 2008, with a special focus on the effects of social class on ideology. For trends the full series of annual SOM surveys are employed. The SOM surveys are mail questionnaires delivered by the academic SOM Institute at the University of Gothenburg.[4] The SOM surveys have been launched annually since 1986, with nationwide representative samples. This survey has several advantages for the present analysis. First of all, it is a survey conducted by mail rather than face to face, and this is believed to have a somewhat lesser bias regarding sympathies for the populist right, which is not altogether socially uncontroversial. Second, it focuses on party sympathy rather than voting, and does so before the election campaigns have started. We consider this an advantage here, as it focuses on the more underlying trend in support of the party, rather than short-term effects of campaigning and mobilization.

Previous research

Sweden Democrats is not unique as a populist/nationalist party receiving strong support from the working class. All around Europe, multiple studies have reported a clear working-class bias in the support for populist/nationalist parties (Ivarsflaten 2005; see also Lubbers *et al.* 2002; Oesch 2008) This could be described as a puzzle, as the working class is generally seen as closely linked to the political left, and not least to social democratic parties (Blomqvist and Green-Pedersen 2004; see also Rydgren 2007; Swank and Betz 2003). On a general level the success of populist/nationalist parties, not the least among the working class, could be seen as a consequence of the decline of class voting.

The political alignment of the working class to the social democratic parties was formed in the early days of European democracy, and has formed something of a baseline for most party systems (Bartolini and Mair 1990; see also Korpi 1983; Lipset and Rokkan 1967). However, for several decades now the alignment has weakened, as discussed in the massive research on the decline of class voting (Clark and Lipset 2001; see also Evans 1999; Franklin *et al.* 1992; Knutsen 2006; Manza *et al.* 1995; Nieuwbeerta and Ultee 1999; Oskarson 2005). The decline of class voting has been explained by changes in the societal structures and conflict lines among citizens due to modernization and globalization, increasing educational levels and changes in people's value structures. However, the existence of class voting is not only related to the voter side (demand side). In order for class-related interests to matter for voting the parties themselves must differ in respect to these interests and values, so the explanation to decreasing or changing class voting might found on the party side as well as on the social or individual side. Multiple studies have shown that parties—not least social democratic parties—have changed in terms of ideological outlook, organization and links to interest groups. Party systems are also found to be less polarized, not the least along the traditionally class-based economic left–right dimension. These explanations are discussed below in relation to working-class support for populist/nationalist parties.

Demand side

In the literature it is often stated that social marginalization and economic risk exposure are important determinants for working-class right populist party (RPP) support, linked to a model of globalization where a group of "losers" is put up against another group of "winners" (Betz 2004; see also Rydgren 2007; van der Brug 2003). The argument states that, due to modernization and globalization, people in low-qualified jobs, in nation-bound or in traditional sectors and with low education risk losing in a situation where competition for jobs and resources has become global due to open borders and migration. The winners, on the other hand, are people with high education and in internationally competitive sectors of the labour market. This transformation of social cleavages is expected to be reflected politically in (at least) three regards, presenting possible explanations for the labour-class support of populist/nationalist parties.

A first line of explanations takes hold of the parties' anti-immigrant profile, and sees the working-class bias as an expression of economic conflict in terms of competition in the labour market from immigrants. The economic conflict explains working-class support for populist/nationalist parties through the effect of open borders on competition for jobs. Immigration and open borders are seen as a threat to the traditional production industry, and thereby to working-class jobs (Fireside 2002). A second line of explanations rather focuses on the nationalist/traditionalist aspect of the parties, and explains the working-class support more in terms of defence of traditionalist and also authoritarian values (Lipset 1959; see also Napier and Jost 2008). This cultural-conflict explanation rather focuses on immigration and open borders as a threat to national culture and a rejection of multiculturalism. A third line of explanations rather sees the populist/nationalist parties as protest parties, opposing the "political establishment" in defence of the "ordinary people", and accordingly focuses more on the anti-political or anti-elite aspect of the parties (Abedi 2004).

Daniel Oesch presents a most relevant analysis of working-class support of populist/nationalist parties in five West European countries (Austria, Belgium, France, Norway and Switzerland), where he employs three lines of explanations: economic conflict; cultural conflict; and alienation. The third line of explanations in Oesch's study sets focus on discontent with the political system and social alienation. His analysis finds the strongest support for the hypothesis stating cultural conflict as the motive behind working-class votes for populist/nationalist parties, even though discontent with the way democracy works is also part of the explanation for Belgium, France and Norway. In in Oesch's study both the economic conflict and cultural conflict are understood as being directly related to immigrants, rather than to the wider ideological dimension of authoritarian vs libertarian values, opposing libertarian values of tolerance and openness with more traditional and nationalistic values (Oesch 2008). Many studies have found strong correlations between low education and support for populist/nationalist parties as well as of more authoritarian ideological leanings. Danish political scientist Rune Stubager examines these parties, and mainly the Danish People's Party, from a cleavage perspective, and shows educational differences as a main explanation for support of the Danish party (Stubager 2006, 2009, 2010). As education is in general very closely associated with class position, this could indicate that the mechanism behind working-class support for RPP parties is education rather than class-related factors in the labour market. The relatively high support from the working class for this kind of party could be a reflection of low educational levels among the working class.

Support side

The weakening of "class voting" is also reflected in party systems, as most systems have seen a weakened political polarization between left and right in traditional economic terms. Rather, new issue areas such as environment, European integration, multiculturalism and immigration, as well as libertarian values, have led to a change in ideological competition between the parties (Albright 2010; see also Green-Pedersen and Mortensen 2010).

In a now well known study (Kriesi *et al.* 2006) it is shown that the potential political tension between the "losers" and the "winners" in globalization processes has been incorporated in the existing two-dimensional national political spaces. The cultural dimension has been gaining importance, as it has become the primary basis for new populist parties. But that bias has been around since the 1970s and the competition in most West European countries has been tripolar for some time: left, right and cultural. The new populist/nationalist parties have managed to constitute a "new" third pole only in France, which is, however, the most left–right-dimensional country in Western Europe except Sweden. According to Kriesi *et al.*, the concept of "winners and losers" has not added any value to earlier explanations.

Instead, globalization's new potential for mobilization has been directed through established competition patterns, irrespective of being fed through new party organizations. This result implies that it is plausible to explain working-class support—provided "losers" are to be found in the working class—for populist/nationalist parties through the third pole in Kriesi *et al.*'s study: the changing cultural dimension.

Party position (supply-side explanations) link the successes for populist/nationalist parties to general changes within the party systems and not the least the social democratic parties. The argument is in short that social democratic parties responded to the mobilization of the new left movement in the 1970s by incorporating more libertarian positions in order to gain (or keep) support from the middle classes. As a result of the articulation of libertarian positions, their counterpart—more traditionalistic, communitarian—was also mobilized, and provided the fertile soil for modern populist/nationalist parties (Bornschier 2010a; see also Kitschelt 1997; Kriesi *et al.* 2006; Lubbers *et al.* 2002). With increased immigration this position was linked to communitarian and nationalistic values, defining immigration as a threat to national values and culture. However, the mobilization and repositioning of parties along the authoritarian–libertarian dimension does not mean that the more traditional economic left–right dimension has disappeared. The position of populist/nationalist parties along this dimension has been widely disputed, not least in the decision to position such parties to the right. Rather than being right-wing parties in economic terms (anti-tax, anti-state, pro-market), these parties have been found to hold something of a middle position, putting lesser salience on economic issues that cannot be linked to immigration (Ivarsflaten 2005).

The ambition in this chapter is to explore working-class sympathy for populist/nationalist parties in the Swedish case. Does its political context—being a social democratic welfare state, having historically a high level of mobilized class voting and a history of extensive labour immigration—have any significant impact on the pattern of support for Sweden Democrats among the working class? Can we distinguish one of the former discussed models as a leading explanation? Is the explanation of class profile for the Sweden Democrats different from equivalent explanations for comparable countries in previous research? The chapter proceeds with a short discussion of the political context of Sweden in 2010 and of class voting in Sweden. It next discusses material and analytical strategy, as well as measurement and models. The analytical strategy is to examine the correlations between class position and support for the Sweden Democrats through a series of binomial regression with different blocs of intermediate variables (Aneshensel 2002). The chapter ends with a discussion of the results and their implications for our understanding of the Sweden Democrats.

The Swedish political context

As stated in the introduction, the populist/nationalist party Sweden Democrats has a clear working-class bias among its supporters. Table 10.1 presents the party support in different class categories in the fall of 2008, and Table 10.2 presents the class composition of the parties' sympathizers.

The main over-representation in support for the Sweden Democrats comes from people in so-called lower technical work, which means, for example, occupations within transport, inventories and workshops (skilled blue collars). The Sweden Democrats was the second-largest party in the sympathies of skilled blue-collar workers (lower technical), outnumbered only by the Social Democrats. Among people occupied in lower sales and service the support was weaker, while sympathy for the party among routine workers was equal to the average level of support. This means that the Sweden Democrats receive its strongest support from what at least used to be the Social Democrats' core groups. In terms of composition of party sympathizers, the Sweden Democrats leaned heavily on the working class, as Table 10.2 shows.

Slightly over 50 per cent of the sympathizers of the Sweden Democrats came from people in lower sales and service or in lower technical occupations. This is

Table 10.1 Party sympathy among social classes (ESeC) in Sweden 2008 (per cent, Sweden Democrats highlighted)

	V	Soc. Dem.	C	Lib.	Cons	CD	Green	SD	Oth.	Sum	N
Managers and professionals	6	26	6	14	32	4	10	1	1	100	700
Intermediate occupations	5	41	3	6	23	4	11	5	2	100	368
Small employers and self-employed (incl. farmers)	2	17	20	6	43	4	3	5	0	100	112
Lower sales and service	5	45	6	5	16	5	8	7	3	100	385
Lower technical	7	46	6	1	12	2	8	15	3	100	179
Routine workers	7	49	9	7	11	4	4	5	4	100	224
Total	6	36	6	8	24	4	9	5	2	100	1,968

Source: Klass-SOM 2008. V = Left Party (left socialist), Soc. dem. = Social Democratic Party, C = Centre Party (agrarian), Lib. = People's Party (liberal), Cons = Moderate Party (liberal conservative), CD = Christian Democratic Party, Green = Environmental Party, SD = Sweden Democrats (populist/nationalist party).

Table 10.2 Class composition (ESeC) among party sympathizers in Sweden 2008 (per cent, Sweden Democrats highlighted)

	V	Soc. Dem.	C	Lib.	Cons	CD	Green	SD	Oth.
Managers and professionals	38	25	30	60	49	37	41	10	12
Intermediate occupations	18	21	9	13	18	19	23	17	23
Small employers and self-employed (incl. farmers)	2	3	17	4	10	6	2	6	0
Lower sales and service	16	24	19	12	13	24	19	27	27
Lower technical	11	12	9	1	5	4	9	28	15
Routine workers	15	15	16	10	5	10	6	12	23
Sum	100	100	100	100	100	100	100	100	100
N	109	718	127	159	467	79	171	98	40

Source: Klass-SOM 2008. V = Left Party (left socialist), Soc. Dem. = Social Democratic Party, C = Centre Party (agrarian), Lib. = People's Party (liberal), Cons = Moderate Party (liberal conservative), CD = Christian Democratic Party, Green party = Environmental Party, SD = Sweden Democrats (populist/nationalist party).

a clearer working-class bias than for any of the other parties, leading us to ask if we here see another kind of class voting than the traditional.

The opportunity structure for the Sweden Democrats

Sweden was long considered one of the countries where the social democratic hold of the working class is strongest. The party system of Sweden has been characterized as strongly uni-dimensional, organized around the left–right dimension based in the class cleavage (Knutsen 2006; see also Nieuwbeerta and Ultee 1999; Oskarson 2005). The Swedish Social Democrats has over time managed to keep its strong support in the working class and among labour union members, while at the same time also receiving considerable support from the middle layers. One explanation for this successful strategy has been claimed to be a strong connection between the Social Democrats and the encompassing welfare state. First of all, the party has traditionally held issue ownership of welfare politics as well as employment politics. Second, Swedish welfare politics has through its universal and generous character also included the middle class and thus received a strong support from wide strata of the population. In particular, support from those employed in the public sector has been quite strong since the late 1970s, when there was intense expansion of the welfare state. The association between voters' class position and party sympathy has long been among the strongest in the Western world, even though a decline in this association has been discussed over several decades, not least in relation to younger generations (Oscarsson and Holmberg 2008; see also Oskarson 1994, 2005). However, within the working class the support for the Social Democratic Party has varied over the years, but for the last twenty years no clear trend can be found, as illustrated in Figure 10.1.

As is clear from Figure 10.1 the support for the Social Democrats among the groups that form the working class is higher than the parties' total support among the entire population, and generally follows the overall trend closely. But with the decreasing overall support for the Social Democratic Party, this means that in many years less than 50 per cent of the working class support the Social Democrats, even in the traditional "core group" of skilled workers (lower technical). The Social Democrats' strong grip of the Swedish working class is no longer that firm, in other words.

As most populist/nationalist parties in Europe, the Sweden Democrats mobilize on criticism of immigration. However, the party's growing strength is not due to increasing levels of immigration-negative attitudes in the Swedish electorate. Rather, Swedish attitudes on immigration and receiving refugees have been getting more tolerant for almost two decades. Swedes are now more tolerant towards foreigners of all kinds than they were in the 1990s (Demker 2011). Figure 10.2 shows that the attitude towards refugees in 2010 is more open and welcoming than at any time since the study began in 1990, even though there is a clear pattern of more positive attitudes in the higher salariat. In all classes presented in Figure 10.2, the proposal of "receiving fewer immigrants" shows

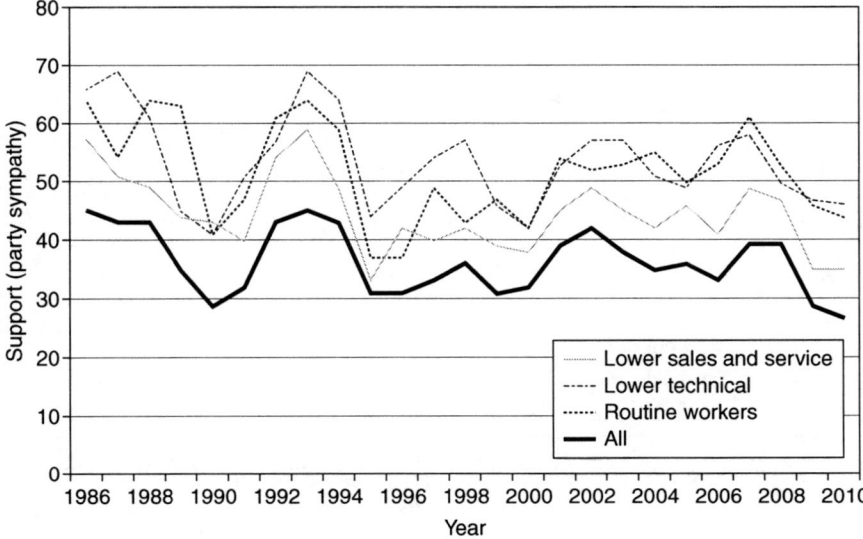

Figure 10.1 Support (party sympathy) for Social Democrats in the working class 1986–2010 (source: SOM surveys 1986–2010).

decreasing popularity between 1990 and 2010. The trend is basically the same in all groups. In other words, working-class support of the Sweden Democrats is not explained by a sudden rise of immigration-negative attitudes in the working class. Rather, it could be argued that the mobilization of immigration negativism was possible due to a weaker left–right mobilization.

The Swedish Social Democratic Party has, like most other similar parties, adopted libertarian values and a clear support for multiculturalism in recent years, while at the same time in many respects becoming more market oriented (Keman 2010; see also Kitschelt 1994). The Conservative Party on the other hand has in later years tuned down its neo-liberal profile and put more focus also on welfare issues, leading these two main parties to be more similar. An illustration of this development is presented in Figure 10.3, where the changing emphasis in election manifestos between the Social Democratic Party and the Conservative Party are compared (Klingemann *et al.* 2006; see also Volkens *et al.* 2010).

The columns in Figure 10.3 illustrates the difference between the two parties in terms of the share of their respective election manifestos devoted to matters regarding market economy and welfare. Positive values indicate that the Conservative Party devotes more space, and negative that the Social Democratic Party devotes more space. It is clear that the difference between the parties has decreased in terms of the emphasis they place on these issues. The Conservative Party is less dominant on issues regarding the market economy, and the Social Democratic Party is less dominant on welfare issues. Also in voters' placement

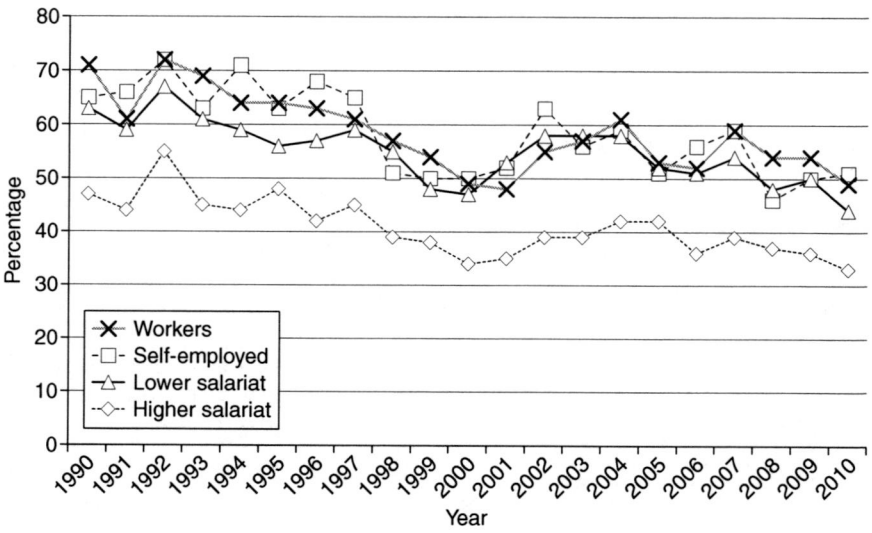

Figure 10.2 Swedish attitudes among social groups to receiving fewer refugees to Sweden 1990–2010 (per cent thinking fewer is a good suggestion) (source: SOM surveys 1990–2010. The graph presents answers "very good proposal" and "good proposal" combined).

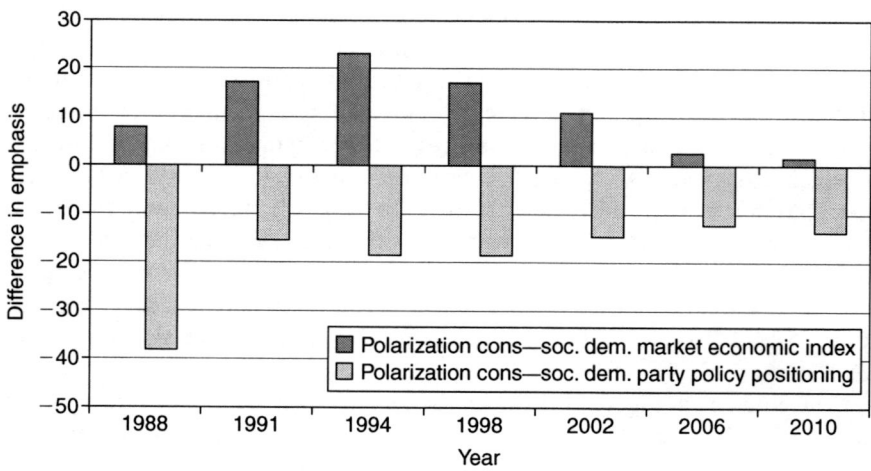

Figure 10.3 Difference in emphasis of economy versus welfare in election manifestos of the Social Democratic Party and Conservative Party 1988–2010 (source: Manifesto project Database http://manifestoproject.wzb.eu/).

of the parties on a left–right scale, the two main opposing parties are perceived to be slightly closer together (Oscarsson and Holmberg 2008). In spite of both increasing tolerance and efforts to "block" the Sweden Democrats, the ideological climate together with the increasing similarities between left and right could be seen as providing a favourable opportunity structure for the Sweden Democrats (Bornschier 2010b; see also Kitschelt 1997).

While the polarization on market economy and welfare policies has become less pronounced in Swedish politics, immigration issues have not been much politicized in the traditional Swedish party system. In advance of the election of 2006 the four right-wing parties (the Conservative Party, the Liberal Party, the Centre Party and the Christian Democratic Party) formed a firm alliance, which proved successful and won the majority in the election. One of their main themes was to take hold of the labour market policy area and introduce what they labelled "the work line", incorporating reforms of unemployment policies as well as of the social insurance system. This meant that "issue ownership" of labour market policies and welfare policies was successfully challenged, and in these central respects the Social Democratic Party and the Conservative Party were considered as standing much closer than in previous years—at least on a rhetorical level (Blomqvist and Green-Pedersen 2004; see also Martinsson 2009).

The Sweden Democrats have put forward immigration issues in their election campaigns, both in 2006 (when the party did not manage to win any seats nationally) and in 2010. During the party's year in the parliament it has broadened its agenda to care about the elderly and criminal policy, subjects that are not new for the party but are now more emphasized. The Sweden Democrats did nearly twice as well in the national election of 2010 than in 2006, gaining twenty seats and 5.7 per cent in the Swedish parliament, the Riksdag. The result in the 2010 national election was not unexpected, since the Sweden Democrats have been present in an increasing number of municipalities ever since the election of 2002, and have also received increasing support in opinion polls since the national election of 2006. The Centre-Right Alliance (composed of the Conservative Party, the Liberal Party, the Centre Party, and the Christian Democrats) was re-elected, but without a majority of the seats in the parliament. However, the challenging opposition of the Social Democrats, the Left Party and the Green Party did not have a majority either, as the Sweden Democrats received seats and ended up in a somewhat pivotal role. The ambition of the established parties has so far been to try to isolate the Sweden Democrats, and several discussions and adjustments crossing the line between the alliance and the opposition have taken place.

With this broad picture of the Swedish political context that is the opportunity structure for the Sweden Democrats, we now proceed to testing the main micro-explanations for working-class support for populist/nationalist parties as discussed above.

Methods and measurements

The test of various explanations for working-class support for the Sweden Democrats is performed through a series of binomial logistic regressions of successive models, following previous research. By statistical elaboration we have tried to decompose the correlation between class position and sympathy for the Sweden Democrats (Aneshensel 2002). In other words, a successful explanatory model would decrease the effect of class position significantly, and instead capture significant effects of intermediate factors. The initial step is to state what should be explained—that is, describe the class base of support for the Sweden Democrats—and includes accordingly the focal association between class position and sympathy for the Sweden Democrats compared to sympathy for any other party. Class is here understood as based on position in the labour market, and is measured using the European Socio-economic Classification (ESeC), theoretically derived mainly from John Goldthorpe's work (Goldthorpe 2000; see also Goldthorpe *et al.* 1980; Harrisons 2006). The classification bears upon the respondents' present occupation. In case of absence from the labour market (unemployment, sick or parental leave, retirement) the classification bears upon previous occupation. Additional variables for being a student or not, and active on the labour market or not, are also added to the base model in order to incorporate all relevant groups. This model is controlled for compositional effects of gender and age (four categories) in order to state the effect of class. Previous studies have found a clear gender pattern in support for populist/nationalist parties, so the class effects might be reflecting the gendered structure of the Swedish labour market. Also, support for populist/nationalist parties have been found to be stronger among younger citizens, and in unqualified jobs young people tend to be over-represented since developing a career usually takes time.

The analysis proceeds as follows. Four main explanations for working-class support based on previous research will be tested on the Swedish case: class-related factors; education; political alienation; and ideology (Oesch 2008). In a sense, the explanatory power of the separate models can tell us something about the character of the party. If the explanation based on political alienation and political marginalization is valid, the populist character of the party is verified. If, on the other hand, ideological values reflecting nationalism and authoritarianism have explanatory power, this could be taken as a verification of the nationalist character of the parties. Finally, if values reflecting the economic conflict in terms of left and right have explanatory value, the "right" aspect of the party is verified (Ivarsflaten 2005). The analysis starts out by taking each of these explanations separately, in order to avoid over-controlling. In a final model all four explanations are tested simultaneously.

A first model tries to discern to what degree the association between class position and support for Sweden Democrats is related to factors in the working life, or whether it is a reflection of class-related educational differences. Educational level is one of the main factors behind occupation and thereby for class position. At the same time, educational level has proved to be central for many aspects of how an individual relates to politics, for value orientations as well as interest and engagement. According to Rune Stubagers' studies of authoritarian values and support for the Danish People's Party, it is educational level rather than class position that matters (Stubager 2006, 2010). Also for Sweden, previous research has found class differences in position along the authoritarian–libertarian dimension to be explained mainly by differences in education (Berglund and Oskarson 2010). Education is measured in four levels: low education (compulsory); medium low (high school); medium high (education above high school but not a university degree); and high education (university degree).

The next model focuses on subjective feelings of class and exposure to unemployment risk, and incorporates controls for working-class identification and fear of unemployment (dichotomies), where the hypothesis is that it is feelings of risk exposure and exploitation rather than actual occupational factors that explain the class bias in support of the Sweden Democrats.

In the third model, the explanation based on political alienation is tested. Many previous studies showing how an individual's relation to the political sphere matters for sympathy for populist/nationalist parties stress a discontent with the political system and politicians as an explanation for voting for populist/nationalist parties (Hainmueller and Hiscox 2007; see also Mayer 2005; Rydgren 2002; Swank and Betz 2003). However, low trust for politics or discontent with how democracy works does not really suffice as an indicator of political alienation. An individual's report on low trust or discontent could be an expression of a sound but initiated criticism of how present politics works, rather than an indication of distance or *Entfremdung* from the political system (Dalton 2004; see also Norris 1999, 2011). Low or decreasing political trust has different consequences depending on personal dispositions and individual resources. While low political trust might be a basically necessary and mobilizing attitude to politics among well educated citizens with a high political interest and engagement, it might reflect an exit from politics altogether among citizens with fewer political resources, low political interest and low engagement. For this reason, Model 4 also controls for political interest.

The final explanatory category focuses on ideology as the explanation for working-class support for the Sweden Democrats: first the general left–right orientation and then the orientation along the authoritarian–libertarian dimension (Berglund and Oskarson 2010). The left–right dimension is associated with what Lipset and Rokkan (1967) once called the owner–worker cleavage—i.e. class conflict—which they regarded as an almost universal conflict line in Western societies, and one that is especially salient in the Swedish context. This dimension can be regarded as a basic test case for the significance of class position. However, one main critique of the relevance of class is that new issues have entered the political arena. Political challenges and issues related to globalization, environmental problems and migration have actualized other social divisions and stressed complementary ideological dimensions in most European countries (Flanagan 1987; see also Flanagan and Lee 2003; Kitschelt 1994; Kriesi *et al.* 2006; Kriesi 2010; Stubager 2008). One important dimension in this regard is the authoritarian–libertarian dimension, regarding issues of tolerance and hierarchical social relations. Survey questions were posed on policy proposals expected to capture the two ideological dimensions, in line with previous research (Evans *et al.* 1996; see also Knutsen and Kumlin 2005; Lachat and Dolezal 2008).

Ideological positions will here be measured from dimensions based on attitude questions, following previous studies (Berglund and Oskarson 2010). The respondents were asked to evaluate the proposals on a five-point scale ranging from a "very good" to a "very bad" proposal. Two scales were then created (summated indexes, transformed to vary between 0 and 10). The first consists of seven items measuring the left–right orientation ($\alpha=0.72$). These reflect attitudes to policy proposals on income inequalities, the strictness of employment protection, the size of the public sector, privatization of health care, the selling of state-owned companies, the level of unemployment benefits and the introduction of a six-hour work day. The higher the value on the scale, the more a person's political beliefs are leaning to the right. The second scale measures the authoritarian–libertarian dimension and is a summation of five items ($\alpha=0.63$). It consists of attitudes to policy proposals about the right to free abortion, gays' right to marriage, the introduction of the death penalty, the safeguarding of Swedish traditions and values and whether fewer refugees should be received in Sweden. Higher values indicate more authoritarian opinions. To state the causal order between attitudes and party sympathy is not easy, since party sympathy might form the individuals' attitudes on matters. However, the general assumption in previous research, which is also followed here, assumes ideology to be the prior (Oesch 2008). The final model incorporates all factors. Since ideology is causally more closely related to party sympathy than factors prior in the analysis, the final model with all factors included is expected to decrease the effects of prior variables—not least education, as earlier research has found this to be a major explanatory factor for authoritarian–libertarian ideological position (Berglund and Oskarson 2010; see also Stubager 2008).

Results

Table 10.3 presents the results from the binominal logistic regression regressions. The three class positions making up the working class—lower sales and service, lower technical (skilled workers) and routine workers—are highlighted in the table. The main purpose here is *not* to explain support for the Sweden Democrats per se, but to test the four explanations of working-class support discussed above. This means that we wish to discompose the effects of a working-class position by other variables, and thus the effect of working-class position would diminish or totally vanish in order to draw the conclusion that we have an explanation.

Model 1 confirms that a working-class position is associated with stronger support for the Sweden Democrats. It is the more qualified positions within the working class, however, that show significant effects. "Routine worker", as well

Table 10.3 Explaining sympathy for the Sweden Democrats (binomial logistic regression b coefficients)

	Model 1	Model 2	Model 3	Model 4	Model 5	Model 6
Managers and professionals	ref.	ref.	ref.	ref.	ref.	ref.
Intermediate occupations	1.07*	0.57	1.09*	0.78	0.16	-0.01
Small employers and self-employed (incl. farmers)	0.78	0.28	0.77	0.63	-0.18	-0.61
Lower sales and service	1.34***	0.79*	1.38***	1.05**	0.73	0.51
Lower technical	1.89***	1.27**	1.95***	1.48***	1.10*	0.93
Routine workers	0.55	-0.05	0.6	0.1	-0.18	-0.39
Students	-0.11	0.17	-0.10	-0.17	0.71	0.59
Outside of labour market	0.35	0.27	0.39	0.06	0.63	0.69
Age 15–19	1.88**	1.93**	1.76**	1.95**	2.05**	1.79*
Age 20–49	0.68	1.06*	0.61	0.68	1.02*	1.07*
Age 50–65	0.11	0.31	0.06	0.13	0.11	0.06
Age 66–85	ref.	ref.	ref.	ref.	ref.	ref.
Sex	0.45	0.4	0.46	0.35	0.35	0.13
Low education		**1.60****				**1.04**
Medium-low education		**1.35***				**1.15**
Medium-high education		**0.6**				**0.62**
High education		**ref.**				**ref.**
Fear of unemployment			**0.48**			**0.36**
Working-class identification			**-0.14**			**-0.61**
Political trust (index)				**-0.46****		**-0.34****
Political interest (index)				**-0.01**		**0.09**
Left–right ideology					**-0.01**	**0.05**
Authoritarian–libertarian ideology					**0.93****	**0.84****
Intercept	*-5.02****	*-5.92****	*-5.01****	*-2.67****	*-9.38****	*-8.69****
Nagelkerke's R²	0.11	0.14	0.12	0.21	0.37	0.42
N	1,605	1,605	1,605	1,605	1,605	1,605

Source: Klass-SOM 2008. Significance levels * <0.05, ** <0.01, *** <0.001. All variables are dichotomies except political trust (index 0–10), political interest (index 0–10), left–right ideology (index 0–10) and authoritarian–libertarian ideology (index 0–10). All indexes are presented in the text.

as a position outside of the labour market, does not show significant effects. We also have a significant effect of "intermediate occupations" (supervisors, lower white collars). Apart from the effect of class position, the only other significant factor is age, and to be younger (fifteen to nineteen years) compared to being older (over sixty-six years). These results indicate that it is not the most socially marginalized groups that support the Sweden Democrats, but rather quite well established working-class people.

In the second model, education is added. As expected from previous studies cited above, we have a clear effect from low and medium-low education. Even if the effects of a class position in "lower sales and service" or "lower technical" is somewhat weaker than in Model 1, the effects are still significant, and the raise in total variance explained is modest. In other words, the extra contribution of educational level is quite limited.

Model 3 adds the subjective class factor of working-class identification and fear of unemployment. None of these factors are significant, but it is notable that the class factors are actually slightly reinforced under control for these subjective factors.

The fourth model focuses on explanations regarding political alienation in terms of political interest and trust, and thereby the populist explanation. By adding these variables to model 1, the explained variance goes up from 0.11 to 0.21, indicating that overall political trust and interest matters, and that part of the support might be interpreted as something of a "protest vote". The effect of political trust is clearly significant, while political interest is not. The effects of working-class position do, however, remain significant. Even though Model 4 indicates that part of the explanation for sympathizing with the Sweden Democrats could be found in sentiments of political distrust, this is not the main reason why the party has its strongest support from among the working class.

Model 5 focuses instead on ideology. In general, left–right position is central to party choice in Sweden, but in terms of sympathy for the Sweden Democrats this does not seem to matter. It does indicate, in other words, that it is not as a "right party" that the Sweden Democrats attract supporters. Of course it might be added here that the definition and measurement of the left–right dimension used in this analysis quite strictly refers to state interference and labour-market issues, and does not incorporate moral or nationalistic items, which are also sometimes referred to in terms of left and right. Rather, these aspects are here defined as reflecting authoritarian-traditionalist/nationalist values, forming the other ideological dimension in Model 5. The effect of position on the authoritarian–liberalism dimension is highly significant, indicating that a position close to the traditionalist/nationalist and immigration-negative end is closely related to support for the Sweden Democrats. The explained variance goes up to 0.37 when this control is added, which also confirms the strong explanatory power of this variable. The effect of a class position in "lower sales and service" is now no longer significant, but a class position in "lower technical" still is, even if it is somewhat weaker than in previous models. We also have significant effects of age under forty-nine years old, and these are actually reinforced compared to

Model 1, indicating that the effect of an authoritarian position is stronger among younger persons.

The final model includes all factors simultaneously. The significant effects of age, political trust and authoritarian–libertarian ideological position remain, but the class effects have decreased and are now insignificant, as are the coefficients for education. The interpretation of this result is that working-class support for the Sweden Democrats is due to class differences in the other factors in the model, and most notably in political trust and authoritarian–libertarian ideological position. The educational differences between people in different class positions matters mainly for ideological position, not for party support per se.

Concluding discussion

Even in Sweden, once characterized as one of the most stable left–right class voting countries in the Western world, today we have a populist/nationalist party with over-representation in the working class. Our analysis points to authoritarian leanings within the working class together with low political trust as bearing a strong part of the explanation. These sentiments within the working class are nothing new, but the present political context of Sweden has presented a "window of opportunity" for the Sweden Democrats to mobilize significant parts of the working class. That members of the working class tend to be more authoritarian than especially academics in the middle class has been known for some time, but as long as the political debates and conflicts are mainly mobilized and articulated along the economic left–right dimension this has not been of any major significance for party sympathy. But as the left–right polarization in the traditional Swedish party system has decreased, and at the same time most parties have moved towards a libertarian position, the authoritarian ideological position has become available to articulate, which the Sweden Democrats have done. Our test supports the nationalist character of the party and indicates that with mobilization of these layers of the working class it is possible to align to new cleavages. The ideological distance between authoritarian-leaning parts of the working class and libertarian middle-class academics in forming a discourse of "us" and "them", together with retrenchment policies and increasing cleavages, is most probably reflected in the low political trust driving sympathies for the Sweden Democrats.

Notes

1 This chapter is a written collaboration between the research projects "Not Just Populism. The establishment and success of xenophobic parties from a Lipset-Rokkan point of view", financed by FAS, the Swedish Council for Working Life and Social Research and "Social Class and Political Attitudes. A study of the political impact of experiences in working life", financed by the Swedish Research Council.
2 www.folkpartiet.se/Vi-behover-dig/Vara-konferenser/valet-2010/valaffischer-2010/.
3 With this figure, the Sweden Democrats became larger than the Left Party (5.6 per cent) and the Christian Democrats (5.6 per cent), and just slightly smaller than the Liberal Party (7.1 per cent), and the Centre Party (6.6 per cent, formerly agrarians).
4 For further information, see www.som.gu.se.

11 Mobilizing the workers?

Extreme right party support and campaign effects at the 2010 British general election

Matthew J. Goodwin and David Cutts

Introduction

One story of the 2010 British general election was the possibility of a break-through by the extreme right-wing British National Party (BNP).[1] Over the previous decade, the BNP had made a series of advances in second-order local, devolved and European elections. While less successful than radical right parties elsewhere in Europe, the party surpassed the performance of any of its predecessors by gaining over fifty local councillors, one seat on the Greater London Assembly and two Members of the European Parliament. At the 2010 general election, the party sought to build on these gains by setting its sights on what had long eluded the extreme right in Britain: a breakthrough at a national election. The BNP was not the only extreme right party contesting the election, but it was easily the most prominent.[2] The goals behind the BNP campaign were threefold: to gain elected representation in Westminster (particularly in its two target seats of Barking and Stoke Central); to achieve several second-place finishes; and to emerge ahead of the UK Independence Party (UKIP) as the fourth-largest party in British politics.[3] To this end the BNP fielded 338 candidates: the largest number of candidates stood by an extreme right party in British electoral history.

Prior to the contest, explanations for the rise of the BNP often implicitly recruited the sociological model of voting (Butler and Stokes 1969; see also Heath *et al.* 1991). Seen from this angle, radical and extreme right-wing parties in Europe have mainly rallied deprived and disillusioned members of the working classes and the unemployed, who feel insecure and abandoned amidst wider socio-structural change such as a post-industrial globalized economy (Betz 1994; see also Kriesi *et al.* 2006). Confronted with this change, and resentful towards the emergence of "New" Labour, which focused more on the middle classes, the argument was that sections of the "white working classes" shifted behind the BNP to express their frustration, discontent and economic insecurity. Across Europe, however, comparative studies have demonstrated how this sociological model is a poor predictor of support for the radical right (Norris 2005; see also van der Brug *et al.* 2005). In short, the sociological profile of radical right voters only takes us so far in terms of understanding what motivates their electoral behaviour. In response, scholars have turned to stress the importance of what is loosely termed the "policy model". This posits that citizens who vote for the radical right are like voters more generally: they are driven by a relatively coherent and rational set of policy and ideological preferences. Foremost, however, they support the radical right to express their opposition to immigration and rising ethno-cultural diversity (Ivarsflaten 2008; see also Norris 2005; Rydgren 2008). After controlling for the profile of voters, these studies and others show how the most powerful predictor of whether somebody will turn out for a radical right party is whether they are concerned about, or hostile towards, immigration and rising diversity.

These broad arguments, however, tend to portray radical right electorates as homogeneous and passive bodies, which simply switch allegiance to these parties either in response to unsettling social change or to the emergence of increasingly salient issues, such as immigration. Much less attention has been devoted to explaining *how* these parties mobilize support, and the extent to which their campaigns have an actual impact on electoral support. Like other parties, those on the radical and extreme right are not passive entities but play an active role in attempting to mobilize votes at elections. For three reasons, therefore, it appears surprising that the effects of these campaigns have been largely ignored. The first is that in the wider study of party politics it is now widely accepted that campaigning can have important electoral effects: see Cutts and Shryane 2006; see also Denver and Hands 1997; Fieldhouse and Cutts 2008; Pattie *et al.* 1995; Whiteley and Seyd 2003. These studies and others provide convincing evidence that the more a party delivers its message to particular types of voters in particular types of areas, the more likely it is that these voters will shift behind the respective party (Johnston and Pattie 2011; see also Pattie and Johnston 2010). Second, the importance of campaigns is underscored by broader trends that are taking place in party systems, namely the declining importance of partisan identification, the growing hesitancy of voters and their tendency to make vote choices closer to elections and the continuing professionalization of parties (Fisher and Denver 2009; see also Fisher *et al.* 2011). In contrast to earlier decades, declining party loyalty and the increased volatility of voters has meant that parties must arguably work harder to "get out the vote" during the campaign period. Third, in the study of the radical right there appears a consensus that—by themselves—"demand-side" arguments that emphasize the role of social and economic conditions provide only a partial account for why citizens have turned towards these parties (Eatwell 2003). This has led scholars to devote more attention to examining the effect of "supply-side" factors, such as the role of organization, ideology and how radical right parties frame their opposition to immigration and minority groups (Carter 2005; see also Kitschelt 1995; Rydgren 2008). Until now, however, this growing body of research on the supply side has largely ignored the electoral impact of actual campaigns by radical right parties.

In this chapter, we begin to address this gap by examining the impact of an electoral campaign by an extreme right party. How effective was the BNP campaign at the 2010 British general election? Drawing on innovative data and ordinary least squares regression (OLS), the chapter proceeds as follows: section one briefly summarizes research on campaign effects; section two examines the electoral context of the 2010 general election; section three investigates the electoral impact of the campaign; and the final section discusses the findings and their implications for the study of extreme and radical right parties in modern Europe.

Campaigning effects and the radical right

In the study of radical right parties it is now well established that their support tends to be most heavily concentrated among particular social groups, mainly skilled and unskilled blue-collar workers and the lower-middle classes (Arzheimer 2009a; see also Kitschelt 1995; Norris 2005). Much less attention, however, has focused on the extent to which campaigns by these parties influence their support at elections. The wider study of electoral behaviour tells us that there are good reasons to expect that where these parties campaign, citizens will be more likely to turn out for them on polling day. In fact, the effect of local campaigns on electoral outcomes has become the "accepted truth", with numerous studies demonstrating that—all other things being equal—the harder a party campaigns, the greater its share of the vote (Johnston and Pattie 1995; see also Johnston 1987; Cutts 2006; Denver and Hands 1997). To gauge the impact of these campaigns, studies routinely utilize campaign spending data, surveys of party agents or members. Analyses of these data have shown how "a party tends to win more votes in seats where it campaigns hard than in seats where it puts in little effort, *ceteris paribus*" (Pattie and Johnston 2003: 385). For example, we now know that variations in the amount that parties spend across different areas during the pre-election period are closely related to their electoral success. Put simply, the more intensively a party campaigns the greater the electoral benefits (Johnson *et al.* 2011).

To what extent do campaigns by radical and extreme right parties have similar effects? Building on the literature above, we similarly investigate the impact of an extreme right party campaign by utilizing three measures of campaign effort. First, we utilize spending data on the basis of its repeated validity and reliability, universal coverage and evidence that it correlates strongly with direct measures of activism (Pattie and Johnston 2009).[4] While extremist parties such as the BNP are often starved of financial resources, we similarly expect to find that where the party invested money this had a significant and positive impact on its support. Second, we include a measure for whether the party had achieved *local* electoral success in the area prior to the 2010 campaign. Particularly for minor parties, success at local elections often assumes an important role by helping to cultivate an image of credibility and attracting new recruits. For example, Mudde (2007) suggests that one important factor in determining whether a radical right party will mobilize a sustained challenge is organization and local implantation. To underscore the point, he highlights how several of the most successful radical right parties have anchored their campaigns in local bastions of support. Gaining representation in local elected office is likely to enhance the prospects of a wider breakthrough by raising the party's profile, promoting an image of electoral credibility and fostering relations with voters. One example is the Liberal Democrats in Britain, who based their national strategy on demonstrating an ability to make local gains (Fieldhouse *et al.* 2006; see also Russell and Fieldhouse 2005). While there is some limited evidence to suggest that support for extreme right parties has been stronger in areas where they have been locally successful (Borisyuk *et al.* 2007; see also Goodwin 2010), the impact of local gains is unclear.[5] For the reasons above, we expect that BNP success in local elections—measured as whether the party has won at least one local council seat in the constituency since 2005—will have a significant positive effect on the party's performance at the 2010 general election.

Third, we also examine the impact of membership, which is included as a predictor variable on the expectation that where the party has larger numbers of members, it is likely to be more visible and have higher rates of activism and stronger local infrastructures. This is based on studies that demonstrate how larger than average memberships can encourage higher rates of activism and improved electoral performances (Seyd and Whiteley 1992; see also Whitely and Seyd 1994). Clearly, endogeneity may be inherent within this relationship, given that members may be contributing to success while success may also attract new members. Separating out this dynamic is difficult and it may be that both factors are operating. It is also important to note that since its formation in 1982 and until a change of policy in 2010, the BNP operated a "whites-only" membership. This requires the measure of membership to be adjusted to take account of the fact that potential party recruits will only be drawn from the white British population. To investigate membership we utilize a list of BNP members that was leaked onto the Internet in 2008 by disaffected activists, and confirmed as genuine by the party leadership. The document contains over 10,000 names and addresses, including postcodes, which allows individual members to be matched to different levels of electoral geography (in this case constituencies). These data allow us to test a third hypothesis, namely that alongside spending and local success, membership will have a significant and positive impact on the BNP's performance at the 2010 general election.

Electoral context: the BNP and the 2010 British general election

As in other European states, from 2001 onwards the electoral resurgence of the extreme right in Britain coincided with the emergence of a more favourable issue agenda for parties that pursue anti-establishment and exclusionary campaigns. Alongside a considerable increase in the salience of immigration (McLaren and Johnson 2007), the first decade of the twenty-first century saw a cluster of security-related issues surge to the forefront of the British public mindset (Clarke *et al.* 2009).[6] While voters became increasingly anxious over immigration and minority groups, there emerged evidence of widespread public dissatisfaction with the policies and performance of the 1997–2010 Labour governments on these specific issues. Numerous surveys and polls revealed that upwards of 70 per cent of respondents rejected the suggestion that Labour had developed sensible policies on immigration and asylum, or that the government was being "open and honest" about the scale of immigration into Britain (Goodwin 2011). Pointing towards these trends and evidence of significant public support for xenophobic, ethnic nationalist and authoritarian positions, some argued there had emerged significant electoral potential for the extreme right (Ford 2010).

It was in this climate that the BNP attracted rising support. Though founded in 1982, it was not until a change of leader in 1999 that the party overhauled its electoral strategy and shifted from an identity-seeking to a vote-seeking stage of development. Rather than devote its scarce resources to contesting costly national elections, the party sought to replicate the strategies of the Front National (FN) in France and the Liberal Democrats in the UK. The result was the "ladder strategy", whereby the BNP sought to use community-based activism and success in second-order elections as a springboard into a breakthrough at the national level. Over several local election cycles, BNP branches were instructed to target local issues, forge links with community groups, establish face-to-face contact with voters and cultivate an image of credibility at the grassroots (BNP 2010b). While not active across the country, these community-based campaigns led the party to attempt to incentivize activism by developing a "voting membership scheme". The scheme, which was partly influenced by similar structures in radical right parties in Sweden, aimed to increase rates of activism by rewarding active members with influence over policy (Goodwin 2011).

Many of the party's early gains at local elections came at the expense of Labour incumbents, and at both the 2001 and 2005 general elections BNP candidates polled strongest in seats that were controlled by Labour (and where Labour incumbents often had large majorities). Within some of these "Labour heartlands", qualitative research revealed how vibrant grassroots campaigning and party competition had either stagnated or was virtually non-existent (Wilks-Heeg 2009). Though BNP campaigns were often haphazard and lacked resources, they increasingly came to be focused on mobilizing skilled and unskilled workers, and the unemployed. Rather than spread across the country, campaigns focused on particular regions and constituencies that had a long history of Labour incumbency, and had often been targeted by the extreme right in earlier decades. Mainly in Greater London, the Midlands, Yorkshire and regions of the North West, the BNP attempted to frame Labour as a party that had abandoned "ordinary working people", and was "more interested in 'gays', ethnics and their rich money-bags backers". In contrast, the BNP sought to reach out to disillusioned ex-Labour voters by framing itself as "the Labour Party your grandfathers voted for" (Ford and Goodwin 2010: 6).

While the party polled significant levels of support at local elections and also gained one seat on the devolved Greater London Assembly (GLA) in 2008, a more significant breakthrough arrived the next year at elections to the European Parliament. Aside from continuing public concern over immigration, the elections were held amidst recession and public outrage over a parliamentary expenses scandal. Seeking to translate these conditions into electoral dividends, the BNP focused its campaign on two pledges: to provide "British jobs for British workers" and "punish the pigs" in Westminster. The party failed to match the performance of its rival, the UK Independence Party, which pushed Labour into third place and recruited thirteen Members of the European Parliament. However, two BNP candidates in the North West and Yorkshire regions were elected. Aside from funding, the result attracted unprecedented amounts of media coverage that culminated in October 2009 with the party leader Nick Griffin appearing in front of over eight million viewers on the flagship television programme "Question Time".

Early aggregate-level analyses suggested BNP support was strongest in urban deprived working-class districts, where levels of education are low, there are large populations of skilled workers and elderly citizens and large Muslim communities of Bangladeshi or Pakistani heritage (Bowyer 2008; see also John *et al.* 2006). Individual-level analysis revealed that the party recruited the bulk of its support from "angry white men": middle-aged and elderly working-class men, citizens who lack formal qualifications and are pessimistic about their economic prospects. BNP support is heavily concentrated among skilled manual workers when compared with its predecessor in the 1970s, the National Front (NF), whose support was more evenly distributed across skilled and unskilled workers and citizens dependent on state benefits (Ford and Goodwin 2010). Consistent with the wider literature, however, it was shown that while BNP supporters share a distinct sociological profile and tend to congregate in particular social contexts, these were not the most important predictors of their support. After controlling for their background characteristics, these voters were motivated chiefly by hostility towards immigration and political dissatisfaction (Ford and Goodwin 2010; see also Cutts *et al.* 2011; Goodwin 2011).

Having assembled an initial electorate and made progress in second-order elections, the BNP set its sights on the 2010 general election at which the issue agenda remained favourable. Though public concerns over the financial crisis and economy dominated, immigration remained highly salient throughout the campaign. According to the British Election Study (BES), only the financial crisis and state of the national economy were more important to voters than immigration. When these respondents were asked their views about the "immigration situation", exactly two-thirds described the situation as either "a little worse" or "or a lot worse". Similarly, one regular measure of British public opinion ranked immigration as the second most important issue for voters: in the month that preceded polling day, more than quarter of the electorate (29 per cent) ranked the issue as one of the most important issues facing the country.[7] During the election month, however, this figure jumped to 38 per cent, which arguably owed much to "Duffygate".

In the months prior to the election, Labour had sought to bolster core support in target areas by pledging greater investment in approximately 130 "white working-class" areas. Shortly afterwards, the Labour Prime Minister Gordon

Brown aimed to connect with citizens who were anxious over immigration by underscoring his party's commitment to controlled immigration and adopting a tougher stance on illegal immigrants. Only a few days prior to the election, however, this attempt to reconnect with disillusioned Labour voters was seriously undermined. While on the campaign trail in the northern town of Rochdale, Brown was asked a series of questions about immigration and other issues by an elderly working-class voter named Gillian Duffy. After leaving the meeting Brown was recorded in his car describing Duffy as "a bigoted woman" and the conversation as "ridiculous" (Kavanagh and Cowley 2010: 174). The BNP subsequently claimed that "a window of opportunity" had opened and quickly sought to appeal to disgruntled Labour voters who may have been offended by Brown's comments.[8] This took the form of a specially tailored newspaper that was distributed around the party's target areas of Barking, Stoke, Barnsley and parts of Leicestershire and Manchester.

More generally, the BNP campaign sought to mobilize its core base while extending its reach to voters who had not previously supported the party. Overall, it is estimated that the party spent in the region of £55,655 during the long campaign, and £159,388 in the short campaign.[9] Clearly, the party was unable to compete financially with the three main parties and more affluent minor parties. Across campaign as a whole, the average BNP candidate spent only £750, compared with an average spend of £1,278 per UKIP candidate and £1,839 per Green Party candidate (Johnston *et al.* 2011). Furthermore, most of the party's resources were devoted to Nick Griffin's campaign in Barking, which was the only seat where the BNP spent almost the entire amount allowed on the short campaign. As at previous elections, the party targeted core voters by pledging to halt all further immigration, deport illegal immigrants and implement a system of voluntary repatriation, whereby "immigrants and their descendants are afforded the opportunity to return to their lands of ethnic origin, assisted by generous financial incentives both for individuals and for the countries in question" (BNP 2010a: 20). Unlike previous elections, however, it also sought to capitalize on evidence of anti-Muslim sentiment among the population (Voas and Ling 2010). A pledge to "counter the Islamic colonisation of Britain" led the party to offer a more detailed set of policies, which included banning the burka, halting the construction of any further mosques and deporting radical Islamist preachers, as well as "any other members of their community who object to these reasonable security measures" (BNP 2010a).

In an attempt to expand its bases of support, the party offered voters a broader range of policies that included: economic protectionism; opposition to "climate change theory"; renationalizing the welfare state; creating an English parliament; abolishing political correctness; restoring capital punishment; protecting civil liberties by repealing human rights legislation; returning to traditional teaching methods; increasing the state pension; and withdrawing from the European Union (BNP 2010a). In media interviews, the BNP Chairman Nick Griffin also focused on a pledge to establish a penal colony in South Georgia for criminals, and the party's opposition to the war in Afghanistan. However, the campaign was frequently undermined by factionalism, infighting and political amateurism. During the immediate pre-campaign period, several events meant that the party was often the subject of negative media coverage: an ex-party member in Yorkshire was imprisoned for eleven years after stockpiling weapons and explosives; Griffin was roundly criticized after questioning whether Britain should provide aid to victims of the Haiti earthquake; there emerged a debate about whether BNP members should be banned from teaching in schools; the party's director of publicity was sacked after allegedly threatening to kill Griffin; and the party was criticized in a documentary for exploiting murder victims after claiming there were racial elements to their cases without obtaining consent from the families.[10] The extremist image of the party was further underscored when a former organizer in the target area of Stoke defected amidst claims that there was "a vein of Holocaust denying within the BNP".[11] Beyond Stoke, factionalism was also evident within other key branches, such as Bradford and Kirklees. As the election approached, discontent among grassroots members was further fuelled when the party was forced to modify its "whites-only" policy in response to pressure from the Equality and Human Rights Commission (EHRC). While hardliners interpreted the change as an abandonment of core principles, other influential activists voiced their dissatisfaction with the employment of a business consultant, who they claimed was financially corrupt, and Griffin, who they contended was politically incompetent. The campaign was further undermined on polling day, when the BBC published footage of the BNP London organizer and a parliamentary candidate brawling in the street with Asian youths.[12]

Aside from internal problems, in its top target seat of Barking in outer East London the BNP met strong opposition from Labour and the anti-fascist network Hope Not Hate. Utilizing online social media, the network claimed to have recruited 142,000 supporters and 20,000 regular online campaigners (Lowles 2010a: 17, 2010b: 6, 2010c: 7). The anti-fascist campaign focused much of its effort on mobilizing members of social groups that were traditionally underrepresented in the BNP electorate, by pitching less aggressive and more positive literature to women and minority groups. Organizers of the Hope Not Hate campaign claimed that one "day of action" mobilized in the region of 500 volunteers, who distributed over 90,000 newspapers across Barking, Dagenham and Havering. On the actual day of the election, over 150 volunteers were specifically deployed to mobilize a targeted list of 6,000 non-BNP voters in key wards. Strong opposition to the BNP was similarly evident in the national tabloid newspaper the *Mirror*, which ran a story entitled "Five Reasons Not to Vote BNP".[13]

Assessing the electoral impact of the BNP campaign

How did the BNP perform at the 2010 general election? In the aftermath of the election, many commentators described the party's performance as a failure. Most noticeably in Barking, Griffin failed in his quest to cause an upset and finished in third place with 14.8 per cent of the vote. Moreover, at local elections that were held on the same day the party lost all twelve of its councillors on

Table 11.1 Support for the BNP in general elections, 1983–2010

Year	Votes received	Percentage of total vote	Constituencies contested	Average in seats contested	Highest vote (%)	Deposits retained
1983	14,621	0.0	54	0.6	1.3	0
1987	553	0.0	222	0.5	0.6	0
1992	7,005	0.1	13	1.2	3.6	0
1997	35,832	0.1	56	1.4	7.5	3
2001	47,129	0.2	33	3.9	16.4	7
2005	192,746	0.7	119	4.9	16.9	34
2010	564,331	1.9	338	3.8	14.6	73

Source: Ford and Goodwin (2010); BBC Election Archive.

Barking and Dagenham Council, while nationally its total number of councillors slumped from over fifty to twenty-eight. Even Griffin conceded that the local election results were "disastrous".[14]

However, closer inspection of the result suggests that it would be incorrect to view the campaign as a failure. Due to the striking increase in the number of candidates, the party was able to more than double its number of votes to over 560,000, and increase its share of the total vote in Britain to 1.9 per cent (see Table 11.1). In England, however, where the party contested 306 seats, it received 3.9 per cent of the total vote compared with 3.0 per cent at the 2005 general election, when it contested only 158 seats. The party contested a total of 126 seats at both the 2005 and 2010 elections; at the latter, it improved its share of the vote in these seats by an average of 1.9 per cent.

Furthermore, in some areas of the country BNP candidates rallied significant support. The party met or surpassed the 5 per cent threshold (that is required if candidates are to retain their deposits) in a total of seventy-three seats, compared to only seven at the 2001 general election. In some seats the BNP polled much stronger, including over 10 per cent in three seats, over 9 per cent in three seats, and 8 per cent or over in a further six seats (see Table 11.2).[15]

Table 11.3 details the overall performance of the party and the regional breakdown of its support. It reveals how the party polled strongest in regions that were targeted during the campaign, and where historically extreme right parties have been most active (Goodwin 2011). The Yorkshire and Humber, West Midlands, North East and North West regions saw the strongest performances by the BNP. This provides further evidence that support for the extreme right has shifted towards Northern England. Whereas in the 1960s and 1970s, extreme right parties tended to focus most heavily on Greater London, in 2010 the BNP was weaker in Eastern and Southern England and stronger in the Midlands and Northern regions (Ford and Goodwin 2010). Compared with the general election in 2005, the party made most progress in the East Midlands and North East regions while, as above, it failed to achieve noticeable gains in Southern England.

How effective was the BNP campaign? To address this question, we analyse constituency-level data derived from the British Constituency Election database

Table 11.2 Top ten BNP performances at the 2010 general election

Constituency	Region	Share of the vote 2010 (%)	% change since 2005
Barking	Greater London	14.6	−2.4
Dagenham and Rainham	Greater London	11.2	+1.9
Rotherham	Yorkshire	10.4	+3.8
Stoke-on-Trent South	West Midlands	9.4	+0.7
West Bromwich West	West Midlands	9.4	−0.5
Burnley	North West	9.0	−1.3
Barnsley Central	Yorkshire	8.9	+4.0
Barnsley East	Yorkshire	8.6	n/a
Normanton, Pontefract & Castleford	Yorkshire	8.4	+3.1
Leeds Central	Yorkshire	8.2	+4.1

Note
The 2005 share of the vote is based on notional results as some of the constituencies above experienced boundary revisions in 2010 (see Rallings and Thrasher 2007).

Table 11.3 2010 BNP performance in England, overall and by region

Regions	BNP 2010 vote share (%)	BNP 2005 vote share (%)	% change 2005–2010
South East	2.3 (26)	1.1 (8)	+0.3 (2)
East of England	3.1 (40)	2.9 (8)	+1.8 (8)
Greater London	3.3 (34)	3.1 (15)	+1.9 (12)
South West	2.2 (19)	1.0 (4)	+0.9 (2)
West Midlands	4.5 (38)	3.3 (35)	+1.7 (24)
East Midlands	4.2 (34)	1.7 (13)	+2.9 (11)
Yorkshire and the Humber	5.0 (48)	3.8 (41)	+1.7 (38)
North West	4.4 (38)	3.5 (22)	+1.9 (17)
North East	4.5 (29)	2.3 (12)	+2.6 (12)
England	3.9 (306)	3.0 (158)	+1.9 (126)

Note
(number of candidates in parentheses).

and other sources.[16] To investigate the role of demand-side factors at constituency level, eight socio-economic variables are obtained from the 2001 census.[17] Given that evidence of collinearity between these variables was found, a principal components analysis was run and two factors were extracted that describe the characteristics of the parliamentary constituencies.[18] Factor 1 reflects the urban character of the area and level of deprivation, whereas Factor 2 captures the class structure and education levels in areas that depend on the manufacturing sector. Consistent with our earlier studies that highlight the importance of disaggregating minority groups (Ford and Goodwin 2010; see also Cutts *et al.* 2011; Bowyer 2008), we include measures of the percentage of the population in the constituency that is Muslim, non-Muslim Asian and Black.[19] These are included separately, as are variables that capture migration from outside the country and the proportion of the population that is of retirement age.

Table 11.4 Explaining BNP 2010 general election support in England

Variables	Model 1: socio-economic predictors and region	Model 2: 2010 BNP performance	Model 3: controlling for prior vote
Constant	3.65**	2.74**	4.16**
Socio-economic predictors			
Factor 1: Urban deprived areas	0.04	0.10	0.02
Factor 2: Working-class manufacturing areas	1.48**	1.11**	1.28**
% Retired	0.12	0.01	−0.01
% Migration from outside UK	−0.43*	−0.26	0.06
Log Black	0.02	−0.10	−0.16
Log Muslim	0.60**	0.56**	−0.23
Log non-Muslim Asian	0.01	−0.09	−0.23
Region (base = SW/SE/Eastern)			
North East	0.11	0.25	−0.89
North West	0.10	0.10	−0.00
Yorkshire and Humberside	0.70**	0.51**	−0.31
West Midlands	−0.10	0.02	−0.50
East Midlands	0.11	0.08	−0.63
London	1.97**	1.62**	2.05**

	(1)	(2)	(3)
Local success and campaign effort			
BNP local election success under Griffin	—	0.81**	0.50*
Log BNP membership	—	1.23**	1.12**
BNP spending	—	0.08***	0.07***
UKIP spending	—	-0.01**	-0.01
Conservative Party spending	—	-0.01**	-0.01**
Labour Party spending	—	-0.01**	-0.01*
Liberal Democrat Party spending	—	-0.01**	-0.01**
Prior vote share			
BNP 2005 vote	—	—	0.14**
R^2	0.57	0.73	0.79
Adjusted R^2	0.55	0.71	0.74
F ratio	29.42**	39.08**	18.34**
N	306	306	126

Notes

** 0.05; *0.10 p-value. We only model England because we don't have membership and legacy variables in Wales and Scotland.
It was decided to create two factors from eight socio-economic variables. No qualifications were included here because it was 0.84** correlated with semi-routine and routine occupations (working class).

The linear models are built incrementally to gauge how the main variables of interest are affected following the introduction of other covariates. Each linear model is built over three stages. The first stage (Model 1) includes the main demand-side variables of interest: (i) two socio-economic factors that capture the effects of social cleavages on voting; (ii) two socio-economic variables (migration from outside the UK and the percentage of the population of retirement age); (iii) ethnic diversity variables; and (iv) regional influences. To examine the importance of supply-side variables on BNP support, the second stage (Model 2) incorporates our measures of BNP activism, namely party spending, local electoral success and membership. The inclusion of these variables allows us to test our hypothesis that the BNP campaign had a strong and positive effect on its support. The final stage (Model 3) includes both demand-side and supply-side variables but also takes account of the party's prior vote share in 2005. This changes the interpretation of the model by detailing the effects of other variables on BNP vote change from 2005 to 2010, where the continuity of support is held constant. The R^2 statistics are reported for each individual regression and reveal an improvement in fit when supply-side predictors are included. The inclusion of these variables along with demand-side predictors explains 73 per cent of the variation in BNP support at the 2010 general election. This increases to 79 per cent when we take account of the prior BNP vote share, although it is important to note that the final model is on a reduced sample size because the BNP stood fewer candidates in 2005.

The results in Model 1 reveal that, at the 2010 general election, the BNP continued to perform strongest in economically insecure and working-class areas that depend more heavily than other areas on the manufacturing sector. There also remains a clear regional pattern to BNP support: it is strongest in the Yorkshire and London regions. The significance of London is likely owe much to the campaign by Nick Griffin in Barking, which attracted considerable media coverage and several "days of action" by grassroots BNP activists. The results in Model 1 also provide further evidence concerning the importance of disaggregating minority ethnic groups: while support for the BNP was significantly stronger in areas where there are large Muslim communities, non-Muslim Asian and Black populations had a less pronounced impact on the party's support (Bowyer 2008; see also Ford and Goodwin 2010).

Importantly, when measures of campaign effort are incorporated into the model (Model 2) the effectiveness of the BNP campaign becomes evident. Though campaigning by rival parties had a negative effect on BNP support, where the party campaigned and was active, and had previously achieved local electoral success, its share of the vote improved. This provides evidence that local electoral breakthroughs appear to have played an important role, by attracting support and enhancing electoral credibility. Furthermore, the party received a higher share of the vote in areas that contained large numbers of BNP members. These findings provide evidence that, at the general election, the BNP performed strongest in areas where it had built a local infrastructure, established a local electoral presence and recruited larger clusters of members. In fact, even after controlling for the prior BNP vote at the 2005 general election, most of the campaign-related variables remain significant. When support at the 2005 general election was controlled for, local campaigning, party membership and (to a lesser extent) local success still had significant effects on BNP support at the 2010 general election. In contrast, demand-side variables remained less salient, with support for the BNP only improving in London and the more economically insecure working-class and manufacturing areas.

Discussion and conclusions

In this chapter, we have shed light on the impact of electoral campaigns that has largely remained hidden in the wider study of radical right parties. This is despite a growing body of research demonstrating that campaigns can have important and significant electoral effects.

In the aftermath of the 2010 general election, various commentators moved to dismiss the BNP as a spent electoral force. Some suggested the party had been "wiped out", while others claimed a "national collapse in the BNP vote".[20] Our findings, however, tell a different story. While the party failed in its quest to achieve its goal of parliamentary representation, and subsequently imploded from within, it still rallied more votes than any previous extreme right campaign. Moreover, by drawing on unique data and regression analysis, we show how the BNP campaign had important and positive effects on its electoral support. Put simply, where the party spent money, achieved local electoral success and had larger than average memberships, it performed more strongly.

These findings are consistent with a wider body of research, which shows how constituency-level campaigns can have a significant electoral impact. Other things being equal, the more that a party actively campaigns in a particular area, the more votes it wins and the fewer its rivals gain (Denver and Hands 1997; see also Pattie and Johnston 2009). Yet despite the fact that campaigns are now integral to parties' broader strategies, until now we have actually known little about the electoral impact of radical or extreme right party campaigns. Instead, studies have tended to assume that voters simply switch allegiance to these parties, either in response to disruptive socio-structural change or as a result of some form of economic or immigration-related grievance. Though studies often hint at the importance of campaigns—for example, stressing the role of ideological appeals, organization and framing—their actual electoral impact is rarely examined (if at all). The broader implications of our findings are that the more intensively a radical right party campaigns, the better it will perform at elections. Where these parties invest resources, build local bastions of support and nurture local memberships, they are likely to receive electoral dividends. This speaks to debates over how radical right parties shift from the stage of local electoral breakthroughs to mobilizing a durable electoral presence (Mudde 2007). It also highlights potential avenues for future research, including comparative studies of campaign effects and how these are influenced by the broader dynamics of party competition.

Appendix

Appendix A11.1 Rotated component matrix

	Component	
	1	2
% renting council housing	0.754	0.401
% overcrowding	0.823	−0.402
% population density	0.841	−0.307
% owner occupied	−0.938	−0.079
% semi-routine and routine	0.019	0.951
% no qualifications	0.278	0.890
% manufacturing	−0.227	0.817
% unemployment	0.808	0.426

Notes
Extraction method: principal component analysis.
Rotation method: varimax with Kaiser normalization.
Rotation converged in three iterations.
Component 1 = 45.986% of variance.
Component 2 = 36.299% of variance.
Cumulative % = 82.285.

Notes

1 Consistent with debates in the wider literature, we draw a distinction between "radical right" and "extreme right" parties. Specifically, we refer in this chapter to our case study (the British National Party) as "extreme right" on the basis of the definition set out by Carter (2005) and the work of Goodwin (2011).
2 The BNP had a total of 338 candidates, compared with 17 candidates from the National Front (NF) and two candidates from the Democratic Nationalists (DN) in Bradford, a breakaway faction from the BNP.
3 Interview 3 with Nick Griffin, December 2009: "Election—BNP 'expects' to be UK's fourth biggest party", BBC News, 5 May 2010. Available online: http://news.bbc.co.uk/2/hi/uk_news/politics/election_2010/8658251.stm (accessed 14 September 2011).
4 Parties are legally required to submit election expenses and make them publicly available. Spending is legally capped and attempts are made to differentiate between the costs of campaigning in borough constituencies and those of less urban constituencies. The assumption is that the latter costs are lower. Because the amount a candidate can legitimately spend is partly a reflection of the local electorate, it is possible to standardize this measure by calculating a candidate's spending as a percentage of the legal maximum permitted in the constituency (Johnston and Pattie 1995; Pattie and Johnston 2009). It is this measure that we utilize in the chapter.
5 One aggregate-level study finds that where the BNP had contested a ward in 2002 we should expect its vote share in 2004 to be at least 24 per cent larger than in a comparable ward that did not have a BNP candidate in 2002 (Borisyuk *et al.* 2007: 670; Joseph Rowntree Charitable Trust 2004).
6 For example, according the British Election Study, whereas in 2001 only 2 per cent of respondents considered immigration the *most* important issue facing the country, by 2005 the figure had risen to 20 per cent. Meanwhile, over the same period the number of respondents rating a cluster of security-related issues as important to them, and which also featured heavily in BNP literature—namely crime, terrorism, the war

in Iraq and immigration—increased almost eightfold to 39 per cent (Clarke *et al.* 2005: 56).

7 These figures are taken from the Ipsos-MORI Issues Index. Available online: www. ipsos-mori.com (accessed September 14 2011). A pre-election poll by Ipsos-MORI also suggested that 14% of the electorate considered asylum and immigration as being 'very important' to their decision about which party to support.

8 "BNP claim 'window of opportunity' from Brown bigot slur", BBC News, 30 April 2010. Available online: http://news.bbc.co.uk/2/hi/uk_news/politics/election_2010/8654914.stm (accessed 14 September 2011).

9 These figures for amounts spent were obtained from the great majority of candidates by returning officers, and forwarded to the Electoral Commission. They are based on 69 returns related to the long campaign and 255 (out of 315) related to the short campaign. They were originally cited in Johnston *et al.* (2011).

10 BBC News, "Bomb cache bus driver Gavan 'obsessed with weapons'". Available online: http://news.bbc.co.uk/1/hi/uk/8462205.stm (accessed 16 September 2011).

11 BBC News, "Former Stoke-on-Trent BNP man criticizes party". Available online: http://news.bbc.co.uk/1/hi/england/staffordshire/8579023.stm (accessed 20 September 2011).

12 BBC News, "Scuffle during BNP East London Campaigning". Available online: http://news.bbc.co.uk/2/hi/uk_news/politics/election_2010/8663695.stm (accessed 14 September 2011).

13 *Mirror*, 5 May 2010. The article associated the BNP with racism, Nazi nostalgia and political violence.

14 Lead author interview with Nick Griffin, June 2010.

15 BNP candidates polled 9.4 per cent in Stoke-on-Trent South, 9.4 per cent in West Bromwich West, 9.0 per cent in Burnley, 8.9 per cent in Barnsley Central, 8.6 per cent in Barnsley East, 8.4 per cent in Normanton, Pontefract and Castleford, 8.2 per cent in Leeds Central, 8.1 per cent in Walsall North and 8.0 per cent in Stoke-on-Trent North.

16 The data was compiled by the authors from the British Constituency Election database and the BBC. The authors would particularly like to thank Pippa Norris and her team, Charles Pattie and Ron Johnston, and John Curtice, Stephen Fisher and Robert Ford for making available some of the data used in the paper.

17 Eight socio-economic variables were used to capture established social cleavages. These included: the percentage of the constituency population that is unemployed; percentage employed in the more economically insecure manufacturing sector; constituency population with no formal educational qualifications; percentage living in council rented accommodation; population density; percentage of constituency population living in overcrowded housing conditions; percentage of the population who are owner-occupiers; and the percentage of the constituency population working in semi-routine and routine occupations.

18 There was strong evidence of collinearity between the socio-economic variables (for example, the correlation between working class as measured—semi-routine and routine occupations—and the percentage of the constituency population with no qualifications was 0.84). Due to this collinearity between the variables, we ran a principal components analysis (PCA). The factor classification axes were rotated and two components were extracted using orthogonal rotation, thus ensuring that the factors stayed uncorrelated. Two factors were required to reproduce 82.29 per cent of the variance (all with eigenvalues greater than one based on the Kaiser criterion).

19 Due to non-normality (positive skewness), we carried out log transformations of all the ethnic diversity variables.

20 See Taylor and Muir 2010; on collapse of the BNP vote, see Hamilton 2010. On coverage more generally, see also Milmo 2010.

12 The radical right in Central and Eastern Europe

Class politics in classless societies?

Michael Minkenberg and Bartek Pytlas

Introduction

While the overall electoral fortune of radical right parties in post-Communist Central and Eastern Europe is similar to their West European counterparts, they are distinct in ideological and organizational terms as well as in the degree of fluidity within the party family (see Minkenberg 2002, 2009a). As the cases of Poland, the Czech Republic, Hungary and others tell, radical right parties come and go, they reorganize and rename themselves. This suggests less stable cleavage structures than in Western Europe where many such parties can count on a solid bloc of faithful voters, which stem disproportionately from the working class.

As Geoffrey Evans puts it:

> In contemporary Central and Eastern Europe, the debate about class politics takes on a very different form than in the West: it concerns not whether class divisions have declined with the transition from industrialism to postindustrialism, but whether they have increased as the ex-communist countries – with their former ideology of classlessness – undergo the uneasy transition from command economy to free market democracy.
>
> (Evans 1999: 18)

Hence the article addresses the question of to what extent the legacy of a "classless society" in post-Communist countries is reflected by an absence of class structures and class appeal in those parties' electoral performance. A first glance at the social characteristics of their electorates reveals a mix of working-class or lower-class and rural support in addition to specific regional variations. The article attempts to provide longitudinal data on the radical right electorate's class composition in Central and Eastern European countries where these parties have entered parliaments (Poland, Hungary, and Slovakia) and to link it to class-based framing efforts of the radical right. We argue that in our cases, a market-liberal agenda retreats behind social nationalist appeals designed to bridge class differences and to exploit anti-capitalist as well as anti-modernization sentiments.

The radical right in Central and Eastern Europe and the legacies of the "classless society": some conceptual remarks

Most experts agree that the radical right can be defined as a radically exclusionist political force, which, more than other political currents and movements, employs rigid historical references in the imagination of the community it claims to fight for. In this vein, the core political programme or ideology of the radical right is a populist and romantic ultranationalism. More specifically, the radical right is involved in an effort to construct an idea of nation and national belonging by radicalizing ethnic, religious, lingual, other cultural and political criteria of inclusion and exclusion, that is, to condense the idea of nation into an image of extreme collective homogeneity and to bring about a congruence between the state and the nation in these exclusionary terms (Minkenberg 1998: 29–47, 2000, 2008; see also Carter 2005: 14–20; Kitschelt and McGann 1995: chapter 1; Kitschelt 2007: 1179; Mudde 2007: 15–26). As the main definitional criterion is not the opposition to democracy, this concept of the radical right is rather inclusive in that it covers more extreme variants of openly anti-democratic or fascist movements and parties, as well as the more vaguely defined currents of right-wing populism, or religiously based nationalism (Minkenberg 2008: 12–15; see also Mudde 2007: 138–157).

As in the case of established Western democracies, Central and Eastern European radical right parties need also to be seen as a modern and modernization-related phenomenon (Mudde 2000b: 44; see also Minkenberg 2002: 335). Admittedly, the counter-pluralist ideology of these actors is not as much related to post-material value shifts, typical for Western societies (dubbed the "silent counter-revolution" by Ignazi 2003). In the context of Central and Eastern Europe, the modernization shift results from processes of post-communist consolidation. The exclusionary idea of a homogeneous nation is introduced in the still salient discourse on the direction of state and nation (re)building. There, it forms the antithesis to liberalization and pluralization processes of the economy and society.

The comparative literature on the radical right in post-1989 Central and Eastern Europe employs some or most of these definitional characteristics and combines them with the region's experience of regime change and transformation and its particular state-socialist or Leninist past (Minkenberg 2002, 2009a; see also Mudde 2000a; Ost 2005; Ramet 1999). But while the importance of history or particular legacies for the trajectory of the radical right in the region is regularly emphasized in the literature, there is both fuzziness in the application of the legacy concept and the lack of a more conceptually grounded analysis or a systematic testing of its effects (or absence thereof) (Minkenberg 2009a). Such research is still in its infancy (Tismaneanu 1998). If at all, the role of the past is typically operationalized in sequential terms, as historical reference points, such as when some experts suggest to create new typologies of right-wing radical parties in Central and Eastern Europe by classifying them according to the (historical) origins of their ideological identity (Mudde 2000a; see also Shafir 2000).

This debate will not be pursued further here. But approaches that analyze the role of the past in the transition and outcome of "1989", summarily called "legacy approaches", need to be discussed for their usefulness in determining how the "class politics" of the old regimes that assumed having established a "class-less society" inform and shape the region's party politics today and in particular the radical right. A closer look at this debate reveals a certain under-evaluation of the legacies of the classless society. The emphasis seems to be more on cultural or individual-psychological than societal-structural aspects of the socialist legacies.

In his seminal essay, Kenneth Jowitt argued that Leninist legacies, which all former Eastern Bloc European countries share, favor an authoritarian rather than liberal, democratic and capitalist way of life (Jowitt 1992a: 293). Leninism as an institutional arrangement (or political regime) and its accompanying cultural traits (or cultural regime) consisted of traditional culture and a sharp distinction between private and public realms and virtues, the institutionalization of charisma through the rule of "the Party", the fragmentation of society, lack of established elites, and mutual distrust among members of society. Jowitt anticipated troubling effects of this system of rule on the prospects for democracy in the region:

> The Leninist legacy in Eastern Europe consists largely – not exclusively – of fragmented, mutually suspicious, societies with little religio-cultural support for tolerant and individually self-reliant behaviour, and of a fragmented region made up of countries that view each other with animosity. The way Leninists ruled and the way Leninism collapsed contributed to this inheritance.
>
> (Jowitt 1992a: 304)

Following this idea, a number of scholars, though at times quite critical of Jowitt's own approach and pessimism, applied the logic of his argument and focused on the Communist era as the independent variable in studying the prospects of liberalization, capitalism, party system stability and democratic consolidation in the region (Crawford and Lijphart 1997; see also Ekiert and Hanson 2003; Tismaneanu *et al.* 2006). In most of these approaches, the variation of post-Communist outcomes, such as successful or unsuccessful regime change, is related to the nature of post-Communist regimes. A particularly instructive application of this approach is the comparative analysis of party competition in selected countries, relating the degree of structured party systems and cleavage divides to the role of bureaucracy and rationality in the old regime (Kitschelt *et al.* 1999: 69–77). A rather different approach is taken by those who widen the concept of legacies to include various further dimensions and layers. For example, in the introduction to their book on *Liberalization and Leninist Legacies*, Crawford and Lijphart identify and explore six key legacies (Crawford and Lijphart 1997: 11f.): (a) the cultural legacy—the history of backwardness, victimization, and intolerance; (b) the social legacy—the absence of an established successor elite; (c) the political legacy—weak party systems with shallow roots in society; (d) the national legacy—the interrupted process of nation-building; (e) the institutional legacy—the survival of Leninist institutions; and (f) the administrative and economic legacy—centralized states and command economies (as well as the related question of universalistic, yet weak welfare states—see Standing 1996).

The program and the reality of a classless society—i.e., the dismantling of previous cleavage structures, which were rooted in, among other things, distinctions of social class—do not figure prominently in Crawford and Lijphart's list. If at all, such a reality can implicitly be found among the characteristics of political and economic legacies. Due to the assumed premise of little or no loyalty between parties and voters advocated by the early legacy scholarship (Crawford and Lijphart 1997: 19ff.), class, as a factor relevant for vote choice per se, does not seem to be approached to a large extent. Barbara Geddes, for example, pessimistically argued that shallow partisan identification and post-communist extension of suffrage onto the general electorate would work as factors that would rather facilitate catch-all or non-interest-based than class-based parties (Geddes 1997). While analyzing the intertwinement between social structure and voting behavior, Kitschelt *et al.* 1999 start with a similar premise, without assuming, however, the widespread and long-lasting prevalence of non-interest politics. Even if the authors fail to identify high direct effects of class on voting behavior, they note its indirect influence correlated with political preferences, i.e., the interest-based vote (Kitschelt *et al.* 1999: 293). Supplementing this argument, Evans and Whitefeld (2000) also point out that social divisions and derived interests play the decisive role for self-reflected political preferences. Nonetheless, they assume rather multidimensional divisions, which cut across interests that might result from economic positions and depend on questions of ethnic, national and religious identity as well as social values (Evans and Whitefeld 2000: 59). Finally, pointing out the explicit importance of class, a case study performed by Mateju *et al.* (1999) showed an increase in direct class-specific, programmatic voting between the 1992 and 1996 elections in the Czech Republic.

Summing up, the question of to what extent the term "class" is applicable for post-communist societies seems of secondary importance to the scholarship. Rather, the focus is put on one of the most visible effects of this societal factor—the character of voting patterns and programmatic politics (i.e., class voting and class politics), ranging from none, via mediated to direct class-based voting. The second related question is the nature of the societal divisions that shape the Central and Eastern European party systems. Thus, the literature on party systems in Central and Eastern Europe after 1989 raises the issue of political representation based on cleavages, the return or remodeling of class, region, religion and other factors, as well as pointing at the differences with regard to Western party systems. This includes, explicitly or implicitly, the relevance of class cleavage structures for the radical right in CEE.

Class cleavage and the radical right in transition: legacies of state socialism?

In their seminal article, Seymour Martin Lipset and Stein Rokkan (1967) under-lined the role of structural cleavages, or societally embedded, persistent conflict lines, for shaping the programmatic division of political parties as "alliances in conflicts over policies and value commitments within the larger body politic" (Lipset and Rokkan 1967: 93). The growing salience or closure of cleavages creates a value "grid" or constellation that determines the structure of a party system.

Much of the comparative party literature comparing East and West after 1989 points out that the Central and Eastern European cleavage structures and party system differ markedly from those in Western democracies (for an overview, see Evans and Whitefeld 2000: 48ff.), also with regard to the radical right. Part of the scholarship (Sztompka 1992, 1993) proposed the "tabula rasa" hypothesis, arguing that programmatic party creation along cleavage lines will not emerge for a long period of time, being instead dominated by charismatic and clientelist parties, an assumption that was soon proved wrong (Kitschelt 1995; see also Evans and Whitefeld 2000). Political cleavages also did not simply "unfreeze" in their pre-authoritarian shape, as could be assumed from earlier democratization waves, e.g., in Latin America. If Lipset and Rokkan's "freezing hypothesis" was already questionable for Western party systems in the 1970s and 1980s, then it is even more difficult to apply to Eastern Europe, simply because there were hardly any stable party systems in the 1920s that could have frozen. Traditional cleav-ages reemerged only in those countries where the most dominant conflict—that between supporters of the old regime and supporters of the new order—was settled, and democratic consolidation had advanced (Beichelt 2001). The next wave of scholarship constituted a "middle path" position, emphasizing the important but not deterministic role of "classical" or pre-authoritarian cleavages, adjusted and reframed in the course of post-communist transition (von Beyme 1996; see also Stöss and Segert 1997; Beichelt 2001). Accordingly, Klaus von Beyme identifies eight cleavages in the East but hastens to add that the older, pre-socialist ones (urban–rural, state–church, monarchist–republican) have been eroded by state socialist modernization policies (von Beyme 1996: 424f.). This leaves four others. Among these are center–periphery and workers–owners, which von Beyme suggests are irrelevant for the radical right, as well as West-erners–indigenists and internationalists–nationalists, which are better seen as two sides of the same coin than two distinct cleavages (Stöss and Segert 1997).

In the West, the new radical right is situated at the right-wing pole of a New Politics cleavage that cuts across the older class-based and religion-based cleav-ages (e.g., Kitschelt and McGann 1995; Minkenberg 1992, 1998). Most research on party systems in post-socialist Central and Eastern Europe identifies some central cleavages such as the one between forces that promote the ideas of market liberalism and those that favor political redistribution, or between mod-ernizers and opponents to modernization (Kitschelt 1992: 31; see also Plasser *et al.* 1997: 134; Stöss and Segert 1997: 398ff.). But there is disagreement about the number and characteristics of other cleavages that are not related to the first one, and where to situate parties of the radical right. For example, Plasser *et al.* suggest considering two more cross-cutting cleavages: one between transformation losers and transformation winners, and another between orientations of self-reliance and the need for guidance. But self-reliers, transformation winners and market liberals do not appear sufficiently distinct as a basis for different cleavages. On the other hand, Glaeßner (Stöss and Segert 1997: 400) suggests condensing all conflict types into one between "structural conservatives" (including ex-communists, nationalists, social populists, etc.) and "modernizers" (market liberals, forum parties, etc.). This approach, however, oversimplifies the conflict structure and overlooks the variety of cleavages within and across countries. Thus, the idea of a dual modernization conflict along a socio-economic axis and along a socio-cultural or value-related axis seems more persuasive because of the distinct logical and historical differences of the two cleavages (Stöss and Segert 1997: 400). For the case of Central and Eastern Europe, Kitschelt and collaborators have adjusted his earlier model to the context of transformation and redefined the two main cleavages as one between market liberals and social protectionists on the one hand, and secular libertarians and religious authoritarians on the other (Kitschelt *et al.* 1999). When applied to the radical right in Central and Eastern Europe, this model suggests to situate the parties at the authoritarian end of the libertarian–authoritarian axis and closer to the state end than the market end of the other axis. So far, however, the evidence is not conclusive. While Kitschelt *et al.* show that in Poland and Hungary the parties in question are situated at the far end of the authorianism scale (with the exception of the Czech SPR-RSC) but in the center of the protectionism scale, others support that these parties are situated at the far end of both cleavages (Dieringer 1998: 656; see also Brendgens 1997: 77). This, in fact, is congruent with the findings for the new radical right in Western democracies but it does not determine the degree of electoral success of these parties. Instead, a closer look at the particular role of state socialist legacies on cleavages is needed.

One such approach is the analysis by Lenka Bustikova and Herbert Kitschelt (2009), which addresses a wide range of phenomena, both in terms of country cases included in their comparative investigation as well as the variables they test as causal factors for the electoral success of the radical right. They follow Kitschelt's earlier work on post-communist party competition and the type of communist regimes (Kitschelt *et al.* 1999) and suggest a political-economic perspective, rather than one based on cultural and identity politics, for the explanation of voting for the radical right. Their argument is that in countries with a legacy of national-accommodative communism, which implemented to a certain degree cross-class social policies and, following 1989, provided a welfare state safety net for the losers of regime change, the radical right receives only limited support. The opposite is true for countries with a patrimonial communist legacy. Here, "red-brown" authoritarian and exclusionary programs resonate in significant segments of the public, mixed with anti-capitalist positions (Ishiyama 2009).

Bustikova and Kitschelt test these propositions for seventeen countries and find that these legacies cast a shadow over the processes after 1989 and account for the general patterns of radical right mobilization. But, they readily admit, their analysis is restricted to the demand side of the radical right and warrants a complementary study of the strategic moves of these parties and how they are constrained by the respective legacies in the electoral arena. Nonetheless, their analysis provides a starting point for a closer consideration of the legacies of "class-less societies" and their impact on the radical right's campaign strategies and performances. The analysis that follows in a two-step manner will first address the demand side and explore class-related characteristics of the support for the radical right in selected CEE countries. In a second step we will consider to what extent the radical right in these countries attempts to frame its political message in terms of class-based rhetoric and agenda.

Demand-side analysis—the radical right and class voting

Looking at the demand side of radical right support in the context of class position needs, in a first step, to take into consideration the distribution of voters along the ideological spectrum of a given party system. The relationship between attitudes and voting behavior is a crucial field of right-wing radicalism research that includes a plethora of interpretations and explanations of radical right support (Minkenberg 1998: 312f.).[1] Approaches arguing in favor of branding radical right support merely as protest vote (e.g., Betz 1994) have soon been amended by empirical analyses that have provided evidence for programmatic voting and the importance of ideological issues (such as immigration, law and order, European integration), voter left–right placement as well as other attitude-related aspects (Minkenberg 1998: chapter 8; see also Lubbers *et al.* 2002; van der Brug and Fennema 2003; van der Brug *et al.* 2005; Arzheimer 2009a). The research on Central and Eastern Europe has yet to provide such a wide range of model-based analyses. Nonetheless, several studies also provide evidence for programmatic right-wing voting. One early study (McManus-Czubińska *et al.* 2001) found significant correlations between the radical right party sympathy in Poland and pro-Church and anti-EU attitudes. Similarly, for the Polish case, de Lange and Guerra (2009: Tables 2 and 3 on pp. 543f.) identified much higher salience levels and a distinct ideological positioning of right-wing radical voters on issues such as abortion, birth rate, the role of the Church, and settlement of foreigners (but, interestingly, not on economic issues). In Hungary, attitudes on euroskepticism, revisionist nationalism, and anti-Roma sentiments were most distinctive for Jobbik voters (Bíró Nagy and Róna 2011: 15, Table 4).

Most notably, left–right self-placement has been applied to operationalize political preferences on a variety of individual issues (Laponce 1981). Despite different trajectories of the development of party systems in Western and Eastern Europe, the newest research (Rudi 2010: 69, 132–141) has shown that the left–right scale as a measure for a general ideological orientation of voters and an indicator of their political positions can also be applied to post-socialist democracies in Central and Eastern Europe.

Table 12.1 shows the voter self-placement on the eleven-grade left–right scale, relative to their professional status. The time of the analysis for each country has been chosen at the period of biggest electoral success of a right-wing radical party. This analysis should make it possible to determine first whether crucial discrepancies in left–right placement arise between different occupational groups (which would allow for the assumption of strong class-based ideological polarization), and second whether one can speak of a particular group as especially oriented to the rightmost pole of the ideological spectrum.

In all countries some levels—stronger in the Slovak Republic and Poland than in Hungary—of class-based polarization can be found. Nonetheless, the divergence from the overall population is not sufficiently strong to allow for identification of clear ideological clusters. In Slovakia, manual workers orient themselves much closer to the leftmost end of the scale, whereas individual entrepreneurs seem to be the group most oriented to the right. White-collar workers tend to assume a centrist position, whereas intellectuals seem to affiliate themselves with the positions adjacent to the middle, slightly further to the right than the left.

In Poland, manual workers (and also, to a similar extent, farmers) are rather evenly distributed on the left–right scale in comparison with the overall population, but with a slight over-representation at the rightmost end. Individual entrepreneurs in Poland lean toward both the right-wing and left-wing ends of the scale. Intellectual professionals are the group with the weakest identification with the right, whereas managers are over-represented at the right-wing pole.

In Hungary, manual workers also lean to the right, being under-represented at the leftmost end of the scale. The divergence from the overall population is nonetheless lower. Individual entrepreneurs tend toward the center, whereas white-collar workers place themselves at positions adjacent to the middle, both just to the left and right. An interesting aspect is the strong right-wing orientation of intellectual professionals and a very strong rightmost affiliation of the unemployed and farmers. The manager group in Hungary is the most strongly left-leaning occupational group in the country.

The left–right self-placement data can serve as an introductory step in establishing potential demand groups for right-wing ideology, but is not enough to assess the relation between the radical right and class voting. On the one hand, respondents in general place themselves either in the neutral middle position or to the ends of the scale. A large number of missing data (non-response) is also a factor. On the other hand, the left–right scale does not give any information on particular party choice. This is why a second step in the demand-side analysis is needed.

Table 12.2 depicts the socio-demographic profile of respondents declaring that they would for a radical right party if elections were held next Sunday. In each case, self-declared voters of the biggest RRP at the time were taken under consideration (League of Polish Families in Poland; Slovak National Party in

Table 12.1 Voter self-placement on the left–right scale related to occupational status in the Slovak Republic, Poland, and Hungary (in percent)

Left–right scale	Left (1)–2			3–5			Center (6)		
	SK 1999	PL 2001	HU 2009	SK 1999	PL 2001	HU 2009	SK 1999	PL 2001	HU 2009
Overall	**10.2**	**14.9**	**7.3**	**21.1**	**27.0**	**15.6**	**50.9**	**29.7**	**21.3**
Unemployed	10.9	8.8	4.6	25.5	18.0	15.1	47.3	37.8	21.9
Farmers	–	10.7	9.5	–	30.1	4.6	–	33.2	36.5
Manual workers	10.5	14.9	6.1	22.5	23.2	13.7	52.6	34.3	22.6
Retailer/individual entrepreneurs	8.0	17.4	6.5	10.7	32.3	13.3	48.0	23.8	45.5
White-collar workers	4.1	13.1	6.0	21.4	15.3	20.1	55.0	26.3	16.8
Intellectual professionals	7.8	17.2	8.2	25.2	28.7	16.4	45.6	23.6	15.0
Management	0.0	13.5	31.3	28.6	22.5	15.0	42.8	21.6	13.9

	7–8			9–10			Right (11)		
	SK 1999	PL 2001	HU 2009	SK 1999	PL 2001	HU 2009	SK 1999	PL 2001	HU 2009
Overall	–	**10.9**	**13.4**	**13.1**	**10.7**	**20.7**	**4.7**	**6.7**	**12.3**
Unemployed	–	10.2	14.0	12.7	11.5	20.8	3.6	6.4	22.9
Farmers	–	10.2	7.2	–	6.7	21.7	–	8.1	23.9
Manual workers	–	14.4	14.0	11.5	13.2	21.0	3.5	7.2	12.5
Retailer/individual entrepreneurs	–	8.0	16.8	29.3	8.4	11.7	5.3	9.3	6.2
White collar workers	–	18.2	11.3	15.0	9.6	24.8	4.5	4.3	12.1
Intellectual professionals	–	11.8	16.5	19.4	11.9	31.9	2.9	6.9	10.3
Management	–	16.1	10.1	28.6	19.8	14.5	0.0	8.3	8.9

Sources (for database references, see Survey Appendix): GESIS 1999; PGSW 2001; DKMKA HES 2009.

Table 12.2 Stratification of right-wing radical party voters in Slovakia, Poland, and Hungary (over-representation and under-representation in percent of voters)

	Slovakia				Poland				Hungary			
	1999	2002	2006	2010	2001	2002	2005	2007	2001	2003	2005	2009
Overall	**12**	**4**	**12**	**5**	**6**	**13**	**3**	**1**	**3**	**2**	**2**	**3**
Education												
Primary	−2	−	−	+2	+1	+9	+1	+0	−1	−1	−1	−1
Vocational	+1	−2	−1	−	+3	+0	+0	+0	+2	+0	+2	+0
Secondary	+1	+1	−1	+1	−2	−5	−1	+0	+0	+0	+1	+2
Higher/university	−2	+0	−4	−2	−1	−7	−2	+1	+2	−1	−2	+1
Occupation												
Unemployed	+1	−	+0	−	+0	+2	+0	+0	+0	+0	+4	+0
Farmers	−	−	−6	−	+3	+2	+0	+0	+2	−2	+2	+0
Manual workers	+2	−	+3	−	+1	−4	+1	+0	+1	+1	+3	+0
White-collar workers	−4	−	−	−	−2	−	−2	−1	−2	+0	+0	+2
Intellectual professionals	−2	−	−	−	−1	−	−2	+0	−1	+0	+0	+3
Self-employed/entrepreneurial	−3	−	−1	−	+2	−3	+0	−1	+1	+0	+2	−1
Management	+0	−	−5	−	−2	−9	−	+0	−	+2	−2	+0
Age												
18–24	+2	−1	+3	+0	−1	+0	+1	+0	+0	+1	+0	+2
25–34	+2	+0	−2	+1	+1	−1	+0	−1	+0	+0	+0	+1
35–54	−1	+1	−1	+1	−1	−3	−1	+0	+0	+0	+1	0
55–64	−3	+2	−2	−1	+2	−1	+2	−1	−1	−1	−	−1
65+	−	+0	+2	−	+1	+6	−1	+0	+1	−1	−1	−1

Sources (for database references see Survey Appendix): **PL**: PGSW 2001; OBOP 2002; PGSW 2005; PGSW 2007; **SK**: GESIS 1999; Gyárfášová/Velšic 2002; Bútorová and Gyárfášová 2006: 137; **HU**: GESIS 1990–2001; DKMKA HES 2003; TÁRKI 2005; DKMKA HES 2009.
Bútorová and Gyárfášová 2010: 175; Bútorová and Gyárfášová 2006: 137; **HU**: GESIS 1990–2001; DKMKA HES 2003; TÁRKI 2005; DKMKA HES 2009.

Slovakia and in Hungary—the Hungarian Justice and Life Party until 2006 and Jobbik after 2007). Row percentages were used to calculate the under-representation and over-representation of RRP voters in each age, occupational, and educational cohort relative to overall RRP support. This method—instead of looking at the percentaged stratification of the overall RRP electorate (column percentages)—was chosen given the (at times) fairly low number of respondents declaring their vote for a particular party, as the resulting skewed data might otherwise have lead to discrepancies in comparisons between different cases and times.

As is visible in Table 12.2, neither a synchronic nor a diachronic comparison of data allows the identification of a clear and stable class-related voter profile of right-wing radical parties in Central and Eastern Europe (confirming the findings for the time period of 1996–2001 in Norris 2005: chapter 6). Overall, these results do not come as a surprise, given the relatively high levels of voter volatility in the region (see Grotz 2000; see also Beichelt 2007; Tiemann 2011). Nonetheless, several trends are observable for particular cases in Table 12.2.

Regarding age, radical right parties are generally elected by younger, particularly first-time, voters. Especially in Poland the trend of attracting this part of the electorate proved successful, with an under-representation in the late 1990s shifting toward a slightly higher ratio of the youngest voters supporting the League of Polish Families (also due to the high activity of LPR's youth organization, the All-Polish Youth). Also in Hungary, Jobbik managed to achieve what its predecessor, MIÉP, had failed to accomplish for a long time (see Norris 2005: Table 6.6), namely attracting first-time voters. In the elections of 2010, support from the youngest Jobbik voters reached 23 percent (Bíró Nagy and Róna 2011: 11). This has come in the wake of a direct campaign by the Hungarian radical right at young voters. The party's chairman Gábor Vona, himself only thirty-two years old at the time of his election, led a campaign that was much more modern, dynamic, and oriented toward young people than had been the case for MIÉP and its much older leader István Csurka. In Slovakia, despite generally stronger support from the youngest voters, the success has not been sustainable. Regarding the oldest strata, only in the Polish case is it possible to see a clear over-representation of voters over sixty-five years of age. This has to do with accommodating the—mostly elderly—followers of the fundamentalist Catholic radio station, Radio Maryja, a support base lost by the LPR to the national-conservative Law and Justice Party just before the 2005 elections. Romania's PRM also noted a shift from younger to older voters between 2004 and 2007 (Sum 2010: 23).

With regard to education, no general relationship can be traced. In the late 1990s, all parties received fairly large support from voters with vocational training, though this trend could not be upheld. In general, all parties did not receive stable, sustainable support from the lower-educated strata, which were under-represented in the first time period under research. Only in Poland (as well as in the Czech Republic, see Norris 2005: Table 6.3; and Romania, see Sum 2010: 23) has the ratio of voters with lower education been decisively higher than in other countries, with the highest-educated strata strongly under-represented. On the opposite side, Jobbik again managed to attract much more highly educated voters than had been the case for MIÉP between 2001 and 2007.

Finally, looking at the professional profile of right-wing radical voters in Central and Eastern Europe, the first observation from the analyzed data shows that unemployed voters do not tend to vote above average for the radical right. In Hungary and Slovakia their support has remained stable and close to the overall sample, with the exception of MIÉP and LPR at the beginning of the 2000s. Especially in Poland, farmers were one of the important voter strata for the LPR. Still, this trend diminished after the country joined the European Union in 2004. With time, the LPR also lost the initial support of the self-employed/ entrepreneurial voters. Manual workers were also generally over-represented among radical right voters, mostly in the case of Slovakia and Poland. In the Czech Republic the radical right vote among skilled workers was twice as strong as the national average (Norris 2005: 140, Table 6.2); however, the Czech case is one of the few in Central and Eastern Europe where a radical right party—i.e., the Republicans—failed to establish itself in the party system. Hungary provides one of the most interesting results, where the more blue-collar and self-employed-based MIÉP gave way to a stronger white-collar and intellectual-oriented Jobbik. The results partially correspond to findings reported in Norris (Norris 2005: 140, Table 6.2), which show that in Hungary, as in Romania, it was the lower-middle class that voted disproportionately for the radical right. For Romania, the latest analyses also show growing support for the PRM from industrial workers (Sum 2010: 23).

When comparing the results from Tables 12.1 and 12.2, we can note that, in the case of Poland and Hungary, rightmost affiliations were to a certain extent compatible with class-based voting for radical-right parties. In Slovakia, on the other hand, this measure proved to be an insufficient indicator. As Table 12.3 further shows, radical right parties' support from particular occupational groups remained in flux. In the case of the Polish LPR only the support among manual workers remained stable, with the strata of farmers and the self-employed stepping away from the party. In Hungary, the previously mentioned shift away from

Table 12.3 Potential RRP voters based on left–right affiliations vs declared RRP voters, in comparison

	Voter potential			*Voter over-representation*		
	SK 1998	PL 2001	HU 2009	SK	PL	HU
Unemployed	0	0	+	+ → 0	0	0
Farmers	NA	+	+	NA	+ → 0	0
Manual workers	0	+	0	+	+	+ → 0
Self-employed	+	+	−	−	+ → −	+ → −
White-collar workers	0	−	+	−	−	− → +
Intellectual professionals	0	0	+	−	− → 0	− → +
Management	0	+	−	0 → −	−	0

blue-collar to white-collar workers is the most visible outcome of Jobbik's taking over the relay baton from MIÉP.

Taking these differences into consideration, it seems clear that a closer look at the demand side of the support for the radical right does not suffice. Therefore, the second step of the analysis focuses on the supply side, bearing in mind the party competition for rightmost oriented voters by several mainstream parties (PiS in Poland, SMER in Slovakia, FIDESZ in Hungary) and the ideological diffusion of right-wing radical frames in the political arenas in Central and Eastern Europe (see Bustikova and Kitschelt 2009; see also Pytlas 2009). This step will also make it possible to integrate the criticism of class-vote research formulated by Peter Mair (Mair *et al.* 1999: 310ff.). It will thus focus not on the question of class voting—i.e., whether certain strata consistently tend to vote for a particular party—but rather on the question of class politics—i.e., whether parties themselves touch upon class-relevant issues or frame them in a manner attractive to particular voter groups.

Supply-side analysis: the radical right and class politics

In Poland, the League of Polish Families never pursued a clear class-oriented politics. The party's socio-economic rhetoric, focusing on redistributive appeals, with notable importance attached to the traditional role of families and the need for their protection embedded in social Catholic teaching, remained in the ideal and timeless cultural sphere with little mobilization potential against a particular "out-group" (except perhaps the European Union). As an example, the party's economic program issued in the year 2003—the only bigger socio-economic document released—is directed not at a particular class but to the "independent Poland, a sovereign Polish Nation" (LPR 2003). The only group mentioned explicitly in the program—mostly in the protectionist, euroskeptic context— were the farmers (LPR 2003: chapter 6). Elsewhere, the terms "Polish nation" and "Polish family," as well as measures aiming at preserving these two entities and securing their economic well-being, abound in the document.[2] When introducing the bill on a special maternity state allowance of 250 euros for each newborn child, the party's leader declared:

> The most important fundament of our program is family, existing in our party's name. A family that needs protection, shield, help. A family that needs support (…). We need to support it through the tax system. We need to support it through the protection of life, through the protection of values.
>
> (Giertych 2006, transl. B.P.)

Nonetheless, the law turned out to be the one singular success in LPR's socio-economic policy. By 2005, the issue of EU integration that had elevated LPR to success became almost obsolete and lost salience, giving way to socio-economic issues and the polarization between "social" and "liberal" Poland spurred by the Law and Justice Party (de Lange and Guerra 2009: 537). Law and Justice managed to integrate the radical right frame into current political debate, depicting Polish reality as a dichotomized struggle between the two blocks: on the one hand the "solidaristic", traditionalist Catholic defenders of the "truly Polish" character and state; on the other hand the "liberal" establishment and winners of modernization aiming to deconstruct the Church, Catholicism, and with it the core value foundations of the state and society. By directing the rhetoric of defense of the Church and Catholic values against an internal enemy, salient socio-economic divisions have been parallelized with and reciprocally enhanced by cultural-axiological interpretations. Elements of radical right ideology, although not present at the core of the political argument, have been used as an auxiliary proxy to legitimize the main axis of political conflict (Pytlas 2009). LPR's further pursuit of their old anti-EU frame and singular attempts to touch upon family politics were not strong enough to break the issue ownership of PiS in the socio-economic sphere. This led to the decisive flow of voters from LPR to PiS and the demise of the party in the 2007 elections (Pytlas 2009; see also de Lange and Guerra 2009).

In Slovakia, the SNS was also unable to break the ownership over socio-economic issues of the mainstream parties. On the one hand, the party programs address the questions of class-based politics to a bigger extent than in Poland. In their 1998 and 2002 programs (SNS 1998; see also SNS 2002), the party—despite focusing mostly on their traditional questions of "national principles", minority issues, historical legacy, Christian roots, or sovereignty—turns attention to the question of "social" and "solidaristic" state economy. Apart from general statements, the farmers as well as self-employed craftspeople and owners of small and middle enterprises are addressed explicitly, touching upon protectionism on the one hand and the call for the fostering of the entrepreneurial spirit and individual freedom on the other. In the terms of social security, "family" is again mentioned as the main addressee. The 2006 program dropped the explicit mention of the self-employed voter strata (SNS 2006).

Despite taking a considerable amount of space in the party programs, socio-economic, class-oriented policies were not in the focus of SNS' daily politics. It was much more oriented around nationalist issues of protecting Slovak interests and discriminatory politics against the Hungarian minority in the south of the country, as well as law-and-order issues, with only sporadic redistributive-populist statements (Haughton 2003; see also Sulik 2006). Since 2002, issue ownership in this matter went to the social-populist Smer, founded only three years before. After 2002, Smer, led by Robert Fico, turned its programmatic appeal to the socio-economic dimension, with the main rhetorical thrust aimed against the liberal reforms implemented by the Dziurinda government in the years 1998–2006. The articulated need for social solidarity was wrapped in populist packaging—for example, when in 2002 one party slogan stated "As they stole under Mečiar, so they steal under Dzurinda" (Rybář and Deegan-Krause 2008: 6) or when during the 2006 parliamentary campaign the party asked whether it was fair that 70 percent of the working population earned less than a statistical prime minister (Sulik 2006: 84). The socio-economic issue polarization became frozen between between Fico's Smer and Dzurinda's SDKÚ, with the future of reforms implemented by the Dzurinda government forming the main area of competition between the parties (Pcolinský and Štensová 2007: 106), which at the same time became the defining issue of the election campaign in general (Gyárfášová 2008: 36). The ethnic competition dimension of identity politics remained occupied by the SNS, which consequently applied an anti-Hungarian stance, directing its campaign against the SMK (Pcolinský and Štensová 2007: 107). Because of the clearly divided, cluster-like structure of political competition, the parties remained in their own, familiar areas and repeatedly competed with their clearly identified traditional enemies, both inside and outside Slovakia's borders (Pytlas 2009).

In Hungary, as is apparent from the analysis above, Jobbik was able to win support from young, highly educated voters (see also Bíró Nagy and Róna 2011), as well as those working mostly in the white-collar and intellectual professional sectors. Thus, they are the first radical right party in Central and Eastern Europe that has been able to attract these strata to such a large extent. In terms of the economy (which, in the party's nationalist fashion is extended onto the whole Carpathian basin, i.e., the former territories of Greater Hungary), Jobbik coined the term "eco-social national economy, which means tailoring the economy, through controls which lead it to serve the interests of Hungarians, so as to provide both the environment and the living standards that people deserve" (Jobbik 2010: 2). Its program mentions most of the occupational groups, referring to "the Hungarian people's industriousness", manufacturing, production, and agricultural sectors as well as "local and domestic businesses." In terms of social policies, the party presents itself as having a much more liberal stance than is the case for other RRPs in the region: "We must be endeavoring to guarantee work opportunities rather than access to benefits. Those capable of labor, should only be entitled to receive state support, through the completion of some form of work" (Jobbik 2010: 10). Also in terms of fighting unemployment, the pressure is not only put on creating new job places but also on ending the exploitation of employees, "to ensure, that a person's occupation doesn't merely serve the function of providing the foundations for financial survival; in addition it should ideally be a source of dignity, gratification and feelings of self-satisfaction." (Jobbik 2010: 11). Together with strong anti-corruption and anti-establishment, as well as law-and-order, rhetoric (Bíró Nagy and Róna 2011: chapter 2), Jobbik formulated a message resonant with active young university graduates, who expected higher standards of living after completing their education and were disenchanted by the previous government. The rebellious and dynamic, quasi-counter-revolutionary image fostered by the party's street activism—most notably the participation in the 2006 Hungarian anti-government protests—combined with a young, professional and well educated leadership additionally contributed to the party's success. This image stuck so well, it could not even be undermined by the party's overt nationalism, irredentist claims, discriminatory anti-Roma rhetoric, and militaristic display of power by the Magyar Gárda, which functioned as the paramilitary and extra-parliamentary wing of Jobbik.

Conclusions

Our article has addressed the question of to what extent the legacy of a "classless society" in post-Communist countries is reflected by the absence of class structures and class appeal in the radical right's electoral performance. The still visible fluidity of the party systems as a whole, the legacies of the previous regimes (among others, weak party-voter loyalties or welfare states with a universal yet low level of benefits), as well as region-specific cleavage constellations, led us to expect limited effects of social stratification. Congruent with some findings in the literature (Norris 2005), the longitudinal data on the class composition of these electorates in countries where these parties have entered parliaments (Poland, Hungary, and Slovakia) show no clear pattern. Nonetheless, one of the most important observations is the Hungarian case, with a clear shift from lower-educated, older blue-collar, and self-employed strata supporting MIÉP to higher-educated, young, white-collar, and intellectual professionals voting for Jobbik.

Rather than finding a sustainable class aspect in voting behavior (i.e., the demand side of the radical right parties), we can to some extent detect specific appeals on the supply side, i.e., the program and the issue framing of these parties. In general, right-wing radical parties in Central and Eastern Europe articulate a populist-solidaristic, social protectionist agenda. At the same time, though, this rhetoric is not directed at any specific class. Rather, it is "the Family" or "the Nation" that is being addressed. As a result, socio-economic class divisions are often being parallelized or bridged with a cultural, axiological, and counter-modernization agenda. In other words, appeals for social protection are equated with the need to protect "national economic interests" against "traitors" and groups not adhering to the traditional values and the radicalized vision of "the Nation". In so doing, the radical right, in its effort to exploit some legacies of the socialist past, prolongs them into the present.

But to what extent the framing efforts by the radical right translate into a more or less continuous absence of a class-based profile of their electorates, or whether the latter is merely the effect of a high level of fluidity in the party system and volatility in the electorate, can only be answered by further and more rigorous scrutiny.

Survey appendix

Poland

PGSW 2001
Polskie Generalne Studium Wyborcze 2001
Data were collected and rendered accessible by the staff of PGSW – Polskie Generalne Studium Wyborcze 2001 (Polish National Election Study 2001) affiliated with the Institute of Political Studies of Polish Academy of Sciences. The research was financed by Scientific Research Committee (grant no. 5 H02E 021 20) and

subsidized by the Economic and Social Research Council (ESRC) and the Warsaw School of Social Psychology (SWPS). Polish Social Data Archive (distribution).

PGSW 2005

Polskie Generalne Studium Wyborcze 2005

Polskie Generalne Studium Wyborcze (PGSW) 2005 afiliowane przy Instytucie Studiów Politycznych PAN finansowane przez Ministerstwo Nauki i Informatyzacji (Komitet Badań Naukowych)—grant nr 1 H02E 060 28 oraz dofinansowywane przez Fundację im. Stefana Batorego, Fundację Centrum Badania Opinii Społecznej (CBOS), Instytut Filozofii i Socjologii PAN i University of Glasgow (Department of Politics & Department of Central and East European Studies).

PGSW 2007

Polskie Generalne Studium Wyborcze 2007

Polskie Generalne Studium Wyborcze 2007, pod kierownictwem Radosława Markowskiego, afiliowane przy Instytucie Studiów Politycznych PAN, dofinansowane przez tę instytucję, oraz przez: Ministerstwo Nauki i Szkolnictwa Wyższego, Wissenschaftszentrum Berlin fur Sozialforschung (WZB), Polską Konfederację Pracodawców Prywatnych Lewiatan, Fundację Batorego, Instytut Filozofii i Socjologii PAN oraz instytucję badawczą realizującą sondaż—PBS DGA.

Hungary

GESIS 1990–2001

ZACAT GESIS Study No. ZA 4054. Consolidation of Democracy in Central and Eastern Europe 1990–2001: Cumulation PCP I and II.

DKMKA HES 2003

TÁRKI Joint Research Center—*TDATA-G35: DKMKA Election Study, 2003: "A" file.* Data sheet. Version: 18 March 2011; TÁRKI Social Research Institute Inc.; Median. Funded by the Hungarian Center for Democracy Foundation. Distributed by the TÁRKI Joint Research Center.

TÁRKI 2005

TÁRKI Joint Research Center—*TDATA-G21: TÁRKI Omnibus 2005/1. Social-political attitudes in Hungary among the adult population.* Data sheet. Version: 4 November 2010. Funded by Századvég Center for Political Analysis, Hungarian Center for Democracy Foundation, Central European Opinion Research Group Foundation, Auto News Ltd. Distributed by the TÁRKI Joint Research Center.

DKMKA HES 2009

DKMKA Election Study Database 2009.

Slovakia

GESIS 1999
ZACAT GESIS Study No. ZA4065. Current Problems of Slovakia 1999.

Notes

1 For a discussion of the relationship between right-wing attitudes and voting behavior, see further (among others): Arzheimer 2009a; Falter 1994; Minkenberg 1998: chapter 8; Norris 2005; Spier 2010; Stöss 1994, 2005.
2 As an example: "We will support Polish families, especially through the tax system, financial help and welfare redistribution for education and raising children" (LPR 2003: 5, transl. B.P.).

13 Social class and the radical right

Conceptualizing political preference formation and partisan choice

Herbert Kitschelt

Introduction

A sensible discussion of the strategic opportunities for growth as well as containment of the radical right in post-industrial democracies and those surrounding them (i.e., Central and Eastern Europe) requires an adequate conceptualization of social structure that makes "locations" (asset endowments, competences, experiences) relevant for the formation of politically relevant "preferences" and "interests." Moreover, it calls for a sophisticated analysis of supply configurations of policy alternatives on the playing field of partisan competition. Only where demand and supply meet will socio-structural dispositions translate into actual vote choices.

I will try to make this concluding essay controversial with some bald and incompletely backed assertions (no empirical evidence provided here!). Think of its heuristic value as one of stimulating further research, even if some of its assertions are overdrawn or turn out to be plain wrong. When it comes to *demand-side considerations*, I will be the champion of intellectual innovation against the majority of the contributions in this volume: the old theory, of understanding political preference through class structure, as provided by the Erikson-Goldthorpe-Portocarero (EGP) framework, simply will not do to account for political preference formation and the demand-side explanation of radical right party support. Moreover, I will claim that we have to go beyond the ad-hocism of two dimensions of political preference formation and analytically think in terms of three dimensions. While two dimensions have been sufficient to map relevant party positions empirically in the past, strategic options for the radical right and its competitors are now beginning to unfold in a three-dimensional space. In the end, my proposals will be at odds with every contribution in this volume, either because (1) I object to the papers' occupation-based conception of social structure, and/or (2) because I begin to stray away from a two-dimensional rendering of the relevant preference space in post-industrial politics.

Relatively few papers in this volume venture into *supply-side considerations*, to which I will devote a bit of space in my response paper. Here I will be the champion of theoretical conservatism and restraint. I prefer to stay as close as possible to an old-fashioned spatial-positional conceptualization of party competition and vote choice, albeit with some behavioral extensions. Once these behavioral extensions have been taken into account, special additive theoretical frameworks that invoke valence, salience, and issue ownership as genuinely distinct considerations and rationale in party competition may contribute too little to be worth the effort, or may appear to be plain wrongheaded. All of this sets aside, of course, non-rational vote choice considerations, which clearly do play a role in citizens' empirical choices among parties. They involve, however, psychological mechanisms available to strategic manipulation by all partisan competitors and therefore do not uniquely reward the radical right. Or they involve mechanisms that are just not strategically manipulable by politicians at all (such as party identification due to socialization and/or religious devotion), and therefore have to be accepted as simple facts of life ("constraints") by the various partisan contenders.

My earlier work on radical right parties (Kitschelt and McGann 1995 specifically) has been blamed, also on the pages of this book, for proposing a "winning electoral formula" that either never was winning or made itself obsolete for the radical right by the time my work appeared in print, just as Hegel's *Owl of Minerva* embarked on its flight only at dusk. Against the backdrop of these earlier considerations, my paper here will conclude by speculating on whether there ever was and currently still is a "winning electoral formula" (or shall we say: "equilibrium strategy"?) for the radical right and its competitors, and what may be its implications for the future of the radical right's conventional competitors.

As a corollary to this discussion, I conclude by seconding Kay Arzheimer's empirical conclusion that the conventional European center left will not be able to win back their erstwhile core electorate, i.e., the bulk of the remaining manual skilled and unskilled blue-collar workers. Instead there will be a multiplicity of partisan lefts in European party systems, only some of which will be able to attract bits and pieces of the working class; while the plurality, if not majority, of what can still be conceptualized as "working-class" voters—and some—will decisively opt for non-leftist parties, and particularly radical right parties. Political entrepreneurs will try to construct a "progressive political coalition" beyond a working-class support base.

Since my piece has more the character of a polemic with analytical, but heuristic, objectives, it will include few references. Moreover, I will not take up definitional issues of what is or is not "radical right" or "right" with different adjectives.

Mapping political preferences onto social experiences: is there still a role for "class"?

Debates about social class in political analysis are motivated by a simple hypothesis: in contemporary post-industrial capitalism, *extra-political social experiences*—whether people make them in the sphere of producing and distributing material goods and services to earn a money income or in the sphere of the self-reproduction of social actors through families (broadly conceived), social networks, and cultural associations—*affect the articulation of preferences and the modes of collective mobilization involved in politics and its ultimate result*, collectively binding authoritative decisions enforced under the shadow of a monopoly of violence, the state. In Marx's terms: "Das Sein bestimmt das Bewußtsein"—"being determines consciousness." Even if we set aside basic challenges to the validity of this claim advanced by theorists of political dealignment and "cartel party" formation—chains of arguments asserting a disconnection between citizens' preferences and politicians' policy commitments and hence a breakdown of political representation, which I will not confront here (but see Kitschelt and Rehm 2011a)—what exactly are the experiences of "being" that affect "consciousness?" And more precisely, how do we construct the space of "consciousness" that is affected by the experiences of "being?"

As a positive or negative reference point for theoretical reasoning and empirical analysis in the papers of this volume, let me introduce a stripped-down version of the model supplied by Goldthorpe (2000), here embellished a bit in a crisp rational-choice language:

1   Individuals are *utility maximizers* who seek to achieve the highest level of income, discounted over their lifetime.

2   Individuals bring a variety of *assets* like education, professional skills, and work experience to bear on their income maximization. These assets lead them to hold different market and organizational positions. Most importantly, professionals have skills that involve judgment and local knowledge and therefore cannot be specified in detailed work contracts. Their "asset-specific" endowments, therefore, command more income and different organizational insertions than those who lack them. The social structure disaggregates basically into a hierarchy of non-manual classes from highly skilled asset-specific professionals (salariat I), via intermediately skilled (salariat II) to routine non-manual wage earners (III), a hierarchy of manual labor (V technicians, VI skilled workers, VII unskilled workers in different sectors a/b/c), and finally a parallel hierarchy of the small self-employed with or without employees in different sectors (IV a/b/c).

3   People form *political partisan preferences primarily over the maximization of market income and they vote on market income.* People's immersion in markets and as holders of assets (skills, capital) constitutes their "class position," and this is critical for their political consciousness. Ultimately, their market-defined and asset-defined class positions make them vote on advancing their prospects for market incomes. They advocate redistribution by political means, if their expected income falls short of the mean income net of a dead loss incurred by redistributive taxation (the "Meltzer–Richard" theorem), while they prefer markets without political redistribution if their class positions yield incomes above that threshold.

4   Certain lifestyle choices and tastes may be influenced by certain *occupation-based "status" hierarchies of esteem* that are separate from class-based relations of income, asset control, and asset specificity. But these status hierarchies are entirely inconsequential for political partisan choices (Chan and Goldthorpe 2007).

Two facts fly in the face of the political sociology implied by the EGP model of preference formation:

- A fair number of people in class positions that should predestine them to vote for a redistributive "left" party fail to do so and vote over-proportionally for radical "right" parties that do not embrace vigorously redistributive positions, or do not even attribute much salience to questions of distribution. This applies to both the manual working class (EGP V–VII) and low-skilled clerical employees (EGP III).
- A fair number of citizens in class positions that should predispose them to oppose redistribution and instead support "rightist" parties consistent with their attributed interests instead support "leftist" parties that have mild or vigorous redistributive appeals and track records. This applies to many citizens in the professions (EGP I and II).

There are at least three responses to this empirical conundrum that progressively undermine the EGP frameworks:

- What matters is not just political demand for redistributive policies, but *also the political supply of partisan alternatives*. Maybe a party system simply does not supply redistributive political stances any longer and therefore releases (class) voters who have such predilections, but are forced to choose on other policy dimensions, as there are no stark alternatives on economics.
- In order to predict partisan choice, on the demand-side the voters' market and asset characterizations of the EGP model need to be supplemented by other experiences made in the spheres of economic production or social redistribution that begin to affect distributive preferences and/or additional dimensions of preferences with consequences for partisan choice.
- The EGP scheme's core characterization of actors' experiences in the economic sphere of gainful employment itself is problematic as a predictor of political preferences, whether over redistributive or other preference dimensions.

All three of these extensions and revisions have some analytical value. I will discuss these ways to deal with "anomalies" undercutting the political-sociological predictive power of the EGP scheme in reverse order, because I want to make a point that some of the extensions discussed in paper contributions to this volume really mask the need for a new construction of the occupational experiences relevant for political preference formation in post-industrial democratic capitalism.

Occupational experiences and preference formation

Occupational experiences are characterized not only by the (1) degree of autonomy and control actors have over their situation and the range of discretion
they enjoy in their occupations, but also (2) by the ambiguity and openness of
the situation: How much do they "understand" how their own actions bring
about outcomes (goods, services), and how much do they rely on the "under-
standings" of other players to define the situation (jointly) and to bring about
such outcomes? These experiences may affect not only preferences over (1) the
appropriate kinds and amount of *reward* ("distribution") that should be allotted
to different contributors, but also preferences over (2) the appropriate *rules*
("governance"), and (3) the appropriate participants (group identity) involved in
the work process.

Autonomy and control of the situation is awarded to actors based on the tangible assets they bring to the collective enterprise (ownership), the skills they
contribute (level, specificity), and the scarce resources they allocate. People with
strong assets and responsibility for the use of scarce resources will allocate a
large share of the output to themselves (preferences against redistribution:
"greed"). More arguably, and net of countervailing forces, they may also want to
keep tight surveillance over the use of resources (advocating a more "authoritarian" process in which people submit to tight and encompassing rules set by the
highest authority, preferences over governance: "grid") and monitor the habits
and orientations of those who participate in the process (discretionary powers
over drawing the line between those who are in and out of the process: inclusive
and exclusive conceptions of "group").

Actors in work organizations may operate in *situations with greater or lesser
understanding of the work technology, with "technology" defined in a purely
cognitive way as cause-effect knowledge.* Situations tend to be ill-understood,
when (1) the causal chains that link actors (and machinery) together combine
many steps and elements in recursive and interactive feedback loops, and (2) the
causal relationships among the steps are uncertain and ill-specified. This happens
to be the case particularly in *"human" and "social" technologies that involve
healing, teaching, persuading, and enlightening,* but in also some material technologies with physical outputs. Most of the ill-understood social and material
technologies pervade fields that are intense in terms of social interaction: the
"object" of the work process is other human beings as clients, with complicated
capacities and aspirations. In health and social policy areas, clients mostly do not
contract for well specified, tangible, intersubjectively well specified services, but
for transformative experiences that affect their sense of self and empower them
to become different people.

Let me submit now that political preference formation is to a substantial
extent *a process of abstraction and generalization from an actor's own
everyday-life occupational experiences* and the imperatives of a "correct" and
"just" order that these experiences generate for that actor: the less a work process
is causally understood and instead relies on experimentation and open-ended

reciprocal interaction with other human beings, the less can it be governed by clear-cut rules and the less it can be surveyed and monitored by some central authority. Generalizing from these experiences, *actors caught up in ambiguous, uncertain work situations may prefer loosely coupled authority structures and a "libertarian" philosophy of social governance that relies on the lateral reciprocity and mutual recognition of participants in a process tolerant to diversity and experimentation ("grid" or governance).* This is also *likely to predispose actors toward a more egalitarian distribution of resources ("greed"),* as many people share in the process in diffuse capacities and therefore may be seen as earning similar rewards for participation in the work. Moreover, the collaborative work process will benefit from the incorporation of diverse talents, thus *predisposing participants toward universalism and inclusiveness on the "group" (or "citizenship") dimension.*

Couched in references to classical sociological theory, I would claim that in causally uncertain task structures, actors negotiate a process of symbolic interaction that involves the mutual recognition of participants. The locus of experience, therefore, is *not primarily class* in the sense of Marx or Weber, conceived as an insertion in markets and hierarchies of control, but of *profession and occupation,* in the sense of Durkheim, as concrete transformative undertaking in the work process ("task structures"), yielding a continuum of modes of action that ranges from instrumental and strategic (inter)actions in well understood environments, to symbolic-interactive and communicative interactions in less well understood environments in which the recognition of the Other becomes a constitutive element of success in the work process, to draw on Habermas' (1981) and Honneth's (1995) further revisions and transformations of the Durkheimian perspective.

In other words, concrete occupational work processes (tasks) may shape political preferences on at least three dimensions, namely concerning criteria over membership in a collaborative process ("group"), the procedural governance of that process ("grid"), and the distributive rewards flowing from that process ("greed"). As a first step, let us consider only a *two-dimensional scheme* in which experiences contributing to distributive preferences are differentiated from experiences that operate primarily on grid/group (governance/citizenship) preferences.

- Those with *few assets, resources and occupational autonomy, as well as with highly structured, well understood occupational tasks,* tend to articulate redistributive political preferences, as well as also authoritarian views over procedures and exclusionary conceptions of access and entry. This is the case with many blue-collar and white-collar low-skill occupations (classes III, IVb, IVc, VI and VII in the EGP scheme).
- Actors with *more assets, resources, and autonomy working with structured, understood occupational tasks oppose redistribution and express more authoritarian-exclusionary grid-group conceptions* (elements in classes I, II, IVa, and V of the EGP scheme, particularly managerial, legal, business, and technical professionals).

- By contrast, actors with *more assets, resources, and autonomy but also less well understood occupational tasks* tend to be more redistributive and especially more libertarian and inclusionary (elements of classes I, II, IVa, and V of the EGP scheme, particularly in socio-cultural professions situated in the health/wellness, education, communication, travel, fashion/style, and entertainment sectors).
- As a residual and quantitatively smaller category, there are those who have *few assets, resources, and autonomy in less-well understood occupational task structures* who are expected to be both more redistributive and more libertarian-inclusive. They are likely to be situated in classes III and VII of the EGP scheme and involve unskilled personal services in homes, medical, and educational institutions.

In other words, in my scheme, political preference formation by and large cuts across the classes of the EGP scheme. This applies especially to the "salariat" (EGP I+II).[1] *This class blows apart*: its diverse constitutive elements are stretched far across the greed, grid, and group preference dimensions. The business-managerial element is clearly against redistribution and somewhere in the middle on the grid/group dimension, whereas the socio-cultural professionals are extreme on the grid/group dimensions and center "left" on the greed dimension.[2] Most of the papers in this volume cannot detect these differences as they build on the EGP scheme, which does not accommodate occupational differentiation of task-structure-based experiences. Conversely, at the low end of skill and asset control, there is no reason to distinguish between manual and non-manual labor (i.e., EGP III, IVc, and VI–VII), as these groups do not experience analytically relevant differences in their occupational task structures. This assertion matches also with findings in some, but not all, of the papers included in this volume: The difference between "manual" and "non-manual" labor in terms of political preferences is immaterial (see, e.g., in this volume, Oesch and Gougou/Mayer, but against that Bornschier/Kriesi, Table 1.1, and van der Brug et al., Table 3.5). The manual/non-manual distinction is a leftover that Goldthorpe imported ad hoc from an older Marxist debate about "productive" and "unproductive" labor and from the later difference between manufacturing and clerical "white-collar" occupations, which to a large extent masked skill and gender differences in the labor force.

If a very rough simplification is permissible, then, we encounter a tripolar configuration of occupational experience clusters, differentiated on two dimensions, yielding three broad groups contrasting in their occupational profiles and consequently their political preferences: (non-)manual, low-skilled occupational autonomy wage earners in highly structured, certain occupational environments; high-skilled, high-autonomy wage earners and independents in structured environments; and high-skilled, high-autonomy wage earners and independents in low-structure/high-uncertainty socially and culturally interactive environments.

But this logic does not suffice to differentiate interests on three dimensions, including that between libertarian/authoritarian grid-governance and inclusive, universalistic versus exclusive, particularistic group-identity preferences. While this distinction becomes practically important in the empirical distribution of preferences in recent years, it cannot be derived from occupational experiences alone. It requires an *external shock* that interacts with occupational experiences: *the more or less great willingness of (growing) ethnic minorities to embrace a libertarian or authoritarian grid-governance structure.* Where ethnic minorities—whether immigrants or not—tolerate or embrace libertarian governance, indigenous libertarians will also accept cosmopolitan conceptions of citizenship. Where, by contrast, ethnic minorities embrace authoritarian conceptions of governance, however, indigenous libertarians may be inclined to embrace exclusionary membership (group) preferences, as a defensive move to protect libertarian domestic socio-political governance structures, whether with regard to religious freedoms, permissive gender and family relations, cultural pluralism, or nonpunitive views of law enforcement. I envision this perspective to be in some ways derivative of what Jürgen Habermas (1992) once coined as "constitutional patriotism," a sense of identity (and exclusionary boundary drawing) not based on ascriptive cultural markers, but a shared understanding of libertarian cultural governance that rejects authoritarian intolerance. I will return to the differentiation of grid/group positions in my analysis of the supply side of the strategic opportunities radical right-wing parties may seize upon.

It will not have escaped readers of this volume that my perspective on the relationship between occupational task structures and political preferences is similar to what Oesch and Bornschier/Kriesi propose. Consider my rendering of the underlying mechanisms of preference formation as friendly amendments to their analyses in two regards:

- More so even than Oesch, I am desperately struggling to find an analytical, deductive, generalizeable, and parsimonious basis to characterize occupational experiences that are involved in the process of political preference formation. We need to go beyond the ad-hocisms of simply positing an "economic" and a "social" dimension of politics, as is typically done in much of American political science, typically on purely empiricist, inductive grounds (see, e.g., Treier and Hillygus 2009).
- Bornschier and Kriesi in their chapter in this book (Chapter 1), and even more so in their other works (Kriesi *et al.* 2006, 2008b) operate with only two dimensions of preference formation, the familiar "economic" and "social" dimensions. But they amend the analysis by claiming that the issues that map onto the "social" dimensions have changed from questions of morality to questions of globalization and particularlistic or collective identities. They quite correctly reject a reductionism that sees conflicts over immigration and globalization simply as issues of income distribution, pitting winners and losers of globalization in capitalist labor and product markets against each other[3] and instead insist on seeing the conflict as one over citizenship and collective identity. But by *conceiving of the relationship between governance and citizenship issues as a temporal sequence of*

issue mappings on the same dimension, they miss the potential strategic and coalitional complications that occur when they appear simultaneously, and actually in configurations where libertarians on governance are not necessarily also cosmopolitan universalists, or where authoritarians are parochial on immigration. This is a point to which I will return in the analysis of racial right-wing party strategies.

The critical point of my discussion, however, is that those who build an analysis of political preference formation, and ultimately party choice, on the tools provided by the EGP scheme, or use the EGP scheme to introduce class/occupational controls to isolate the empirical significance of "additive" factors, miss that the EGP scheme itself is wrong-headed and misleading as a construct to capture experiences and preference formation in the sphere of economic activity in post-industrial capitalism. Because it misconceives the mechanisms of preference formation, its categories are more or less useless in explanatory and predictive regards to account for the foundations of political partisan alignments. Most egregiously, the political sociology applications of the EGP scheme myopically confine themselves to political preference formation over asset distribution ("greed"), while falsely claiming that questions of governance and citizenship are either irrelevant for partisan alignments (as asserted by Chan and Goldthorpe 2007) or are simply derivatives of distributive preferences.

A question I will not raise here, but have addressed elsewhere, concerns the endogeneity of occupational choice: are people showing particular greed/grid/group preferences not because of their occupational exposure, but are their occupational choices a reflection of pre-existing political preferences? Even if endogeneity prevailed, one would have to wonder why there is such a striking match between people's preferences and their choice of occupational experiences (the "weak" theory of occupational preference formation). But there is, in fact, some clinching evidence based on time-series data of occupational careers and political preferences, showing that not just self-selection into an occupation, but prolonged occupational exposure leaves a net effect on people's political preferences (the "strong" theory of occupational preference formation).[4]

I shall also dwell here only in very cursory terms on the unique situation in post-communist countries. As touched upon, but not elaborated, in Minkenberg and Pytlas' contribution (chapter 12), we are dealing here with not-quite post-industrial economies, generally with rather modest-sized pockets of socio-cultural or technical professionals, but a very large low-skilled and intermediate-skilled blue-collar and white-collar clerical labor force. Not only is the center of gravity of preference formation in these polities substantially closer to leftist-redistributive "greed" positions, authoritarian "grid" positions, and particularist "group" positions than in Western post-industrial democracies;[5] but also the occupational structure, considered alone, suggests that economic-distributive issues may be more at the forefront of political contestation than the other dimensions. If active divisions over grid and group issues do then occur, they may be prompted much more directly by the strategic calculations of political parties and their trajectories on the supply side of democratic politics than grounded in sociologically deeper clashes of occupational and lifestyle experiences that look for an outlet on the plane of party competition. Hence we observe a sociologically more amorphous alignment of citizens around political parties.

Political preference formation beyond occupational experience

It goes without saying that political preference formation does not exhaust itself in occupational experiences. Nor may the impact of occupational experiences on the radical right work entirely through political preferences.[6] But in order to identify correctly the size and calibration of the effect exerted by these additional mechanisms of preference formation, we need an adequate baseline model of occupational experiences to begin with. If papers in this volume followed this strategy, I would venture to postulate that the effect of additional preference mechanisms promoting radical right vote choice, net of the class experiences measured with the EGP scheme, would be absorbed by occupational experiences. This does not imply that the mechanisms identified by the authors of this volume have no causal force, but it changes their quantitative calibration: to a considerable extent, these variables pick up the impact of occupational experiences for which there are no controls, as I will argue briefly for several of the papers. I will then, however, turn to an inverse puzzle, namely that occupational experience appears to affect radical right vote choice not only *through* policy preferences, but also *net of* such preferences. Other than measurement error in the empirical observation of policy preferences, this may be due to the fact that occupation also works through other channels that affect partisan choice net of preferences, particularly associational memberships and networks into which voters are tied. More so than in this volume, the mediating role of unions and churches, but also residential neighborhood networks, may deserve some attention.

Overestimating the impact of factors additive to occupational experiences

Ivarsflaten and Stubager (Chapter 7) argue in their contribution that education provides a unique mechanism of political preference formation and partisan choice that is separate from occupational status or class. Moreover, the impact of education cannot be accounted for with an instrumental model of rational income maximizers. Economic vulnerability cannot be the exclusive or even main basis of the link between lower education, greater aversion to immigration, and higher propensity to vote for the radical right. While I second this general conclusion and see it partially confirmed by Bornschier and Kriesi's contribution (Chapter 1), I would, however, posit that better concepts to capture occupational experiences than the EGP scheme would reduce the size of the education coefficients in the statistical estimations substantially. The same amendment applies to the estimations presented in Gougou/Mayer that show large educational and birth cohort effects, but control for occupational experiences in the spirit of conventional EGP categories.

Coffé (Chapter 8) provides an instructive empirical analysis of the distinctive impact of gender on radical right voting preferences. But also here the EGP scheme looms large, and some of the gender differences may be particularly striking because there is no control for occupational experiences. After all, among highly educated people, women are concentrated in the tier of socio-cultural professionals for which one may postulate strong libertarian-cosmopolitan and mildly redistributive preferences. A telling tracker that gender may mask occupational experiences emerges from the paper's comparison of the impact of education on radical right vote propensities for men and women. Without holding constant for attitudes toward immigration, women display a much larger difference in right-wing voting propensity across levels of education than men (Table 13.1), an effect that mostly disappears when immigration attitudes are controlled for. Since female professionals are much more likely to work in people-processing social services than men, I would expect the initial gender difference in educational impact on the vote to disappear at least partly, when an adequate occupational model is used as control. Of course, some of the gender difference is likely to be genuine, having to do with women's differential insertion in reproductive life (childrearing) and the contested power balance in family relations that may be only loosely correlated with occupational experiences.

Why political preferences and policy preferences may not capture the entire effect of occupational experiences on the radical right vote

While occupations loom large in providing experiences that feed through political preference formation into vote choice, not all occupational impact on partisan choice is mediated through political preferences. One additional plausible mechanism running from experiences to vote choice may have to do with the mediating role of associational ties and networks, particularly that of labor unions and religious associations. Empirically, occupational membership may correlate with associational networks. But what these networks contribute to the process of partisan choice may not show up in people's preference formation alone. Furthermore, inasmuch as it shows up in their preference formation and vote choice, associational memberships may in part contradict and counteract the spontaneous experiences of the work life.

As a general template, let us assume that labor unions are led by sophisticated political entrepreneurs, who have a bent not only to resonate with their members' concerns for redistributive demands but also to counteract the authoritarian and particularistic propensities of low-skilled, low-education wage earners in highly structured occupational situations. Net of all occupational factors and other factors, labor unionism may make members more redistributive, libertarian, and cosmopolitan than non-members. Moreover, where unions are affiliated with conventional parties of the center left, union members may remain more loyal to established parties than non-unionists. This may in part be due to associational ties, in part due to the mediating impact of union membership on policy preferences.

Similar causal complications may apply to religious affiliation. While Christian religions may instill acceptance of the political-economic status quo and therefore may exert a net force nudging people away from income redistribution ("greed") and toward more authoritarian governance ("grid"), the Christian influence on "group" issues may be more ambivalent: hostile to the acceptance of competing religious cultural templates, but inviting to an influx of people who can be incorporated in the churches, consistent with the universalistic and egalitarian encompassing conception of the Christian community. Organizational affiliations and intellectual doctrines may hence make practicing Christians support radical right-wing parties in lesser numbers than non-believers or adherents of other religious faiths.

How do the various contributions in the book speak to the mediating impact of associational affiliation on political preferences over the greed/grid/group dimensions and ultimately the act of partisan choice for the radical right? Surprisingly, neither labor union membership nor religious practice appear as systematic control in all of the studies, as they should, at least in my view. Bornschier and Kriesi provide the most explicit treatment, albeit not when they compare partisan choice across national population samples. They report the odd finding that, net of preferences, both voters with low and high education have a lesser tendency to support the radical right than voters with medium education (Table 13.1, column 3). I wonder whether the negative coefficient for low-education voters is not simply masking the fact that it is the impact of higher-than-average union affiliation on low-education members that reduces the propensity of this group to support the radical right. We cannot tell whether that is true even from the authors' later estimation that *among* workers union membership has no effect on the propensity to vote for the extreme right. The effect could run through political preferences that are controlled for in Bornschier and Kriesi's estimation (Table 1.2).[7]

The decline of union-based associational ties as a cause of working-class votes for the radical right is also strongly hinted at in Gougou and Mayer's piece on intergenerational change in the determinants of radical right voting. Had the authors been able to control for associational memberships, it may be the decline of union affiliation—not birth cohort by itself—that explains the greater availability of French voters to the radical right.

In Coffé's piece on gender, the large size and resilience of the negative statistical relationship between social sector employment and radical right voting among women, even when controlling for preferences over economics (greed) and immigration (group), may suggest not only occupational roots of preference formation (women in the social sector are more likely to be professional care deliverers rather than merely general administrators), but also an intervening associational mechanism: women tend to be more organized in social services than in other areas, and even those with low skill may be predisposed as a result of union affiliation against supporting radical right parties.

Coffé's chapter (Chapter 8) is intriguing because it shows a robust negative net association between religious devotion and support of the radical right, both with and without attitudinal controls. Christian religious commitment and universalistic doctrines, at least in the way practiced in Western Europe, may at times predispose devout voters against ethnocentrism ("group"), even though they tend to be more authoritarian on questions of political governance ("grid").[8] Here we have an example where the need for a distinct third dimension of preference formation shows up. Regrettably, in some papers religious practice does not show up as mechanism at all (Bornschier and Kriesi, Chapter 1; Oskarson and Demker, Chapter 10). The opposite problem may apply to van der Brug *et al.* (Chapter 3, especially Table 3.5). The regressions on vote choice include so many religious variables, some with opposite signs, that it is unclear what substantive conclusions should be drawn from them.

Overall, the message of my discussion should be obvious: we have to re-theorize the constitutive role of work and economy for the formation of political preferences beyond the Marxian or Weberian approaches incorporated in the EGP scheme. Against that backdrop, we can then calibrate the independent contribution of asset endowments in the production sphere (especially education, but also income), as well as preference-forming experiences in the spheres of social reproduction (gender and family status, possibly age) and associational intermediation (especially professional and religious associations).

From preference distributions to partisan alignments: the role of supply-side factors in the emergence of electoral coalitions around radical right parties

If we follow the sociological intuition that political preferences are anchored outside the sphere of politics itself, strategic politicians who aspire to power and office can persuade people to act only on preferences that are already spontaneously present. Nevertheless, this does not make partisan politics a mirror image of social structure, as politicians may assemble different coalitions of voters, characterized by overlapping preferences. Whether or not distinct radical right parties emerge in this process depends on a number of conditions that are not identified by sociological and political-economic circumstances, but they are genuinely part and parcel of the political-institutional sphere. I propose an incomplete yet fairly parsimonious model of supply-side analysis, but claim that commonly voiced additional considerations provide too little empirical explanatory power and traction to be worth in-depth consideration. Against this backdrop, I will then consider the strategic choices faced by radical right parties and their competitors in post-industrial democracies in the early decades of the twenty-first century.

A minimalist supply-side model

The supply-side model makes several assumptions about the demand side that should first be brought into the open. They conform to assumptions made in behavioral models of party competition recently proposed by Laver (2005), Laver and Serengeti (2011), and Budge *et al.* (2010).

- Voters act on parties' *spatial proximity in policy positions*, either "naively," by supporting the closest party in a sense yet to be specified for multidimensional spaces, or "strategically," by supporting a party that is likely to enter coalitions pulling the resulting policy output close to the voter's ideal position (Kedar 2009).[9]
- But parties' perceived policy positions are not instantly and freely chosen; they are based on ideology and reputation. Parties build up a cumulative stock of perceptions that shapes people's views of their policy positions. Given citizens' limited information processing, parties can effectively change their perceived policy appeal only very gradually and without leap-frogging established competitors.
- "*Money matters most* (3M)," even though partisan competition may involve multiple dimensions. In the political sphere, citizens are most concerned with the impact of policy on the size and certainty of their income flow. The greater they perceive the impact of differences between the competing parties' positions on economic policies and incomes ("greed"), relative to the differences they anticipate to flow from the parties' rival conceptions of governance ("grid") or citizenship universalism ("group"), the greater will be the weight of economic considerations in their vote choice. Narrow perceived partisan differences on economics releases voters to prioritize other dimensions.

The critical move here is *to postulate priority of economics, but then partially to endogenize the salience of issue dimensions for the vote choice.* Rather than treating salience as a separate consideration, salience is a function of partisan polarization (non-convergence of party positions). A simple empirical test undergirds this assertion: in Benoit and Laver's (2006) expert data survey of party appeals, a party's extremism on a policy issue correlates in the experts' judgments with the salience that party attributes to the issue. The correlation is not perfect, but while almost *all parties* that take an extreme position on an issue are *also* judged to *consider that issue highly salient for their pursuits*, the reverse does not necessarily apply: moderate positions too sometimes become highly salient for a party.

The main supply-side hypotheses that flow from this framework for vote- or office-maximizing politicians, then, are the following:

- The more the existing mainstream parties *converge on economic issues of (re)distribution,* the more citizens are willing to vote on another dimension of political issues, *provided politicians offer alternatives on that dimension.*

- Because voters react to *reputation and ideological cues*, politicians cannot adjust their parties' positions rapidly to changing issue demands.
- Where parties converge on economic positions, new party entry becomes likely, if existing parties differentiate stances on additional dimension(s) but cannot service all the relevant options.

These hypotheses are somewhere between my earlier hypothesis that it is *exclusively economic convergence of conventional parties* that matters for the rise of radical right parties with pronounced extreme positions on grid and/or group issues (Kitschelt 2007), and the alternative position that it is only issue priming by conventional parties with divergent positions on the grid/group dimensions that precipitates voter crystallization around a radical right alternative (Ignazi 2003). It is informed by the recent analysis of Spies and Franzmann (2011), even though I do not trust their use of Comparative Manifesto Project party positions for the more fine-grained analysis of parties' issue positions on policy dimensions. They find that indeed the Ignazi immigration divergence thesis, and not my original more simplistic economic convergence thesis, is empirically borne out,[10] but that there is a substantial interaction effect along the lines postulated in my modified hypothesis: only when (the salience of) the economic-distributive policy dimension has shrunk, because parties' positions have converged, a greater polarization on non-distributive group issues will boost the performance of radical right parties.

The critical question, of course, that is raised by the supply-side hypothesis is this: why would existing parties ever converge on the dominant economic dimension, well knowing that it might open up opportunities for a polarized competition on a second dimension they cannot sufficiently control to preempt the entry of new challengers? This question has given rise to a variety of answers through the lens of which we can also examine contributions to the radical right literature, including papers in this volume. Several authors have raised the question of why there are so few electorally substantial left-authoritarian parties (if any), although there are plenty of voters with political preferences clustering around such positions (in this volume, e.g., van der Brug *et al.*, Bornschier and Kriesi).

1   *The first answer is that new party entry happens in institutionally permissive electoral systems with low thresholds to entry.*[11] Applied to the radical right, this proposition rallies support (e.g., Golder 2003), but also rejection (e.g., van der Brug *et al.* 2005; Arzheimer 2009a; Spies and Franzmann 2011). Testing the proposition adequately may be beset by a fundamental asymmetry and discontinuity: while radical right parties are unsuccessful in systems with the most restricted entry conditions—single-member district plurality winner systems—all other systems offer little predictive value for the presence or absence of successful radical right parties. Very high electoral thresholds may restrict the number of parties and may impose a "forced choice" (Huber and Stanig 2010) on citizens. Nevertheless, the skeptics may be right that in all other instances electoral system specifications do not explain radical right success or successful new party entry more generally.

2   Another, in my view unsatisfactory, explanation of dimensional proliferation and new party entry was offered by Meguid (2005). It infuses Downs (1957)
with Riker (1982) and relies on a *heresthetic manipulation of dimensional issue
salience in the party competition*. In order to weaken its main competitor on the
dominant (economic) dimension of competition, a party may invoke an issue on
another issue dimension that is bound to divide its competitor, but not itself.
Thus, in France the Socialists highlighted a pro-immigrant position, well
knowing that it would force the Gaullists to take a stance on an issue in which
the party is divided between anti-immigrants and indifferents, and thus open the
opportunity for anti-immigrants to defect to a third alternative.

But most of the time any of the major parties will incur the risk that invoking
issues on a new preference dimension is likely to divide not only its competitors,
but also the party itself, internally. This is Odmalm's (2011) point regarding why
conventional Swedish parties never invoked immigration. Meguid's one and
only unambiguous case, that of France in the 1980s, is unique in that the left
could externalize its division over immigration by being divided into a (potentially anti-immigrant) communist and a pro-immigrant socialist left. Moreover,
Meguid does not control for convergence of parties on the dominant dimension.
It is telling that the second dimension led to the surge of a new party success
only after the economic policy convergence of the existing alternatives. This
happened in France after the governing socialists withdrew from their redistributive economic policies and in Sweden after more than a decade of economic and
social policy convergence between right and left, as shown in this volume by
Oskarson and Demker (chapter 10).

3   A third possibility is to invoke the strategic incapacity of established
parties to change their appeals dramatically in the face of new issues. It is to
invoke the *path-dependent articulation of party ideologies and electoral reputations*. Convergence of parties is not a problem as long as: (1) there are no exogenous shocks to the accommodations parties and constituencies may have worked
out on the dominant dimension of competition; and (2) there are no plausible
and pressing second- or third-dimension issues that would offer themselves for
politicization. Thus, the dominance of "cross-class" Christian democratic and
National Rally parties in continental Europe, institutionally manifested in comprehensive, but only moderately redistributive welfare states, became an issue of
disssatisfaction only when unemployment and economic stagnation reduced
popular support for existing economic and social policy. Under these conditions,
the rise of a new issue (such as immigration) and the interaction with the old
issue dimension (Spies and Franzmann 2011) could become the point of crystallization for new party entry on a new dimension.

*In addition to reputational constraints, the objective nature of economic chal-
lenges may make it difficult for conventional parties to reestablish polarized politics on economic issues.* This may ultimately have forced even the hand of
politicians in Sweden to converge on economic and social policy issues and
create a space for the rise of a radical right-wing party. Questions of intergenerational justice due to the demographic transition to low-fertility societies or access

to increasingly sophisticated medical services do not easily lend themselves to politicization on the familiar economic-distributive dimension. Similar complications arise with trade globalization and financial globalization, and the management of technological innovations. They often defy simple distributive formula that could be politicized in party competition.

The power of strategic path dependence, partisan reputation, and objective political-economic conditions may also help to explain *why it is so difficult to establish left-authoritarian parties*. Where welfare states have grown to limits and problems of demography and human capital formation dominate the agenda of social policy makers, even new radical right party entrants cannot run for office with the hope that leftist-populist economic policy rhetoric demanding more economic security and redistribution will resonate with substantial voter groups.[12]

A framework that examines the interaction between narrower competition on familiar issue dimensions and gaining salience of new dimensions may also help to account for the post-communist radical right. The nature of the post-communist economic problems and options for their resolution made redistributive politics not an option, particularly in countries where the nature of the old regime and reform politicians emerging from it, rather advanced levels of development, and proximity to the EU suggested a quick adoption of Western capitalism. Here politicians had particularly strong incentives to politicize new issue dimensions, especially against the backdrop of the existing parties' weak reputations on the economic dimension. Because parties have weak reputations, post-communist polities have also experienced the successful entry of new left-authoritarian parties with cheap populist talk. When in government, however, they have invariably been unable to redeem their promises. Instead, they rather moved on to grid/group issues, when questions of economic (re)distribution have proven too hard to politicize to the benefit of the parties' electoral constituencies.

4   This leaves finally *internal, organizational processes* to account for the strategic inability of parties to take advantage of electoral opportunities and gather up "homeless" electorates. Internal organizations may hamper strategic adjustment both in existing mainstream parties I have analyzed for European social democracy (Kitschelt 1994: chapter 5), as well as in new radical right parties that I only touched upon in passing in my earlier work (Kitschelt and McGann 1995), but that have recently been put front and center in Art's (2011) study of radical right-wing party organization. Indeed, the recruitment of activists and the organizational mobilization of radical right parties may be a genuine causal contributor to their electoral fates, independent of their programmatic pitch and the socio-economic constituencies to which they might appeal.

While the ability to assemble more or fewer organizational resources is a proximate explanation for the success of radical right parties, it is more difficult, however, to explain in turn why radical right-wing parties have differential success in mobilizing organizational resources. The *cordon sanitaire* argument that new party entrants are less successful and attract fewer high-quality contributors, when all established parties uniformly shun their collaboration, looks now less plausible than just a few years ago, inspecting the list of *cordon sanitaire* party systems in Art's (2011: 44) study. Where that *cordon* is claimed to have sanitized coalition politics in the past (often since the 1980s), very few observations still find radical right parties weakened: in some instances, the *cordon* has never prevented the sustained rise of radical right parties (e.g., Flanders, France). In other instances, the *cordon* appears recently to have failed to stop radical right contenders and/or to have broken down (e.g., Netherlands, Sweden). By Art's count, among countries with a *cordon sanitaire*, empirically consistent with the argument are now only: (1) the United Kingdom where, following Goodwin and Cutts in this volume (chapter 11) politicians anyway should not easily worry about the rise of a third party alternative; as well as (2) Germany, where an idiosyncratic explanation building on the nature and legacy of German National Socialism and its effect on the available cadre of radical right parties may be the more convincing explanation for a low-quality radical right.

In summary, what I bet on is a supply-side explanation for radical right parties that considers the constrained strategic flexibility of conventional parties in light of new exogenous shocks (demographics, technological innovation, immigration, etc.) and ancient legacies (prominence of cross-class parties and emergence of the welfare state, combined with corresponding partisan ideologies and reputations) as the key, supplemented by an organizational analysis of radical right-wing mobilization. I put less stock on institutional explanations (electoral laws) and on competition theories that emphasize issue salience, issue ownership, or a combination of the two, a directional theory of voting in which politicians earn issue ownership by making issues salient.[13] These factors have either quite limited empirical relevance or are altogether endogenous to other determinants.

From preferences to radical right political parties: is there (still?) a "winning formula"? Consideration of the demand side alone

In this concluding section, let me apply the demand- and supply-side model considerations to the current strategic situation of the radical right and explore its implications for more or less electoral success. Based on data for the 1980s, I had proposed a supply-side "winning formula" in many West European countries—other than those affected by clientelistic exchange relations—according to which an electorally successful radical right combined a market-liberal distributive position with an authoritarian governance and citizenship position. Let me emphasize that this was always a supply-side characterization in order to bring together a demand-side electoral coalition of rather disparate constituents: petty bourgeois based on authoritarian and market-liberal preferences, but blue-collar and clerical employees based on authoritarianism, with an emphasis on anti-immigration views. I never posited the "market-liberal worker," as presumed by some earlier critics (such as Ivarsflaten 2005) and in this volume by Arzheimer (Chapter 4). Already in the 1980s, the working-class voters of the radical right were no market liberals. But in places such as France, they found themselves in a strategic situation in which the major conventional parties had sufficiently converged on economics to make a substantial subset of workers, and maybe mostly those not affiliated with labor unions, indifferent between the major parties on merely economic policy grounds and therefore available to a strong messenger on a second dimension of competition. Radical right-wing parties were always coalitions of market-liberal petty bourgeois and non-market-liberal workers. Because my rendering has so often been distorted in the literature, let me insert one citation from the analysis of the French Front National electorate:

> We infer from these data that the National Front builds a social coalition that relies primarily on small businesspeople and farmers, who are motivated by strong procapitalist and authoritarian preferences as well as xenophobic resentments, and on elements of the working class whose decisive criterion of affiliation with the National Front is authoritarianism and racism, yet not procapitalism.
>
> (Kitschelt and McGann 1995: 112)

Interestingly, even now in this volume quite a few of the papers find that being right-wing on economics is, *ceteris paribus*, one predictor of radical right party choice, albeit not the strongest one. This is suggested at least by Bornschier and Kriesi's data, Oesch's analysis, and Gougou and Mayer's French survey. Oskarson and Demker see no impact of market liberalism on radical right party choice in Sweden, and van der Brug *et al.*'s over-controlled estimations defy interpretation, burdened with a multiplicity of (re)distributive policy items, as well as subjective class that is often more a tracer of issue positions than occupational practice, and with a heterogeneous set of surveys from both Western and Eastern post-communist countries aggregated into one analysis.

Nevertheless, I am ready to admit that what might have been a "winning formula" from the vantage point of the political supply side in the 1980s may no longer be so today. What has changed since then? And is there still a winning formula? Finally, what are the implications for conventional parties?

On the demand side, my analysis of 1980s data was predicated on the assumption that there was still a numerically substantial traditional petty bourgeoisie worth catering to as an aspiring radical right party. Moreover, the structural crisis of the blue-collar and white-collar clerical working class through the information technology revolution had just begun. Furthermore, the 1980s was still a decade of expanding welfare states, particularly in health care and education, so that in many countries large shares of highly skilled professionals went into public social services, increasing the economic leftism of well educated socio-cultural professionals. What has changed since then?

• *The traditional petty bourgeoisie has shrunk almost to insignificance.* But with the IT revolution progressing, we see a *new small entrepreneurial stratum of the self-employed* that is characterized by high education and highly varied occupational task structures, including many people-processing and culture-producing services that predispose professionals against authoritarianism and parochialism. Based on the occupational analysis I offered earlier, these people should be unavailable to radical right parties. Self-employed voters are no longer a particularly auspicious constituency for the radical right.

• *The decline of the blue-collar working-class and the white-collar clerical occupations has accelerated since the early 1990s.* It has released a quantitatively more substantial share of the labor force into a state of economic uncertainty and unemployment. Hence the share of the population with economically redistributive, but authoritarian grid and parochial group interests should have increased. Furthermore, especially the younger cohorts of this stratum have not been socialized into associational channels of unions (or churches?) that would make them resilient against the lures of radical right parties, net of their policy preferences. In contrast to the 1980s, low-skilled manual and non-manual wage earners, and especially the younger and less associationally affiliated tiers of this group (Gougou and Mayer, chapter 9 in this volume) are the backbone of radical right party support.

My original model also tacitly made some supply-side assumptions that are no longer true or have become relevant only recently. These changes have affected the menu of radical right-wing party choices:

• I tacitly assumed that *parties of the radical right were in the opposition to governments constituted by conventional parties.* It is easier to build broad programmatic coalitions as opposition parties, when leaders can remain ambivalent about a party's programmatic elements that divide their following. For the radical right, this clearly applied to questions of economic liberalism. Since the mid-1990s, however, radical right parties have participated several times in national government coalitions with cabinet ministers that signed off on market-liberal reforms (e.g., Austria, Italy). Invariably these experiments deeply shocked the working-class supporters of the radical right, especially in Austria, and led to a precipitous decline in right-wing party support in subsequent elections.

• As already indicated above, *the demographic transition, in conjunction with the "maturity" of the welfare state and labor-saving technological innovations, probably more so than ongoing globalization, and most recently the 2008 financial crisis,* have constrained the redistributive leeway of governments in advanced capitalist polities. On the supply side, parties that have a programmatic reputation to defend and that have a time horizon longer than one electoral term cannot possibly suddenly endorse reckless populist campaigns to redistribute resources that are patently unavailable. Even new radical right parties may find that left-wing populist slogans would too obviously lack credibility to help their bid for electoral support. While on the demand side the hearts of many voters may call for economic redistribution in combination with authoritarian and parochial grid/group politics, on the supply side this combination is difficult to sell as a partisan package.

• Finally, on the supply side, the *specter of an Islamist fundamentalist challenge undercutting Western libertarian individualism*, starkly highlighted by the events of 9/11, subsequent attacks in Europe, and the (brief) prominence of Al Qaeda, has opened opportunities *for a new rhetorical heresthetics*. With some semblance of credibility, radical rightist political leaders now claim that an exclusionary policy on immigration and multiculturalism is needed to prevent the influx of Islamic immigrants that may undermine the foundations of a Western libertarian, individualistic social order. This train of reasoning may make it possible for radical right-wing parties to split constituencies with libertarian "grid" beliefs into those that stick to inclusive, universalistic "group" perspectives on immigration and multiculturalism and those that are willing to embrace exclusionary, parochial "group" views of national or Western civilizational identity in ways that can be assimilated into the electoral fold of the radical right. Pim Fortuyn's electoral list in 2001 was the first trial balloon to test this strategy.

Due to the interplay of demand- and supply-side conditions, *strategic opportunities for radical right parties*, erstwhile confined to a market-liberal authoritarianism, multiply and cover a range of programmatic variants. In a similar vein, *parties on the libertarian left are caught up in a differentiation of strategic opportunities*. Table 13.1 schematically summarizes this unfolding of options over time.

Until the aftermath of the student movements of 1968 and the 1973–4 oil crisis, three broad streams of political parties dominated the politics of Western capitalist democracies: Social Democracy, Christian Democracy, and Liberalism. They distinguished themselves primarily on economics/greed issues and secondarily on select religion/grid issues. The advent of postindustrial society (1970s–1990s), and especially of welfare states with large social service sectors opened opportunities for the creation of left-libertarian parties. Right-authoritarian alternatives emerged partly in backlash against the socio-cultural change in governance epitomized by the libertarian left, partly in reaction to the economic dislocation and plight of small business and blue collar workers in the postindustrial transformation.

In the most recent era (1990s–2010s), the accelerating demographic transition, IT-induced structural reorganization of production and service industries, and the fundamentalist religious challenge to libertarianism, finally, permitted a further differentiation of partisan opportunities. On the left, it opens the possibility for a libertarian party current with less intense redistributive commitments. Moderate libertarian currents, in turn, may also revise their inclusive "group" positions in the spirit of "constitutional patriotism" (or European civilizational identity?).

Table 13.1 Strategic differentiation of party camps with changing demand-side and supply-side conditions

	1950s–1970s			1970s–1990s			1990s–2010s		
	Group	Grid	Greed	Group	Grid	Greed	Group	Grid	Greed
Radical right							+	–	–
Authoritarian right left							+	=/–	=
Authoritarian center							+	+	=/+
Authoritarian right				+	+	+			
Mainstream									
Liberals	=	=/–	+	=/–	=/–	+	=	–	+
Christian democrats	=	+	=	=	+	=/+	=/+	=/+	=/+
Social democrats	=	=	–	=/–	=/–	+	=	–	=
Radical left									
Libertarian left				=	–	–	–	–	=/–
Libertarian center							=	–	=
Libertarian right							+	–	=/+

On the right, radical parties back-pedal from economic market liberalism, intensify their anti-immigrant and anti-pluralistic "group" appeal, while giving up on parts of the authoritarian "grid" positions about family, gender roles, and the punitive character of the justice system. As several papers in this volume suggest, the newest radical right configures itself around starkly exclusionary conceptions of "group" identity, but more moderate "grid" positions on authoritarian governance and more centrist "greed" positions less enthusiastic about the market place. As Betz and Meret highlight, radical right parties insist on primarily *domestic* market liberalism with a small tax-and-spend state, albeit with some social safeguards for indigenous national citizens. However, they vigorously reject *international* market liberalism ("globalization") and the universalistic welfare state.

Most importantly, parties such as the *Dansk Folkeparti* under Pia Kjaersgaard or the *Front National* under Marine Le Pen, have tried to split "group" from "grid" radicalism, up to the point where they may be all but reversing some of the parties' authoritarian-traditionalist Christian family values and morality "grid" positions in favor of a libertarian individualism. The purpose of this ideological move is to broaden the prospective electoral coalition attracted by radical right politicians to include also those who endorse a hard line only on exclusionary "group" stances, but otherwise defend libertarian "grid" positions. The trailblazer of this programmatic profile was the assassinated Dutch right-wing politician *Pim Fortuyn*. In this instance, however, his programmatic mix of libertarian and xenophobic appeals, unprecedented in the strategy set of the radical right until then, made it doubly difficult and ultimately impossible for his heterogeneous followers to configure his party around a coherent message after his premature death.

Even on the far left, there may be efforts to embrace an exclusionary "group" agenda together with libertarian "grid" and redistributive "greed" appeals. An effort in this direction has come from the "new left" Dutch Socialist Party's (not to be mixed up with the social democratic Dutch Labor Party) that began to embrace anti-immigrant positions with the justification to defend liberty and welfare state. Even Oskar Lafontaine, a leader of the German *Left Party*, an assembly of activists from the former East German post-communist successor party and leftist defectors of the German social democrats, has made antiimmigration noises hinting at the combination of an exclusionary "group" agenda with a left wing distributive ("greed") with a libertarian governance ("grid") appeal.

Where does this leave *the possibility of parties in the "empty quadrant" of authoritarian left positions over which so many contributions to this book are puzzling?* In a way, this quadrant has already been filled by parties in flesh and blood, yet not in the West, but in the postcommunist East. A nationalist or dominant-ethnic group appeal tends to be the programmatic configuration most favored by unreconstructed former communist ruling parties, such as the Communist Party of Russia or the Communist Party of the Czech Republic. These parties are militantly redistributive ("greed") and they are libertarian on issues of social governance ("grid"), no doubt fueled by their anti-clericalism and atheism; but they also embrace exclusionary parochial "group" positions. In Western democracies, prospects of parties appealing to radical populist left-wing nationalism and xenophobia are limited not only by the share of the population economically threatened by dislocations.[14] As suggested above, such leftist economic agenda appeals lack a sense of empirical credibility and realism even for people with left-authoritarian yearnings that would be indispensable to attract a steady and substantial flow of electoral support.

In Figures 13.1 and 13.2, I try to depict the movement of demand side preference distributions mapped in the three-dimensional vectors given in Table 13.1 from the first formation (1950s–1970s) to the second formation (1970s–1990s) and then on to the post-1990 period in a two-dimensional space, although an emerging three-dimensional space would be more accurate. As in Laver's (2005) agent based models of party competition, the two dimensional landscape of demand-side preference distributions with multiparty competition does not yield a single unambiguous Nash-equilibrium. Parties may fan out over the whole space, but instead of constant cycling of partisan positions, the operational continuity of party ideology and partisan reputation restrains the effortless flexibility of even the most unprincipled catch-all parties. Different kinds of parties will inscribe themselves in different fields and regions of the electoral space and adjust their political appeals based on trial-and-error processes using simple rules-of-thumb deployed to increase the future electoral share of parties.

The arrows grafted onto Figure 13.2 indicate what may be the central tendencies of radical right-wing strategies since the 1990s. The solid arrow pointing North-West indicates a movement of radical right parties to the economic center and more libertarian grid positions, defending Western individualism. Being a

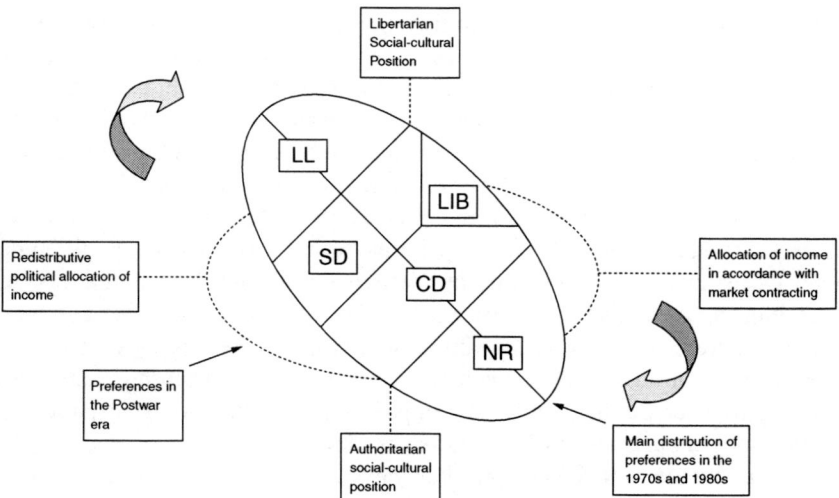

Figure 13.1 Distribution of political preferences from the postwar decades to the 1970s and 1990s.

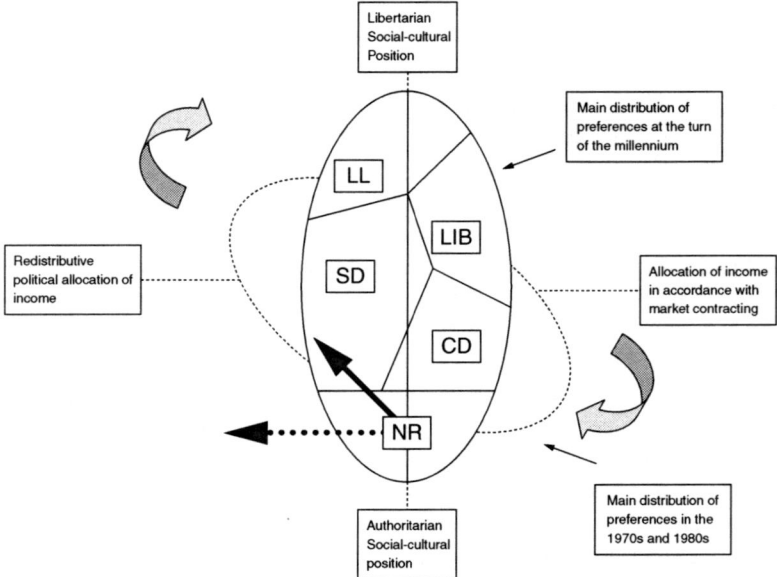

Figure 13.2 Distribution of political preferences from the 1980s into the twenty-first century.

two-dimensional rendering of what effectively becomes a three-dimensional dynamic, however, it does not separately depict the location and movement of the parties on the third, the "group," where radical right parties have remained at the exclusionary-particularlistic pole.

In Figure 13.2, an additional dotted line indicates the direction of a conceivable straight leftist movement of parties on economic distribution, yielding an authoritarian and xenophobic right that almost resembles the thrust of the left periphery of fascist movements in Italy and Germany in the 1920s or of unreconstructed post-communist successor parties, such as the Czech Communists, today. I believe, however, that this configuration of policy appeals (group+; grid-; greed-) is not feasible as a winning electoral strategy on the radical right outside the postcommunist Eastern European realm with still rather different circumstances than those prevailing in Western Europe and North America. A far-reaching redistributive economic agenda, defending and extending comprehensive welfare states, combined with an authoritarian conception of political governance and an exclusionary vision of nationhood and citizenship, however, lacks cognitive credibility, and thus empirical plausibility to be capable of attracting substantial shares of West European electorates.

Let us finally return to the *plight of European social democracy, or more generally the challenges encountered by all three of the major conventional legacy programmatic issue families*, namely social democratic, Christian Democratic-"cross class" and liberal market economic appeals, as they venture to contain their loss of electoral market share due to the onslaught of novel left-libertarian and right-authoritarian parties. Easiest, of course, would be a *re-polarization of political competition around economic partisan politics*. But except in residual welfare states with great income inequality and a patchy social security network that allows a substantial share of the population to fall into poverty and economic destitution, as in the United States and, to a lesser extent, in Australia, Canada, and New Zealand, the agenda of partisan repolarization on "greed" (liberal) and "grid" authoritarian positions in party competition in 2010+ is unlikely to resonate with large electoral constituencies. Empirically it may be true that the moderation of social democratic issue stances on economic redistribution through the "Third Way" agenda of market-oriented social reform and activation of labor market participation has undercut the backing social democrats traditionally received from blue-collar working class constituencies (Keman 2010; Evans and Tilley 2012). But social democrats face an electoral trade-off: a return to the old social democratic welfare and redistributive agenda might help social democrats to woo back some traditional core blue-collar constituencies, but the parties would surely shed other and potentially more numerous electoral constituencies in medium- to higher-skilled service sector occupations, attracted precisely by the Third Way social democrats' moderately redistributive appeals combined with a mildly libertarian perspective on governance issues and a more sympathetic policy on multicultural citizenship—all positions not well received by the parties' traditional core low-skilled manual and clerical electoral constituencies.

The dilemma of social democracy in postindustrial capitalism is thus obvious. As Arzheimer's analysis suggests, only a reduction in the ideological salience of immigrant "group" issues agreed on by all of the conventional political parties through withdrawal from polarizing issue positions,[15] combined with a renewed partisan polarization on "greed" issues among the very same parties, could somewhat rejuvenate social democratic electoral support. If, however, partisan repolarization on redistributive economic and social policy choices is not a credible partisan strategy under the conditions of most mature welfare states, then social democracy may be finally trapped in a process of inevitable structural decline that is mediated, but not overcome, by strategic partisan choices.

While in the 1970s and 1980s social democracy still could take advantage of multiple adjustment strategies to changing demand profiles (Kitschelt 1994), it appears to be running out of options in the twenty-first century. What appears to take its place is a diversified field of smaller, programmatically more focused political parties spread across the three-dimensional space that stretches from an all-dimensional centrist origin toward redistributive economic positions, libertarian views of political governance and inclusive-universalistic views of multicultural citizenship. In that set of political parties, it may remain the essential specialty and task of social democratic parties, however, to compete for the median voter over several issue dimensions simultaneously and thus make it hard, if not impossible, to form government coalitions against its consent. Even in a world populated by multiple left-libertarian and centrist-libertarian parties and by center-left-authoritarians, right-centrists and right-liberal authoritarian parties, an electorally shrunken, deflated social democracy may thus sustain an extraordinary weight in the actual process of bargaining over government formation and hammering out legislative policy projects.

Notes

1 For empirical evidence, see Kitschelt and Rehm (2011b).
2 It is not at the authoritarian and exclusionary pole, because education (see below) has a countervailing influence, net of occupational experience.
3 As prominent points of reference they can draw on Mayda and Rodrik (2005) and Hainmueller and Hiscox (2010). Of course, this does not imply that self-regarding economic calculations of competition in the global marketplace are altogether irrelevant for actors' assessments of the desirability or acceptability of immigration and free trade.
4 For a discussion of existing evidence in this regard and the preparation of additional new evidence, see Kitschelt and Rehm (2011b).
5 This is partially obscured in Minkenberg and Pytlas' contribution (Chapter 12) because of the occupational categorizations available and the use of a general left–right scale to represent preferences (e.g., Table 12.1). In Slovakia, where left–right has a more economic-distributive "greed"-based popular meaning, a much larger percentage of the respondents situates itself center left, whereas in Hungary, where the meaning of left and right is primarily "group"-based and secondarily "grid"-based, half of the population is on the right. Poland is somewhere in between both in terms of the meaning of left and right as well as the popular distribution.
6 In this regard, Bornschier and Kriesi (Chapter 1, this volume: Table 1.1) find that political preferences reduce, but do not cancel out the predictive power of occupation for party choice. Here experiences in the associational and the reproductive spheres that may be associated with occupation, but are not controlled for in Bornschier and Kriesi's study, may play a role.
7 As far as I can tell, Bornschier and Kriesi offer no evidence that unions do not make their members more impervious to hostility against immigrants. Therefore I do not find their assertion completely justified that "[b]eing a member of a labor union no longer immunizes workers from the appeal of the extreme right." I would like to see this demonstrated.
8 Also in the general literature on religion and partisan alignment, religion is often seen as orthogonal to the concerns of radical right politics, whether for reasons of programmatic appeal (Knutsen and Kumlin 2005) or organizational association with Christian parties that make religious voters unavailable to the radical right (see Arzheimer and Carter 2009).
9 This may explain backlash voting for an extreme party, even if a voter supports a more moderate position. For radical right parties in Eastern Europe, see Bustikova (2011).
10 There are, however, difficult endogeneity questions not addressed in their estimation: could it be that the conventional parties spread out on "group" questions of immigration only because a serious radical right party has already made an appearance, not the other way round?
11 The institutional argument is made more generally about second-dimension politics by de la O and Rodden (2008).
12 The situation is obviously different where changes in taxation and corporate governance have facilitated a vast concentration of wealth, such as in the United States and, to a lesser extent, in Britain, over the past generation. Here a renewed polarization on the economic-distributive policy dimension of party competition is plausible.

13 Interestingly, Budge in his recent theory of party competition (Budge *et al.* 2010) makes no reference to issue ownership theory as his own earlier brainchild, but pretty much adopts a spatial model of party competition with behavioral constraints imposed.

14 This share is actually rather large, especially if we add in pensioners whose income is threatened by the consequences of the demographic transition.

15 Once again, I present salience as endogenize to configurations of partisan issue positions.

References

Aarts, K. and J. Thomassen. 2008. "Dutch Voters and the Changing Party Space 1989–2006". *Acta Politica*, 43: 203–234.

Abedi, A. 2004. *Anti-Political Establishment Partie. A Comparative Analysis*. London: Routledge.

Adorno, T. W., E. Frenkel-Brunswik, D. Levinson, and N. Sanford. 1950. *The Authoritarian Personality*. New York: Harper and Row.

Akkermann, T. and A. Hagelund. 2007. "Women and Children First! Anti-Immigration Parties and Gender in Norway and the Netherlands". *Patterns of Prejudice*, 41: 197–214.

Albright, J. J. 2010. "The Multidimensional Nature of Party Competition". *Party Politics*, 16: 699–719.

Allan, J. P. and L. Scruggs. 2004. "Political Partisanship and Welfare State Reform in Advanced Industrial Societies". *American Journal of Political Science*, 48: 496–512.

Allardt, E. 1968. "Past and Emerging Political Cleavages", in O. Stammer, ed. 1968. *Party Systems, Party Organizations, and the Politics of New Masses, Beiträge zur 3. Internationalen Konferenz über Vergleichende Politische Soziologie, Berlin, 15–20*. Berlin: Institut für politische Wissenschaft an der Freien Universität Berlin.

Allen, N. 2011. "Labour's Third Term: A Tale of Two Prime Ministers", in N. Allen and J. Bartle, eds. *Britain at the Polls*. London: Sage.

Allison, P. D. 2002. *Missing Data*. Thousand Oaks: Sage Publications.

Altemeyer, B. 1988. *Enemies of Freedom. Understanding Right-Wing Authoritarianism*. San Francisco: Jossey-Bass.

Amable, B. 2011. "Ouvriers, sales et méchants", *Libération*, May 17, available online at www.liberation.fr/economie/01012337750-ouvriers-sales-et-mechants (viewed June 15, 2011).

Andersen, J. G. and T. Bjørklund. 2000. "Radical Right-Wing Populism in Scandinavia: From Tax Revolt to Neo-liberalism", in P. Hainsworth, ed. 2000. *The Politics of the Extreme Right: From the Margins to the Mainstream*. London: Pinter.

Andersen, J. G. and T. Bjørklund. 1990. "Structural Change and New Cleavages: The Progress Parties in Demark and Norway". *Acta Sociologica*, 33: 195–217.

Aneshensel, C. 2002. *Theory-Based Data Analysis for the Social Sciences*. Thousand Oaks, CA: Pine Forge Press.

Art, D. 2011. *Inside the Radical Right. The Development of Anti-Immigrant Parties in Western Europe*. Cambridge: Cambridge University Press.

Arzheimer, K. 2009a. "Contextual Factors and the Extreme Right Vote in Western Europe, 1980–2002". *American Journal of Political Science*, 53: 259–275.

Arzheimer, K. 2009b. "Protest, Neo-Liberalism or Anti-Immigrant Sentiment: What Motivates the Voters of the Extreme Right in Western Europe?". *Zeitschrift für Vergleichende Politikwissenschaft/Comparative Governance and Politics*, 2: 173–197.

Arzheimer, K. and E. Carter. 2009. "Christian Religiosity and Voting for West European Radical Right Parties". *West European Politics*, 32: 985–1011.

Arzheimer, K. and E. Carter. 2006. "Political Opportunity Structures and Right-Wing Extremist Party Success". *European Journal of Political Research*, 2006: 419–443.

Auer, S. 2000. "Nationalism in Central Europe—A Chance or a Threat for the Emerging Liberal Democratic Order?". *East European Politics and Societies*, 14: 213–245.

Austria Documentation. 1994. *The Nationalrat Election in Austria*, Information on October 9. Vienna: The Federal Press Service.

Balch, A. 2009. "Labour and Epistemic Communities: The Case of 'Managed Migration' in the UK". *British Journal of Politics and International Relations*, 11: 613–633.

Bale, T. 2008a. *Immigration and Integration Policy in Europe: Why Politics—and the Centre-Right—Matter*. Abingdon: Routledge.

Bale, T. 2008b. "Turning Round the Telescope. Centre-Parties and Immigration and Integration Policy in Europe". *Journal of European Public Policy*, 15: 315–330.

Bale, T. 2003. "Cinderella and her Ugly Sisters: The Mainstream and Extreme Right in Europe's Bipolarising Party Systems". *West European Politics*, 26: 67–90.

Bale, T., C. Green-Pedersen, A. Krouwel, K. Luther, and N. Sitter. 2010. "If You Can't Beat Them, Join Them? Explaining Social Democratic Responses to the Challenge from the Populist Radical Right in Western Europe". *Political Studies*, 58: 410–426.

Bale, T., J. Hampshire, and R. Partos. 2011. "Having One's Cake and Eating It Too: Cameron's Conservatives and Immigration". *Political Quarterly*, 82: 398–406.

Bale, T. and P. Webb. 2011. "The Conservative Party", in N. Allen and J. Bartle, eds. *Britain at the Polls*. London: Sage.

Bartolini, S. 2000. *The Political Mobilization of the European Left, 1860–1980. The Class Cleavage*. Cambridge: Cambridge University Press.

Bartolini, S. and P. Mair. 1990. *Identity, Electoral Competition and Electoral Availability: The Stabilization of European Electorates 1885–1995*. Cambridge: Cambridge University Press.

Bastow, S. 1997. "Front National Economic Policy: From Neo-Liberalism to Protectionism". *Modern & Contemporary France*, 5: 61–72.

Beck, P. A. 1974. "A Socialization Theory of Partisan Realignment", in R. G. Niemi, ed. *The Politics of Future Citizens*. San Francisco: Jossey-Bass, 199–219.

Beichelt, T. 2007. "Zum Nutzen des Challenge-Response-Ansatzes im Hinblick auf die Parteientwicklung in Mitteleuropa", in D. de Nève, M. Reiser, K.-U. Schnapp, eds. 2007. *Transformation—ein Dauerphänomen*. Baden Baden: Nomos.

Beichelt, T. 2001. *Demokratische Konsolidierung im Postsozialistischen Europa. Die Rolle der politischen Institutionen*. Opladen: Leske Budrich.

Beichelt, T. and M. Minkenberg. 2002. "Explaining the Radical Right in Transition: Theories of Right-Wing Radicalism and Opportunity Structures in Post-Socialist Europe". FIT Paper 3/2002. Frankfurter Institut für Transformationsstudien: Frankfurt Oder.

Beirich, H. and D. Woods. 2000. "Globalization, Workers and the Northern League". *West European Politics*, 23: 130–143.

Belanger, E. and K. Aarts. 2006. "Explaining the Rise of the LPF: Issues, Discontent and the 2002 Dutch Elections". *Acta Politica*, 41: 4–20.

Bélanger, S. and M. Pinard. 1991. "Ethnic Movements and the Competition Model. Some Missing Links". *American Sociological Review*, 56: 446–457.

Benoit, K. and M. Laver. 2006. *Party Policy in Modern Democracies*. London: Routledge.

Bergh, J. 2004. "Protest Voting in Austria, Denmark, and Norway". *Scandinavian Political Studies*, 27: 367–389.

Berglund, T. and Oskarson, M. 2010. "Klass och ideologiska dimensioner", in M. Oskarson, M. Bengtsson, and T. Berglund, eds. *En fråga om klass—levnadsförhållanden, livsstil, politik*. Malmö: Liber.

Berlin, I. 1976. *Vico and Herder: Two Studies in the History of Ideas*. London: Hogarth.

Betz, H-G. 2005. "Against the System: Radical Right-Wing Populism's Challenge to Liberal Democracy", in J. Rydgren, ed. *Movements of Exclusion: Radical Right-Wing Populism in the Western World*. New York: Nova.

Betz, H.-G. 2004a. *La droite populiste en Europe: extrême et démocrate?* Paris: Autrement.

Betz, H.-G. 2004b. "Exclusionary Populism in Western Europe in the 1990s and Beyond. A Threat to Democracy and Civil Rights?" *Identities, Conflict and Cohesion*. Paper nr 9, UNRISD.

Betz, H-G. 2003. "The Growing Threat of the Radical Right", in P. H. Merkl and L. Weinberg, eds. *Right-Wing Extremism in the Twenty-First Century*. London: Frank Cass, 74–93.

Betz, H.-G. 2002a. "Contre la mondialisation: xénophobie, politiques identitaires et populisme d'exclusion en Europe occidentale". *Politique et Sociétés*, 21 (2): 9–28. Available online: www.erudit.org/revue/ps/2002/v21/n2/000477ar.pdf.

Betz, H.-G. 2002. "The Divergent Paths of the FPÖ and the Lega Nord", in M. Schain, A. Zolberg and P. Hossay, eds. *Shadows Over Europe: The Development and Impact of the Extreme Right in Western Europe*. New York: Palgrave, 61–81.

Betz, H.-G. 2001. "Radikaler Rechtspopulismus im Spannungsfeld zwischen neoliberalistischen Wirtschaftskonzepten und antiliberaler autoritärer Ideologie", in D. Loch and W. Heitmeyer, eds. *Schattenseiten der Globalisierung. Rechtsradikalismus, Rechtspopulismus und separatistischer Regionalismus in westlichen Demokratien*. Frankfurt am Main: Suhrkamp.

Betz, H.-G. 1998. "Introduction", in H.-G. Betz and S. Immerfall, eds. *The New Politics of the Right: Neo-Populist Parties and Movements in Established Democracies*. London: Macmillan.

Betz, H.-G. 1994. *Radical Right-Wing Populism in Western Europe*. New York: St Martin's Press.

Betz, H.-G. 1993. "The New Politics of Resentment: Radical Right-Wing Populist Parties in Western Europe". *Comparative Politics*, 25: 413–427.

Betz, H.-G. and C. Johnson. 2004. "Against the Current—Stemming the Tide: The Nostalgic Ideology of the Contemporary Radical Populist Right". *Journal of Political Ideologies*, 9: 311–327.

Betz, H.-G. and S. Meret. 2009. "Revisiting Lepanto: The Political Mobilization against Islam in Contemporary Western Europe". *Patterns of Prejudice*, 43: 313–334.

Beyme, K. 1988. "Right-Wing Extremism in Post-War Europe", in K. Beyme, ed. 1988. *Right-Wing Extremism in Western Europe*. London: Frank Cass.

Biorcio, R. 2010. *La Rivincita del Nord. La Lega dalla contestazione al governo*. Torino: Editori Laterza.

Bíró Nagy, A. and D. Róna. 2011. "Rational Radicalism. Jobbik's Road to the Hungarian Parliament, 2003–2010". Paper presented at the Workshop "On the Moderation and Immoderation of Religious Political Parties in Democratic Politics", University of Eichstätt, Germany, 16–18 June.

Bjørklund, T. 2011. "The Radical Right in Norway. The Development of the Progress Party", in N. Lagenbacher and B. Schellenberg, eds. *Is Europe on the 'Right' Path?*. Berlin: Friedrich Ebert Stiftung.

Bjørklund, T. 2009. "To mål på arbeiderklasse: Yrke og klassetilhørighet Norske velgere og partier fra 1965 til 2005". *Norsk Statsvitenskapelig Tidsskrift*, 1: 5–30.

Bjørklund, T. and J. G. Andersen. 2002. "Anti-Immigration Parties in Denmark and Norway: The Progress Parties and the Danish People's Party", in M. Schain, A. Zolberg, and P. Hossay, eds. *Shadows over Europe: The Development and Impact of the Extreme Right in Western Europe*. New York: Palgrave Macmillan.

Blomqvist, P. and C. Green-Pedersen. 2004. "Defeat at Home? Issue-Ownership and Social Democratic Support in Scandinavia". *Government and Opposition*, 39: 587–613.

Blondel, J. 1968. "Party Systems and Patterns of Governments in Western Democracies." *Canadian Journal of Political Science* 1: 180–203.

Blunkett, D. 2002. "The Right is our True Enemy". *Guardian*, 2 April.

BNP. 2010a. *Democracy, Freedom, Culture and Identity: British National Party General Election Manifesto 2010*. Powys: British National Party.

BNP. 2010b. *Activists' and Organisers' Handbook: Education and Training*. Powys: British National Party.

Bobbio, N. 1996. *Left and Right: The Significance of a Political Distinction*. Chicago: University of Chicago Press.

Boomgaarden, H. G. and R. Vliegenthart. 2007. "Explaining the Rise of Anti-Immigrant Parties: The Role of News Media Content". *Electoral Studies*, 26: 404–417.

Borisyuk, G., C. Rallings, M. Thrasher, and H. Van der Kolk. 2007. "Voter Support for Minor Parties: Assessing the Social and Political Context of Voting at the 2004 European Elections in Greater London". *Party Politics*, 13: 669–694.

Bornschier, S. 2010a. *Cleavage Politics and the Populist Right. The New Cultural Conflict in Western Europe*. Philadelphia: Temple University Press.

Bornschier, S. 2010b. "The New Cultural Divide and the Two-Dimensional Political Space in Western Europe". *West European Politics*, 33: 419–444.

Boswell, C. and D. Hough. 2008. "Politicizing Migration: Opportunity or Liability for the Centre-Right in Germany". *Journal of European Public Policy*, 15: 331–348.

Bourdieu, P. 1984. *Distinction: A Social Critique of the Judgment of Taste*. London: Routledge.

Bovens, M. and A. Wille. 2010. "The Education Gap in Participation and Its Political Consequences". *Acta Politica*, 45: 393–422.

Bowyer, B. T. 2008. "Local Context and Extreme Right Support in England: The British National Party in the 2002 and 2003 Local Elections". *Electoral Studies*, 27: 611–620.

Brendgens, G. 1997. "Demokratische Konsolidierung in der Tschechischen Republik". Unpublished Master's Thesis. Heidelberg: University of Heidelberg, Institute for Political Sciences.

Brooks, C. and J. Manza. 2006. "Why Do Welfare States Persist?". *The Journal of Politics*, 68: 816–827.

Broughton, D. 2000. "The first Six *Länder* Elections of 1999: Initial Electoral Consequences and Political Fallout of the *Neue Mitte* in action". *German Politics*, 9: 51–70.

Brown, R. 1995. *Prejudice: Its Social Psychology*. Oxford: Blackwell.

Brubaker, R. 1997. *Nationalism Reframed. Nationhood and the National Question in the New Europe*. Cambridge: Cambridge University Press.

Brubaker, R. 1992. *Citizenship and Nationhood in France and Germany*. Cambridge, MA: Harvard University Press.

Bryson, A., B. Ebbinghaus, and J. Visser. 2011. "Introduction: Causes, Consequences and Cures of Union Decline". *European Journal of Industrial Relations*, 17: 97–105.

Budge, I. and D. Farlie. 1983. *Explaining and Predicting Elections: Issue Effects and Party Strategies in Twenty-Three Democracies*. London: Allen and Unwin.

Budge, I., L. Ezrow, and M. D. McDonald. 2010. "Ideology, Party Factionalism, and Policy Change: An Integrated Dynamic Theory". *British Journal of Political Science*, 4: 781–804.

Bürgisser, R. 2011. "Auswirkungen der Globalisierung auf den Wahlentscheid. Von der Globalisierung geformte individelle Policy-Präferenzen und deren Einfluss auf die Wahlentscheidung". Research seminar paper, Institute for Political Science, University of Zurich.

Burke, P. J. 2004. "Identities and Social Structure: The 2003 Cooley–Mead Award Address". *Social Psychology Quarterly*, 67: 5–15.

Bustikova, L. 2011. "Revenge of The Radical Right: When Tolerance Breeds Hatred. Explaining the Electoral Success of Radical Right Parties in Post-Communist Democracies". Paper prepared for delivery at the Annual Meeting of the American Political Science Association, Seattle, 1–4 September.

Bustikova, L. and H. Kitschelt. 2009. "The Radical Right in Post-Communist Europe. Comparative Perspectives on Legacies and Party Competition", in M. Minkenberg, ed. "Legacies and the Radical Right in Post-1989 Central and Eastern Europe", special issue of *Communist and Post-Communist Studies*, 42: 459–484.

Butler, D. and D. Stokes. 1969. *Political Change in Britain: Forces Shaping Electoral Choice*. Basingstoke: Macmillan.

Bútorová, Z. and O. Gyárfášová, O. 2011. "Trendy vo verejnej mienke a voličskom správaní", in Z. Bútorová, O. Gyárfášová, G. Mesežnikov, and M. Kollár, eds. *Slovenské volby '10. Šanca na zmenu*. Bratislava: Institút Pre Verejné Otázky.

Bútorová, Z. and O. Gyárfášová. 2006: "Trendy vo verejnej mienke a volebnom správaní", in G. Mesežnikov, O. Gyárfášová, and M. Kollar, eds. *Slovenské voľby '06. Výsledky, príčiny súvislosti*. Bratislava: Institút Pre Verejné Otázky.

Campbell, A., P. E. Converse, W. E. Miller, and D. E. Strokes. 1960. *The American Voter*. New York, London, Sydney: John Wiley.

Capdevielle, J. and E. Dupoirier. 1981. "L'effet patrimoine", in J. Capdevielle, E. Dupoirier, G. Grunberg, E. Schweisguth, and C. Ysmal, eds. *France de gauche, vote à droite*. Paris: Presses de Sciences.

Carter, E. 2005. *The Extreme Right in Western Europe: Success or Failure?*. Manchester: Manchester University Press.

Casellato, A. and G. Zazzara. 2010. "Veneto Agro. Operai e sindacato ala prova del leghismo (1980–2010)". Treviso: Istituto di ricerche economiche e sociali.

Castells, M. 1996. *The Rise of the Network Society*. Oxford and Malden: Blackwell.

Cattacin, S., B. Gerber, M. Sardi, and R. Wegener. 2006. *Monitoring Misanthropy and Rightwing Extremist Attitudes in Switzerland. An Explorative Study*. Geneva: University of Geneva, Sociograph, no. 1.

CBS, SKON, H. van der Kolk, K. Aarts. M. Rosema and M. Brinkman (2012) *Dutch Parliamentary Election Study 2010*, The Hague: CBS/SKON.

Center for Politiske Studier (CEPOS). 2011. "Negativt nettobidrag på 16 mia. Kr. på de offentlige finanser fra indvandrere og efterkommere fra mindre udviklede lande—potentialer for forbedring". Available online: www.cepos.dk/fileadmin/user_upload/_temp_/

Negativt_nettobidrag_paa_16_mia._kr._paa_de_offentlige_finanser_fra_indvandrere_ og_efterkommere_fra_mindre_udviklede_lande_-_potentiale_for_forbedring.pdf (viewed September 15, 2011).

Chan, T. W. and J. H. Goldthorpe. 2007. "Class and Status: The Conceptual Distinction and its Empirical Relevance". *American Sociological Review*, 72: 512–532.

Chavaneux, C. 2011. "La tentation de la 'démondialisation'". *Alternatives Économiques*, June: 56–58.

Clark, T. N. and S. M. Lipset. 2001. *The Breakdown of Class Politics. A Debate on Post-Industrial Stratification*. Washington, DC: Woodrow Wilson Center Press.

Clark, T. N., S. M. Lipset, and M. Rempel. 1993. "The Declining Political Significance of Social Class". *International Sociology*, 8: 293–316.

Clarke, H. D., D. Sanders, M. C. Stewart, and P. F. Whiteley. 2009. *Performance Politics and the British Voter*. Cambridge: Cambridge University Press.

Clarke, H. D., M. C. Stewart, M. Ault, and E. Elliott. 2005. "Men, Women and the Dynamics of Presidential Approval". *British Journal of Political Science*, 35: 31–51.

Coenders, M. and P. Scheepers. 2003. "The Effect of Education on Nationalism and Ethnic Exclusionism: An International Comparison". *Political Psychology*, 24: 313–343.

Coffé, H. 2008. "Social Democratic Parties as Buffers against the Extreme Right: The Case of Belgium". *Contemporary Politics*, 14: 179–195.

Coffé, H. and C. Bolzendahl. 2010. "Same Game, Different Rules? Gender Differences in Political Participation". *Sex Roles*, 62: 318–333.

Cole, A. 2005. "Old Right Or New Right? The Ideological Positioning of Parties of the Far Right". *European Journal of Political Research*, 44: 203–230.

Commission Nationale Consultative des Droits de l'Homme. 2009. *La lutte contre le racisme, l'antisémitisme et la xénophobie. Année 2009*. Paris: La documentation Française.

Crawford, B. and A. Lijphart. 1997. "Old Legacies New Institutions. Explaining Political and Economic Trajectories in Post-Communist Regimes", in Crawford, B. and A. Lijphart, eds. *Liberalization and Leninist Legacies. Comparative Perspectives on Democratic Transitions*. Berkeley: The Regents of the University of California Berkeley.

Crepaz, M. L. 2008. *Trust Beyond Borders: Immigration, the Welfare State, and Identity in Modern Societies*. Ann Arbor: The University of Michigan Press.

Crouch, C. 1999. *Social Change in Western Europe*. Oxford: Oxford University Press.

Curtice, J., S. Fisher, and R. Ford. 2010. "Appendix 2: An Analysis of the Results", in D. Kavanagh and P. Cowley. 2010. *The British General Election of 2010*. Basingstoke: Palgrave Macmillan.

Cutts, D. 2006. "Continuous Activism and Electoral Outcomes: The Liberal Democrats in Bath". *Political Geography*, 25: 72–88.

Cutts, D., R. Ford, and M. Goodwin. 2011. "Anti-Immigrant, Politically Disaffected or Still Racist After All? Examining the Attitudinal Drivers of Extreme Right Support in Britain in the 2009 European Elections". *European Journal of Political Research*, 50: 418–440.

Cutts, D. C. and N. Shryane. 2006. "Did Local Activism Really Matter? Liberal Democrat Campaigning and the 2001 British General Election". *British Journal of Politics and International Relations*, 8: 427–444.

Dalton, R. J. 2004. *Democratic Challenges, Democratic Choices. The Erosion of Political Support in Advanced Industrial Democracies*. Oxford: Oxford University Press.

Dalton, R. J. 1996. "Political Cleavages, Issues, and Electoral Change", in LeDuc, L., L. R. Niemi, and P. Norris, eds. *Comparing Democracies. Elections and Voting in Global Perspective*, Thousand Oaks, CA: Sage.

Dalton, R. J., S. C. Flanagan, and P. A. Beck. 1984. *Electoral Change in Advanced Industrial Democracies. Realignment or Dealignment?*. Princeton: Princeton University Press.

Dansk Folkeparti, Arbejdsprogram. Available online: www.danskfolkeparti.dk/Arbejdsprogram.asp (viewed September 15, 2011).

Dansk Folkeparti, Principprogram, København: Nyhavns Tryk og Kopi Center 1997.

Darlington, R., ed. 2010. "Open Verdict Why Voters Left Labour". London: Demos. Available online: www.openleft.co.uk/wp-content/uploads/2010/09/Open-verdict-FINAL.pdf.

Davies, J. C. 1966. "The J-Curve of Rising and Declining Satisfaction as a Cause of Some Great Revolutions and a Contained Rebellion", in H. D. Graham and T. R. Gurr, eds. *The History of Violence in America: Historical and Comparative Perspectives*. New York: Praeger.

de Lange, S. L. 2007. "A New Winning Formula? The Programmatic Appeal of the Radical Right". *Party Politics*, 13: 411–435.

de Lange, S. L. and S. Guerra. 2009. "The League of Polish Families between East and West, Past and Present", in M. Minkenberg, ed. "Legacies and the Radical Right in Post-1989 Central and Eastern Europe", special issue, *Communist and Post-Communist Studies*, 42: 527–550.

de la O, A. and J. Rodden. 2008. "Does Religion Distract the Poor? Income and Issue Voting Around the World". *Comparative Political Studies*, 41: 437–477.

Decker, O., M. Weißmann, J. Kiess, and E. Brähler. 2010. *Die Mitte in der Krise. Rechtsextreme Einstellungen in Deutschland 2010*. Berlin: Friedrich Ebert Stiftung.

Demker, M. 2011. "Scandinavian Right-Wing Parties. Diversity more than Convergence?", in A. Mammone, E. Godin, and B. Jenkins, eds. *Mapping the Extreme Right in Contemporary Europe. From Local to Transnational*. London: Routledge.

Demos. 2010. "Open Verdict: Why Voters Left Labour". London: Demos. Available online: www.openleft.co.uk/wp-content/uploads/2010/09/Open-verdict-FINAL.pdf (viewed August 20, 2011).

Denver, D. and G. Hands. 1997. *Modern Constituency Electioneering*. London: Frank Cass.

Derks, A. 2004. "Are the Underprivileged Really that Economically Left? Attitudes Towards Economic Redistribution and the Welfare State in Flanders". *European Journal of Political Research*, 43: 509–521.

Dieringer, J. 1998. "Die ungarischen Parlamentswahlen 1998", in *Zeitschrift für Parlamentsfragen*, 29.

Dorling, D. 2010. "All Connected? Geographies of Race, Death, Wealth, Votes and Births". *The Geographical Journal*, 176: 186–198.

Downs, A. 1957. *An Economic Theory of Democracy*. New York: Harper.

Dustman, C. and I. P. Preston. 2007. "Racial and Economic Factors in Attitudes to Immigration". *The B.E. Journal of Economic Analysis & Politics*, 7: 1–39.

Eatwell, R. 2004. "Introduction: The New Extreme Right Challenge", in R. Eatwell and C. Mudde, eds. *Western Democracies and the New Extreme Right Challenge*. London: Routledge.

Eatwell, R. 2003. "Ten Theories of the Extreme Right", in P. Merkl and L. Weinberg, eds. *Right-Wing Extremism in the Twenty-First Century*. London: Frank Cass.

Ekiert, G. and S. E. Hanson. 2003. *Capitalism and Democracy in Central and Eastern Europe Assessing the Legacy of Communist Rule*. Cambridge: Cambridge University Press.

Erikson, R. 1984. "Social Class of Men, Women and Families". *Sociology*, 18: 500–514.

Erikson, R. and J. H. Goldthorpe. 1992. *The Constant Flux: A Study of Class Mobility in Industrial Societies*. Oxford: Clarendon Press.

Esping-Andersen, G. 1999. "Politics Without Class? Postindustrial Cleavages in Europe and America", in H. Kitschelt, P. Lange, G. Marks, and J. D. Stephens, eds. *Continuity and Change in Contemporary Capitalism*. Cambridge: Cambridge University Press.

Esping-Andersen, G. 1993. "Post-Industrial Class Structures: An Analytical Framework", in G. Esping-Andersen, ed. 1993. *Changing Classes. Stratification and Mobility in Post-Industrial Societies*. London: Sage, 7–31.

Evans, G. 1999. "Class and Vote: Disrupting the Orthodoxy", in G. Evans, ed. *The End of Class Politics? Class Voting in Comparative Context*. Oxford: Oxford University Press, 323–334.

Evans, G. 2000. "The continued significance of class voting." *Annual Review of Political Science* 3: 401–417.

Evans, G. 1999. "Class Voting: From Premature Obituary to Reasoned Appraisal". In Evans, G. eds. *The end of class politics? Class voting in comparative context*. Oxford: Oxford Univ. Press.

Evans, G. 1999. *The End of Class Politics? Class Voting in a Comparative Context*. Oxford: Oxford University Press.

Evans, G. 1997. "Class Inequality and the Formation of Political Interests in Eastern Europe". *Archive of European Sociology*, 38: 207–234.

Evans, G., A. Heath, and M. Lalljee. 1996. "Measuring Left-Right and Libertarian-Authoritarian Values in the British Electorate". *British Journal of Sociology*, 47: 93–112.

Evans, G. and S. Whitefeld. 2000. "Explaining the Formation of Electoral Cleavages in Post-Communist Democracies", in H.-D. Klingemann, eds. *Elections in Central and Eastern Europe. The First Wave*. Berlin: Sigma.

Evans, G. and S. Whitefeld. 1999. "The Emergence of Class Politics and Class Voting in Post-Communist Russia", in G. Evans, eds. *The End of Class Politics? Class Voting in Comparative Context*. Oxford: Oxford University Press.

Evans, G. and J. Tilley. 2012. "How Parties Shape Class Politics: Explaining the Decline of the Class Basis of Party Support". *British Journal of Political Science*, 42: 137–161.

Evans, J. 2000. "Le vote gaucho-lepéniste: le masque extrême d'une dynamique normale". *Revue française de science politique*, 50: 21–51.

Evans J., K. Arzheimer, G. Baldini, T. Bjorklund, E. Carter, S. Fisher, and G. Ivaldi. 2001. "Comparative Mapping of Extreme Right Electoral Dynamics: An Overview of EREPS". *European Political Science*, 1: 42–53.

Facchini, G. and A.-M. Mayda. 2006. *Individual Attitudes Towards Immigrants: Welfare-State Determinants Across Countries*. Bonn: Institute for the Study of Labor, IZA DP.

Falter, J. 1994. *Wer wählt rechts? Die Wähler und Anhänger rechtsextremistischer Parteien im vereinigten Deutschland*. München: Beck.

Fennema, M. 2010. *Geert Wilders: Tovernaarsleerling*. Amsterdam: Bert Bakker.

Fennema M. 2005. "Populist Parties of the Right", in J. Rydgren, ed. *Movements of Exclusion: Radical Right-Wing Populism in the Western World*. New York: Nova.

Fennema, M. 1997. "Some Conceptual Issues and Problems in the Comparison of Anti-Immigrant Parties in Western Europe". *Party Politics*, 3: 473–492.

Fennema, M. and C. Pollmann. 1998. "Ideology of Anti-Immigrant Parties in the European Parliament". *Acta Politica*, 33: 111–138.

Fieldhouse, E. and D. Cutts. 2008. "The Effectiveness of Local Party Campaigns in 2005: Combining Evidence from Campaign Spending and Agent Survey Data". *British Journal of Political Science*, 39: 367–388.

Fieldhouse, E., D. C. Cutts, and A. Russell. 2006. "Neither North nor South: The Liberal Democrat Performance in the 2005 General Election". *Journal of Elections, Public Opinion and Parties*, 16: 77–92.

Fireside, H. 2002. "The Demograhic Roots of European Xenophobia". *Journal of Human Rights*, 1: 469–479.

Fisher, J., D. C. Cutts, and E. Fieldhouse. 2011. "The Electoral Effectiveness of Constituency Campaigning in the 2010 British General Election: The 'Triumph' of Labour?". *Electoral Studies*, forthcoming.

Fisher, J. and D. Denver. 2009. "Evaluating the Electoral Effects of Traditional and Modern Modes of Constituency Campaigning in Britain 1992–2005". *Parliamentary Affairs*, 62: 196–210.

Flanagan, S. C. 1987. "Value Change in Industrial Societies". *American Political Science Review*, 81: 1303–1319.

Flanagan, S. C. and A.-R. Lee. 2003. "The New Politics, Culture Wars and the Authoritarian—Libertarian Value Change in Advanced Industrial Democracies". *Comparative Political Studies*, 36: 235–270.

Flecker, J., G. Hentges, and G. Balazs, G. 2007. "Potentials of Political Subjectivity and the Various Approaches to the Extreme Right: Findings of the Qualitative Research", in J. Flecker, ed. *Changing Working Life and the Appeal of the Extreme Right*. Aldershot: Ashgate.

Flynn, D. 2005. "New Borders, New Management: The Dilemmas of Modern Immigration Policies". *Ethnic and Racial Studies*, 28 (3): 463–490.

Folch, A. 2011. "Immigration: ce que coûtent vraiment les clandestins". *Valeurs actuelles*, June 30. Available online: www.valeursactuelles.com/dossier-d039actualit%C3%A9/dossier-d039actualit%C3%A9/immigration-ce-que-co%C3%BBtent-vraiment-clandestins20110630.

Folch, A. 2010 "Pourquoi elle fait peur à la droite". *Valeurs actuelles*, December 9: 12–14.

Fondation pour l'innovation politique (Fondapol). 2011. "Le sentiment européen chez les Français", April. Available online at www.fondapol.org/wp-content/uploads/2011/05/Sentiment-europ%C3%A9en_R%C3%A9sultats-d%C3%A9taill%C3%A9s.pdf (viewed August 28, 2011).

Fontana, M.-C., A. Sidler, and S. Hardmeier. 2006. "The 'New Right' Vote: An Analysis of the Gender Gap in the Vote Choice for the SVP". *Swiss Political Science Review*, 12: 243–271.

Ford, R. 2010. "Who Might Vote BNP? Survey Evidence on the Electoral Potential of the Extreme Right in Britain", in R. Eatwell and M.-J. Goodwin, eds. *The New Extremism in Twenty-First Century Britain*. London: Routledge.

Ford, R. and M. J. Goodwin. 2010. "Angry White Men: Individual and Contextual Predictors of Support for the British National Party". *Political Studies*, 58: 1–25.

Franklin, M. N., T. Mackie, and H. Valen. 1992. *Electoral Change. Responses to Evolving Social and Attitudinal Structures in Western Countries*. Cambridge: Cambridge University Press.

Fremskrittspartiet, Prinsipp- og handlingsprogram 2005–2009, p. 5.

Frey, T. 2009. *Die Christdemokratie in Westeuropa. Der schmale Grat zum Erfolg.* Baden-Baden: Nomos.

Front National. 2011. "Projet économique du Front national. Les grandes orientations", April. Available online: www.frontnational.com/pdf/projet-eco-fn.pdf (viewed July 20, 2011).

Fuchs, D. and H.-D. Klingemann. 1989. "The Left-Right Scheme", in K. Jennings and J. van Deth, eds. *Continuities in Political Action. A Longitudinal Study of Political Orientations in Three Western Democracies.* Berlin: de Gruyter.

Gaasholt, Ø. and L. Togeby. 1995. *I syv sind. Danskernes holdninger til flygtninge og indvandrere.* Aarhus: Politica.

Gallagher, M., M. Laver, and P. Mair. 2011. *Representative Government in Modern Europe*, fifth edn. London: McGraw-Hill.

Ganzeboom, H. B. G. and D. J. Treiman. 1996. "Internationally Comparable Measures of Occupational Status for the 1988 International Standard Classification of Occupations". *Social Science Research*, 25: 201–239.

Geddes, B. 1997. "A Comparative Perspective on the Leninist Legacy in Eastern Europe", in B. Crawford and A. Lijphart, eds. 1997. *Liberalization and Leninist Legacies. Comparative Perspectives on Democratic Transitions.* Berkeley: The Regents of the University of California Berkeley, 142–183.

Gesthuizen, M., T. van der Meer, and P. Scheepers. 2008. "Ethnic Diversity and Social Capital in Europe: Tests of Putnam's Thesis in European Countries". *Scandinavian Political Studies*, 32: 121–142.

Gibson, R. K. 2002. *The Growth of Anti-Immigrant Parties In Western Europe.* Lewiston: Edwin Mellen Press.

Giddens, A. 2010. "The Rise and Fall of New Labour". *New Statesman*, May 17. Available online: www.newstatesman.com/uk-politics/2010/05/labour-policy-policies-blair (viewed July 17).

Gidengil, E. 1995. "Economic Man–Social Woman? The Case of the Gender Gap in Support for the Canada-United States Free Trade Agreement". *Comparative Political Studies*, 28: 384–408.

Gidengil, E. and M. Hennigar. 2005. "The Gender Gap in Support for the Radical Right in Western Europe". Paper prepared for presentation at the annual meeting of the American Political Science Association, Washington DC.

Gidengil, E., M. Hennigar, A. Blais, and N. Nevitte. 2005. "Explaining the Gender Gap in Support for the New Right". *Comparative Political Studies*, 38: 1171–1195.

Giertych, R. 2006. "Program Polityczny LPR. A Speech by Roman Giertych". Paper presented at the Kongres Ligi Polskich Rodzin, Warszawa, March 11.

Givens, T. E. 2004. "The Radical Right Gender Gap". *Comparative Political Studies*, 37: 30.

Golder, M. 2003. "Explaining Variation in the Electoral Success of Extreme Right Parties in Western Europe". *Comparative Political Studies*, 36: 432–466.

Goldthorpe, J. H. 2002. "Globalisation and Social Class". *West European Politics*, 25: 1–28.

Goldthorpe, J. H. 2000. *On Sociology. Numbers, Narratives, and the Integration of Research and Theory.* Oxford: Oxford University Press.

Goldthorpe, J. H., C. Llewellyn, and C. Payne. 1980. *Social Mobility and Class Structure in Modern Britain.* Oxford: Clarendon Press.

Goodhart, D. 2004. "Is Britain Becoming too Diverse to Sustain the Mutual Obligations behind a Good Society and the Welfare State?". *Prospect Magazine*, February: 30–37.

Available online: www.carnegiecouncil.org/media/goodhart.pdf (viewed July 20, 2011).

Goodwin, J. and J. M. Jasper. 2007. "Emotions and Social Movements," in J. E. Stets and J. H. Turner, eds. *Handbook of the Sociology of Emotions*. New York: Springer.

Goodwin, M. 2011. *New British Fascism: Rise of the British National Party*. Abingdon: Routledge.

Goodwin, M. J. 2010. "Activism in Contemporary Extreme Right Parties: The Case of the British National Party". *Journal of Elections, Public Opinion and Parties*, 20: 31–54.

Gougou, F. 2011. "La droitisation du vote des ouvriers en France: Désalignement, réalignement et renouvellement des generations", in J.-M. De Waele and M. Vieira, eds. Forthcoming. *Une droitisation de la classe ouvrière en Europe?*. Paris: Economica.

Gougou, F. 2008. "The 2008 French Municipal Elections. The Opening and the Sanction". *French Politics*, 6: 395–406.

Gougou, F. and S. Labouret. 2010. "The 2010 French Regional Elections: Transitional Elections in a Realignment Era". *French Politics*, 8: 321–341.

Gougou, F. and G. Roux. 2011. "Political Change and Cleavage Voting in France: Class, Religion, Political appeals and Voters Alignments (1962–2007)", in G. Evans and N. D. De Graaf, eds. Forthcoming. *Political Choice Matters: Explaining the Strength of Class and Religious Cleavages in Cross-National Perspective*. Oxford: Oxford University Press.

Goul Andersen, J. 1992. "Denmark: The Progress Party—Populist Neo-Liberalism and Welfare State Chauvinism", in P. Hainsworth, ed. 1992. *The Extreme Right in Europe and the USA*. London: Pinter, 193–205.

Green, S. 2007. "Divergent Traditions, Converging Responses: Immigration and Integration Policy in the UK and Germany". *German Politics*, 16: 95–115.

Green, S. 2004. *The Politics of Exclusion: Institutions and Immigration Policy in Contemporary Germany*. Manchester: MUP.

Green-Pedersen, C. and P. B. Mortensen. 2010. "Who Sets the Agenda and Who Responds to it in the Danish Parliament? A New Model of Issue Competition and Agenda-Setting". *European Journal of Political Research*, 49: 257–281.

Griffin, R. 2000. "Interregnum or Endgame? Radical Right Thought in the 'Postfascist' Era". *Journal of Political Ideologies*, 5 (2):163–78.

Grotz, F. 2000. *Politische Institutionen und post-sozialistische Parteiensysteme in Ostmitteleuropa. Polen, Ungarn, Tschechien und die Slowakei im Vergleich*. Opladen: Leske+Budrich.

Grunberg, G. and E. Schweisguth. 1990. "Libéralisme culturel et libéralisme économique", in CEVIPOF. 1992. *L'électeur français en question*. Paris: Presses de la Fondation Nationale de Sciences Politiques.

Grunberg, G. and E. Schweisguth. 1997. "Recompositions idéologiques", in D. Boy and N. Mayer, eds. *L'électeur a ses raisons*. Paris: Presses de la Fondation Nationale de Sciences Politiques.

Guilluy, C. 2010. *Fractures françaises*. Paris: François Bourin.

Gyárfášová, O. 2008. "National Populism in Slovakia: Political Attitudes and Views of the Public", in G. Mesežnikov and O. Gyárfášová, eds. *National Populism in Slovakia*. Bratislava: IVO.

Gyárfášová, O. and M. Velšic. 2002. "Slovenskí voliči a parlamentné voľby 2002 – III. Časť. Analýza výskumných zistení". Working paper, Inštitút pre verejné otázky.

Habermas, J. 1992. "Staatsbürgerschaft und nationale Identität", in *Faktizität und Geltung*. Frankfurt, Main: Suhrkamp.

Habermas, J. 1981. *Theorie des kommunikativen Handelns.* Frankfurt, Main: Suhrkamp.

Hainmueller, J. and M. J. Hiscox. 2010. "Attitudes Toward Highly Skilled and Low-Skilled Immigration: Evidence from a Survey Experiment". *American Political Science Review*, 104: 61–84.

Hainmueller, J. and M. J. Hiscox. 2007. "Educated Preferences: Explaining Attitudes Toward Immigration in Europe". *International Organization*, 61: 399–442.

Hamilton, F. 2010. "BNP Hopes of a Breakthrough Dashed as Party Defeated in Target Seats". *Times* online, May 7.

Hansen, R. S. 2000. *Citizenship and Immigration in Post-War Britain: The Institutional Origins of a Multicultural Nation.* Oxford: Oxford University Press.

Harris, L. 2006. "L'observatoire de l'opinion", May. Available online: www.lh2.fr/_upload/ressources/sondages/politique_nationale/lh2libeobservatoire2mai06.pdf(viewed July 26, 2011).

Harrison, E. and D. Rose. 2006. "The European Socio-economic Classification", ESeC User Guide.

Harrits, G. S., A. Prieur, L. Rosenlund, and J. Skjott-Larsen. 2009. "Class and Politics in Denmark: Are Both Old and New Politics Structured by Class?". *Scandinavian Political Studies*, 33: 1–27.

Haughton, T. 2003. "'We'll Finish What We Started': The 2002 Slovak Parliamentary Elections". *Journal of Communist Studies and Transition Politics*, 19: 65–90.

Häusermann, S. 2010. *The Politics of Welfare State Reform in Continental Europe: Modernization in Hard Times.* Cambridge: Cambridge University Press.

Hays, J. C., S. D. Ehrlich, and C. Peinhardt. 2005. "Government Spending and Public Support for Trade in the OECD". *International Organisation*, 59 (2): 473–494.

Heath, A., R. Jowell, J. Curtice, G. Evans, J. Field, and S. Witherspoon. 1991. *Understanding Political Change: The British Voter 1963–1987.* Oxford: Pergamon.

Heinrich, G. and S. Schoon. 2007. "The 2006 Landtag Election in Mecklenburg-Western Pomerania". *German Politics*, 16: 526–533.

Hines, J. R. 2006. "Will Social Welfare Expenditures Survive Tax Competition?". *Oxford Review of Economic Policy*, 22: 330–348.

Hobsbawm, E. 1990. *Nations and Nationalism Since 1780. Programme, Myth, Reality.* Cambridge: Cambridge University Press.

Hogwood, P. 2000. "Citizenship Controversies in Germany; The Twin Legacy of Völkisch Nationalism and the Alleinvertretungsanspruch". *German Politics*, 9: 125–44.

Holmes, D. R. 2000. *Integral Europe: Fast-Capitalism, Multiculturalism, Neofascism.* Princeton, NJ: Princeton University Press.

Hooghe, L., R. Bakker, A. Brigevich, C. de Vries, E. Edwards, G. Marks, J. Rovny, M. Steenbergen, and M. Vachudova. 2010. "Reliability and Validity of Measuring Party Positions: The Chapel Hill Expert Surveys of 2002 and 2006". *European Journal of Political Research*, 49: 687–703.

Hooghe, L., G. Marks, and C. J. Wilson. 2002. "Does Left/Right Structure Party Positions on European Integration?". *Comparative Political Studies*, 35: 965–989.

Honneth, A. 1995. *The Struggle for Recognition. The Moral Grammar of Social Conflicts.* Cambridge, MA: MIT Press.

Hough, D. 2011. "Small but Perfectly Formed? The Rise and Rise of Germany's Smaller Parties". *German Politics*, 20: 186–199.

Houtman, D., P. Achterberg, and A. Derks. 2008. *Farewell to the Leftist Working Class.* New Brunswick, NJ: Transaction Publishers.

Howard, M. M. 2006. "The Leninist legacy revisited", in V. Tismaneanu, M. M. Howard, and R. Sil, eds. 2006. *World Order After Leninism*. Seattle and London: University of Washington Press.

Huber, J. E. and P. Stanig. 2010. "Individual Income and Voting for Redistribution Across Democracies". Unpublished paper, Columbia University, March 13.

IFOP. 2011. "Les Français, le protectionnisme et le libre-échange", May. Available online: www.ifop.com/media/poll/1535-1-study_file.pdf (viewed August 29, 2011).

IFOP. 2009. "Les Français et la construction des mosquées et des minarets en France", December. Available online at www.lefigaro.fr/assets/pdf/Sondage-minaret.pdf (viewed August 12, 2011).

Ignazi, P. 2003. *Extreme Right Parties in Western Europe*. New York: Oxford University Press.

Ignazi, P. 2002. "The Extreme Right: Defining the Object and Assessing the Causes", in M. Schain, A. Zolberg, and P. Hossay, eds. *Shadows over Europe: The Development and Impact of the Extreme Right in Western Europe*. New York: Palgrave Macmillan.

Ignazi, P. 1992. "The Silent Counter-Revolution: Hypotheses on the Emergence of Extreme Right-Wing Parties in Europe". *European Journal of Political Research*, 22: 3–34.

Inglehart, R. 1977. *The Silent Revolution. Changing Values and Political Styles Among Western Publics*. Princeton, NJ: Princeton University Press.

Ipsos/Mori. 2009. "Doubting Multiculturalism", May. Available online: www.ipsos-mori.com/_assets/pdfs/Multiculturalism-Briefing.pdf (viewed August 13, 2011).

Ipsos/Mori. n. d. Online: www.ipsos-mori.com/researchpublications/researcharchive/poll.aspx?oItemId=19&view=wide.

Ishiyama, J. 2009. "Historical Legacies and the Size of the Red-Brown Vote in Post-Communist Politics", in M. Minkenberg, M. ed. "Legacies and the Radical Right in Post-1989 Central and Eastern Europe". Special issue, *Communist and Post-Communist Studies*, 42: 485–504.

Ivaldi, G. 2001. "L'analyse comparée des soutiens électoraux du national-populisme en Europe occidentale. Apports et limites des grands programmes d'enquêtes transnationales (1990–1998)", in P. Perrineau P. ed. 2001. *Les croisés de la société fermée. L'Europe des extrêmes droites*. La Tour d'Aigues: l'Aube.

Ivarsflaten, E. 2008. "What Unites the Populist Right in Western Europe? Re-Examining Grievance Mobilization Models in Seven Successful Cases". *Comparative Political Studies*, 41: 3–23.

Ivarsflaten, E. 2007. "Party Pasts, Immigrant Policies, and Voter Mobilization in the 2002 Swedish Election Campaign", in S. Gloppen and L. Rakner, eds. 2007. *Globalization and Democratization: Challenges for Political Parties*. Bergen: Fagbokforlaget: 175–192.

Ivarsflaten, E. 2005. "The Vulnerable Populist Right Parties: No Economic Realignment Fuelling their Electoral Success". *European Journal of Political Research*, 44: 465–492.

Ivarsflaten, E., S. Blinder, and R. Ford. 2010 "The Anti-Racism Norm in Western European Immigration Politics: Why Consider It and How to Measure It". *Journal of Elections Public Opinion and Parties*, 20: 421–445.

Jasiewicz, K. 2009. "The Past is Never Dead, Identity, Class and Voting Behaviour in Contemporary Poland". *East European Politics and Societies*, 23: 491–508.

Jensen, C. 2011. "Conditional Contraction: Globalisation and Capitalist Systems". *European Journal of Political Research*, 50: 168–189.

Jobbik. 2010. "Radical Change. A Guide to Jobbik's Parliamentary Electoral Manifesto for National Self-Determination and Social Justice". Budapest: Jobik Foreign Affairs Committee.

John, P. and H. Margetts. 2009. "The Latent Support for the Extreme Right in British Politics". *West European Politics*, 32: 496–513.

John, P., H. Margetts, D. Rowland, and S. Weir, S. 2006. *The British National Party: The Roots of its Appeal*. University of Essex: Democratic Audit.

Johns, R., L. Bennie, and J. Mitchell. 2011. "Gendered Nationalism: The Gender Gap in Support for the Scottish National Party". *Party Politics*, forthcoming. Online.

Johnston, R. 1987. *Money and Votes: Constituency Campaign Spending and Election Results*. London: Croom Helm.

Johnston, R. and C. Pattie. 2011. "Where did Labour's Votes Go? Valence Politics and Campaign Effects at the 2010 British General Election". *British Journal of Politics and International Relations*, 13: 283–303.

Johnston, R. and Pattie, C. 2010. "The Local Campaigns and the Outcome", in J. Bartle, and N. Allen, eds. 2010. *Britain at the Polls 2010*. London: Sage.

Johnston, R. and C. Pattie. 2006. *Putting Voters in their Place: Geography and Elections in Great Britain*. Oxford: Oxford University Press.

Johnston, R. and C. Pattie. 1995. "The Impact of Spending on Party Constituency Campaigns at Recent British General Elections". *Party Politics*, 1: 261–273.

Johnston, R., C. Pattie, D. Cutts, E. Fieldhouse, and J. Fisher. 2011. "Local Campaign Spending at the 2010 General Election and Its Impact: Exploring what Wider Regulation has Revealed". *Political Quarterly*, 82: 169–192.

Joseph Rowntree Charitable Trust. 2004. *539 Voters' Views: A Voting Behaviour Study in Three Northern Towns*. York: JRCT.

Jowitt, K. 1992a. "The Leninist Legacy", in K. Jowitt, ed. 1992. *New World Disorder. The Leninist Extinction*. Cambridge: The University of California Press, 284–305.

Jowitt, K. 1992b. "The Leninist Extinction". in K. Jowitt, ed. 1992. *New World Disorder. The Leninist Extinction*. Cambridge: The University of California Press.

Judt, T. 2005. *Postwar. A History of Europe Since 1945*. London: Penguin.

Jun, W. 2011. "Volksparteien Under Pressure: Challenges and Adaptation". *German Politics*, 20: 200–222.

Juvin, H. 2010. "Le renversement du monde. Politique de la crise". Paris: Gallimard.

Kahanec, M. and K. F. Zimmermann. 2008. "Migration and Globalization: Challenges and Perspectives for the Research Infrastructure". Bonn: Institute for the Study of Labor, IZA DP no. 3890, December.

Kahn, J.-F. 2011. "La gauche libérale en plein racisme social". *Le Monde*, July 5. Available online: www.lemonde.fr/idees/article/2011/07/05/la-gauche-liberale-en-plein-racisme-social_1544975_3232.html (viewed July 10, 2011).

Kavanagh, D. and P. Cowley. 2010. *The British General Election of 2010*. Basingstoke: Palgrave Macmillan.

Kedar, O. 2009. *Voting for Policy, Not Parties*. Cambridge: Cambridge University Press.

Keman, H. 2011. "Third Ways and Social Democracy: The Right Way to Go?". *British Journal of Political Science*, 41: 671–680.

Keman, H. 2010. "Cutting Back Public Investment after 1980: Collateral Damage, Policy Legacies and Political Adjustment". *Journal of Public Policy*, 30: 163–182.

Kemper, T. 2001. "A Structural Approach to Social Movement Emotions", in J. Goodwin, J. M. Jasper, and F. Polletta, eds. *Passionate Politics: Emotions and Social Movements*. Chicago: University of Chicago Press.

Kingston, P. W. 2000. *The Classless Society*. Stanford: Stanford University Press.

Kintz, M. 2010. "The Landtag Election in Saxony". *German Politics*, 19: 230–236.

Kitschelt, H. 2010. "The Comparative Analysis of Electoral and Partisan Politics: A Comment on a Special Issue of *West European Politics*". *West European Politics*, 33: 659–672.

Kitschelt, H. 2007. "Growth and Persistence of the Radical Right in Postindustrial Democracies. Advances and Challenges in Comparative Research". *West European Politics*, 30: 1176–1207.

Kitschelt, H. 2004. *Diversification and Reconfiguration of Party Systems in Postindustrial Democracies*. Bonn: Friedrich Ebert Stiftung.

Kitschelt, H. 2003. *Diversification and Reconfiguration of Party Systems in Postindustrial Democracies*. Bonn: Friedrich Ebert Stiftung.

Kitschelt, H. 1997. *The Radical Right in Wstern Europe. A Comparative Analysis*. Ann Arbor: Michigan University Press

Kitschelt, H. and A. McGann 1995. *The Radical Right in Western Europe: A Comparative Analysis*. Ann Arbor: University of Michigan Press.

Kitschelt, H. 1994. *The Transformation of European Social Democracy*. Cambridge: Cambridge University Press.

Kitschelt, H. 1992. "The Formation of Party Systems in East Central Europe". *Politics and Society*, 20: 7–50.

Kitschelt, H., Z. Mansfeldova, R. Markowski, and G. Tóka. 1999 *Post-Communist Party Systems. Competition, Representation and Inter-Party Cooperation*. Cambridge: Cambridge University Press.

Kitschelt, H. and P. Rehm. 2011a. "Occupation as a Site of Economic and Non-Economic Preference Formation." Paper presented at the Eighteenth Conference of Europeanists, Barcelona, June 20–22.

Kitschelt, H. and P. Rehm. 2011b. "Party Alignments. Change and Continuity". Paper prepared for the Conference on "The Future of Democratic Capitalism", University of Zurich, June 16–18.

Klingemann, H.-D., A. Volkens, J. Bara, I. Budge, and M. D. McDonald. 2006. *Mapping Policy Preferences II. Estimates for Parties, Electors, and Governments in Eastern Europe, European Union and OECD 1990–2003*. Oxford: Oxford University Press.

Knigge P. 1998. "The Ecological Correlates of Right-Wing Extremism in Western Europe". *European Journal of Political Research*, 34: 249–279.

Knutsen, O. 2006. *Class Voting in Western Europe. A Comparative Longitudinal Study*. Lanham: Lexington Books.

Knutsen, O. 2005. "The Impact of Sector Employment on Party Choice: A Comparative Study of Eight West European Countries". *European Journal of Political Research*, 44: 593–621.

Knutsen, O. 1995. "Value Orientations, Political Conflicts and Left-Right Identification: A Comparative Study". *European Journal of Political Research*, 28: 63–93.

Knutsen, O. and S. Kumlin. 2005. "Value Orientations and Party Choice", in J. Thomassen, ed. 2005. *Europan Voter. A Comparative Study of Modern Democracies*. Oxford: Oxford University Press, 125–166.

Kohn, M. and C. Schooler. 1969. "Class, Occupation, and Orientations". *American Sociological Review*, 34: 659–678.

Koopmans, R. and P. Statham, eds. 2000. *Challenging Immigration and Ethnic Relations Politics: Comparative European Perspectives*. Oxford: Oxford University Press.

Kopstein, J. 2003. "Postcommunist Democracy. Legacies and Outcomes". *Comparative Politics*, 35: 231–250.

Korpi, W. 1983. *The Democratic Class Struggle*. London: Routledge.

Kriesi, H. 2010. "Restructuration of Partisan Politics and the Emergence of a New Cleavage Based on Values". *West European Politics*, 33: 673–685.

Kriesi, H. 1999. "Movements of the Left, Movement of the Right: Putting the Mobilization of Two Types of Social Movements into Political Context", in H. Kitschelt, P. Lange, G. Marks, and D. Stephens, eds. 1999. *Continuity and Change in Contemporary Capitalism*. Cambridge: Cambridge University Press.

Kriesi, H. 1998. "The Transformation of Cleavage Politics—The 1997 Stein Rokkan Lecture". *European Journal of Political Research*, 33: 165–185.

Kriesi, H. 1993. *Political Mobilization and Social Change. The Dutch Case in Comparative Perspective*. Aldershot: Avebury.

Kriesi, H. 1989. "New Social Movements and the New Class in the Netherlands". *American Journal of Sociology*, 94: 1078–1116.

Kriesi, H., E. Grande, R. Lachat, M. Dolezal, S. Bornschier, and T. Frey. 2006. "Globalization and the Transformation of the National Political Space: Six European Countries Compared". *European Journal of Political Research*, 45: 921–956.

Kriesi, H., E. Grande, R. Lachat, M. Dolezal, S. Bornschier, and T. Frey. 2008a. "Globalization and its Impact on National Spaces of Competition", in H. Kriesi, E. Grande, R. Lachat, M. Dolezal, S. Bornschier, and T. Frey. 2008. *West European Politics in the Age of Globalization*. Cambridge: Cambridge University Press.

Kriesi, H., E. Grande, R. Lachat, M. Dolezal, S. Bornschier, and T. Frey. 2008b. *West European Politics in the Age of Globalization*. Cambridge: Cambridge University Press.

Kymlicka, W. and K. Banting. 2006. "Immigration, Multiculturalism, and the Welfare State". *Ethics & International Affairs*, 20: 281–304.

Lachat, R. and M. Dolezal. 2008. "Demand Side: Dealignment and Realignment of the Structural Political Potentials", in H. Kriesi, E. Grande, R. Lachat, M. Dolezal, S. Bornschier, and T. Frey. 2008. *West European Politics in the Age of Globalization*. Cambridge: Cambridge University Press.

Landré, M. 2011. "Le programme éco passéiste et irréaliste du FN", *La Croix*, June 10. Available online: http://blog.lefigaro.fr/social/2011/04/le-programme-eco-passeiste-et.html (viewed September 2, 2011).

Lange, S. L. 2007. "A New Winning Formula? The Programmatic Appeal of the Radical Right". *Party Politics*, 13: 411–435.

Laponce, J. A. 1981. *Left and Right. The Topography of Political Perceptions*. Toronto: University of Toronto Press.

Larsen A. C. 2011. "Ethnic Heterogeneity and Public Support for Welfare". *Scandinavian Political Studies*, 34: 332–353.

Laver, M. 2005. "Policy and the Dynamics of Party Competition". *American Political Science Review*, 99 (2), May: 263–282.

Laver, M. and E. Serengeti. 2011. *Party Competition. An Agent-Based Model*. Princeton, NJ: Princeton University Press.

Lawson, K. 1988. "When Linkage Fails", in K. Lawson and P. H. Merkle, eds. 1988. *When Parties Fail: Emerging Alternative Organizations*. Princeton, NJ: Princeton University Press.

Le Hay, V. and M. Sineau. 2010. "Effet patrimoine: 30 ans après, le retour?". *Revue française de science politique*, 60: 869–900.

Le Pen, J.-M. 1989. *L'espoir*. Paris: Editions Albatros.

Le Pen, M. 2011a. "Discours d'investiture". Tours, January 17. Available online: www.frontnational.com/?p=6295 (viewed August 17, 2011).

Le Pen, M. 2011b. "Discours premier mai". Paris, May 1. Available online: www.frontnational.com/?p=6863 (viewed August 17, 2011).

Le Pen, M. 2011c. "Discours social". Bompas, March 11. Available online: www.frontnational.com/?p=6622 (viewed August 17, 2011).

Le Pen, M. 2011d. "Le Pen présente son plan pour améliorer le pouvoir d'achat". *Le Monde*, May 13. Available online: www.lemonde.fr/politique/article/2011/05/13/marine-le-pen-presente-son-plan-pour-ameliorer-le-pouvoir-d-achat_1521856_823448.html.

Le Pen, M. 2011e. "Le mondialisme est un totalitarisme". *Causeur*, January 10. Available online: www.causeur.fr/%C2%AB-le-mondialisme-est-un-totalitarisme-%C2%BB,8280 (viewed August 20, 2011).

Letty, E. 2011. "Le virage à gauche du Front National", *Le choc du mois*, May: 36–37.

Lewis-Beck, M. S. 1998. "Class, Religion and the French Voter: A Stalled Electorate?" *French Politics and Society*, 16: 43–51.

Lind, M. 2007. "The Centre-Ground's Shift to the Left", *Financial Times* online, November 27: Available online: www.ft.com/cms/s/0/4afdfafe-9cf7-11dc-af03-0000779fd2ac.html#axzz1XA8D1BXD (viewed July 3, 2011).

Linz, J. and A. Stepan. 1996. *Problems of Democratic Transition and Consolidation*. Baltimore: Johns Hopkins University Press.

Lipset, S. M. 1960. *Political Man. The Social Bases of Politics*. London: Heinemann.

Lipset, S. M. 1959. "Democracy and Working-Class Authoritarianism". *American Sociological Review*, 24: 482–501.

Lipset, S. M. and Rokkan, S. 1967. *Party Systems and Voter Alignments*. New York: The Free Press.

Lipset, S. M. and R. Stein. 1967. "Cleavage Structures, Party Systems and Voter Alignments", in S. M. Lipset and R. Stein, eds. 1967. *Party Systems and Voter Alignments*. New York: Free Press.

Lööw, H. 2011. "The Extreme Right in Sweden: Growing Slowly", in N. Lagenbacher and B. Schellenberg, eds. *Is Europe on the 'Right' Path*. Berlin: Friedrich Ebert Stiftung.

Louis, H. 2006. "L'observatoire de l'opinion", May. Available online: www.lh2.fr/_upload/ressources/sondages/politique_nationale/lh2libeobservatoire2mai06.pdf(viewed July 26, 2011).

Lowles, N. 2010a. "The Politics of Hope and Hate". *Searchlight Magazine*, 418 (April).

Lowles, N. 2010b. "Record Breakers". *Searchlight Magazine*, 419 (May).

Lowles, N. 2010c. "Routed". *Searchlight Magazine*, 420 (June).

LPR. 2003. *Skrót programu gospodarczego Ligi Polskich Rodzin. Dla niepodległej Polski i suwerennego Narodu Polskiego*. Warszawa: LPR.

Lubbers, M. 2001. *Exclusionistic Electorates: Extreme Right-Wing Voting in Western Europe*. Nijmegen: Katholieke Universiteit Nijmegen.

Lubbers, M., M. Gijsberts and P. Scheepers. 2002. "Extreme Right-Wing Voting in Western Europe". *European Journal of Political Research*, 41: 345–378.

Lubbers, M. and P. Scheepers. 2000. "Indvdiual and Contextual Characteristics of the German Extreme Right-Wing Vote in the 1990s: A Test of Complementary Theories". *European Journal of Political Research*, 38: 63–94.

Lucardie, P. 1998. "The Netherlands: The Extremist Center Parties", in H.-G. Betz and S. Immerfall, eds. *The New Politics of the Right. Neo-Populist Parties and Movements in Established Democracies*. New York: St Martin's Press.

Mair, P. 2001. "The Green Challenge and Political Competition: How Typical is the German Experience?". *German Politics*, 10: 99–116.

Mair, P., S. M. Lipset, M. Hout, and J. H. Goldthorpe. 1999. "Critical Commentary: Four Perspectives on The End of Class Politics?", in G. Evans, ed. *The End of Class Politics? Class Voting in Comparative Context*. Oxford: Oxford Univ. Press.

Manza, J. H., M. Brooks, and B. Clem. 1995. "Class Voting in Capitalist Democracies Since World War II: Dealignment, Realignment, or Trendless Fluctuation?". *Annual Review of Sociology*, 21: 137–162.

Marks, G., L. Hooghe, M. Nelson, and E. Edwards. 2006. "Party Competition and European Integration in the East and West: Different Structure, Same Causality". *Comparative Political Studies*, 39: 155–175.

Martin, P. 2000. *Comprendre les évolutions électorales: La théorie des réalignements revisitée*. Paris: Presses de Sciences Po.

Martinsson, J. 2009. *Economic Voting and Issue Ownership. An Integrative Approach*. Göteborg: Statsvetenskapliga institutionen, Göteborgs Universitet.

Mateju, P., B. Rehakova, and G. Evans. 1999. "The Politics of Interests and Class Realignment in the Czech Republic, 1992–1996", in G. Evans, ed. *The End of Class Politics? Class Voting in Comparative Context*. Oxford: Oxford University Press.

Mayer, N. 2007. "Comment Nicolas Sarkozy a rétréci l'électorat Le Pen". *Revue française de science politique*, 57: 429–445.

Mayer, N. 2005. "Radical Right Populism in France. How Much of the 2002 Le Pen Votes does Populism Explain?". Presented at the Symposium on Globalization and the Radical Right Populism, Ben Gurion University, April 11–12.

Mayer, N. 2002 (1999). *Ces Français qui votent Le Pen*. Paris: Flammarion.

Mayer, N. 1998. "The Front National in the Plural". *Patterns of Prejudice*, 32: 4–24.

Mayer, N., G. Michelat, and V. Tiberj. 2010. "Le racisme à l'heure de la crise", in Commission nationale consultative des droits de l'homme, ed. *La lutte contre le racisme et la xénophobie: 2009*. Paris: La Documentation française, 102–123.

Mayda, A. and D. Rodrik. 2005. "Why Are Some People (and Countries) More Protectionist than Others?". *European Economic Review*, 6: 1393–1430.

McClosky, H. and A. Brill. 1983. *Dimensions of Tolerance: What Americans Believe About Civil Liberties*. New York: Russell Sage Foundation.

McGann, A. J. and H. Kitschelt. 2005. "The Radical Right in The Alps. Evolution of Support for the Swiss SVP and Austrian FPO". *Party Politics*, 11:147–171.

McLaren, L. and M. Johnson. 2007. "Resources, Group Conflict and Symbols: Explaining Anti-Immigration Hostility in Britain". *Political Studies*, 55: 709–732.

McManus-Czubińska, C., W. Miller, R. Markowski, and J. Wasilewski. 2001. "The New Polish 'Right'?". *Journal of Communist Studies and Transition Politics*, 19: 1–23.

Meguid, B. 2005. "Competition between Unequals: The Role of Mainstream Party Strategy in Niche Party Success". *American Political Science Review*, 99: 347–359.

Meret, S. 2010. *The Danish People's Party, the Italian Northern League and the Austrian Freedom Party in a Comparative Perspective*, Party Ideology and Electoral Support, SPIRIT PhD series. Aalborg: Aalborg University.

Merrill, S. and B. Grofman. 1999. *A Unified Theory of Voting*. Cambridge, NY: Cambridge University Press.

Michelat G. and M. Simon. 1977. *Classe, religion et comportement politique*. Paris: Presses de la FNSP/Editions sociales.

Michelat G. and M. Simon. 2004. "Les ouvriers et la politique: Permanence, ruptures, réalignements". Paris: Presses de Sciences Po.

Milmo, C. 2010. "Griffin's Future in Doubt as BNP Campaign Implodes". *Independent*, May 8.

Minkenberg, M. 2009a. "Leninist Beneficiaries? Pre-1989 Legacies and the Radical Right in Post-1989 Central and Eastern Europe. Some Introductory Observations". *Communist and Post-Communist Studies*, 42: 445–458.

Minkenberg, M. 2009b. "Legacies and the Radical Right in Post-1989 Central and Eastern Europe". *Communist and Post-Communist Studies*, 42: 445–448.

Minkenberg, M. 2008. *The Radical Right in Europe. An Overview*. Gütersloh: Verlag Bertelsmann Stiftung.

Minkenberg, M. 2002. "The Radical Right in Post-Socialist Central and Eastern Europe: Comparative Observations and Interpretations". *East European Politics and Societies*, 16: 335–362.

Minkenberg, M. 2001. "La nouvelle droite radicale, ses électeurs et ses milieux partisans: Vote protestataire, phénomène xénophobe ou 'modernization losers'", in P. Perrineau, ed. *Les croisés de la société fermée*. La Tour d'Aigues: l'Aube.

Minkenberg, M. 2000. "The Renewal of the Radical Right: Between Modernity and Anti-Modernity". *Government and Opposition*, 35: 170–188.

Minkenberg, M. 1998. *Die neue radikale Rechte im Vergleich. USA, Frankreich, Deutschland*. Opladen/Wiesbaden: Westdeutscher Verlag.

Minkenberg, M. 1997. "The New Right in France and Germany. Nouvelle Droite, Neue Rechte, and the New Right Radical Parties", in P. H. Merkl and L. Weinberg, eds. 1997. *The Revival of Right-Wing Extremism in the Nineties*. London: Frank Cass.

Minkenberg, M. 1992. "The New Right in West Germany: The Transformation of Conservatism and the Extreme Right". *European Journal of Political Research*, 22: 55–81.

Minkenberg, M. and P. Perrineau. 2007. "The Radical Right in the European Elections 2004". *International Political Science Review*, 28: 29–55.

Mitra, S. 1988. "The National Front in France—a Single-Issue Movement?", in K. von Beyme, ed. *Right-Wing Extremism in Western Europe*. London: Frank Cass.

Monroe, K. R., J. Hankin, and R. B. Van Vechten. 2000. "The Psychological Foundations of Identity Politics". *Annual Review of Political Science*, 3: 419–447.

Mossuz Lavau, J. 1997. "Les Françaises et le Front national", in C. Lessselier and F. Venner, eds. *L'extrême droite et les femmes: enjeux et actualité*. Villeurbanne: Golias.

Mudde, C. 2007. *Populist Radical Right Parties in Europe*. Cambridge: Cambridge University Press.

Mudde, C. 2004. "The Populist Zeitgeist." *Government and Opposition*, 39 (4): 541–63.

Mudde, C. 2000a. "Extreme-Right Parties in Eastern Europe". *Patterns of Prejudice*, 34: 5–27.

Mudde, C. 2000b. "In the Name of the Peasantry, the Proletariat, and the People: Populisms in Eastern Europe". *East European Politics and Societies*, 14: 33–53.

Mudde, C. 1999. "The Single-Issue Party Thesis: Extreme Right Parties and the Immigration Issue". *West European Politics*, 22: 182–197.

Mudde, C. 1996. "The War of Words. Defining the Extreme Right Party Family". *West European Politics*, 19: 225–248.

Mughan, A., C. Bean, and I. McAllister. 2003. "Economic globalization, job insecurity und the populist reaction." *Electoral Studies, 22*: 617–633.

Mughan, A. and P. Paxton. 2003. "Immigrants, Prejudice and Politics: A Model of Populist Party Voting". Paper presented at the ECPR Joint Sessions.

Müller, W. 1999. "Class Cleavages in Party Preferences in Germany – Old and New." in

Evans, G. ed. 2000. *The End of Class Politics? Class Voting in Comparative Context.* Oxford: Oxford University Press.

Mulvey, G. 2010. "When Policy Creates Politics: The Problematizing of Immigration and the Consequences for Refugee Integration in the UK". *Journal of Refugee Studies,* 23: 437–62.

Nannestad, P. 1999. *Solidaritetens pris. Holdninger til indvandrere og flygtninge i Danmark 1987–1993.* Aarhus: AarhusUniversitetsforlag.

Napier, J. L. and J. T. Jost. 2008. "The 'Anti-Democratic Personality' Revisited: A Cross-National Investigation of Working-Class Authoritarianism". *Journal of Social Issues,* 64: 595–617.

Neu, V. 2009. *Bundestagswahl in Deutschland am 27. September 2009.* Berlin: Konrad Adenauer Stuftung.

Nie, J. and K. Stehlik-Barry. 1996. *Education and Democratic Citizenship in America.* Chicago: University of Chicago Press.

Nielsen, J. H. 2007. "Hvilken slags af indvandrere ønsker man?", in G. Andersen, J. Andersen, O. Borre, K. M. Hansen, and H. J. Nielsen, eds. 2005. *Det nye politiske landskab. Folketingsvalget 2005 i perspektiv.* Aarhus: Academica.

Nieuwbeerta, P. and N. D. Graaf. 2001. "Traditional Class Voting in Twenty Postwar Societies", in G. Evans, ed. 2000. *The End of Class Politics? Class Voting in Comparative Context.* Oxford: Oxford University Press.

Nieuwbeerta, P. and W. Ultee. 1999. "Class Voting in Western Industrialized Countries, 1945–1990: Systematizing and Testing Explanations". *European Journal of Electoral Research,* 35: 123–160.

Nordlinger, J. 2010. "Among the Progs". *National Review Digital,* July 19. Available online: www2.nationalreview.com/nordlinger/nordlinger_progs07–19–10.asp (viewed July 28 2011).

Norris, P. 2011. *Democratic Deficit. Critical Citizens Revisited.* Cambridge: Cambridge University Press.

Norris, P. 2005. *Radical Right. Voters and Parties in the Electoral Market.* Cambridge: Cambridge University Press.

Norris, P. 1999. *Critical Citizens. Global Support for Democratic Governance.* Oxford: Oxford University Press.

Nunn, C. Z., J. Harry, J. Crockett, and A. Williams. 1978. *Tolerance for Nonconformity.* San Fracisco: Jossey-Bass Publishers.

OBOP. 2002. *Preferencje partyjne Polaków w grudniu 2002 r.* Warszawa: TNS OBOP.

Odmalm, P. 2011. "Political Parties and 'The Immigration Issue': Issue Ownership in Swedish Parliamentary Elections 1991–2010". *West European Politics,* 34: 1070–1091.

OECD. 2004. *Quarterly Labour Force Statistics (Heft 4).* Paris: OECD.

OECD. 2003. *OECD Employment Outlook. Towards More and Bettter Jobs.* Paris: OECD.

OECD. 2002. *Benefits and Wages. OECD Indicators.* Paris: OECD.

OECD. 1992. *Trends in International Migration. SOPEMI.* Paris: OECD.

Oesch, D. 2008. "Explaining Workers' Support for Right-Wing Populist Parties in Western Europe: Evidence from Austria, Belgium, France, Norway, and Switzerland." *International Political Science Review,* 29: 349–373.

Oesch, D. 2006a. "Coming to Grips with a Changing Class Structure: An Analysis of Employment Stratification in Britain, Germany, Sweden and Switzerland". *International Sociology,* 21: 263–288.

Oesch, D. 2006b. *Redrawing the Class Map. Stratification and Institutions in Britain, Germany, Sweden and Switzerland.* Basingstoke: Palgrave Macmillan.

Oesch, D. and L. Rennwald. 2010. "The Class Basis of Switzerland's Cleavage between the New Left and the Populist Right". *Swiss Political Science Review,* 16: 343–371.

Oesch, D. and J. Rodriguez Menes. 2011. "Upgrading or Polarization? Occupational Change in Britain, Germany, Spain and Switzerland, 1990–2008". *Socio-Economic Review,* 9: 503–532.

Olsen, J. 2007. "The Merger of the PDS and WASG: From Eastern German Regional Party to National Radical Left Party?". *German Politics,* 16: 205–221.

Onfray, M. 2011. "Pour on finir avec la gauche de droite". *Marianne,* June 25: 78.

Oosterwaal, A. and R. Torenvlied. 2010. "Politics Divided from Society? Three Explanations for Trends in Societal and Political Polarisation in the Netherlands". *West European Politics,* 33: 258–279.

Oscarsson, H. and S. Holmberg. 2008. *Regeringsskifte. Väljarna och valet 2006.* Stockholm: Norstedts Juridik.

Oskarson, M. 2005. "Social Structure and Party Choice", in J. Thomassen, eds. *The European Voter. A Comparative Study of Modern Democracies.* Oxford: Oxford University Press.

Oskarson, M. 1994. *Klassröstning i Sverige. Rationalitet, lojalitet eller bara slentrian.* Stockholm: Nerenius & Santerus.

Ost, D. 2005. *The Defeat of Solidarity. Anger and Politics in Postcommunist Europe.* Ithaca: Cornell University Press.

Palier, B. 2010. "Ordering Change: Understanding the 'Bismarckian' Welfare Reform Trajectory", in B. Palier, ed. *A Long Goodbye to Bismarck? The Politics of Welfare Reform in Continental Europe.* Amsterdam: Amsterdam University Press.

Pattie, C. and R. Johnston. 2010. "Constituency Campaigning and Local Contests at the 2010 UK General Election". *British Politics,* 5: 481–505.

Pattie, C. and R. Johnston. 2009. "Still Talking, But is Anyone Listening? The Changing Face of Constituency Campaigning in Britain, 1997–2005". *Party Politics,* 15 (4): 411–434.

Pattie, C. and R. Johnston. 2003. "Local Battles in a National Landslide: Constituency Campaigning at the 2001 British General Election". *Political Geography,* 22 (4): 381–414.

Pattie, C., R. Johnston, and E. Fieldhouse. 1995. "Winning the Local Vote: The Effectiveness of Constituency Campaign Spending in Great Britain, 1983–1992". *American Political Science Review,* 89: 969–83.

Pcolinský, V. and A. Štensová. 2007. "Slovak Parliamentary Elections 2006", in *Central European Political Studies Review,* 9: 102–113.

Pech, T. 2011. "Front national: La grande illusion". *Alternatives Économiques,* May: 42–44.

Perrineau, P. 1997. *Le symtôme Le Pen. Radiographie des électeurs du Front National.* Paris: Fayard.

Perrineau P. 1995. "La dynamique du vote Le Pen: Le poids du gaucho-lepénisme", in P. Perrineau and C. Ysmal, eds. *Le vote de crise: L'élection présidentielle de 1995.* Paris: Presses de Sciences.

Plasser, F. and P. A. Ulram. 2000. "Rechtspopulistische Resonanzen: Die Wählerschaft der FPÖ", in F. Plasser, P. A. Ulram, and F. Sommer, eds. 2000. *Das Österreichische Wahlverhalten.* Wien: Signum.

Plasser, F. and P. A. Ulram. 1997. *Politischer Kulturwandel in Ost-Mitteleuropa. Theorie und Empirie demokratischer Konsolidierung.* Opladen: Leske & Budrich.

Plasser, F., A. P. Ulram, and F. Sommer. 2000. *Das Österreichische Wahlverhalten.* Wien: Signum Verlag.

Plasser, F., A. P. Ulram, and Waldrauch, 1999. *Analysis of the 1999 Parliamentary Elections. Patterns, Trends and Motives.* Wien: ZAP.

Policy Network. 2011. "Exploring the Cultural Challenges to Social Democracy: Anti-Migration Populism, Identity and Community in an Age of Insecurity". Available online: www.policy-network.net/publications_download.aspx?ID=7374.

Prowe, D. 1994. " 'Classic' Fascism and the New Radical Right in Western Europe: Comparisons and Contrasts". *Contemporary European History,* 3: 289–313.

PvdA. 2009. ' "Verdeeld verleden, gedeelde toekomst. Resolutie Integratie". Partij van de Arbeid resolution on integration, Utrecht, March.

PvdA. 2006. "Het Nederland van morgen". Parliamentary election manifesto Partij van de Arbeid 2006. Available online: http://dnpp.eldoc.ub.rug.nl/FILES/root/programmas/vp-per-partij/PvdA/pvda06.pdf, accessed 15–09–2011.

PvdA. 2002. "De kaasstolp aan diggelen. De PvdA na de dreun van 15 mei". Partij van de Arbeid evaluation report regarding parliamentary election of 2002, Amsterdam, September.

Pytlas, B. 2009. "The Diffusion of Radical Right Ideology in Central-Eastern Europe: The Case of Poland and Slovakia". Paper presented at the fifth ECPR General Conference, Potsdam, September 10–12.

Quillian, L. 1995. "Prejudice as a Response to Perceived Group Threat: Population Composition and Anti-Immigrant and Racial Prejudice in Europe". *American Sociological Review,* 60: 586–611.

Rallings, C. and M. Thrasher, eds. 2007. *Media Guide to the New Parliamentary Constituencies.* Plymouth: LGC Elections Centre.

Ramet, S. 1999. *The Radical Right in Central and Eastern Europe Since 1989.* University Park: The Pennsylvania State University Press.

Reynié, D. 2011. *Populismes: La pente fatale.* Paris: Plon.

Riedlsperger, M. 1998. "The Freedom Party of Austria: From Protest to Radical Radical Right Populism", in Betz, H.-G. and S. Immerfall, eds. 1998. *The New Politics of the Right. Neo-Populist Parties and Movements in Established Democracies.* New York: St Martin's Press.

Riker, W. H. 1982. *Liberalism against Populism. A Confrontation between the Theory of Democracy and the Theory of Social Choice.* Prospect Heights, IL: Waveland Press.

Rippeyoung, P. L. F. 2007. "When Women are Right. The Influence of Gender, Work and Values on European Far-Right Party Support". *International Feminist Journal of Politics,* 9: 379–397.

Rodrik, D. 2007. "Sense and Nonsense in the Globalization Debate". *Foreign Policy,* 107: 19–37.

Rudi, T. 2010. *Wahlentscheidungen in postsozialistischen Demokratien in Mittel- und Osteuropa. Eine vergleichende Untersuchung.* Baden-Baden: Nomos.

Russell, A. and E. Fieldhouse. 2005. *Neither Left Nor Right? The Liberal Democrats and the Electorate.* Manchester: Manchester University Press.

Rybář, M. and K. Deegan-Krause. 2008. "Slovakia's Communist Successor Parties in Comparative Perspective". *Communist and Post-Communist Studies,* 41: 497–519.

Rydgren, J. 2008. "Immigration Sceptics, Xenophobes or Racists? Radical Right-Wing Voting in Six West European Countries". *European Journal of Political Research,* 47: 737–765.

Rydgren, J. 2007. "The Sociology of the Radical Right". *Annual Review of Sociology*, 33: 241–262.

Rydgren, J. 2005. "Is Extreme Right-Wing Populism Contagious? Explaining the Emergence of a New Party Family". *European Journal of Political Research*, 44: 413–37.

Rydgren, J. 2003. "Meso-level Reasons for Racism and Xenophobia. Some Converging and Diverging Effects of Radical Right Populism in France and Sweden". *European Journal of Social Theory*, 6: 45–68.

Rydgren, J. 2002. "Radical Right Populism in Sweden: Still a Failure but for How Long?". *Scandinavian Political Studies*, 25: 27–56.

Rydgren, J. and P. Ruth. 2011. "Voting for the Radical Right in Swedish Municipalities: Social Marginality and Ethnic Competition?". *Scandinavian Political Studies*, 34: 202–225.

Sacchi, S. 1998. *Politische Potenziale in modernen Gesellschaften. Zur Formierung linksgrüner und neokonservativer Bewegungen in Europa und den USA*. Frankfurt/New York: Campus.

Sawicki, F. 2011. "Le prolo, l'expert et le mépris de classe". *Libération*, June 10. Available online: www.liberation.fr/politiques/01012342430-le-prolo-l-expert-et-le-mepris-de-classe (viewed June 15, 2011).

Schain, M., A. Zolberg, and P. Hossay. 2002. *Shadows Over Europe: The Development and Impact of the Extreme Right in Western Europe*. New York: Palgrave.

Schedler, A. 1996. "Anti-Political-Establishment Parties." *Party Politics*, 2 (3): 291–312.

Scheve, K. F. and M. J. Slaughter. 2004. "Economic Insecurity and the Globalization of Production". *American Journal of Political Science*, 48: 662–674.

Scheve, Kenneth F. and M. J. Slaughter. 2001a. *Globalization and the Perceptions of American Workers*. Washington: Institute for International Economics.

Scheve, Kenneth F. and M. J. Slaughter. 2001b. "What Determines Individual Trade-Policy Preferences?". *Journal of International Economics*, 54 (2): 267–292.

Schmitt, H., E. Scholz, I. Leim, and M. Moschner. 2009. *The Mannheim Eurobarometer Trendfile 1970–2002*. Data set edition 2.01, codebook and unweighted frequency distributions, updated by I. Leim and M. Morschner, ZA Cologne, Gesis. Available online: http://info1.gesis.org/dbksearch/file.asp?file=ZA3521_cod_v2–0–1.pdf.

Schuyt. 2009. "Verdeeld verleden, gedeelde toekomst". *Socialisme & Democratie*, 2009 (1–2).

Seyd, P. and P. Whiteley. 1992. *Labour's Grassroots: The Politics of Party Membership*. Oxford: Clarendon.

Shafir, M. 2000. "Marginalization or Mainstream? The Extreme Right in Post-Communist Romania", in P. Hainsworth, ed. 2000. *The Politics of the Extreme Right: From the Margins to the Mainstream*. London: Pinter.

Simpson, I. H., D. Stark, and R. A. Jackson. 1988. "Class Identification Processes of Married, Working Men and Women". *American Sociological Review*, 53: 284–293.

Sineau, M. 2004. "Les paradoxes du gender gap à la française", in B. Cautrès and N. Mayer, eds. *Le nouveau désordre électoral: Les leçons du 21 avril 2002*. Paris: Presses de Sciences.

Smith, A. 2001. *Nationalism. Theory, Ideology, History*. Cambridge: Polity Press.

Sniderman, P. M. and L. Hagendoorn. 2007. *When Ways of Life Collide. Multiculturalism and its Discontents in the Netherlands*. Princeton: Princeton University Press.

Sniderman, P. M., L. Hagendoorn, and M. Prior. 2004. "Predispositional Factors and Situational Triggers: Exclusionary Reactions to Immigrant Minorities". *American Political Science Review*, 98: 35–50.

Sniderman, P. M., P. Peri, R. J. P. de Figueiredo, and T. Piazza. 2000. *The Outsider: Prejudice and Politics in Italy*. Princeton: Princeton University Press.

Snow, D. A., D. M. Cress, L. Downey, and A. W. Jones. 2010 (1998). "Disrupting the 'Quotidian': Reconceptualizing the Relationship between Breakdown and the Emergence of Collective Action", in D. McAdam and D. A. Snow, eds. *Readings on Social Movements: Origins, Dynamics, and Outcomes*. Oxford: Oxford University Press.

SNS. 2006. "Volebny Program Slovenskej Národnej Strany. Sme Slováci Slovákom Slovenskú Vládu". Bratislava.

SNS. 2002. "Program Národnej Obnovy. Pre volebné obdobie 2002–2006". Bratislava.

SNS. 1998. "Program Slovenskej Národnej Strany". Bratislava.

Sommerville, W. 2007. *Immigration under New Labour*. Bristol: Policy Press.

Sørensen, A. 1994. "Women, Family and Class". *Annual Review of Sociology*, 20: 27–47.

Spier, T. 2010. *Modernisierungsverlierer? Die Wählerschaft rechtspopulistischer Parteien in Westeuropa*. Wiesbaden: VS Verlag für Sozialwissenschaften.

Spies, D. 2010. "Why the Working-Class Turned Right". *GK Soclife*, working paper series, 1 (September).

Spies, D. and S. T. Franzmann. 2011. "A Two-Dimensional Approach to the Political Opportunity Structure of Extreme Right Parties in Western Europe". *West European Politics*, 5: 1044–1069.

Squire, V. 2008. "Acounting for the Dominance of Control: Inter-party Dynamics and Restrictive Asylum Policy in Contemporary Britain". *British Politics*, 3: 241–261.

Standing, G. 1996. "Social Protection in Central Eastern Europe. A Tale of Slipping Anchors and Torn Safety Nets", in G. Esping-Andersen, ed. 1996. *Welfare States in Transition. National Adaptations in Global Economies*. London: Sage.

Stears, M. 2011. "This is not the Blue Labour View on Immigration". Available online: www.ippr.org/articles/56/7747/this-is-not-the-blue-labour-view-on-immigration.

Stefanini, P. 2010. *Avanti Po. La Lega Nord alla riscossa nelle regioni rosse*. Milano: Il Saggiatore.

Stiglitz, J. 2003. "Globalization and the Economic Role of the State in the New Millennium". *Industrial and Corporate Change*, 12: 3–26.

Stöss, R. 2005. *Rechtsextremismus im Wandel*. Berlin: Friedrich-Ebert-Stiftung.

Stöss, R. 1994. "Forschungs- und Erklärungsansätze – ein Überblick", in W. Kowalsky and W. Schroeder, eds. *Rechtsextremismus. Einführung und Forschungsbilanz*. Opladen: Westdeutscher Verlag.

Stöss, R. and D. Segert. 1997. "Entstehung, Struktur und Entwicklung von Parteiensystemen in Osteuropa nach 1989—eine Bilanz", in S. Dieter, R. Stöss, and O. Niedermayer, eds. *Parteiensysteme in postkommunistischen Gesellschaften Osteuropas*. Opladen: Leske & Budrich.

Stubager, R. 2010. "The Development of the Education Cleavage: Denmark as a Critical Case". *West European Politics*, 33: 505–533.

Stubager, R. 2009. "Education-Based Group Identity and Consciousness in the Authoritarian-Libertarian Value Conflict". *European Journal of Political Research*, 48: 204–233.

Stubager, R. 2008. "Education Effects on Authoritarian-Libertarian Values: A Question of Socialization". *British Journal of Sociology*, 59: 327–50.

Stubager, R. 2006. *The Educaton Cleavage: New Politics in Denmark*. Aarhus: Institut for Statskundskab, Aarhus Universitet.

Sulik, R. 2006. "Socialna Politika", in G. Mesežnikov and M. Kollar, eds. 2006. *Vol'by 2006. Analýza volebných programov politických strán a hnutí*. Bratislava: IVO.

Sum, P. E. 2010. "The Radical Right in Romania: Political Party Evolution and the Distancing of Romania from Europe". *Communist and Post-Communist Studies*, 43: 19–29.

Swank, D. 2005. "Globalisation, Domestic Politics, and Welfare State Retrenchment in Capitalist Democracies". *Social Policy & Society*, 4: 183–195.

Swank, D. and H.-G. Betz. 2003. "Globalization, the Welfare State and Right-Wing Populism in Western Europe". *Socio-Economic Review*, 1: 215–245.

Swidler, A. 1986. "Culture in Action: Symbols and Strategies". *American Sociological Review*, 51: 273–286.

Swyngedouw, M. 1998. "The Extreme Right in Belgium: Of a Non-existent Front National and an Omnipresent Vlaams Blok", in H.-G. Betz and S. Immerfall, eds. *The New Politics of the Right. Neo-Populist Parties and Movements in Established Democracies*. New York: St Martin's Press.

Swyngedouw, M. 2001. "The Subjective Cognitive and Affective Map of Extreme Right Voters: Using Open-Ended Questions in Exit Polls". *Electoral Studies*, 20: 217–241.

Synovate. 2010. *Winst- en verliesrekening*. Post-election survey. Available online: www.politiekebarometer.nl/pdf/winst%20en%20verlies.pdf (accessed September 21, 2011).

Szelényi, I., E. Fodor, and E. Hanley. 1997. "Left Turn in Post-Communist Politics: Bringing Class Back In?". *East European Politics and Societies*, 11: 190–224.

Szelényi, S., I. Szelényi, and W. R. Poster. 1996. "Interests and Symbols in Post-Communist Political Culture: The Case of Hungary". *American Sociological Review*, 61: 466–477.

Sztompka, P. 1993. "Civilizational Incompetence: The Trap of Post-Communist Societies". *Zeitschrift für Soziologie*, 22: 85–95.

Sztompka, P. 1992. "Dilemmas of the Great Transition". *Sisyphus*, 8: 9–28.

Taggart, P. 2000. *Populism*. Buckingham: Open University Press.

Taggart, P. 1996. *The New Populism and the New Politics. New Protest Parties in Sweden and in Comparative Perspective*. Basingstoke: Macmillan.

Taguieff, P. A. 1988. *La Force du préjugé. Essai sur le racisme et ses doubles*. Paris: La Découverte.

Tåhlin, M. 2007. "Skills and Wages in European Labour Markets: Structure and Change", in D. Gallie, eds. *Employment Regimes and the Quality of Work*. Oxford: Oxford University Press.

Tajfel, H. 1981. *Human Groups and Social Categories. Studies in Social Psychology*. Cambridge: Cambridge University Press.

Tarrow, S. 1998. *Power in Movement: Social Movements and Contentious Politics*. Cambridge: CUP.

Taylor, M. and H. Muir. 2010. "General Election 2010: The Defeat of the BNP". *Guardian*, May 14.

Terra Nova. 2011. "Gauche: Quelle majorité électorale pour 2012?" Fondation Terra Nova, Projet 2012, contribution n. 1. Available online: www.tnova.fr/sites/default/files/Rapport%20Terra%20Nova%20Strat%C3%A9gie%20%C3%A9lectorale.pdf (viewed June 13, 2011).

Thomsen Frølund, J. P. 2006. *Konflikten om de nye Danskere*. Viborg: Akademisk Forlag.

Tiemann, G. 2011. "Parteiensysteme: Interaktionsmuster und Konsolidierungsgrad", in F. Grotz and F. Müller-Rommel, eds. 2011. *Regierungssysteme in Mittel- und Osteuropa*. Wiesbaden: VS Verlag.

Tillie, J. N. 1995. "Partijvoorkeur, Partijconcurrentie en Stemgedrag", in B. Niemoller and J. van Holsteyn, eds. *De Nederlandse Kiezer 1994*. Leiden: DSWO.

Tismaneanu, V. 2007. "Is East-Central Europe Backsliding? Leninist Legacies, Pluralist Dilemmas". *Journal of Democracy*, 18: 33–39.

Tismaneanu, V. 1998. *Fantasies of Salvation: Democracy, Nationalism, and Myth in Post-Communist Europe*. Princeton: Princeton University Press.

Tismaneanu, V., M. M. Howard, and R. Sil. 2006. *World Order after Leninism*. Seattle/London: University of Washington Press.

TNS Gallup for Berlingske Tidende. 2011. Lyngallup om udlændingedebatten, March 29.

Tomlinson, J. 2003. "Globalization and Cultural Identity. Available online: www.polity.co.uk/global/pdf/gtreader2etomlinson.pdf (viewed July 23, 2011).

Treier, S. and D. Sunshine Hillygus. 2009. "The Nature of Political Ideology in the Contemporary Electorate". *Public Opinion Quarterly*, 73: 679–703.

Tworzecki, H. 2003. *Learning to Choose: Electoral Politics in East-Central Europe*. Stanford: Stanford University Press.

UNHCR. 2002. *2002 UNHCR Statistical Yearbook*. Geneva: United Nations High Commissioner for Refugees.

Van de Werfhorst, H. G. and N. D. de Graaf. 2004. "The Sources of Political Orientations in Post-Industrial Society: Social Class and Education Revisited". *The British Journal of Sociology*, 55: 211–235.

van der Brug, W. 2003. "How the LPF Fuelled Discontent: Empirical Tests of Explanations of LPF-support". *Acta Politica*, 38: 89–106.

van der Brug, W. 1999. "Voters' Perceptions and Party Dynamics". *Party Politics*, 5: 147–169.

van der Brug, W. and M. Fennema. 2007. "What Causes People to Vote for a Radical Right Party? A Review of Recent Work". *International Journal of Public Opinion Research*, 19: 474–487.

van der Brug, W. and M. Fennema. 2003. "Protest or Mainstream? How the European Anti-Immigrant Parties have Developed into Two Separate Groups by 1999". *European Journal of Political Research*, 42: 55–76.

van der Brug, W., M. Fennema, and J. Tillie. 2000. "Anti-Immigrant Parties in Europe: Ideological or Protest Vote?". *European Journal of Political Research*, 37: 77–102.

van der Brug, W., M. Fennema, and J. Tillie. 2005. "Why Some Anti-Immigrant Parties Fail and Others Succeed. A Two-Step Model of Aggregate Electoral Support". *Comparative Political Studies*, 38: 537–573.

van der Brug, W. and J. van Spanje. 2009. "Immigration, Europe, and the 'New' Cultural Dimension". *European Journal of Political Research*, 48: 309–334.

van der Eijk, C., W. van der Brug, M. Kroh, and M. Franklin. 2006. "Rethinking the Dependent Variable in Electoral Behavior—On the Measurement and Analysis of Utilities". *Electoral Studies*, 25: 424–447.

van der Waal, J., P. Achterberg, and D. Houtman. 2007. "Class Is Not Dead—It Has Been Buried Alive: Class Voting and Cultural Voting in Postwar Western Societies (1956–1990)". *Politics and Society*, 35: 403–426.

van der Waal, J., P. Achterberg, D. Houtman, W. de Koster, and K. Manevska. 2010. "'Some are More Equal than Others': Economic Egalitarianism and Welfare Chauvinism in the Netherlands". *Journal of European Social Policy*, 20: 350–363.

van Kessel, S. 2011a. Interview with R. Cuperus, member of the Dutch Social Democratic think tank, Wiardi Beckman Stichting, Utrecht, 8 September, 2011.

van Kessel, S. 2011b. "Explaining the electoral Performance of Populist Parties: The Netherlands as a Case Study". *Perspectives on European Politics and Society*, 12: 68–88.

van Kessel, S. 2011c. *Supply and demand. Identifying populist parties in Europe and explaining their electoral performance* Unpublished D.Phil. Thesis, July 2011, Brighton: University of Sussex.

van Spanje, J. 2010. "Contagious Parties. Anti-Immigration Parties and their Impact on Other Parties. Immigration Stances in Contemporary Western Europe". *Party Politics*, 6: 563–86.

Velfærdskommissionen. 2005. Analyserapport—Fremtidens velfærd og globalisering. Available online: www.fm.dk/db/filarkiv/18665/Analyse_1_hele_rapporten.pdf (viewed September 15, 2011).

Vignal, P. 2011. " 'Barack Obama est plus à droite que moi' dit Marine Le Pen". Reuters, September 1. Available online: http://fr.reuters.com/article/topNews/idFRPAE78008I 20110901 (viewed September 3, 2011).

Villedary, Pierre (2011), Jean d'Arc boutée du 1er mai du FN, minute, April 13, pp. 4–5.

Voas, D. and R. Ling. 2010. "Religion in Britain and the United States", in A. Park, J. Curtice, K. Thomson, M. Phillips, E. Clery, and S. Butt, eds. 2010. *British Social Attitudes: the Twenty-Sixth Report*. London: Sage, 65–86.

Vogelaar, E. 2009. "PvdA, kom uit die kramp", op-ed article, January 20. Available online: www.pvda.nl/opinie/opinie/PvdA+kom+uit+die+kramp.html (accessed September 21, 2011).

Volkens, A., O. Lacewell, S. Regel, H. Schultze, and A. Werner. 2010. *The Manifesto Data Collection. Manifesto Project (MRG/CMP/MARPOR)*. Berlin: Wissenschaftszentrum Berlin für Sozialforschung (WZB).

von Beyme, K. 1996. "Rechtsextremismus in Osteuropa", in J. W. Falter, H.-G. Jaschte, and J. R. Winkler, eds. 1996. *Rechtsextremismus*. Opladen: Westdeutscher Verlag.

Walter, S. 2010. "Globalization and the Welfare State: Testing the Microfoundations of the Compensation Hypothesis". *International Studies Quarterly*, 54: 403–426.

Warwick, P. V. 2002. "Toward a Common Dimensionality in West European Policy Spaces". *Party Politics*, 8: 101–122.

Welch, S. and J. Hibbing. 1992. "Financial Conditions, Fender, and Voting in American National Elections". *Journal of Politics*, 54: 197–213.

Wessel, D. 2011. "Big U.S. Firms Shift Hiring Abroad". *Wall Street Journal*, April 19. Available online: http://economiccrisis.us/2011/04/big-firms-shift-hiring/ (viewed July 7, 2011).

Whiteley, P. and P. Seyd. 2003. "How to Win a Landslide by Really Trying: The Effects of Local Campaigning on Voting in the 1997 British General Election". *Electoral Studies*, 22: 301–302.

Whiteley, P. and P. Seyd. 1994. "Local Party Campaigning and Voting Behaviour in Britain". *Journal of Politics*, 56: 242–251.

Wilks-Heeg, S. 2009. "The Canary in a Coalmine? Explaining the Emergence of the British National Party in English Local Politics". *Parliamentary Affairs*, 62: 377–398.

Wüst, A. 2004. "Naturalised Citizens as Voters: Behaviour and Impact". *German Politics*, 13: 341–359.

YouGov. 2009a. Online: www.channel4.com/news/media/2009/06/day08/yougovpoll_080609.pdf.

YouGov. 2009b. Online: www.yougov.co.uk/extranets/ygarchives/content/pdf/DTresults_OCT_BNP.pdf.

Zaslove, A. 2004a. "Closing the Door? The Ideology and Impact of Radical Right Populism on Immigration Policy in Austria and Italy". *Journal of Political Ideologies*, 9 (1): 99–118.

Zaslove, A. 2004b. "The Dark Side of European Politics: Unmasking the Radical Right". *European Integration*, 26 (1): 61–81.

Index

Page numbers in *italics* denote tables, those in **bold** denote figures.